# Trading System Architecture Explained

*Where Latency Hides and How Design Matters*

Thomas V. Trex

Published by NobleTrex Press


For permissions and other inquiries, write to:
P.O. Box 3132, Framingham, MA 01701, USA

# Contents


**1 Market & Latency Fundamentals** **5**

1.1 Evolution of Electronic Market Structure . . . . . . . . . 5

1.2 Primary Sources of Latency . . . . . . . . . . . . . . . . . . 16

1.3 Order Book Dynamics & Price Discovery . . . . . . . . . 28

1.4 Latency as an Economic Edge . . . . . . . . . . . . . . . . . 39

1.5 Regulatory Impacts on Latency Strategies . . . . . . . . . 49

**2 Market Microstructure Basics** **61**

2.1 Order Types and Attributes . . . . . . . . . . . . . . . . . . 61

2.2 Core Order Types: Market, Limit, Stop, Stop-Limit . . 62

2.3 Time-in-Force: How Long an Order Lives . . . . . . . . . 66

2.4 Visibility: Displayed, Hidden, and Iceberg Orders . . . 69

2.5 Aggressive vs. Passive Combinations . . . . . . . . . . . 71

2.6 Latency as an Implicit Attribute . . . . . . . . . . . . . . 73

2.7 Queue Priority and Matching Rules . . . . . . . . . . . 74

2.8 Quote-Driven vs. Order-Driven Markets . . . . . . . . . 85

2.9 Venue Fragmentation and Routing Logic . . . . . . . . 96

2.10 Life Cycle Events and State Changes . . . . . . . . . . . 108

3 **Latency Definitions, Taxonomy & Measurement** **123**
3.1 Latency Taxonomy and Nomenclature . . . . . . . . . . 123
3.2 Clock Synchronization & Time Sources . . . . . . . . . 136
3.3 Instrumentation & Tap Points . . . . . . . . . . . . . . . 149
3.4 Statistical Analysis & Histograms . . . . . . . . . . . . . 163
3.5 Benchmarking Methodologies . . . . . . . . . . . . . . . 176
3.6 Visualizing Latency Distributions . . . . . . . . . . . . . 188

4 **Trading System Architecture & Components** **199**
4.1 Layered Architecture Overview . . . . . . . . . . . . . . . 199
4.2 Component Interaction Models . . . . . . . . . . . . . . . 212
4.3 State Machines and Event-Driven Design . . . . . . . . 226
4.4 In-Process vs. Distributed Deployment . . . . . . . . . 238
4.5 Risk Management & Kill Switches . . . . . . . . . . . . 251
4.6 Observability Hooks . . . . . . . . . . . . . . . . . . . . . . 264

5 **Network Protocols & Physical Connectivity** **279**
5.1 Optical Paths and Propagation Delay . . . . . . . . . . 279
5.2 Switch Architecture and Buffer Behavior . . . . . . . . 288
5.3 IP, UDP, TCP Trade-offs . . . . . . . . . . . . . . . . . . . 299
5.4 Multicast Market Data Distribution . . . . . . . . . . . 310
5.5 Co-Location and Cross-Connects . . . . . . . . . . . . . 323
5.6 Route Diversity and Disaster Scenarios . . . . . . . . . 334

6 **Operating System, Hardware & Runtime** **347**
6.1 CPU Microarchitecture for Trading . . . . . . . . . . . 347
6.2 NUMA Awareness and Memory Bandwidth . . . . . . . 358
6.3 OS Scheduling and CPU Isolation . . . . . . . . . . . . 368
6.4 Interrupt Handling and Polling Modes . . . . . . . . . 378

6.5 Kernel Bypass Frameworks . . . . . . . . . . . . . . . . . . 390
6.6 Compiler and Runtime Optimizations . . . . . . . . . . . 400

**7 Market Data Handling & Feed Handlers 413**
7.1 Feed Handler Design Patterns . . . . . . . . . . . . . . . 413
7.2 Protocol Decoding Techniques . . . . . . . . . . . . . . . 423
7.3 Gap Detection and Recovery . . . . . . . . . . . . . . . . 435
7.4 Normalization & Aggregation . . . . . . . . . . . . . . . . 448
7.5 Dissemination to Strategy Engines . . . . . . . . . . . . 463

**8 Order Gateways & Lifecycle Engineering 477**
8.1 Session Management and Heartbeats . . . . . . . . . . . 477
8.2 Low-Latency Serialization . . . . . . . . . . . . . . . . . . 489
8.3 Order Validation and Risk Checks . . . . . . . . . . . . . 501
8.4 Cancel-Replace Workflows . . . . . . . . . . . . . . . . . 514
8.5 Acknowledgement Handling and Latency Budgets . . . 527
8.6 Failure Modes and Replay Logic . . . . . . . . . . . . . . 539

**9 Optimization Patterns & Kernel-Bypass Techniques 553**
9.1 Lock-Free Data Structures . . . . . . . . . . . . . . . . . 553
9.2 Cache-Friendly Coding . . . . . . . . . . . . . . . . . . . 566
9.3 Batching vs. Single-Shot Processing . . . . . . . . . . . 576
9.4 User-Space Networking Deep Dive . . . . . . . . . . . . 587
9.5 Latency Anti-Patterns . . . . . . . . . . . . . . . . . . . . 601
9.6 Holistic System Tuning . . . . . . . . . . . . . . . . . . . 611

**10 Reliability, Safety & Production Operations 625**
10.1 Redundancy and Failover Architectures . . . . . . . . . 625
10.2 Monitoring and Alerting for Latency . . . . . . . . . . . 638

10.3 Chaos Testing in Trading Systems . . . . . . . . . . . . . 649
10.4 Compliance, Audit Trails, and Data Retention . . . . . 662
10.5 Incident Response Playbooks . . . . . . . . . . . . . . . . 673
10.6 Capacity Planning and Continuous Improvement . . . 684

# Introduction

Electronic trading underpins modern financial markets, with billions of transactions executed daily across global exchanges. The efficiency, resilience, and profitability of trading operations are critically determined by the architecture of the underlying technology. As market competition intensifies, the significance of latency reduction has become a defining characteristic of contemporary trading system design. This book, *Trading System Architecture Explained: Where Latency Hides and How Design Matters*, systematically examines the architectural foundations, practical trade-offs, and optimization strategies necessary to engineer high-performance trading systems.

In the first chapter, the book delineates the fundamental structure of electronic markets and clarifies how latency has evolved into an economic variable of strategic importance. By tracing the migration from manual trading pits to fully automated, electronic limit-order books, it becomes clear how automation has rendered latency both quantifiable and actionable. The mechanics of latency formation and its direct impact on execution outcomes are explored, including the economic rationale for minimizing delays. Regulatory influences are also assessed, establishing a balanced view of the opportunities and constraints imposed by market oversight.

Subsequent chapters build upon this foundation by introducing the central concepts of market microstructure. Detailed analysis of order types, matching algorithms, and venue fragmentation reveals the technical nuances that shape the life cycle of every order in a fragmented global marketplace. By mapping state transitions and event flows, the text shows precisely where trading logic must intervene to maintain both speed and correctness.

A rigorous taxonomy of latency is established, standardizing measurement techniques and terminology to eliminate ambiguity in both engineering and trading discussions. Clock synchronization, latency instrumentation, and statistical evaluation methodologies are articulated to equip readers with the skills necessary to benchmark, diagnose, and visualize latency distributions across complex production environments.

The architectural core of this book presents a layered model of modern trading stacks, spanning from the strategy layer at the top to the physical network and hardware layers below. Each architectural boundary is scrutinized to uncover sources of latency that may not be apparent at first glance. Component interactions, risk management, observability, and deployment models are analyzed with a focus on balancing performance optimization with system maintainability and operational transparency.

Further technical depth is provided by delving into the physical and protocol-level aspects of market connectivity. Optical paths, switching behavior, and transport protocol selection are examined for their determinative roles in shaping latency envelopes. Practical strategies for co-location, route diversity, and disaster recovery are introduced to inform the design of robust and performant infrastructure.

At the system level, the book explores operating system configuration, hardware tuning, and advanced runtime optimization. Topics such as CPU isolation, memory layout, interrupt processing, and kernel bypass frameworks are presented with a focus on technical rigor and empirical performance impact. Feed handlers, gateway design, and order life cycle engineering are then addressed, demonstrating how throughput and reliability are achieved under strict latency budgets.

Optimization patterns and anti-patterns receive focused treatment, with an emphasis on practical coding and deployment techniques that distinguish elite low-latency systems. Finally, operational best practices for achieving reliability, safety, and regulatory compliance in production environments are established. Monitoring, alerting, failure recovery, and process improvement methodologies are detailed to support sustainable long-term trading operations.

In sum, this book delivers comprehensive and actionable insights for engineers, technologists, and trading professionals committed to building, maintaining, and optimizing low-latency trading systems. Each chapter unpacks the technical and organizational factors that differentiate merely functional solutions from world-class platforms.

# Chapter 1

# Market & Latency Fundamentals

*Markets are not just crowds of opinions; they are physical systems that move information through space, wires, and software-one timestamp at a time. In this chapter you will recast exchanges as distributed computers, see how tiny delays reshape who trades with whom, and learn why a few microseconds can quietly separate profitable strategies from expensive illusions.*

## 1.1 Evolution of Electronic Market Structure

Modern trading systems sit on top of market structures that would be almost unrecognizable to a trader from fifty years ago. To understand where latency hides today, and why microseconds suddenly matter, you need a mental picture of how markets evolved from human-mediated trading floors to fully electronic networks of machines.

This section walks through that evolution in stages. At each stage, we will highlight two things:

- How trades were actually arranged and recorded.
- What "latency" meant in that environment, and how visible (or invisible) it was.

By the end, you should see that the move from people shouting in a pit to servers exchanging timestamped messages did not just speed things up. It turned time itself into a clearly measured, economically meaningful resource that trading systems must manage as carefully as capital or risk.

## Open-Outcry Pits: When Humans Were the Market

For most of the 20th century, major exchanges were physical places. Stocks, futures, and options were traded in "pits" or on trading floors. The core mechanism was *open outcry*: traders stood together, shouting bids and offers and using hand signals to negotiate trades.

**How trading worked**

A simplified sequence on a traditional floor might look like this:

- An investor calls their broker and says, for example, "Buy 1,000 shares of XYZ up to 25.50."
- The broker's assistant writes a paper order ticket and hands it to a floor runner.
- The runner physically carries the ticket onto the exchange floor to thc appropriate pit.
- A floor broker, standing in or near the pit, reads the order and starts shouting: "Bid 25.50 for 1,000 XYZ!"
- Other traders respond with their offers. If someone is willing to sell at 25.50 or less, they consummate the trade verbally and by hand signal.
- The trade is written on a ticket, later typed into the exchange's systems, and eventually reported back to the investor.

The order book—the list of who wanted to buy or sell at each price—largely lived *in people's heads*. Specialists or designated market makers might maintain a more formal record, but they still operated in a noisy, human environment. Quotes were shared by voice, on chalkboards, or later on simple electronic price boards showing best bid and offer. Depth away from the best prices was often invisible to anyone not standing right there.

**What latency meant on the floor**

Speed mattered even then. A fast runner, an attentive broker, and a loud voice could all improve your chance of getting a good trade. But several important features of latency in this world stand out:

- **Human reaction time dominated.** Delays were measured in seconds or tens of seconds: the time to write a ticket, walk it across the floor, shout an order, and negotiate a trade.
- **Latency was not precisely measured.** There were no consistent timestamps from order entry to execution. If you tried to ask, "How many milliseconds did it take for my order to get to the pit?" the question itself would not have made sense.
- **Information was local and fuzzy.** People physically close to the action naturally saw and heard things before people farther away. But that advantage was not quantified in microseconds. Being on the floor was an edge, yet it was more about access and skill than measurable network delay.

In other words, latency existed, but it was almost entirely *implicit*. It lived in human behavior and physical logistics, not in clocks and cables.

## Telephone and Screen-Based Trading: First Steps Toward Electronification

As technology advanced, phones, fax machines, and basic computer terminals began to reshape markets, even while open-outcry floors remained central.

**Remote access and early automation**

Two developments are especially important for our story:

- **Telephone and teletype networks.** Brokers could call floor traders or send instructions via teletype or rudimentary messaging systems, reducing the need for physical presence.
- **Quote screens and electronic reporting.** Exchanges began to disseminate consolidated price information on electronic displays, allowing off-floor participants to see more current market data.

Toward the later decades of the 20$^{th}$ century, some markets introduced basic forms of *computer-assisted order matching* for smaller, more standardized orders. Larger or more complex trades were still handled by humans, but a growing fraction of everyday business started to touch a computer at some stage before or after the floor.

**Latency becomes structured, but still coarse**

Latency in this period started to take on a more structured shape:

- **Multiple hops.** An instruction might move from investor to broker to floor, and then into an electronic reporting system. Each hop added delay.
- **Clock time appears in the record.** Trade reports often carried timestamps (to the nearest minute or, later, to the second). This was still too coarse to measure the impact of short delays on trade outcomes, but it was a first move toward time-aware record-keeping.
- **Batching and queues emerge.** Some early systems handled orders in batches or queues, introducing concepts like "time priority" inside the electronic component even if the traders themselves were not thinking in those terms.

For trading strategy, however, speed was still a background consideration. Few participants were explicitly building systems with the goal of shaving off milliseconds. The typical investor was more concerned with whether their order was filled at all and approximately at what price, not with the exact path and arrival time of their message inside the exchange's computers.

## Electronic Communication Networks (ECNs): From Floors to Digital Order Books

The real structural break began when trading started to move away from the physical floor toward fully electronic venues. In equities, one early manifestation of this shift was the rise of Electronic Communication Networks (ECNs) in the 1990s.

### What is an ECN?

An ECN is an electronic system that matches buy and sell orders from participants, often outside the traditional floor-based exchange. Key features included:

- **Electronic limit order books.** Participants could submit limit orders—specifying a price and quantity—directly into a computer system. The ECN maintained a list of resting orders on each side, ranked by price and time.
- **Automated matching.** When a new order arrived that could trade against existing orders at compatible prices, the system executed the trade automatically, according to pre-defined rules (usually some form of price-time priority).
- **Electronic market data.** The ECN provided a feed of its current best bid and offer, and sometimes deeper book levels, to participants over data lines.

For the first time, the "place where orders meet" was not a human crowd but a computer program running on a server.

### Latency becomes a technical property

Once trading became message-passing between machines, latency started to look different:

- **Messages have timestamps.** Orders, cancels, and trades could now be logged with precise timestamps by the ECN. Over time, this granularity moved from seconds to milliseconds, then to microseconds and beyond.

- **Network delays are observable.** If a participant sent an order and saw it acknowledged a fixed amount of time later, they could begin to measure their round-trip latency to the venue.
- **Matching is deterministic.** The logic determining which order trades first is encoded in software. If two orders arrive at the same price, the one with the earlier timestamp in the matching engine wins. Time order becomes a formal, recorded concept rather than a matter of who shouted first.

The ECN era introduced a profound shift: latency began to transition from something messy and human into something systematic and, at least in principle, measurable and improvable.

## Fully Electronic Limit Order Books: The Exchange as a Matching Engine

As electronic trading proved itself, many markets moved progressively toward fully electronic central limit order books (CLOBs). Some exchanges closed their physical floors entirely; others kept them for a while but shifted the main liquidity to electronic systems.

In a CLOB-based market:

- All displayed bids and offers are stored and managed by an electronic matching engine.
- Participants connect to the exchange via network links (leased lines, cross-connects, or the public internet).
- Orders, cancels, and modifications are standardized electronic messages following a prescribed protocol.

### Price-time priority and the importance of arrival time

Most electronic books adopt some variant of *price-time priority*. This rule says:

- Better prices beat worse prices. A higher bid or lower offer has priority over others.

- Among orders at the same price, the earliest arrival gets served first.

This seemingly simple rule has deep implications for latency:

- A tiny difference in arrival time determines whether you are at the front or back of the queue at a given price.
- Being ahead in the queue often means you get filled when a tradeable opportunity arises, while those behind you may not trade at all.
- When prices move quickly, the ability to submit, update, or cancel orders slightly faster than others can sharply change your fill quality and risk.

In the pit era, "getting there first" meant elbowing into the crowd or shouting louder. In electronic markets, it means having your message reach the matching engine first, and that is a function of hardware, software, and network design.

**Latency is now a design parameter**

In a fully electronic exchange:

- **Every message has a path.** Orders travel from trading systems, through internal networks and gateways, across external links, into exchange gateways, and finally to the matching engine.
- **Each component adds delay.** Network switches, firewalls, operating systems, serialization and deserialization of messages, and the matching engine itself all contribute to total latency.
- **Participants can measure and optimize.** By time-stamping messages at various points along the path, firms can build a latency budget and decide where to invest in improvement.

Crucially, electronic exchanges often expose enough information (through acknowledgements, execution reports, and market data) for participants to infer how fast they are relative to others. This opens the door to treating latency as a controllable variable rather than a background annoyance.

## Fragmented Multi-Venue Ecosystems: Latency as a Relative Advantage

Once markets were electronic, it became easier to launch new venues. Today, many asset classes—equities in particular—trade across multiple exchanges, alternative trading systems, and dark pools at once.

**Multiple books, one market**

In a fragmented market:

- The same security may have active order books on many venues simultaneously.
- Market data is disseminated from each venue, sometimes combined into consolidated feeds.
- Participants may choose to route orders to one venue or another based on fees, liquidity, or speed.

From the point of view of a trading system architect, the market becomes a distributed system. There is no single "place" where price is discovered. Instead, prices and volumes emerge from the interactions of many matching engines, each with its own latency characteristics and connectivity patterns.

**Latency gaps between venues**

In this environment, latency is not just about how fast you are to one exchange. It is also about:

- **Inter-venue delays.** A price change on one venue appears in its market data feed and, after some delay, in consolidated or third-party feeds. Another venue's book may remain temporarily out of sync, showing "stale" prices.
- **Routing delays.** A smart order router deciding where to send an order adds its own processing time. The chosen path—which venue, which physical route—affects how quickly the order hits a particular book.
- **Asymmetric information arrival.** Some participants receive faster data feeds (for example, direct feeds from each venue)

while others rely on slower, consolidated feeds. The former can react to new information before the latter are even aware of it.

Now latency is fundamentally *relative*. The question is not only, "How long does my order take?" but also, "How long does my order take *compared with everyone else's* and compared with the time it takes for information to propagate between venues?"

## From Latency as Nuisance to Latency as Tradable Dimension

With all these elements in place—electronic books, precise timestamps, and multiple venues—latency became something more than a side effect. It became an explicit, tradable dimension of market structure.

**Latency as a measurable quantity**

Because modern systems log events with fine-grained timestamps, firms can compute:

- Time from signal generation to order dispatch.
- Time from order dispatch to exchange acknowledgement.
- Time from external market event (such as a price change) to internal reaction.

These are not abstract notions. They are concrete metrics that firms track over time, optimize, and sometimes even treat as key performance indicators. Traders can ask, "What is our median round-trip latency to Exchange A vs. Exchange B?" and get quantitative answers.

**Latency as a source of edge and risk**

Once latency is measurable, it naturally becomes part of trading strategy:

- **Edge.** If you receive and react to information faster than others, you can update quotes, place orders, or pull resting orders before slower participants do. Over many events, even tiny time leads can accumulate into better average prices and higher fill quality.

- **Risk.** If you are consistently slower, you tend to be filled when the market is moving against you and miss favorable opportunities. Latency then becomes a form of adverse selection: you interact with the book on worse terms than faster counterparts.

Firms invest in faster networks, more efficient software, and closer physical proximity to exchange matching engines not just to "go fast" in some vague sense, but because each incremental improvement can change the statistics of who trades with whom and at what price.

## Co-Evolution of Market Structure and Technology

It is tempting to think of technology as simply reacting to market needs: exchanges go electronic, so traders modernize their systems. In reality, the relationship is two-way. Market structure and technology co-evolved, and latency sat at the center of that evolution.

### Market changes that heightened the role of latency

Several structural shifts amplified the importance of time:

- **Standardized message protocols.** Fixed, well-defined formats for orders and market data made it easier to build automated systems and tune them for speed.
- **Increased automation on the buy and sell sides.** As algorithms took over more of the decision-making, the entire lifecycle from signal to execution compressed, making sub-second delays more consequential.
- **Higher turnover and shorter horizons.** Strategies that rely on small price discrepancies or fleeting opportunities became more common; for these, arriving even a little bit earlier can be the difference between profit and loss.

Each of these developments both relied on and further encouraged investment in lower latency infrastructure.

### Technology responses that reshaped market design

At the same time, technology-driven behavior prompted changes in how venues were designed and regulated:

- **Co-location and proximity services.** Exchanges began offering space in or near their data centers so that participants could reduce physical distance and, therefore, propagation delay.
- **Refinements to matching engines.** As participants pushed the limits of speed, venues optimized their own software and hardware to handle high message rates and minimize internal processing time.
- **New types of venues.** Some platforms aimed at being ultra-fast and low-cost; others experimented with intentional delays or alternative matching rules to reshape competition based on latency.

In other words, as traders started to treat latency as an economic resource, exchanges responded by making latency an explicit parameter of their offerings.

## Why This History Matters for System Architecture

For a trading system architect today, this evolution is not just background color. It explains why your system must treat time as a first-class concern.

In pit-based markets, the main design challenge might have been managing client relationships and ensuring operational reliability. In modern electronic markets, design questions include:

- Where should your trading servers be physically located relative to each venue?
- How should your software be structured to minimize unnecessary processing and queuing?
- Which data feeds should you consume, and how will differences in their latency affect your view of the market?
- How will you measure and monitor latency at each stage of your order's journey?

These are not purely technical questions. Because market structure has made latency observable, measurable, and tradable, your answers directly influence execution quality, risk, and profitability.

As we move into the next sections, we will dissect the end-to-end journey of an order and map out the primary sources of latency along the way. The historical path from shouting in a pit to messages in a matching engine sets the stage: it explains why latency exists where it does, and why thoughtful system architecture can turn time from a hidden constraint into a consciously managed part of your trading strategy.

## 1.2 Primary Sources of Latency

In the previous section we saw how markets evolved from human trading pits to electronic limit order books, and how that evolution turned time into a measurable, tradable resource. We now zoom in from that high-level history to the concrete path a single order takes through a modern trading system.

Our goal in this section is simple but powerful: to decompose the end-to-end journey of an order into understandable stages, and to identify where and why latency is introduced at each stage. Once you can see latency as the sum of many smaller delays, it stops being a vague sense of "slowness" and becomes a set of engineering and design problems you can reason about.

We will follow an order from its origin in a trading strategy or human decision, through internal systems and networks, and finally into the exchange matching engine. Along the way we will distinguish:

- **Physical components** (cables, switches, servers, distance).
- **Logical components** (software logic, risk checks, routing decisions).
- **Fixed vs. variable latency** (what is always there vs. what fluctuates).

By the end of this section, you should be able to sketch an order's path in your own environment and start building a latency budget: an explicit accounting of where time is spent and which parts you can influence.

## From Trading Intent to Outbound Message

Every order begins as an intention: either a human trader decides to buy or sell, or an automated strategy produces a signal. The path from that intent to a concrete order message involves several layers.

### Strategy logic and decision latency

Consider an automated strategy that monitors market data and decides when to place an order. Its latency has several elements:

- **Input acquisition.** The strategy must receive and parse market data messages. This depends on the speed of your market data feed, internal distribution, and any preprocessing.
- **Computation time.** The strategy's logic—from a simple threshold rule to a complex predictive model—requires CPU or specialized hardware time to evaluate.
- **Scheduling and context switching.** The operating system decides when your strategy's process or thread runs. Competing workloads, interrupts, and task scheduling can introduce small but sometimes variable delays.

Even if you do not think of this as "latency," it represents the time between the world changing (for example, a new quote appears) and your system deciding to act. For ultra-fast strategies, this decision time is a major focus of optimization. For slower strategies, it may be less critical but still part of the overall budget.

### Application stack and message construction

Once the strategy decides to send an order, it must construct an outbound message. Typically this involves:

- **Internal APIs or function calls.** The strategy passes an order object to another component (for example, an order management system or execution engine).
- **Business logic checks.** The system may validate the order: symbol, side (buy/sell), quantity, client identifiers, and any strategy-specific constraints.
- **Serialization.** The order is converted from in-memory structures into a standardized message format (for example, a protocol like FIX, or a binary venue-specific format) to be sent over the network.

These steps usually involve memory allocations, data copying, and function calls. Each individual operation is fast, but together they add measurable latency. The more layers your application stack has (adapters, middleware, logging, monitoring hooks), the more opportunities there are for incremental delay.

## Risk Checks and Controls

Before an order leaves your firm, it typically passes through risk controls. These controls are essential: they prevent runaway algorithms, enforce capital limits, and help satisfy regulatory requirements. But they also introduce both fixed and variable latency.

Common risk-related checks include:

- **Pre-trade risk limits.** Verifying that the order does not exceed position limits, notional exposure thresholds, or credit lines.
- **Price reasonability checks.** Ensuring the order price is within a reasonable range of the current market price to avoid obvious errors (so-called "fat finger" protection).
- **Duplicate or replay protection.** Detecting and blocking repeated messages that might indicate a system malfunction.

Each check requires access to internal state (for example, current positions, outstanding orders, risk limits). If this state is in memory and carefully maintained, the checks can be extremely fast and predictable. If it requires database queries or communication with remote services, the latency can be larger and highly variable.

From a design point of view, risk systems illustrate a fundamental trade-off: stronger controls often require more computation and data access, which can increase latency. Architects must balance safety and speed, sometimes designing "fast paths" for low-risk orders and more thorough checks for exceptional cases.

## Smart Order Routing and Venue Selection

In fragmented markets, an order may need to be routed to one of many possible venues. The component responsible for this decision is often called a *smart order router* (SOR) or simply a router.

### Router decision latency

The router considers questions such as:

- Which venues currently display the best price?
- Where is there sufficient depth to fill the desired quantity?
- What are the fees, rebates, or other costs on each venue?
- How likely is each venue to provide a fast, high-quality fill?

To answer these questions, the router needs:

- **Recent market data.** Up-to-date views of each venue's order book.
- **Internal models or rules.** Logic for how to split orders, handle partial fills, and avoid undesirable venues in certain conditions.

Even simple routing logic adds latency: the system must inspect multiple options and choose a destination. More sophisticated routers, which use richer market data or predictive models, can add more.

### Multi-hop routing and aggregation

If an order is split across venues, the router may generate multiple child orders and send them along different paths. Each additional destination introduces its own network and venue-specific latencies. If the parent order's behavior depends on the fills of its children (for example, slowing or canceling remaining slices if early fills are poor), then the timing of acknowledgements and fills feeds back into routing decisions, adding another layer of complexity.

From a latency perspective, routers sit at an important junction: they exist to improve execution quality and reduce costs, but they do so by adding an extra layer between strategy and exchange. In system architecture, this layer must be designed carefully to avoid undoing the benefits it is meant to deliver.

## Network Stack and Physical Transport

Once an order message is constructed and its destination determined, it must travel from your systems to the exchange. This journey introduces some of the most intuitive sources of latency: the network stack and physical distance.

### Within the host: operating system and network stack

Before your message leaves the server, it passes through the operating system's networking layers:

- **System calls.** The application hands the message to the OS via network-related calls.
- **Kernel processing.** The kernel prepares the message, adds protocol headers (for example, TCP/IP), and hands it to the network interface card (NIC).
- **Queuing and buffering.** If the NIC or kernel is busy, your packet may wait briefly in queues before transmission.

These steps are often overlooked, but in low-latency systems the design of the OS and network stack is crucial. Choices about operating system, drivers, interrupt handling, and buffer management can make the difference between highly predictable, low-variance latency and a system with erratic delays.

### On the wire: switches, routers, and distance

After leaving the host, the packet moves through physical links and network devices:

- **Switches and routers.** Each network device that forwards the packet adds a small amount of processing and possible queuing delay.
- **Medium.** The type of physical link matters: fiber optic cables, copper, microwave links, and other media each have different propagation properties.
- **Distance.** Even at the speed of light in fiber, it takes measurable time for a signal to travel between two geographically separated points. For example, a few hundred kilometers can add a millisecond or more of one-way propagation delay.

Some aspects of network latency are essentially fixed: you cannot beat the physical limits of propagation speed over a given distance. Others are variable: congestion, equipment load, and routing changes can cause fluctuations. Architects often work to minimize the number of hops, choose high-quality links, and place trading systems physically close to exchange data centers to reduce this component.

## Exchange Gateways and Access Layers

When your packet reaches the exchange's environment, it usually does not go directly to the matching engine. Instead, it passes through one or more *gateways* or access layers designed to handle participant connectivity.

### Session management and protocol handling

Exchange gateways typically perform tasks such as:

- **Session authentication.** Verifying that the connection is from a known participant and is authorized.
- **Protocol parsing.** Reading the incoming message, validating its format, and translating it into internal structures used by the matching engine.
- **Rate limiting and throttling.** Enforcing limits on how many messages a participant can send in a given time to protect the exchange from overload.

These operations add processing time. Because gateways must handle traffic from many participants, their internal queuing and load can create variability: during busy periods, messages may wait longer in gateway queues before being handed off to the matching engine.

### Exchange-side risk and compliance checks

Many venues also run their own pre-trade checks. These can include:

- **Exchange-level credit limits.** Ensuring that a participant does not exceed limits set by the exchange or a sponsoring broker.
- **Regulatory checks.** Enforcing rules around order types, short sale restrictions, or other market-specific constraints.

From a participant's perspective, these checks are part of the venue's fixed latency profile. You cannot remove them, but you can learn how they behave under different conditions and factor that into your design and strategy.

## The Matching Engine: Final Determination of Time and Priority

At the end of the journey lies the exchange's matching engine: the system that maintains the order book and decides which orders trade.

### Internal queuing and processing

Inside the matching engine, incoming messages (orders, cancellations, modifications) are typically processed one at a time or in small batches. The engine:

- **Updates the order book.** Adds new resting orders, removes filled or canceled orders, and adjusts quantities and positions in queues.
- **Applies matching rules.** When a new order can trade against existing orders, it executes trades according to the venue's rules (often price-time priority).
- **Generates responses.** Sends back acknowledgements, execution reports, and market data updates.

The matching engine introduces both fixed and variable latency:

- **Fixed.** The base processing time required to handle a single message when the system is relatively idle.
- **Variable.** Additional delays when the engine is busy processing a high volume of messages, causing messages to wait in internal queues.

From the viewpoint of your trading system, you only see the external effect: the time between the message reaching the exchange and the responses coming back. But understanding that there is an internal queue helps explain why latency can spike during periods of heavy market activity.

## Putting It Together: Latency as a Budget

We have now outlined the main components of the journey from trader intent to exchange match:

1. Strategy logic and decision-making.

2. Application stack and message construction.
3. Risk checks and controls.
4. Smart order routing and venue selection.
5. Operating system and host network stack.
6. Physical network and distance.
7. Exchange gateways and access layers.
8. Matching engine processing.

Each step adds some latency. Some steps are largely under your control (strategy code, internal risk implementation, host configuration). Others are shared or external (network infrastructure, exchange behavior). All of them interact: a small delay early on might cause you to arrive at the venue during a busier period, exposing you to more queueing later.

A useful way to think about this is as a *latency budget*. You can imagine allocating "time allowances" to each stage, then measuring actual performance and comparing it to your targets. For example:

- Strategy and application: up to a certain number of microseconds.
- Internal risk and routing: another allowance.
- Network: constrained by distance and connectivity choices.
- Exchange path: learned from observation and venue documentation.

When actual measurements exceed your budget in one area, you can decide whether it is worth investing effort or money to improve it, or whether that delay is acceptable given your strategy's time horizon.

## Visualizing the Order Path

To make these concepts concrete, Figure presents a left-to-right diagram of the order's journey, with the major components and their associated latency contributions.

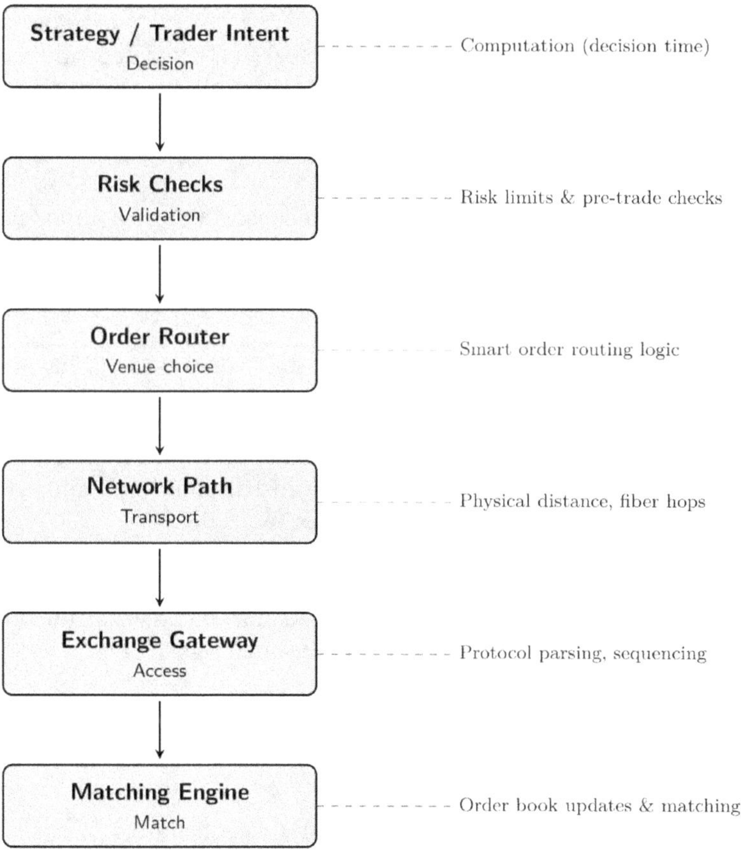

## Fixed vs. Variable Latency, Averages vs. Tails

So far we have focused on the structural placement of latency. To design robust systems, you must also think about *how* latency behaves statistically.

### Fixed vs. variable components

- **Fixed latency** is the portion that remains roughly the same from event to event. Examples include minimum propagation time over a fixed distance or a tightly controlled, in-memory computation that always follows the same path.
- **Variable latency** (often called jitter) fluctuates depending on load, contention, and other dynamic conditions. Examples include waiting in a queue on a busy gateway or contending for CPU with other processes.

In a latency budget, it is often helpful to separate these components. Fixed latency tells you the best you can hope to achieve. Variable latency determines how often you will be slower than that ideal and by how much.

### Average behavior vs. tail events

Many systems are designed and evaluated on average latency. However, in trading, the *tails* of the latency distribution–the unusually slow events–can be just as important. For example:

- If most of your orders reach the exchange quickly but a small fraction are delayed, those delayed orders may be precisely the ones that get filled at bad prices during fast markets.
- Short bursts of high latency can cause your strategy to operate on stale information or to send orders that are no longer appropriate by the time they arrive.

Understanding both the typical and worst-case behavior of each latency component is critical. Some design choices aim to reduce mean latency; others focus on tightening the distribution to reduce extreme outliers.

## What You Can and Cannot Control

Not all sources of latency are under your control, but many are. Roughly speaking:

- **Under your control:** Strategy logic, internal software design, risk check implementation, internal network design, server placement decisions, and operating system configuration.
- **Partially under your control:** Choice of connectivity providers, quality of external networks, selection of venues and order types.
- **Outside your control:** Exchange internal processing, other participants' activity levels, and regulatory requirements that mandate certain checks.

A well-architected trading system focuses optimization on areas where effort and investment can meaningfully reduce latency or variability, while accepting and adapting to the parts of the environment that are fixed.

## From Map to Measurement

This section has given you a conceptual map of where latency comes from along the order path. In later chapters, we will discuss how to measure each component in practice using timestamps, logging, and specialized telemetry tools. For now, the key outcome should be clarity:

- You can describe the journey of an order in your own words.
- You can identify each major physical and logical stage.
- You understand that latency is the sum of many small delays, some fixed, some variable.

Armed with this mental model, you can begin to think like a system architect: every design decision—from data structures in your strategy, to the placement of a risk engine, to the choice of network provider—has a latency footprint. The better you understand that footprint, the more effectively you can design trading systems that align with your strategy's time horizon and performance goals.

## 1.3 Order Book Dynamics & Price Discovery

In the previous sections we treated latency as a sequence of engineering delays between a trader's intent and the exchange's matching engine. We decomposed that path into components and argued that latency is a budget you can analyze and optimize.

In this section we step into the market's side of the interface and ask: once an order reaches the exchange, how does its precise arrival time determine *who* trades first and *at what price*? The answer lives in the mechanics of the limit order book, the rules of queueing, and the reality that modern liquidity is fragmented across many venues.

Our goal is to connect latency directly to observable trading outcomes: fills, slippage, and the path of price discovery.

### From quotes on a screen to a structured queue

Most traders are used to seeing the market through a simple two-sided quote: best bid and best offer, along with their sizes. Behind those two numbers, the exchange maintains a detailed structure: the *limit order book*.

Think of the limit order book as a set of queues, one queue for each possible price level:

- On the bid side, each queue holds buy limit orders at a given price.
- On the offer (ask) side, each queue holds sell limit orders at a given price.

Within each queue, orders are arranged according to the exchange's priority rule. For most modern electronic markets, especially in large equity, futures, and many FX venues, the dominant rule is:

> *Price–time priority:* better prices go first; at the same price, earlier arriving orders go first.

Price–time priority has two powerful implications:

- Your *price* choice determines which queue you join.
- Your *arrival time* determines your position *within* that queue.

The previous chapter's focus on latency now becomes very concrete: the timestamp at which the matching engine receives and orders your message controls your queue position, and queue position controls your chance of trading.

## Queue position and fill priority

Consider the best bid at 100.00 with a displayed size of 500 shares. That 500 might be composed of three separate orders:

| Order | Size | Arrival time |
|---|---|---|
| A | 200 | 09:30:00.100000 |
| B | 100 | 09:30:00.250000 |
| C | 200 | 09:30:00.400000 |

To the outside world, the book simply shows "Bid: 100.00 x 500". Internally, the exchange knows that A is first in line, then B, then C, based purely on arrival time.

If a market sell order for 150 shares arrives and trades at 100.00, the matching engine will:

- Fill order A for 150 shares (leaving 50 remaining in A).
- Leave B and C untouched.

Now suppose you send a new buy limit order D for 100 shares at 100.00. Where does it go? Under price–time priority, D arrives after A, B, and C, so it is placed *behind* them in the queue. Your order D will only trade after the remaining 500 shares ahead of it have been executed or canceled.

At this point, latency has a very visible economic role:

- If your trading system had been able to reach the exchange even a few microseconds earlier, your order might have been placed in front of B or C.
- That improved queue position would materially increase your fill probability and reduce your expected waiting time.

## How latency decides between "almost simultaneous" orders

In engineering terms, two orders that leave the traders' systems at nearly the same moment may arrive at the matching engine in a clearly defined order due to small latency differences along the path. The exchange must break ties, and it does so using the actual arrival times it observes, typically in microsecond or even sub-microsecond resolution.

Imagine two firms, X and Y, both trying to join the bid at 100.00 with 100 shares each:

- X's order leaves its server at 09:30:00.500000 with a path taking 200 microseconds.
- Y's order leaves its server at 09:30:00.500050 with a path taking 150 microseconds.

Although X pushed the send button first, Y's total *end-to-end* latency is smaller. From the exchange's point of view:

- X arrives at 09:30:00.500200.

- Y arrives at 09:30:00.500200 as well, or perhaps a tiny fraction earlier or later.

The matching engine uses its own internal clock and message processing order to assign time priority. If Y's message is processed first, Y gets ahead of X in the queue. A handful of microseconds in network, operating system, or gateway processing has turned into a durable economic edge for Y for as long as both orders rest at that price.

This is where all of the earlier discussion about latencies in switches, kernels, and gateways becomes tangible: those small differences crystallize into *who is first in the book.*

## Cancellations, replacements, and queue reshaping

The order book is not static. Participants constantly cancel and replace orders, react to new information, and adjust their positions. Every such action interacts with the queueing rules and, again, with latency.

- **Cancellation latency:** When you send a cancel message for a resting order, that cancel has to travel to the exchange and be processed before a contra-side order arrives to trade with you. If your cancel is delayed, you might be filled at a price you no longer want.
- **Modification as cancel–replace:** Many venues implement a "modify" as an implicit cancel followed immediately by a new order at the new price or size. This usually *loses* time priority because it is treated as a fresh order. A strategy that constantly tweaks prices may suffer from repeated loss of queue position, especially if its cancel–replace messages are not low-latency.
- **Queue thinning vs. queue jumping:** Fast participants can quickly cancel their stale quotes and repost at new prices, effectively jumping ahead of slower traders who are still trying to exit the old queue.

The concept of "latency arbitrage" often traces back to these timing races: a trader who can update or remove their stale quote faster than others can hit it is less likely to be adversely selected.

## Price discovery as a sequence of queue interactions

So far we have focused on who gets filled first at a fixed price. To connect this to price discovery, recall that the limit order book is the interface where supply and demand meet. Prices move when trades happen or when the best quotes move.

In a price–time priority book, this process unfolds as:

- New information arrives (macro data, news, order flow, correlated asset moves, etc.).
- Some participants interpret this information faster and decide that the current quotes are no longer attractive.
- Fast traders cancel or reprice their resting orders, often pulling away from prices they think are now too cheap or too expensive.
- Others, slower to react, leave their orders resting at old prices.
- Marketable orders arrive (for example, a market buy) and first consume any liquidity that still remains at the old, now-unattractive prices.
- Only after those queues are exhausted do trades occur at updated price levels.

Latency influences *who* ends up trading at the old price versus the new one:

- Fast participants may have already canceled their old quotes before aggressive orders arrive.
- Slower participants are more likely to be "picked off" at stale prices.

In other words, price discovery is not an abstract statistical process; it is literally the outcome of which messages (orders, cancellations, modifications) reach the matching engine first. The path of transaction prices over time is shaped by a continuous race among participants to either be in or out of each price level as new information arrives.

## Fragmented liquidity and cross-venue timing gaps

So far we have imagined a single exchange. In reality, most modern markets are *fragmented*: the same instrument can trade simultaneously on many venues. Liquidity is spread across:

- Traditional exchanges,
- Alternative trading systems or dark pools,
- Electronic communication networks (ECNs),
- Internalizing brokers and systematic internalizers in some jurisdictions.

From the point of view of price discovery, the market now consists of multiple books that are only loosely synchronized by data feeds and order routing. Two key forms of latency emerge:

- **Market data latency:** The time it takes for a price or trade on venue A to be observed by a trader or router at venue B.
- **Routing latency:** The time it takes for an order (or cancel) to travel from the trader to each venue and to be processed there.

These latencies interact in subtle ways:

- When venue A's best offer updates, some routers will see that change earlier than others, depending on their data feeds and processing speed.
- When a router chooses between venues, small differences in estimated queue sizes, prices, and latencies can lead it to send orders to one venue rather than another.
- During fast markets, quotes on one venue can be stale by the time they are seen through the consolidated feed; a trader with lower-latency direct feeds might treat those quotes as "free options" to hit or lift.

From the perspective of your trading system architecture, every additional venue is another end-to-end path with its own latency profile. Your smart order router sits in the middle, trying to make choices based on slightly out-of-date snapshots of many books.

## Latency, stale quotes, and inter-venue arbitrage

A concrete example makes this clearer. Suppose the same stock trades on venues X and Y. At a given instant, the true fundamental value of the stock shifts upward due to new information. Fast participants on venue X react first:

- They aggressively buy at the old offers on X and then raise their bids.
- The best offer on X moves from 100.00 to 100.05 very quickly.

On venue Y, some liquidity providers are slower:

- Their offers are still posted at 100.00.
- The public consolidated feed may still show Y's 100.00 offer even after X has moved to 100.05, due to feed and processing delays.

A trader with low-latency direct feeds and fast routing can now:

- Observe that X has already moved higher.
- Infer that 100.00 on Y is probably stale and underpriced.
- Rapidly send a buy order to Y to lift that 100.00 before the slower liquidity providers there can cancel.

If the order arrives in time, the trader buys at 100.00 and could, in principle, immediately sell at 100.05 on X or simply hold the position at a favorable price. This is a latency-based form of cross-venue arbitrage, and the critical determinant is whose messages reach Y's matching engine first: the fast arbitrageur's marketable buy, or the slower liquidity providers' cancels.

Notice how many separate latencies matter here:

- The time for X's quote change to be observed.
- The computation time to decide that Y's quote is stale.
- The routing and processing time for the arbitrageur's order to reach Y.
- The routing and processing time for Y's liquidity providers' cancels to reach Y.

Each participant is running a small distributed system against the broader distributed system of the market itself. The outcome of the race sets the sequence of trade prices on Y, and hence contributes to the overall trajectory of price discovery across venues.

## Queue position and fill probability: intuitive dynamics

Returning to a single venue, it is useful to internalize how queue position affects *fill probability*, which is a key input to any trading system that relies on passive orders.

Imagine the best bid at 100.00 with a total quantity of 1,000 units. You are contemplating joining this bid. Your expected fill probability over the next short time interval depends on several intuitive factors:

- **Your position in the queue:** If you are at the very front, you are filled first whenever a sell order hits the bid. If you are last, you need a large volume of incoming sells before you see any fills.
- **The rate of incoming contra orders:** If sells are arriving frequently, even deep queue positions may see fills quickly.
- **Cancellation behavior ahead of you:** If participants ahead of you often cancel their orders, your effective position improves over time.

Latency influences all three:

- Faster arrival gets you closer to the front at a given price.

- Faster cancellation lets you abandon a poor queue position and try again at a new price without being picked off.
- Faster reaction to order flow allows your models to infer when a queue is likely to be consumed and position you accordingly.

In practice, many short-horizon strategies build statistical models of fill probability as a function of queue position, recent order flow, and book dynamics. For such strategies, reducing latency directly sharpens the alignment between the state your model uses and the actual state of the book at the time your order arrives.

## Latency and adverse selection

Order book dynamics also clarify the connection between latency and *adverse selection*. You are adversely selected when you are the one providing liquidity exactly when the market is about to move against you.

In the context of a limit order book:

- If you are resting at the best bid and the next trade is a large aggressive sell just before the price ticks down, you have likely been adversely selected.
- If you consistently get filled right before prices move unfavorably, your strategy is effectively providing an option to faster traders.

Latency plays two complementary roles:

- **Protection against adverse selection:** Faster cancellation and repricing reduce the time you spend resting at quotes that have become stale in light of new information. You are less often the one left in the queue when aggressive contra flow arrives.
- **Ability to impose adverse selection on others:** If you receive and process information faster than some liquidity providers, you can choose to trade against their stale quotes immediately before prices move. In aggregate, this is how some market-making and arbitrage strategies earn their edge.

When you quantify realized execution quality—for example, by measuring your average slippage against mid-market prices shortly before and after your fills—you are indirectly measuring how latency and order book dynamics have positioned you in the ecosystem of price discovery.

## Fragmented price discovery and the role of routing logic

In a fragmented market, price discovery is not confined to a single order book. Instead, each venue has its own micro-level dynamic, and routing logic stitches them together into a coherent trading experience for you and your clients.

Your smart order router must make rapid decisions such as:

- Which venue currently offers the best effective price, after considering fees, rebates, and expected queue position?
- Where can I expect a higher fill probability given my latency to each venue?
- How will my order impact future routing choices if it changes the queue composition on a particular book?

Because market data and routing are both subject to latency, the snapshot your router sees is always slightly out of date. A router that is designed without a clear understanding of order book dynamics and latency can systematically send orders into deteriorating quotes, consistently arriving just after faster traders have moved elsewhere.

By contrast, a router that explicitly models:

- feed latencies,
- message-processing delays,
- historical behavior of queues on each venue,

can align its routing decisions with the actual state of each book when the order is likely to arrive. This is another way architecture translates directly into economic outcomes.

## Putting it together: latency as a structural feature of microstructure

We can now see how everything fits together:

- The limit order book organizes supply and demand into price-ranked queues with time-based priority.
- Latency determines which queue you reach and where you stand in that queue.
- Cancellation and modification latencies control how quickly you can exit or reshuffle your queue positions as new information emerges.
- In fragmented markets, cross-venue data and routing latencies create timing gaps that shape arbitrage opportunities and the path of price discovery.
- Across all of these mechanisms, latency influences both your fill probability and your exposure to adverse selection.

From this perspective, latency is not an incidental performance metric; it is woven into the core rules of electronic trading. Every design decision in your trading system architecture—how you connect to venues, how you process feeds, where you host your servers—ultimately shows up as a microsecond here or a millisecond there, and those differences are cemented into queue positions and trade prices.

A disciplined trading firm treats order book dynamics and price discovery as *clients* of its technological design. Rather than optimizing speed in the abstract, you measure and manage latency with clear reference to how it affects your place in the book, your share of fills, and your realized execution costs. Subsequent chapters will build on this foundation, moving from conceptual understanding to concrete measurement and optimization techniques for latency within the trading system.

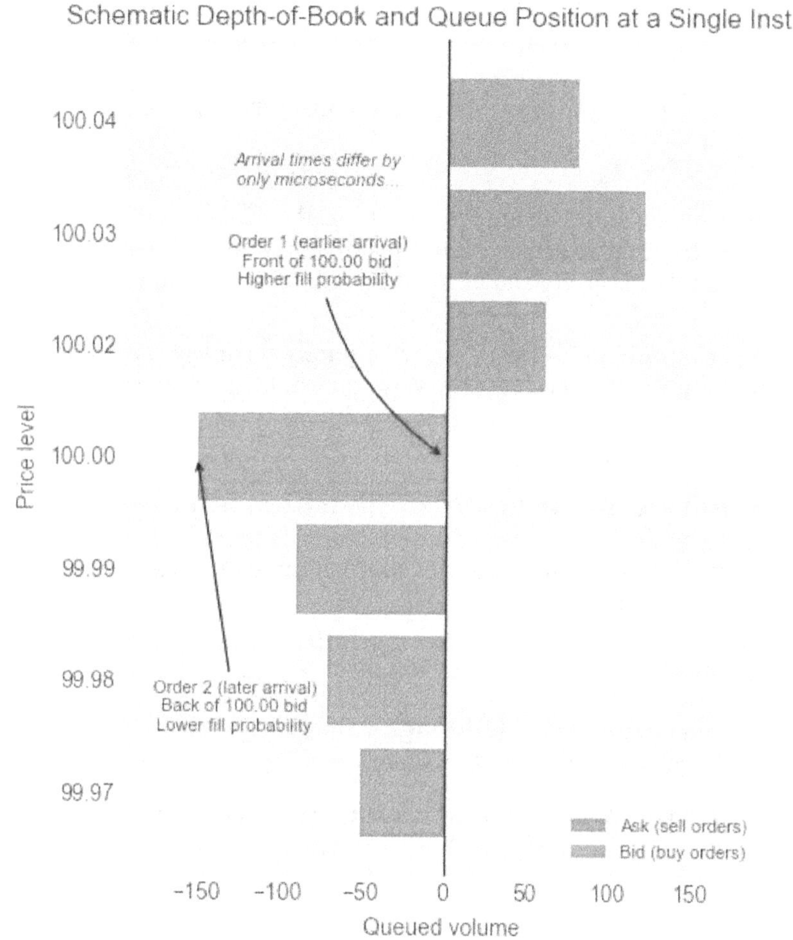


## 1.4 Latency as an Economic Edge

The previous sections established two key ideas. First, latency is not a vague notion of "slowness," but a set of identifiable delays between your trading logic and the exchange's matching engine. Second, once an order reaches the exchange, those delays solidify into queue positions and interaction with the limit order book, shaping who trades first and at what price.

We now move from structure to economics. The central question of this section is:

> How do time advantages, even on the scale of microseconds or milliseconds, translate into measurable differences in fills, slippage, and ultimately trading profits (alpha)?

Answering this turns latency from a purely technical obsession into something you can evaluate the way you would any investment: by its expected return relative to cost and risk.

## Economic channels through which latency matters

Latency affects trading outcomes through three main channels:

- **Fill probability:** whether your orders trade at all, and how completely.
- **Execution price (slippage):** the price you receive versus the price you targeted or the reference price you care about.
- **Information advantage (alpha capture):** whether you tend to be on the right side of price moves or the wrong side.

All of these are tightly linked to the order book and queueing mechanics described earlier. A simple way to think about it is:

> Your latency profile decides which subset of the market's opportunities you are physically able to interact with.

If you cannot get to the book before it moves, you cannot capture certain profitable trades. If you cannot cancel stale quotes before fast traders trade against them, your profits will leak away through adverse selection.

## Latency and fill probability

Consider a strategy that attempts to buy passively by posting limit orders at the current best bid. From the perspective of the last section, every order you submit joins a queue at that bid price. Your position in the queue heavily influences your chance of getting filled.

When your system is faster, two things generally improve:

- **You join queues earlier.** Given the same decision time, a lower end-to-end latency from decision to matching engine gives you a better place in line at a given price.
- **You can target better prices without sacrificing all fills.** If you can reliably be near the front of the queue, you do not always need to "chase" the price aggressively for fills.

Imagine two traders, FastCo and SlowCo, both running the same simple strategy: whenever their model forecasts a short-term upward move, they both try to buy by placing a limit order at the current best bid. The only difference is that:

- FastCo's order round-trip to the exchange is 200 microseconds.
- SlowCo's order round-trip is 2 milliseconds.

When their models trigger simultaneously, FastCo's orders consistently arrive earlier, landing ahead of SlowCo in the queue at that bid. Over thousands of such events:

- FastCo will enjoy a higher *fill rate* at the original bid price.
- SlowCo will more often see the price move up before its order is filled, forcing it to decide between canceling or chasing the price higher.

If both firms measure the percentage of their desired trade size that is actually executed at the target price, FastCo's metric will be better. Those extra partial fills at favorable prices accumulate into a meaningful economic advantage over time.

This is not simply a convenience; for many short-horizon strategies, a modest improvement in fill probability at good prices is the difference between a barely breakeven idea and a robustly profitable one.

## Latency and slippage

*Slippage* is the difference between the price you actually trade at and some reference price you care about. The reference might be:

- The mid-quote at the time your model decided to trade.
- The price at which you sent your order.
- A benchmark such as the volume-weighted average price (VWAP) over a given window.

Latency affects slippage because it determines how much the market can change between the point at which you decide to trade and the moment your order interacts with the book.

Consider a simple scenario where your model decides to buy when the mid-quote is 100.00. There are two broad possibilities:

- **You submit a limit order** at 100.00 (the current best bid).
- **You submit a marketable order** that crosses the spread to buy immediately.

In both cases, your realized price will depend on how the book evolves during your latency window:

- **Limit order case.** If your order arrives quickly and gets a good position in the queue, you are more likely to be filled at 100.00 before the price moves up. If you arrive slowly, someone else may have taken that liquidity, or the offers may have been lifted, causing the best bid to move up. Your limit order might never fill, or it may fill only partially before the price runs away. To eventually get your full size, you may have to reprice at higher levels, increasing your slippage relative to the original mid-quote.

- **Marketable order case.** If your marketable buy arrives quickly, it trades against the liquidity that was visible when your model decided. If it arrives late, the offers you saw may already have been consumed or moved up. You may end up paying a higher price or walking up the book into deeper, worse-priced liquidity to complete your trade.

Even though the decision logic is identical, the slower trader lives in a slightly different world:

- They are systematically more likely to get “after-the-fact” prices, because much of the favorable liquidity disappears during their latency.
- They are more frequently forced to compromise—either forgoing trades (lost opportunity) or accepting worse prices (higher slippage).

Over many trades, if both firms compute their average slippage versus the decision-time mid-quote, FastCo will typically show smaller average slippage and tighter dispersion around that average. SlowCo’s slippage distribution will be more negative and more volatile.

## Latency and alpha capture

Alpha, in this context, is the part of your returns that remains after controlling for market direction and simple risk exposures. It reflects your ability to systematically buy before prices go up and sell before prices go down.

Latency influences alpha because it determines whether you tend to trade *before* or *after* short-term price moves associated with the information your models are exploiting.

Revisit our two firms, FastCo and SlowCo, both using the same signal that predicts an average upward price move of, say, 2 cents over the next few seconds. Suppose that, in a frictionless world with no latency, buying when the signal fires would yield this 2-cent edge on average.

In the real world:

- FastCo's lower latency lets it submit and execute orders closer to the time the signal is generated. Its fills tend to occur while the predicted move is still mostly in the future.
- SlowCo's greater latency means that by the time it trades, part of the predicted move has already happened. The edge has been "used up" by faster participants.

Quantitatively, if you measure the average price change between your actual execution prices and some later reference point (for example, the mid-quote a few seconds after your trade):

- FastCo might still realize, for illustration, 1.5 cents of that expected 2-cent edge.
- SlowCo might only realize 0.3 cents, or possibly nothing at all after transaction costs.

The lost 1.7 cents per share for SlowCo are not random bad luck; they are a structural consequence of being late to implement the same signal. Over millions of shares, the difference in realized alpha becomes substantial.

This logic also works in reverse. If your latency is so poor that your trades consistently occur *after* the short-term move, you might end up systematically *losing* money despite having a signal that, in theory, predicts correctly. In that sense, insufficient speed can turn a good idea into a negative-alpha strategy.

## Adverse selection and the cost of being slow

The order book perspective tells us that not all fills are equally desirable. Being filled right before the market moves in your favor is good; being filled right before it moves against you is bad.

*Adverse selection* occurs when you are consistently on the wrong side of this timing. From the standpoint of latency:

- Faster traders often get to choose whether to trade against *your* quotes after they see new information.

- If you cannot cancel or revise your quotes quickly, you end up being the counterpart when they decide the price is about to move.

Imagine you are providing liquidity by posting a bid. A negative news shock hits:

- Fast traders read the news, reprice their models, and rush to cancel their bids or push them down.
- If your cancel messages are slow, your old bid stays in the book.
- Aggressive sellers from the fast crowd may choose to hit your stale bid exactly because it is still there when others have pulled back.

If you later measure how prices evolve after your fills, you might find a pattern:

- On average, the price tends to drop further after your buy trades.
- On average, the price tends to rise after your sell trades.

This asymmetry is a monetary measure of adverse selection. Reducing latency in quote updates and cancels can directly shrink this drag:

- You spend less time sitting at unattractive prices.
- You are less often the "last man standing" in the queue when fast traders have decided the quote is bad.

From an economic perspective, the key metric is the average post-trade price movement relative to your fill. Bring that closer to zero, and you raise your expected profit per trade, even if nothing else about your model changes.

## Cumulative impact: small edges, many repetitions

Because individual trades often involve tiny price differences, it can be tempting to dismiss latency improvements as marginal. The critical insight is that modern systematic strategies may execute:

- Thousands of trades per day for a single instrument.
- Across hundreds or thousands of instruments.
- Over months and years.

Even very small per-trade benefits accumulate. A fraction of a cent improvement in average execution price, multiplied by millions of shares per year, can easily exceed the cost of meaningful infrastructure upgrades.

Conversely, a small but systematic disadvantage—slightly worse fills, slightly lower fill rates on good prices, slightly more adverse selection—can erode the profitability of an otherwise sound strategy.

When you evaluate latency as an investment, you do not need to justify it with dramatic per-trade gains. You need to understand:

- The *average impact* of speed on your key execution metrics.
- The *volume* of trades over which that impact compounds.
- The *stability* of that advantage across market conditions.

This is a familiar capital budgeting problem in disguise.

## Strategy dependence: where speed truly matters

Not every strategy needs extreme speed. The importance of latency depends on your strategy's characteristics:

- **Time horizon of alpha.** If your signal predicts price moves over days or weeks, microseconds will be irrelevant, and even seconds may not matter much. If your horizon is seconds or less, latency is central.
- **Turnover and trade frequency.** A strategy that trades infrequently may not justify heavy investment in speed, even if it occasionally loses to faster traders. High-turnover strategies amplify any execution advantage or disadvantage.

- **Style of execution.** Strategies that rely heavily on passive liquidity provision (posting quotes) are especially sensitive to cancellation and update latency. Strategies that primarily cross the spread may care more about the speed of routing and market data.

- **Competition.** In markets or instruments where many high-speed players compete, falling significantly behind the speed frontier may preclude certain styles of trading altogether.

Your architectural decisions about latency should be aligned with this profile. For a long-horizon, low-turnover portfolio, investing heavily to shave microseconds may be wasteful. For an intraday, high-frequency strategy, failing to do so may mean the strategy is never economically viable in live trading, even if backtests based on idealized assumptions look strong.

## From technical optimization to capital allocation

With these ideas in mind, you can now frame latency work within your overall investment process:

- **Measure.** For each major strategy, measure how your fills, slippage, and post-trade price movements depend on your current latency profile. This involves instrument-level and venue-level statistics, not just headline averages.

- **Attribute.** Distinguish between losses that come from model errors (bad signals) and those that come from execution (bad timing). Latency improvements can only fix the latter.

- **Estimate benefits.** Ask: If I could reduce certain latencies by a realistic amount, how would my fill rates, slippage, and adverse selection metrics change, given my current trading patterns?

- **Estimate costs.** Quantify the financial and organizational costs of proposed changes: hardware, network lines, exchange connectivity, specialized staff, and operational complexity.

- **Compare and prioritize.** Evaluate latency projects alongside other uses of capital, such as developing new signals, expanding coverage, or improving risk management.

This discipline transforms latency from an engineering race with no finish line into a series of concrete, testable investment decisions. The question is not "How fast can we possibly be?" but:

> "How much speed is economically justified for this particular strategy and trading style, given its alpha horizon, turnover, and competition?"

## Robustness, diminishing returns, and risk

Finally, it is important to recognize that investing in speed has diminishing returns and its own risks:

- **Diminishing returns.** The first big reductions in latency—for example, moving from a distant data center to co-location, or from a generic network stack to an optimized one—often bring substantial improvements in execution quality. Further refinements may produce much smaller incremental benefits, especially if you are already near the speed of your peers.
- **Execution risk.** Extreme optimization can make systems brittle. Aggressive kernel tuning, custom hardware, or complex routing logic may increase the risk of rare but severe failures: missed cancels, runaway quoting, or desynchronization between components.
- **Regulatory and reputational risk.** Some latency techniques push up against regulatory boundaries or public expectations about market fairness. High-speed strategies have occasionally been at the center of policy debates; any design choice that relies heavily on exploiting other participants' slower feeds or routes should be assessed through that lens.

A thoughtful architecture aims for *economically meaningful* speed that is also *operationally robust*. Rather than chasing every last microsecond, you identify the ranges of latency that materially affect your strategies and design systems to be reliably within those ranges, even under stress.

### Summary: latency as a priced parameter

By this point in the chapter, latency should be visible as a priced parameter in your trading business, not just a technical curiosity:

- It shapes your place in the order book and thus your fill probabilities.
- It determines how much of your theoretical signal edge turns into realized alpha before the market moves.
- It influences your exposure to adverse selection when you provide liquidity.
- It compounds over thousands of trades into significant differences in profits and losses.

In the chapters that follow, we will turn this economic understanding into practical design guidelines. We will look at how to measure latency more precisely, how to relate those measurements to execution metrics, and how to build architectures that deliver the level of speed your strategies truly need—no more, and no less.

## 1.5 Regulatory Impacts on Latency Strategies

Up to this point, we have treated latency as a technical and economic variable: an attribute of your trading system and of the market's plumbing that shapes fills, slippage, and alpha. In reality, latency is also a *governed* variable. Market structure is not just the product of technology and competition; it is also the outcome of regulatory choices and venue-specific rules.

This section examines how regulation and venue design influence which latency tactics are available, which are discouraged, and which are deliberately built into the market. The goal is not to provide a legal treatise, but to give you a clear framework: when you design latency-sensitive strategies and architectures, you are operating inside a rule set that can change, and sometimes targets latency itself.

## Latency in the eyes of the regulator

Market regulators and venue operators care about latency for three broad reasons:

- **Fair access and level playing field.** They want to avoid a situation where only a tiny set of participants can realistically compete because of extreme speed advantages that others cannot reasonably obtain.
- **Market integrity and stability.** Very fast, tightly coupled systems can amplify errors or feedback loops, leading to instability or flash crashes. Rules sometimes aim to slow down or dampen destabilizing feedback.
- **Market quality.** Regulators track liquidity, spreads, depth, and volatility. They care whether latency-advantaged strategies improve these metrics (for example by tighter spreads) or degrade them (for example by increased noise or fleeting liquidity).

From a trading system architect's perspective, this means that your choices around speed and topology are not just constrained by physics and budgets, but also by:

- Regulatory requirements on access and connectivity.
- Venue rules about order types, throughput, and timing.
- Mechanisms deliberately inserted to affect latency, such as speed bumps.

Understanding these constraints early in your design process can save you from investing in latency tactics that turn out to be disallowed or fragile under regulatory change.

## Co-location and proximity hosting

Perhaps the most visible intersection between regulation and latency is *co-location*: exchanges and trading venues offer space in or near their data centers so participants can place their own servers as physically close as possible to the matching engine.

From a pure engineering standpoint, co-location is a straightforward service:

- Shorter physical distance means shorter fiber runs and fewer hops.
- Fewer and simpler network segments mean lower and more predictable latency.

From a regulatory standpoint, however, co-location raises questions:

- Is access to co-location offered on fair, non-discriminatory terms?
- Do some participants receive systematically better latency, for example through special cages, custom cross-connects, or private microwave networks?
- Does the combination of co-location and internal venue policies create hidden tiers of access?

In many major jurisdictions, co-location is permitted but subject to principles of *fair access*. This typically means:

- Any qualified participant can request co-location, within capacity limits.
- Pricing and technical specifications are published and standardized.
- The venue does not secretly give one firm a faster physical route than others via the same service tier.

For your architecture, this has two important implications:

- **Latency advantages are partly commoditized.** Once co-location is widely available and roughly symmetric, being in the co-lo facility is no longer a distinct edge by itself—it is a prerequisite. The competitive edge moves to what you build *inside* the rack: hardware choices, software stack, and algorithms.
- **Non-standard arrangements invite scrutiny.** If you seek or are offered special connectivity, custom routing, or privileged access, you must consider regulatory risk: rules and guidance may change to close what regulators perceive as unfair advantages.

Designing a latency-sensitive system therefore means not only selecting co-location where necessary, but also ensuring that your setup is robust to potential changes in how co-location is priced, standardized, or restricted.

## Market data, order protection, and latency asymmetries

Another major regulatory lever is the *market data and order protection regime.*

Most advanced markets have rules specifying:

- How and when trade and quote information must be published.
- Whether venues must protect "best" displayed prices across the system, or whether trades can occur at worse prices on one venue while better prices are available on another.
- Requirements for fair and non-discriminatory access to data feeds.

These rules shape latency strategies in several ways.

**Consolidated feeds vs. direct feeds.**

Regulators often require the existence of a consolidated public data feed that aggregates quotes and trades from all venues and disseminates a unified view of the market. At the same time, venues can sell faster, richer *direct feeds* from their own systems.

This creates a latency hierarchy:

- Direct feeds are typically faster and more detailed, but more expensive.
- The consolidated feed is slower and may omit some microstructural detail, but is accessible to a broader set of participants.

Regulation balances two concerns:

- Allowing venues to innovate and monetize high-quality data.
- Ensuring that the public or smaller participants are not left with dangerously stale or incomplete information.

For latency strategies, the key architectural questions become:

- Which feeds do you subscribe to, and how do you process and synchronize them?
- How do you handle discrepancies between fast direct feeds and slower consolidated data?
- If order protection rules require you to consider the best prices across venues, how does data latency affect your routing logic?

Your system must respect these regulatory constraints while attempting to exploit any legal advantage available from lower-latency or richer feeds.

**Order protection and routing obligations.**

In some jurisdictions, order protection rules require that trades for certain securities do not occur at prices worse than the best displayed quote on any protected venue. This influences latency because:

- Your smart order router must track the protected top-of-book across venues, using whatever feeds are legally permitted.
- Latency in those feeds can cause your view of the "best" price to lag; yet you are still responsible for routing in compliance with the rules.

If your router is designed without careful consideration of feed latencies and regulatory definitions of "protected" quotes, you can inadvertently violate order protection rules or at least expose yourself to execution that regulators or clients may later challenge.

## Speed bumps and intentional delays

In recent years, some venues and regulators have taken a more direct approach to latency: they have introduced *intentional delays*, often called "speed bumps," into parts of the trading process.

A speed bump is a small, fixed delay—often measured in microseconds or milliseconds—inserted into one or more of the following:

- Order entry.
- Order cancellation or modification.
- Matching or routing of orders.

The purpose of such mechanisms varies:

- To reduce the advantage of pure reaction-speed strategies that depend on being marginally faster than others.
- To give liquidity providers slightly more time to react to new information before being picked off.
- To dampen hyper-fast feedback loops that can destabilize markets.

From your perspective as an architect, speed bumps change the effective latency landscape in a targeted way:

- **They cap the benefit of ultra-fine latency improvements.** If every order is delayed by, say, 1 millisecond at the venue, then shaving 50 microseconds from your own system may matter less on that venue than on one without a bump.
- **They create side-specific asymmetries.** Some designs delay only certain types of messages (for example, order entry but not cancellations). Such asymmetries can favor particular strategies over others, and your architecture should be aware of which pathways are slowed.
- **They change cross-venue timing.** A speed-bumped venue may lag non-bumped venues in reacting to market-wide news. That can affect your routing decisions, arbitrage logic, and expectations around fill quality.

Critically, speed bumps are *policy tools*. They may be introduced, modified, or removed as part of broader debates about fairness and quality. A strategy that depends too narrowly on a specific speed bump design may face significant model risk if rules change.

## Order types, throttles, and message-rate limits

Venues and regulators also influence latency strategies indirectly through rules about *order types*, *message rates*, and *throttling mechanisms*.

**Order types as microstructure policy.**

Exchanges define specific order types with embedded behaviors: hidden or partially hidden orders, pegged orders, discretionary orders, and so on. Some of these order types can be exploited in latency-sensitive ways. For example, a pegged order that tracks the best bid or offer might change behavior rapidly as the reference quote moves.

Regulators sometimes scrutinize order types that seem to favor sophisticated, latency-sensitive participants at the expense of others. In response, venues may:

- Modify or retire certain order types.
- Standardize behavior to reduce subtle timing advantages.
- Increase transparency around how order types interact with matching and queue priority.

Architecturally, you must design for the possibility that order-type definitions can change and, with them, the latency characteristics of your strategies.

**Message-rate limits and throttles.**

High-speed strategies can generate enormous volumes of messages: orders, cancels, modifications, and quotes. To prevent overload and abusive behavior, venues and regulators often impose:

- Per-connection or per-firm message-rate limits.
- Throttling mechanisms that slow or reject excess traffic.
- Minimum resting times for orders or fees for excessive cancellations.

These rules shape latency strategies in several ways:

- They limit your ability to "spray and cancel" orders in an attempt to be everywhere at once.
- They force you to prioritize which messages matter most under tight latency budgets.
- They introduce non-linear behavior: once you hit a throttle, your effective latency can spike as messages are queued or rejected.

Robust systems therefore include:

- Real-time monitoring of message rates relative to limits.
- Back-off and prioritization logic that degrades gracefully under constraint.

- Awareness of how throttling affects end-to-end latency during periods of stress.

Ignoring these regulatory and venue-imposed constraints can lead to architectures that perform well in backtests but fail in live markets when confronted with throttling or penalties.

## Fair access, best execution, and client-facing obligations

If you operate as an agency broker or asset manager, regulation also shapes how you deploy latency advantages on behalf of clients.

Two concepts are central:

- **Best execution.** You are generally obligated to seek the best reasonably available execution for clients, considering price, costs, speed, and likelihood of execution.
- **Fair treatment of clients.** You should not exploit latency asymmetries to systematically advantage one set of clients over another, or your firm's proprietary trading over client orders, without clear and acceptable justification.

Latency-sensitive architecture can help you meet best execution obligations by:

- Improving fill rates at good prices.
- Reducing slippage and adverse selection.
- Allowing more precise control of routing and timing.

However, these same capabilities can raise questions if misused, for example:

- Routing profitable, latency-sensitive flow to internal strategies while leaving slower, less favorable routes for clients.

- Designing systems that implicitly favor certain clients' orders in shared execution channels.

From a design perspective, this means:

- Making routing logic transparent and explainable.
- Logging latency-related decisions and outcomes to support regulatory and client review.
- Ensuring that configuration and policy rules governing latency-sensitive behavior are aligned with best execution and fair-dealing obligations.

## Regulatory change as a source of model and design risk

Finally, any latency strategy operates against a moving regulatory backdrop. Over the past decades, several shifts have had direct implications for speed-sensitive trading:

- Changes in tick sizes and lot sizes, altering the economics of providing liquidity.
- Revisions to order protection rules or the definition of protected quotes.
- Introduction or modification of circuit breakers, halts, and volatility controls.
- New transparency requirements for dark pools and internalizers, affecting where and how liquidity can be accessed.

Each such change can:

- Alter the profitability of strategies that rely on specific latency relationships.

- Change which venues or feed types are essential.
- Modify the balance between co-located and non-co-located participants.

Therefore, latency-sensitive architecture must be:

- **Configurable.** Rules about routing, order types, and venue usage should be adjustable without redesigning the entire system.
- **Monitored.** You should be able to observe in real time how regulatory or venue changes affect your latency, fill rates, and slippage.
- **Scenario-tested.** Before new rules go live, simulate or dry-run their effects on your strategies and infrastructure.

Treat regulatory change as a first-class source of risk, on par with model drift or hardware failure, especially for architectures that push hard on the latency frontier.

## Summary: designing speed under rules

Regulation and venue rules do not eliminate latency competition; they channel and shape it. Co-location, data feed regimes, speed bumps, order types, throttles, and best-execution obligations all define the playground in which latency strategies operate.

For a trading system architect, the key takeaways are:

- Every latency advantage you seek should be checked against explicit rules on access, fairness, and market quality.
- Some latency tools (like co-location) have become standardized and regulated; they are now baseline capabilities, not exotic edges.
- Other tools (like speed bumps or complex order types) are policy experiments; building strategies that rely heavily on their current form carries regulatory and design risk.

- Client-facing obligations mean that latency-sensitive design is not just about speed and profit, but also about explainability and fairness.

By understanding latency as both a technical and a regulated dimension of market design, you can build systems that are not only fast and economically effective, but also resilient to the evolving legal and policy environment in which modern electronic markets operate.

# Chapter 2

# Market Microstructure Basics

*Every trading system ultimately crashes into the same hard surface: the exchange rulebook. This chapter peels back the abstractions your code relies on-"send order", "get fill"-and exposes the microstructure beneath: how venues really match orders, where your messages sit in the queue, and which life-cycle events quietly add milliseconds or basis points of slippage. By the end, you'll see that many performance problems aren't in your algorithms at all, but in how those algorithms collide with the market's plumbing.*

## 2.1 Order Types and Attributes

In the previous chapter we treated "an order" almost as a black box: a message that goes from your system to the exchange, and eventually returns with some combination of fills, rejections, or cancellations. To design low-latency systems, that abstraction is too coarse. The matching engine behaves very differently depending on *how* you phrase the instruction.

This section opens that black box. We will:

- Define the main order types and key attributes.
- Explain what the matching engine does with each.
- Connect each variant to three practical concerns:
- fill quality (price and quantity),
- information leakage (what others can infer about your intentions),
- latency risk (how much small timing differences change your outcome).

Throughout, keep one idea in mind: an order is not just "buy or sell." It is a bundle of constraints and preferences. The more you constrain the exchange, the more sensitive you become to microseconds and microstructure details.

## 2.2 Core Order Types: Market, Limit, Stop, Stop-Limit

Most other order types are layered on top of four primitives.

**Market Orders**

A market order says: *"Trade this quantity immediately at the best prices available."* It does not specify a price limit. The exchange matches it against resting orders on the opposite side, walking the book as far as needed to fill the requested quantity.

**Fill quality.**

- You gain immediacy but surrender control over price.
- In a deep, liquid market, the impact may be a fraction of a tick.
- In a thin or stressed market, you may sweep through multiple price levels, producing large slippage.

**Information leakage.**

- Because a market order consumes visible liquidity, it instantly reveals that someone was willing to cross the spread for that quantity.
- Large market orders can telegraph urgency; other traders infer that a sizable trader is active and may adjust quotes defensively.

**Latency risk.**

- A market order's value depends mainly on the state of the book *at arrival*, not on an exact price. That makes it somewhat more robust to modest latency than a very tight limit.
- However, if the book is moving fast, even millisecond delays can move you from trading at the current best price to trading several ticks worse.
- From a system perspective, market orders relax some timing pressure on the client but increase the need for accurate, up-to-date risk checks; the notional traded is uncertain at send time and must be bounded by risk limits.

### Limit Orders

A limit order says: *"Trade this quantity, but only at a price at least this good."* For a buy limit order, the limit is the *maximum* price you will pay; for a sell, the *minimum* price you will accept.

**Fill quality.**

- Limit orders give you price control. You avoid paying above your limit (for buys) or selling below it (for sells).
- When your limit is more aggressive than the current best price (for example, you place a buy limit above the best ask), the order behaves similarly to a market order: it executes immediately, often at prices better than the limit.
- When your limit is inside the book (for example, a buy below the best ask), the order may rest in the book and only fill if the market moves to you or others trade through you.

**Information leakage.**

- A displayed limit order contributes to the visible quote. Others see your price and size.
- If you post large visible size at a level away from the market, you may reveal your interest and invite others to trade ahead or fade before you get filled.
- On the other hand, being passive (providing liquidity) often earns rebates or better average execution prices, especially for market makers, and is less immediately revealing than an aggressive market sweep.

**Latency risk.**

- An aggressive limit (close to or through the current best price) is highly sensitive to latency. If the market moves by a tick before your order arrives, the order may no longer execute or may execute at a worse queue position.
- A passive limit that rests far from the current market is less latency-sensitive at entry, but latency still matters for subsequent modifications and cancels.
- When strategies rely on narrow spreads or fleeting arbitrage opportunities, a few microseconds of additional path length can be the difference between being first in the queue or tenth.

### Stop Orders

A stop order is an instruction that becomes active *only after* the market reaches a trigger price (the stop price). Conceptually it says: *"If the market trades at or through this level, submit a new order for me."*

The most common is the stop-*market* order:

- A sell stop-market below the current price is often used as a protective stop: if the price falls to the stop level, the order activates as a market order and sells immediately.
- A buy stop-market above the current price might be used to enter on a breakout.

**Fill quality.**

- Stops are about conditional execution, not price control. A stop-market may activate at your trigger price but actually fill at a worse price if the market gaps through your level.
- You must treat the stop as a *boundary* for when to trade, not a guarantee of the execution price.

**Information leakage.**

- Many venues keep stop orders off the public book until they trigger. This can reduce information leakage versus equivalent visible resting orders.
- However, when a wave of stops triggers at the same level, the resulting burst of market orders is highly informative to other traders about trapped inventory and forced exits.

**Latency risk.**

- Stop triggering depends on market data: last trade, bid/ask, or other reference. If your own system maintains a synthetic stop (client-side), then your feed latency directly affects when you send the activating order.
- Exchange-native stops reduce that dependency, but there is still internal matching-engine latency between the trigger event and your order entering the book.
- In fast markets, even small delays can cause you to be filled at much worse prices than the stop, or not at all if the market snaps back before the stop order is processed.

### Stop-Limit Orders

A stop-limit order combines a trigger price and a limit price. Once the stop triggers, the order becomes a limit order instead of a market order. This adds a second layer of control:

- You ensure you only trade if the market reaches your stop, *and* you bound the price you are willing to accept.

- The trade-off is that in fast moves your limit may never be hit, leaving you unfilled even though your stop condition was met.

**Fill quality, leakage, and latency.**

- Fill quality is more predictable than a pure stop-market, but at the cost of more non-fills.
- Information leakage is similar to stops: the order is often hidden until triggered.
- Latency risk is higher than either component alone. You suffer from both the timing of the trigger and the usual limit order race for queue position once live.

## 2.3 Time-in-Force: How Long an Order Lives

Order type answers "*how* to trade." Time-in-force (TIF) answers "*how long* should this instruction remain active?"

**Day and Good-Till-Cancelled (GTC)**

**Day orders.** A day order is active until the end of the trading session in which it was submitted. If unfilled, it expires automatically at the close.

**GTC orders.** A good-till-cancelled order persists across trading days until explicitly cancelled or until a venue-specific maximum lifetime is reached.

**Practical effects.**

- Day and GTC orders are suitable for investors and slower strategies that are willing to wait for the market to come to them.
- They are less sensitive to small latency variations at the moment of entry, but require robust state management: your system must track open orders across restarts, sessions, and even software releases.

- From a risk standpoint, long-lived orders expose you to regime changes. When the environment shifts (volatility, event risk), you must cancel or adjust these standing instructions quickly; latency now matters for *exit* rather than entry.

**Immediate-or-Cancel (IOC)**

An IOC order says: *"Fill as much as you can immediately; cancel the rest."* Any portion that cannot be matched instantly at your stated price constraints is removed instead of left resting.

**Fill quality.**

- IOC is a natural fit for tactical liquidity taking, arbitrage, and smart order routing. You take what is there, then move on.
- You avoid lingering residual pieces that might be picked off later under worse information.

**Information leakage.**

- Because IOC orders do not remain in the book, they do not advertise your interest for long.
- However, partial fills still reveal that you were willing to cross the spread for at least some size, and cancellations (and their timing) may be inferred from trade patterns.

**Latency risk.**

- IOC orders are extremely latency-sensitive. Their value collapses if the book changes between the time you observe the quote and when your order arrives.
- This is a direct "stale quote" problem: your decision is based on market data stamped at time $t$, but your order interacts with a book at $t + \Delta t$. The larger $\Delta t$, the more often your IOC returns unfilled.
- Architecturally, IOC usage pushes you toward co-location, low-latency networking, and tight integration between market data and order gateways.

### Fill-or-Kill (FOK)

A FOK order says: *"Fill the entire quantity immediately at my price or better, or do nothing at all."* There is no partial execution.

**Fill quality and leakage.**

- FOK is valuable when partial fills are not useful, for example when a hedge requires a precise size.
- It minimizes information leakage if unfilled: the order arrives, checks the book, and disappears without leaving a resting footprint.
- When filled, though, you reveal a large sudden demand or supply, similar to a big market order, especially if you consume multiple levels.

**Latency risk.**

- FOK combines the latency sensitivities of IOC with an even stricter condition. Any small deterioration in the book before arrival converts a potential full fill into a complete miss.
- Systems sending FOKs must monitor hit ratios closely; a low realized fill rate is often a sign that routing or infrastructure latency is misaligned with the strategy's assumptions.

### Good-Till-Time and Other Variants

Some venues support cxplicit cxpiry timestamps (good-till-time) or more complex conditions (good-till-event). These allow you to encode timing logic directly into the order, reducing the need for client-side timers.

From a design perspective, every extra TIF option you use must be modeled in your order state machine and replay logic. The more conditions are embedded in the exchange, the more you rely on their clocks and their interpretation of expiry versus your own.

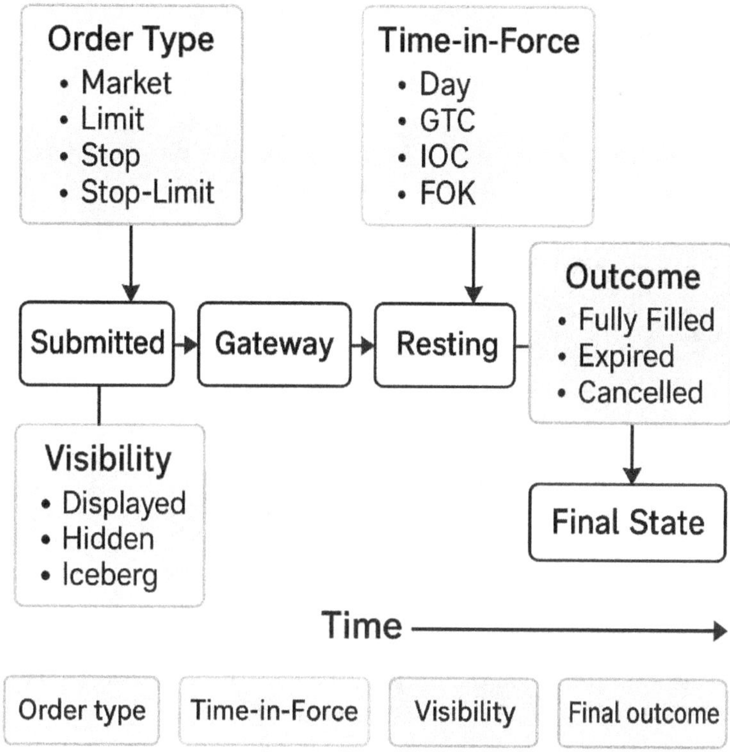


## 2.4 Visibility: Displayed, Hidden, and Iceberg Orders

Beyond type and lifetime, you must also decide whether and how your order is visible to other participants.

**Displayed Orders**

A standard limit order is fully displayed in the order book:

- Its price and full size appear at the appropriate level.

- It contributes to the public best bid or offer if it is at the top of the book.

**Advantages.**

- You gain queue priority at your price according to the venue's matching rules (discussed in the next section).
- You help define the market; other traders see your quote and may trade against it.

**Costs.**

- You fully reveal your intended size at that level, which can invite front-running, gaming, or adverse selection.
- When the market moves toward your level, faster traders can react ahead of you, buying or selling in front of your quote and leaving you filled when it is no longer attractive.

### Hidden and Reserve (Iceberg) Orders

Hidden orders do not appear in the visible book, but can still interact with incoming orders at their price. Iceberg or reserve orders split your size into a displayed peak and a hidden remainder.

**Fill quality.**

- Hidden orders often have lower queue priority than displayed orders at the same price. You trade off some probability of being filled for reduced information leakage.
- Icebergs offer a compromise: you display a small slice to gain some priority while keeping most of the size out of view. Each time the visible slice is filled, the exchange replenishes it from the hidden reserve, usually sending a new peak to the back of the queue.

**Information leakage.**

- Hidden and iceberg orders are tools to mask your true size and intent.

- However, patterns in replenishment and repeated fills at the same price can still signal the presence of a large hidden counterparty to observant participants.

**Latency risk and system design.**

- For hidden liquidity, since you give up queue priority, latency becomes even more crucial when you *do* choose to display or refresh size. Your visible slice competes for priority with others at the same price.
- Iceberg replenishment events are state changes in your order life cycle. Systems must model and log them; otherwise you will mismeasure your exposure and fill statistics.
- Latency in receiving fill reports on the visible slice can delay your decision to cancel the remaining hidden reserve or to hedge the executed portion, increasing risk.

## 2.5 Aggressive vs. Passive Combinations

Most trading strategies can be characterized by whether they seek to *take* liquidity (aggressive) or *provide* liquidity (passive) on average. The combinations of order type, TIF, and visibility encode that choice.

### Typical Aggressive Patterns

Aggressive orders cross the spread or sit at the very front of the queue to ensure rapid execution. Common patterns include:

- Market or aggressively priced limit orders with IOC or FOK TIF.
- Small or no displayed size remaining after the initial attempt (no resting residue).

**Impact on fill quality.**

- You generally achieve high fill rates and low waiting times.
- You may suffer from higher slippage and transaction costs, especially during volatile periods when the book is thin.

**Information leakage and latency.**

- Aggressive behavior reveals more about your urgency and direction, especially when orders are large relative to visible depth.
- These patterns are the most latency-sensitive because they respond to fleeting price discrepancies and arbitrage opportunities. Even small delays can turn a profitable trade into an adverse fill.

### Typical Passive Patterns

Passive orders aim to earn the spread or provide liquidity to others. Typical patterns:

- Limit orders priced at or slightly inside the current best bid or offer.
- Time-in-force set to Day or GTC, sometimes with hidden or iceberg flags.

**Impact on fill quality.**

- When successful, passive orders capture the spread and reduce trading costs.
- The main risk is adverse selection: you are filled precisely when others know something you do not, such as incoming news or hidden order flow.

**Information leakage and latency.**

- Visible passive orders broadcast your willingness to trade at a given level, which may attract informed traders.
- Latency matters in a different way: not just on entry, but on exit. When a quote becomes stale (for instance, after a news shock), your ability to cancel or reprice quickly determines how often you are "picked off" at bad prices.

## 2.6 Latency as an Implicit Attribute

Although "latency" does not appear in any order ticket field, every attribute you choose encodes assumptions about timing:

- A tight IOC limit assumes the book you see now will still exist when you reach it.
- A GTC order assumes you can monitor, cancel, and adjust it whenever the environment changes.
- A hidden order assumes the gain from reduced information leakage exceeds the cost of lower queue priority and higher timing vulnerability.

From an architectural standpoint, supporting this variety has concrete consequences:

- Your gateway interfaces must validate combinations of type, TIF, and visibility according to each venue's rule set, ideally without adding avoidable latency.
- Risk checks must anticipate the worst-case fill behavior of each order type; for example, a stop-market activation can momentarily behave like a large market sweep.
- Routing logic must be aware of how each destination interprets attributes (for example, whether IOC is strictly enforced, how hidden orders are prioritized) to avoid unexpected behavior.

In summary, order types and attributes are the vocabulary with which you converse with the market. To an end investor, these may look like simple drop-down menus. To a trading system designer, they are levers that shape queue position, information footprint, and sensitivity to every microsecond between your decision and the matching engine's response.

## 2.7 Queue Priority and Matching Rules

In the previous section we treated an order as a set of attributes: type, time-in-force, and visibility. We looked at how those choices shaped your exposure to latency and information leakage. In this section we move one step deeper into the matching engine and ask a more specific question:

> Given many orders at the same price, *who* gets to trade first, and how much do they get?

The answer is encoded in the venue's *matching rules*. These rules determine the priority of each order in the queue and how incoming opposite-side volume is allocated. For latency-sensitive trading, this is crucial: a difference of microseconds in arrival time can move you from the front of the queue to the back, changing your fill probability from almost certain to almost zero.

We will:

- Describe the main matching schemes used in modern markets.
- Show, with simple numeric examples, how tiny timing differences change queue position and realized fills.
- Connect those examples to system design: what these rules imply for latency budgets, routing decisions, and risk models.

### Price First, Then Something Else

Almost all electronic order books obey one overarching principle: *better prices trade first*. Among orders at the same price, the venue applies an additional tie-breaking rule. The most common are:

- **Price-time priority** (often called FIFO: first-in, first-out).
- **Pro-rata priority**, which allocates fills in proportion to displayed size.

- **Hybrid schemes**, which mix time and size rules or apply special treatment to specific participants.

From a system perspective, you control your *price* when you choose the limit, and you influence your *priority within that price* by choosing when (and how much) to send. Latency optimization mainly affects that second dimension: at a given price, can you be early enough, or big enough, to get the fills your strategy expects?

## Price-Time Priority (FIFO)

Under pure price-time priority, the book at each price level is a queue ordered by arrival time:

- The first order at a given price sits at the head of the queue.
- Later orders at the same price line up behind it in the order they arrived.
- Incoming opposite-side quantity trades against the queue in that order, exhausting each order before moving to the next.

## A Simple FIFO Example

Imagine the best bid in a stock is $10.00, and three buy orders at that price arrive:

- Trader A sends a buy limit for 100 shares at $10.00 at time $t_0$.
- Trader B sends a buy limit for 200 shares at $10.00 at time $t_0 + 1$ millisecond.
- Trader C sends a buy limit for 50 shares at $10.00 at time $t_0 + 2$ milliseconds.

The queue at $10.00 (best bid) is:

- A: 100 shares (front of the queue).

- B: 200 shares.
- C: 50 shares (back of the queue).

Now suppose an incoming sell market order for 180 shares hits the book.

- A's entire 100 shares trade first.
- There are 80 shares of selling left; they then go to B.
- B receives 80 of their 200 shares; 120 remain resting.
- C is untouched.

The key point: that 1-millisecond advantage allowed A to capture a full fill, while B, with twice the size, received only a partial, and C got nothing. If A and B had swapped arrival times, their fill outcomes would also have swapped.

## Tiny Latency Differences, Big Fill Differences

In FIFO markets, microseconds matter when:

- The volume at the best price is small compared to the volume of informed or urgent flow hitting it, and/or
- Many speed-sensitive traders compete to post at the same price level.

If your strategy assumes that "posting 100 shares at the best bid yields a 70% chance of full execution within 50 milliseconds," that probability is really a statement about:

- Your expected *queue position* when you arrive, and
- The expected *flow* that will hit your price before the market moves away.

Any additional latency in your path — slower market data, slower decision logic, slower gateway — systematically moves you down the queue. The effect compounds over time: many apparently small "almost filled" events add up to a large P&L difference.

## Pro-Rata Matching

Under pro-rata matching, the book at a given price is more like a pool than a strict line. Instead of always serving the earliest order first, the exchange allocates an incoming contra order across all resting orders *in proportion to their displayed size*. Time is either secondary or almost irrelevant for the bulk of the allocation.

## A Simple Pro-Rata Example

Consider a futures contract where the best bid is again $10.00, but the venue uses pro-rata matching. Three buy orders rest at $10.00:

- Trader D: 100 contracts.
- Trader E: 200 contracts.
- Trader F: 50 contracts.

For simplicity, assume all three were in place before any sells arrive. The total quantity at $10.00 is 350 contracts.

Now an incoming sell market order for 140 contracts hits the book. Under strict pro-rata:

- D's share of the resting volume is $100/350$, so they receive $100/350$ of 140 contracts $\approx$ 40 contracts.
- E's share is $200/350$, so they receive $\approx$ 80 contracts.
- F's share is $50/350$, so they receive $\approx$ 20 contracts.

Rounding rules vary by venue, but the idea is that larger orders get proportionally larger fills. A small participant cannot completely block a large participant simply by arriving first.

## Latency vs. Size in Pro-Rata

In a pure pro-rata world:

- *Displayed size* is your main lever for improving fill share.
- *Arrival time* still matters for details (such as tie-breaking on residual contracts after rounding), but much less than in FIFO.

This has several consequences:

- It encourages "quote stuffing" or "size padding," where traders display more size than they truly want in order to win a larger pro-rata share, then quickly cancel unfilled residuals.
- It reduces, but does not eliminate, the value of shaving microseconds off latency; those microseconds mainly influence marginal units of allocation.
- It shifts system design pressure toward very fast quote cancellation and update logic, because your displayed size becomes a critical tactical variable.

## Hybrid and Size-Priority Schemes

Many venues adopt hybrids rather than a pure FIFO or pure pro-rata model. Examples include:

- **Price-time with size thresholds**: orders above a certain minimum size receive preferential placement or a guaranteed minimum allocation.
- **Time-segmented pro-rata**: within time buckets (for example, all orders arriving in the same microsecond), allocation is pro-rata, but across buckets, earlier buckets trade first.
- **Special priority tiers**: some participants (market makers, designated liquidity providers) may receive priority at a price, or enhanced allocation, in exchange for meeting quoting obligations.

These details vary by asset class and venue, but the design message is consistent: *you must know the local rules*. Small differences in matching logic can make a previously profitable latency strategy unprofitable, or vice versa.

## Worked Example: Two Traders, Two Latencies

To make the interaction between latency and matching concrete, consider a simple scenario in a pure FIFO market.

At time $T = 0$:

- The best bid is $10.00 with 0 shares resting.
- Both Trader Fast and Trader Slow decide to place a buy limit order for 100 shares at $10.00 based on the same market data snapshot.

Their systems, however, have different end-to-end latencies:

- Trader Fast's path from decision to matching engine is 300 microseconds.
- Trader Slow's path is 800 microseconds.

## Timeline and Queue Formation

- At $T = 0.00030$ seconds, Fast's order arrives and becomes the only bid at $10.00.
- At $T = 0.00080$ seconds, Slow's order arrives and queues behind Fast, forming a 200-share bid at that price.

Now, at $T = 0.00100$ seconds, a sell market order for 150 shares arrives.

## Outcomes

- Under price-time priority:

  - Fast receives a full 100-share fill.
  - Slow receives the remaining 50 shares.
- If, instead, their orders had arrived in the reverse order (for example, if a network issue temporarily slowed Fast's path), Slow would have received 100 shares and Fast only 50.

A difference of 500 microseconds in system latency flipped the distribution of a valuable liquidity event.

### Pro-Rata Contrast

Now imagine the same scenario on a pro-rata venue, with the same arrival times and sizes, and the same 150-share incoming sell:

- Total resting bid at $10.00: 200 shares (100 Fast + 100 Slow).
- Each trader's share is 50% of the resting quantity.
- Each receives roughly 75 shares, with minor rounding differences.

In this case, arrival time hardly changes the economic outcome; size dominates.

## From Queue Position to Fill Probability

The previous examples were deterministic: given a single incoming order, we could compute exact fills. In reality, many orders arrive over time, and you care about the *probability* that your resting order will be fully or partially filled before one of three things happens:

- The price moves away.
- You cancel or modify the order.
- The session ends.

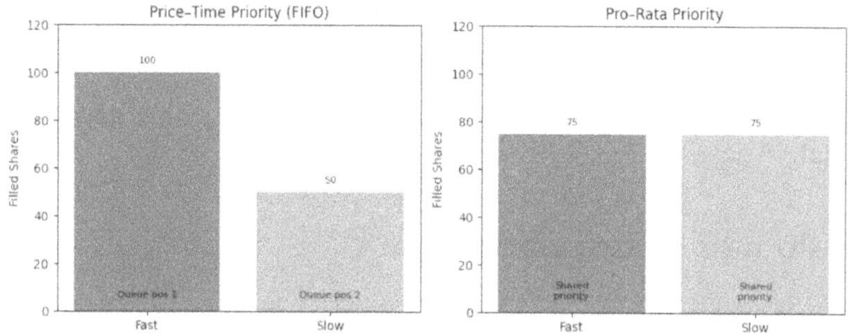


Figure 2.1: Effect of matching rules on fill allocation for two traders submitting similar orders with slightly different arrival times. Under price-time priority, the faster trader captures a larger share of the same liquidity event; under pro-rata, displayed size dominates and fills are shared more evenly.

In a FIFO market, your fill probability at a given price depends on:

- Your position in the queue (how many units are ahead of you).
- The statistical distribution of incoming opposite-side volume while the price is at that level.

If you move just a few ranks back in the queue because of extra latency, your expected fill probability can drop sharply, especially when:

- Opposite-side flow tends to be "just enough" to clear the front of the queue but rarely reaches deeper levels.
- The price level you are quoting is short-lived; the market bounces away before deep queue positions are served.

In pro-rata markets, the key variable is your share of displayed size. Cutting your displayed amount in half roughly halves your expected fill share, all else equal. But if everyone is inflating sizes to chase pro-rata allocations, the environment becomes unstable: rapid cancel/replace cycles mean that your *effective* share of the pool can change millisecond by millisecond.

## Risk, Adverse Selection, and Queue Uncertainty

Matching rules also shape your exposure to adverse selection — being filled when it is bad for you and not filled when it would have been good.

## FIFO and Adverse Selection

In FIFO markets:

- Being at the *front* of the queue is a double-edged sword. You earn more spread on average, but you are also the first to be hit when informed traders arrive.
- If your latency is poor, you are often *not* at the front when good liquidity arrives, but you may still be resting when conditions worsen, leaving you with a low fill rate in favorable periods and a non-trivial fill rate in unfavorable ones.

This pattern means that even modest queue-position uncertainty must be modeled explicitly in your expected-value calculations. A strategy that is marginally profitable assuming "always first in queue" may be unprofitable once realistic latency distributions are applied.

## Pro-Rata and Strategic Sizing

In pro-rata venues:

- Traders often use large displayed sizes to gain allocation, then rely on rapid cancellation to reduce risk if the market moves against them.
- Slow systems that cannot cancel quickly enough are at a disadvantage: they show large sizes but cannot pull them when conditions deteriorate, increasing adverse selection.

Therefore, in a pro-rata environment, the latency race often centers on *cancel/replace* operations rather than only on initial submission.

Matching rules and latency interact across the entire life of the order, not just at entry.

## Architectural Implications

Matching algorithms are often discussed in microstructure theory courses as abstract rules. For a trading system architect, they are concrete design constraints.

## Latency Budgets and Co-Location

In FIFO markets, every extra microsecond between your decision and the exchange's timestamp is a *direct tax* on queue position. This pushes designs toward:

- Co-locating trading servers in the same data center as the exchange.
- Minimizing layers between strategy and gateway (fewer hops, fewer copies).
- Using low-latency network stacks and careful OS tuning to reduce jitter.

If your strategy is sensitive to being first or second in a queue, you must treat end-to-end latency as a first-class design metric, measured and monitored continuously.

## Order Management and State Tracking

Matching rules also influence how you manage order state:

- In FIFO markets, you need visibility into your approximate queue position to forecast fill probabilities. Some venues expose aggregate queue size or your relative rank; others do not, requiring you to infer it from your own order and trade feed.

- In pro-rata markets, you must track your displayed size and the total at your price in near real time to estimate your expected allocation and to decide how aggressively to size your quotes.

This information feeds back into risk and inventory models. For example, a market-making engine may raise or lower quotes based not just on price, but on whether it is currently "over-represented" or "under-represented" in the queue at each side.

## Strategy Design and Venue Selection

Finally, different strategies naturally gravitate to different matching rules:

- Very latency-sensitive strategies (such as arbitrage that depends on being first to a new price) are often focused on FIFO venues, where being early yields a clear edge.
- Strategies that can display larger sizes and tolerate partial fills may find pro-rata venues more attractive, provided they have good cancel performance.
- A smart order router must understand these nuances to route orders intelligently: the "best" displayed price may behave very differently depending on the underlying matching engine.

Queue priority and matching rules translate your technical latency into economic outcomes. At a given price:

- FIFO markets reward being first; microseconds of advantage can change who captures scarce liquidity.
- Pro-rata markets reward displayed size; arrival time plays a smaller, but still non-zero, role.
- Hybrid schemes add further twists, sometimes favoring certain roles or sizes.

For system designers, these rules argue for two disciplines:

- **Measurement**: know your true latency profile and how it affects your typical queue position on each venue.
- **Alignment**: design strategies, order types, and routing behavior that are consistent with those profiles and with the local matching rules.

Only by viewing the matching engine's queue as a central character — not a black box — can you understand where latency really hides and how much it is worth to reduce it.

## 2.8 Quote-Driven vs. Order-Driven Markets

So far we have assumed a central limit order book: many anonymous participants place limit orders, which line up in queues at each price, and the matching engine applies clear priority rules. That world is *order-driven.*

In practice, especially outside the most liquid equities and futures, a large share of trading takes place in *quote-driven* markets. There, your counterparty is not an anonymous crowd but a specific dealer or market maker quoting you a two-sided price. The difference is not just cosmetic. The underlying market design changes:

- how prices are discovered,
- how sensitive you are to latency,
- and what your trading system must do to manage risk and hedge.

Understanding these two archetypes is essential before we look at fragmented venues and routing. If the *same* instrument can trade on both a quote-driven platform and an order-driven exchange, you must design systems that can operate intelligently in both worlds.

## Two Different Market Designs

### Order-Driven Markets: The Central Limit Order Book

In an order-driven market, such as most modern stock and futures exchanges:

- All participants can submit limit and market orders.
- Buy and sell orders rest in a central limit order book (CLOB).
- The best bid and best offer are formed by the top of that book.
- The matching engine applies transparent rules (for example, price-time) to decide who trades when a new order arrives.

Key characteristics:

- **Anonymity:** You typically do not know who is on the other side.
- **Transparency:** You see aggregated depth at each price, at least near the top of the book.
- **Symmetry:** In principle, any participant can provide or take liquidity under the same rule set.

In this setting, microstructure concepts like queue position, hidden liquidity, and time-in-force directly govern your executions. Latency is about where you sit in the queue when the next aggressive order arrives.

### Quote-Driven Markets: Dealers and RFQs

In a quote-driven market, the primary actors are dealers (or liquidity providers) who commit their balance sheet to trade with clients. Typical workflows:

- A client sends a request for quote (RFQ) to one or more dealers: "Bid/offer for 5 million EUR/USD" or "Price for 50 corporate bonds with these identifiers."
- Each dealer responds with a two-sided quote: a bid price, an offer price, and a size for each.

- The client chooses a dealer and trades, often by hitting the dealer's bid or lifting the offer.

In some platforms, dealers continuously stream quotes; in others, quoting is primarily reactive, in response to RFQs.

Key characteristics:

- **Bilateral relationships:** Prices may differ by client, depending on credit, past behavior, and commercial agreements.
- **Limited transparency:** There is usually no public order book; other clients do not see your RFQs or the quotes you receive.
- **Dealer discretion:** Dealers may adjust or withdraw quotes quickly, apply credit limits, or condition execution on internal checks such as last-look.

Here, microstructure is less about your place in a queue and more about how quickly you can obtain and act on quotes from multiple dealers, and how dealers manage the resulting risk.

## Price Discovery and Transparency

The first major contrast between the two designs is how prices are discovered and revealed.

### Order-Driven: Public Aggregation

In a CLOB:

- Every displayed order contributes to the public view of supply and demand.
- Best bid and offer (and often deeper levels) are broadcast to all subscribers in real time.
- Price discovery is *collective*: the interaction of many small and large orders at different prices.

For a trading system, this means:

- You can treat the order book as a shared state observable by all.
- Your own quote is part of that state, visible to competitors and clients alike.
- You can calibrate models (for example, market impact or order arrival rates) using historical book data.

### Quote-Driven: Bilateral Negotiation

In quote-driven markets:

- The price discovery process is distributed across many dealer-client interactions.
- Different clients may receive different prices at the same time, depending on size, urgency, and relationship.
- There may be indicative reference prices (for example, composite feeds), but firm executable prices arrive through RFQ or streams.

From a system design perspective:

- There is no single "book" to watch; instead, you must manage multiple bilateral price streams or quote responses.
- Your information about the market is *personalized* and incomplete; you only see what is quoted to you.
- Historical data for modeling must capture these bilateral outcomes, not just a central set of quotes.

This affects how you estimate fair value and measure slippage. In an order book you can compare your trades to the prevailing bid/offer; in an RFQ world you may benchmark against composite or indicative mid-prices but must recognize that those may not reflect the exact liquidity you could access.

## Latency Sensitivity: Who Wins and Why

Both market types are latency-sensitive, but in different ways.

**Order-Driven: Racing for Queue Position**

In an order-driven market:

- Your latency determines whether your limit order arrives at the top or deeper in the queue.
- For aggressive strategies, latency determines whether you interact with a stale quote before someone else cancels or reprices.
- When news breaks or prices move across venues, latency determines whether you are first to update quotes or exploit an arbitrage.

Thus, latency is tied to *queue priority* and *adverse selection*. Being slow can mean:

- Lower fill rates at attractive prices.
- Higher fill rates at unattractive ones (because you fail to cancel in time).

This is why high-frequency traders invest heavily in co-location, fast networks, and optimized software: small improvements in microseconds change how often they are first or last in the queue, and therefore their realized P&L.

**Quote-Driven: Racing to Respond and to Choose**

In a quote-driven market, the latency race has different stages.

**On the dealer side.**

Dealers compete to win client trades. Their sensitivity is mainly:

- **Response time:** How quickly they can price an RFQ and send a quote.
- **Hedging time:** How quickly they can hedge the resulting position, often in an order-driven market.

If multiple dealers receive the same RFQ, a slow dealer might miss the chance to respond before the client's decision deadline. Even if the platform allows late quotes, being late reduces the chance your quote is chosen.

**On the client side.**

Clients care about:

- **Quote collection time:** How fast they can gather quotes from several dealers for the same RFQ.
- **Decision time:** How quickly they can compare those quotes to reference prices and select the best.

A slow client system might miss a narrow window in which a particularly attractive quote is valid. Dealers often place time limits (for example, a few seconds or less) on RFQ responses, especially in volatile markets.

### Last-Look and Latency Risk

Many quote-driven platforms, especially in FX, allow dealers a "last-look" window:

- After the client attempts to trade against a quote, the dealer has a short period (for example, tens of milliseconds) to accept or reject based on the latest market data and risk checks.
- If the market has moved against the dealer, they may reject or requote; if it has moved in their favor, they usually accept.

This shifts some latency risk from dealer to client:

- For the dealer, last-look reduces the downside of being slightly slow to hedge.
- For the client, it introduces uncertainty: even if they click quickly, the trade may be declined.

System design must account for this:

- Clients may need to manage expectations and statistics on rejections, adjusting routing to favor dealers with lower last-look rejection rates.
- Dealers must implement low-latency risk checks and market data updates within the last-look window to avoid unnecessary rejections or missed hedging opportunities.

## Hedging Tactics Across Market Types

A crucial link between quote-driven and order-driven markets is hedging. Often:

- The *primary* market where a client trades is quote-driven.
- The dealer hedges in a more liquid, order-driven reference market (for example, a futures contract or an underlying equity).

### Dealer Hedging in an Order-Driven Market

Suppose a dealer quotes a client in a corporate bond RFQ platform:

- The client buys 10 million nominal of the bond at the dealer's offer.
- The dealer now has long exposure to the bond.
- To manage risk, the dealer may hedge interest-rate and credit spread exposure using liquid futures or ETFs, or by trading the underlying issuer's stock.

Timing matters:

- There is a delay between when the dealer decides the quote, when the client accepts, and when the trade is confirmed.
- There is additional latency when the dealer sends hedge orders into the order-driven markets.

If the hedge is placed into a CLOB:

- The dealer is now competing in a queue-driven environment.
- Their hedging effectiveness depends on their latency relative to other participants and on their understanding of the matching rules.

In this way, dealer systems must bridge two microstructures: bilateral quote workflows on the client side, and anonymous order books on the hedge side.

### Client Cross-Venue Routing

Clients may also choose between quote-driven and order-driven venues for the *same* product or close substitutes. For example:

- An institutional FX trader may compare RFQ quotes from banks with prices on a central limit order-driven FX ECN.
- A large equity order could be split between displayed order books and RFQ-style block trading platforms.

Their routing logic must consider:

- **Latency:** Sending to a distant exchange might incur higher network delays than hitting a local dealer stream.
- **Market impact:** Displayed orders in an order book may move the visible price; RFQs may be more discreet but rely on dealer balance sheets.
- **Fill certainty:** A firm RFQ quote with no last-look may be more reliable than a top-of-book price that may vanish before an order arrives.

Designing a smart router that evaluates these trade-offs requires explicit models of both microstructures, not just a single "best price" notion.

## System Design Patterns in Each World

By now the microstructural contrasts should suggest different architectural emphases.

### Order-Driven: Market Data and Queue-Aware Engines

For order-driven markets, typical system features include:

**High-fidelity market data ingestion.**

- Depth-of-book feeds, often with sequence numbers, must be processed with minimal latency and loss.
- Normalization logic must preserve order book events (add, modify, delete) so strategies can reconstruct the queue and infer their own position.

**Low-latency routing to matching engines.**

- Gateways must translate internal order models into venue protocols (for example, FIX, binary feeds) with minimal overhead.
- Risk checks must be efficient enough to avoid bloating latency beyond the strategy's tolerance.

**Stateful order management.**

- The system must track partially filled, resting, and replaced orders accurately, as discussed in later sections on life cycle events.
- Queue-aware logic (for example, cancel if too deep in the queue) relies on timely and correct state.

### Quote-Driven: RFQ Orchestration and Dealer Logic

For quote-driven markets, design patterns differ.

On the *client* side:

- **RFQ management:** Systems must generate RFQs, send them to multiple dealers, and collect responses within strict timeouts.

- **Quote evaluation:** Engines compare dealer quotes, adjust for credit, fees, and historical behavior (for example, rejection rates), and decide where to trade.
- **Asynchronous flow handling:** Responses can arrive at different times, and some may be withdrawn; the router must handle partial or late responses gracefully.

On the *dealer* side:

- **Pricing engines:** Systems must transform live market data and risk positions into executable two-sided quotes, possibly differentiated by client.
- **Inventory and risk controls:** Before accepting an RFQ, the system checks limits and projected exposure, often within tens of milliseconds.
- **Hedging interfaces:** Once a quote is traded, automated hedge algorithms send orders into one or more order-driven venues.

Much of the latency budget here is consumed by:

- internal pricing and risk calculations,
- bilateral messaging over protocols tailored to the RFQ platform,
- and the subsequent hedge operations.

## Blended and Evolving Microstructures

Real markets often mix elements of both designs.

### Order Books with RFQ Features

Some order-driven venues offer RFQ functionality on top of the book:

- A client can RFQ a block size larger than what is visible in the book.

- Liquidity providers respond, possibly leaning on the order book for reference and hedge.

Here, your system must:

- Monitor both the lit order book and RFQ channels.
- Avoid double-counting liquidity (for example, a dealer quoting on RFQ might simultaneously adjust their displayed quotes).

**Dealer Streams that Resemble Order Books**

Some quote-driven platforms aggregate continuous dealer streams into a consolidated view resembling a limit order book:

- The top-of-book may show multiple banks' best bids and offers.
- But the underlying execution remains bilateral; when you trade, you trade with one specific dealer.

This hybrid structure:

- Gives clients more transparency while preserving dealer relationships.
- Requires routing logic that can choose not just the best price but the best dealer, taking into account operational and latency characteristics.

## Implications for Latency-Aware Architecture

Bringing the discussion back to latency and design:

- In **order-driven** markets, latency primarily affects your *place in the queue* and how often you interact with the best visible liquidity.
- In **quote-driven** markets, latency primarily affects *who wins an RFQ* and how effectively a dealer can hedge the resulting risk.

This leads to different architectural priorities:

- **Order-driven focus:** network proximity to exchanges, highly optimized market data and order gateways, fine-grained measurement of microsecond-level delays.
- **Quote-driven focus:** efficient RFQ orchestration, robust latency-aware pricing engines, and tight integration between bilateral trading and hedge venues.

Many institutional systems must do both. A buy-side smart order router may:

- send part of a large order to dark or RFQ-style venues to seek size improvement,
- while algorithmically slicing the remainder into child orders for lit order books, competing for queue position.

Designing such a router requires a unified view of microstructure:

- what "fast enough" means in each venue type,
- how to value additional milliseconds saved or lost,
- and how to reconcile different transparency and execution guarantees.

In the next section, when we discuss venue fragmentation and routing logic, we will build directly on this comparison. We will treat quote-driven and order-driven markets as different nodes in a network of liquidity, each with its own latency profile and microstructural rules, and show how a smart router can navigate that network intelligently.

## 2.9 Venue Fragmentation and Routing Logic

In the previous sections we treated trading mostly on a single venue: one order book, one set of matching rules, and one microstructure to understand. Real markets rarely look that simple. The same stock, future, or currency pair often trades simultaneously on many exchanges, alternative trading systems, and dark pools.

This *venue fragmentation* changes the problem you are solving:

- You no longer ask only, "What order should I send?"
- You must also ask, "*Where* should I send it, and in what sequence?"

Answering that question is the job of a *smart order router* (SOR). The SOR sits between strategies and venues, consuming market data from many sources and deciding how to split and schedule orders across them. Fragmentation, fee structures, and dark liquidity together create a landscape where latency is not just about reaching a single book quickly, but about coordinating many paths with different speeds and behaviors.

## Why Markets Fragment

Before we can design routing logic, we need to understand why a single instrument ends up trading on multiple venues in the first place. The reasons are economic, regulatory, and technological.

## Competition and Innovation

Exchanges and trading platforms compete on:

- **Fees and rebates:** Maker-taker pricing (paying liquidity providers, charging takers) or the reverse.
- **Speed:** Matching engine performance, co-location facilities, connectivity options.
- **Features:** Special order types, dark or midpoint books, auction mechanisms.

New venues emerge offering slightly different combinations, attracting specific types of flow. Over time, liquidity fragments: no single venue handles all volume, even if one is dominant.

## Regulation and Best Execution

Regulators may require:

- Fair access and non-discriminatory pricing.
- National best bid and offer (NBBO) concepts, where brokers must consider quotes from multiple exchanges.

This encourages brokers and trading firms to connect to multiple venues to demonstrate that they are seeking best execution, not just trading where it is convenient.

## Dark Pools and Block Trading

Some venues are intentionally less transparent:

- **Dark pools** allow participants to trade without displaying their orders publicly.
- **Block trading platforms** cater to large institutional orders, often using RFQ or negotiation mechanisms.

These venues promise reduced market impact and information leakage, at the cost of less certainty about whether and when you will be filled.

The result is a network: many places where your order *could* go, each with different rules, fees, latencies, and liquidity profiles. The SOR's job is to navigate this network intelligently.

## What a Smart Order Router Actually Does

Conceptually, a smart order router performs three tasks:

1. **Observe** the state of each venue: current prices, available size, and recent fill behavior.
2. **Rank** venues for a given parent order, accounting for price, fees, likelihood of fill, and latency.
3. **Dispatch** child orders (slices of the parent) across venues and adjust them dynamically as conditions change.

Although the basic idea is simple, the details are where latency and architecture matter.

## Inputs: Market Data and Venue Metadata

The router consumes:

- **Top-of-book and depth** from lit exchanges: best bid/offer, size, and deeper levels where available.
- **Dark indications:** Sometimes aggregate dark pool availability, midpoint indications, or historical hit rates.
- **Fee and rebate schedules:** Maker-taker charges, venue-specific surcharges, and any broker-client commission structure.
- **Latency characteristics:** Measured round-trip times to each venue, including gateways and risk checks.
- **Reliability metrics:** Probability of rejection, cancel delays, and historical execution quality.

All of these inputs are *time-sensitive.* A "best" displayed price that is 2 milliseconds old on a fast market may already be stale.

## Outputs: Child Orders and Schedules

Given a parent order, such as "Buy 50,000 shares of XYZ over the next 10 minutes," the router might:

- Send immediate child orders to venues showing the best combination of price and size.
- Park passive orders on venues where rebates are attractive and queue dynamics are favorable.
- Probe dark pools with small midpoint orders to seek hidden liquidity without moving the lit price.
- Rebalance across venues as fills accumulate and market conditions evolve.

The router's decisions implicitly embed assumptions about how each venue behaves and how latency will affect realized execution.

## Latency in a Fragmented World

In a single-venue model, latency is largely a scalar: how long from decision to matching engine. In a fragmented world, latency is a *vector*: you have a different path length and jitter for each venue.

## Stale Prices and "Phantom" Liquidity

Suppose three venues (A, B, C) all show the same best ask of $10.00 for an instrument:

- Venue A: 5,000 shares at $10.00.
- Venue B: 3,000 shares at $10.00.
- Venue C: 2,000 shares at $10.00.

If your measured latencies are:

- A: 500 microseconds.
- B: 1,200 microseconds.
- C: 2,000 microseconds.

then the *effective* likelihood that the $10.00 ask will still be present when your order arrives is different on each venue, even though the NBBO view is identical.

Venue C's quote is more likely to be stale. If many participants are hitting that price, by the time your order reaches C, the 2,000 shares may already have been traded or cancelled. If your router naively ranks venues only by displayed price and size, it might over-allocate to C and suffer higher rejection and slippage.

## Co-Location and Multi-Venue Trade-offs

You can reduce latency to a single venue by co-locating servers in its data center, but you cannot be equidistant from all venues simultaneously:

- Placing servers near Exchange 1 may increase round-trip times to Exchange 2 and 3.
- Building separate co-located instances for each venue adds complexity, cost, and synchronization challenges.

The router's architecture must therefore:

- Maintain accurate, per-venue latency measurements.
- Decide whether the benefit of being faster to one venue outweighs being slower to another, given your strategy mix.

In other words, topology and routing logic are co-designed. Where you put your hardware affects how you should route, and how you intend to route affects where it is worth placing hardware.

## The SOR in the System Architecture

Let us place the smart order router in context. Upstream you have:

- Strategies deciding when and how much to trade.

- Risk and portfolio systems setting limits and objectives.

Downstream you have:

- Exchange gateways and connectivity to each venue.
- Market data adapters feeding both strategies and the router.

The SOR sits in the middle, performing three core functions:

1. **Normalization:** Convert diverse market data and venue rule sets into a common internal model (prices, sizes, fees, latency metrics).
2. **Decision:** For each parent order or slice, choose destinations and order types.
3. **Feedback:** Learn from fills, rejections, and routing outcomes to refine future decisions.

This middle layer is where many latency-quality trade-offs live:

- A more sophisticated routing decision may require more computation and cross-venue state, adding microseconds to the path.
- A very simple, fast router may make naive choices that look best on paper but perform poorly in practice due to stale quotes and venue quirks.

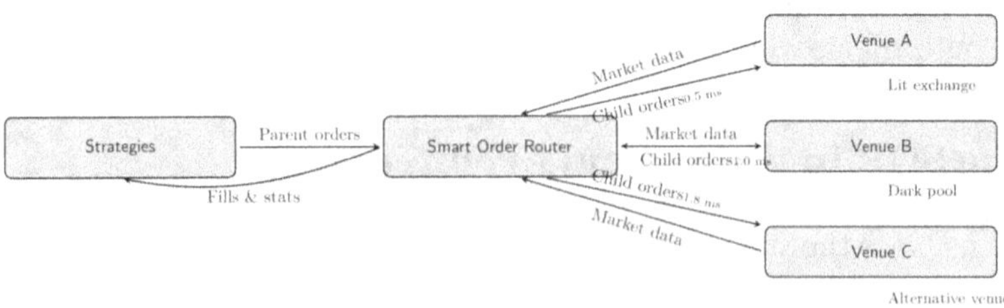

## Fees, Rebates, and "True" Prices

Displayed prices can be misleading if you ignore fees and rebates. A buy at $10.00 on one venue may be *economically* better or worse than the same price elsewhere.

## Maker-Taker and Taker-Maker

Common structures include:

- **Maker-taker:** The venue pays a small rebate to liquidity providers (makers) and charges a fee to liquidity takers. For example, provide at $10.00 and receive $0.002 per share; take at $10.00 and pay $0.003 per share.
- **Taker-maker:** The reverse: takers receive rebates, and makers pay fees.

From the router's point of view, the *effective* price of a trade is:

- Quoted price $\pm$ fees and rebates, plus
- Any broker commissions or internal cost allocations.

Two venues may both show a best ask of $10.00, but if one charges $0.003 per share and the other charges $0.001, the second is strictly better for a liquidity-taking buy, all else equal.

## Routing by Economics, Not Just Quotes

The SOR must:

- Maintain an up-to-date table of per-venue cost structures.
- Convert displayed quotes into net expected execution prices.
- Account for different maker/taker roles depending on order type (for example, passive limit vs aggressive marketable order).

However, this cannot be done in isolation from latency:

- A slightly better net price on a slow venue may be inferior to a marginally worse quote on a faster venue if the slower path significantly increases the chance of missing the liquidity.
- Dark pools that do not charge explicit fees may still impose an *opportunity cost* if they cause long delays waiting for fills that never come.

Thus, venue ranking becomes multi-dimensional: price, fee, latency, and fill probability all interact.

## Dark Liquidity and Information Leakage

Dark venues and hidden order types introduce another dimension. They can reduce information leakage but complicate routing decisions.

## Why Use Dark Venues?

A trader might prefer dark pools when:

- Executing large orders that would move the visible price if displayed.
- Seeking midpoint executions between the best bid and offer.
- Wanting to avoid revealing trading intentions to the wider market.

Dark pools typically reference lit markets for pricing (for example, midpoint of NBBO) but do not advertise their own order book depths.

## Probing vs. Broadcasting

To access dark liquidity, routers may use:

- **Small probes:** Sending small child orders to test whether a pool is active, then scaling up if fills occur.
- **Simultaneous posting:** Placing some size in the dark while also posting or taking in lit markets.

This introduces routing challenges:

- If you probe too aggressively, you risk information leakage: other participants might infer your interest from patterns, even in dark venues.
- If you probe too cautiously, you may miss available dark liquidity, ending up trading more in the lit market with higher impact.

Latency again matters:

- Dark orders often sit longer, waiting for counterparts; slow cancel processing can leave you exposed if conditions change.
- Coordination between dark and lit venues must happen on sub-second timescales to react to price movements and partial fills.

## Routing Policies and Latency Trade-offs

Bringing these elements together, we can describe some common routing styles and their implications.

## Sweep, Then Post

For an urgent parent order, a router might:

1. Aggressively sweep the best lit quotes across multiple venues up to a certain price limit.
2. Then post the remaining size passively on one or more venues.

Latency considerations:

- Sweeping multiple venues in parallel requires sending child orders almost simultaneously, which may cause over-fills if fills come back faster than cancels can be processed.
- Sweeping sequentially (hit A, then B, then C) reduces over-fill risk but increases the time during which the market can move, potentially worsening prices.

System design must choose between:

- **Parallelism:** Higher technical complexity and risk of race conditions, but better use of fleeting liquidity.
- **Sequential routing:** Simpler but more exposed to adverse market moves over the routing horizon.

## Dark-First vs. Lit-First

Another trade-off is the order in which you access dark and lit venues:

- **Dark-first:** Try to fill passively in dark pools, then send remaining size to lit markets.
- **Lit-first:** Execute a core amount in visible markets to lock in liquidity, then try to improve remaining execution cost with dark fills.

Dark-first can reduce impact but risks delay:

- If dark pools are inactive, you may waste valuable time waiting.
- Meanwhile the lit price can move away, worsening later fills.

Lit-first protects against delay but may reveal your intentions and move the market.

The routing logic must therefore encode a *time budget* and an *impact budget*, deciding how long to wait in dark venues before pivoting to lit. Latency in feedback (how quickly you learn that dark probes are failing) sets a lower bound on how responsive this logic can be.

## Embedding Routing Logic into Architecture

From an architectural viewpoint, smart routing is not just an algorithm; it is a set of services and data flows.

## Data Cohesion and Time Stamping

To make latency-aware routing decisions you need:

- Precise time stamps on all market data and order events.
- Consistent clock synchronization across systems that feed the router (for example, between strategy servers, SOR, and gateways).
- Real-time monitoring of per-venue latencies and rejection rates.

Without this, any attempt to model "liquidity persistence" or "quote freshness" will be unreliable, and the router may systematically over- or under-value certain venues.

## Modularity and Extensibility

Venues evolve: fee schedules change, new order types appear, dark pools launch and shut down. The routing layer should be modular:

- Each venue adapter encapsulates protocol details, fee models, and microstructure quirks.
- The core routing engine works with abstracted metrics: net price, latency, expected fill probability.
- Adding a new venue mostly means adding a new adapter and calibrating its metrics, not rewriting routing logic.

This modularity also helps you experiment with alternative routing policies (for example, changing dark-first thresholds) without disrupting the lower-level connectivity.

Venue fragmentation turns trading into a multi-dimensional routing problem. The smart order router becomes the bridge between microstructure theory and system design:

- It interprets displayed and dark liquidity, fee structures, and matching rules across many venues.
- It incorporates latency measurements directly into venue ranking and order scheduling.
- It balances competing objectives: price improvement, execution certainty, information leakage, and market impact.

For a latency-focused architect, the key lesson is that speed is not one number. It is a profile across venues, paths, and routing decisions. Well-designed routers make that profile explicit and use it to turn microseconds into measurable execution quality, rather than letting fragmentation turn those same microseconds into hidden slippage and risk.

## 2.10 Life Cycle Events and State Changes

In the earlier sections of this chapter we looked at the building blocks of trading: order types, matching rules, venues, and routing. We treated an order mostly as a message that interacts with these mechanisms. In a real system, however, an order is better understood as a *process* that passes through a series of states over time.

Each transition between states is triggered by an event:

- a decision in your strategy,
- a response from a venue,
- a risk limit being hit,
- a timeout or a scheduled expiry.

At every such transition, two things matter for realized execution quality:

- How quickly the event occurs (exchange and network latency).
- How quickly and correctly your software reacts (internal latency and logic).

This section maps the typical life cycle of an order from creation to final state, highlighting where latency and software reactions directly affect P&L and risk.

## A Standard Order Life Cycle

Different firms use slightly different labels, but most electronic trading systems recognize a core set of states. For our purposes we will use:

- **Created**
- **Risk-Checked**
- **Sent**
- **Acknowledged**
- **Resting**
- **Partially Filled**
- **Fully Filled**
- **Cancelled**
- **Rejected**
- **Expired**

Not every order passes through every state. For example, an order can be rejected before it ever rests, or it can go directly from acknowledged to fully filled. But any realistic trading system must be able to represent and react to each of these possibilities.

Right after we list the states, it is useful to visualize them as a state machine.

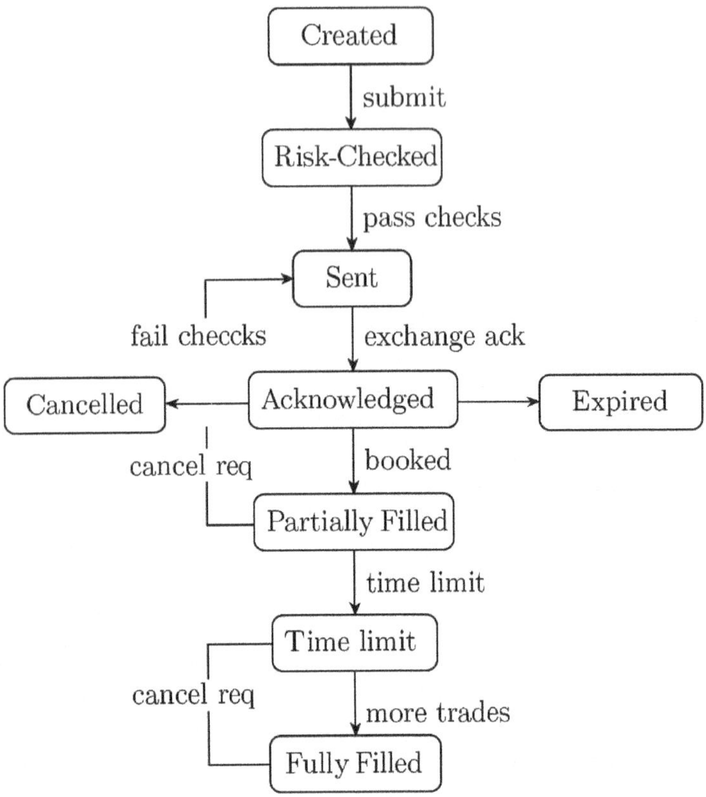


With this map in mind, we now walk through each state and its transitions, emphasizing where latency hides and how your system should behave.

## From Decision to the Exchange: Created, Risk-Checked, Sent

### Created

An order enters the **Created** state the moment your strategy decides to trade:

- The strategy specifies instrument, side, quantity, price, order type, and any special attributes.
- An internal order object is instantiated in your order management system (OMS).

This step is mostly under your control. Latency here comes from:

- Strategy computation time (for example, signal evaluation, portfolio optimization).
- Internal messaging between strategy and OMS.

Although this latency does not show up on exchange logs, it still affects when the order reaches the book. For latency-sensitive strategies, reducing the gap between "decide to trade" and "order is created" is as important as network tuning.

**Risk-Checked**

Before an order can be sent externally, it usually passes through pre-trade risk checks. The order is in the **Risk-Checked** state while it is being evaluated against:

- Position and exposure limits.
- Credit limits and regulatory constraints (for example, maximum leverage).
- Fat-finger checks (for example, maximum order size, price bounds).

Two outcomes are possible:

- **Pass:** The order moves on to the **Sent** state.
- **Fail:** The order goes to **Rejected** with an internal reason, and is never transmitted.

Latency here is delicate:

- Slow risk checks improve safety but increase the chance that the market moves away before you even submit.
- Over-aggressive optimization (for example, skipping checks) increases operational and regulatory risk.

Well-designed systems balance these by:

- Implementing risk checks in efficient, in-memory data structures.
- Pushing simple checks to the gateway layer, closer to the exchange, while centralizing more complex ones.
- Caching commonly used values (for example, current positions, limits) to avoid repeated database calls.

### Sent

Once risk passes, the order transitions to **Sent** when your gateway transmits it to the venue:

- The order is serialized into the venue's protocol (for example, FIX, binary).
- It travels over the network to the exchange's gateway, then through internal hops to the matching engine.

From your perspective, this is a "black-box" period:

- You no longer control the order, but you also have not yet received any confirmation.
- Network or gateway problems here may cause retransmissions, timeouts, or unknown state.

Key latency elements:

- Network round-trip time and jitter.

- Serialization and deserialization overhead.
- Exchange gateway and internal routing delays.

Monitoring this segment is crucial. If it lengthens unexpectedly, you may need to adjust strategy parameters that assume certain maximum times between decision and book interaction.

## Acknowledgment and Book Interaction: Acknowledged, Resting

### Acknowledged

When the venue receives your order and successfully accepts it into their system, they send an *acknowledgment*. Your OMS then transitions the order to **Acknowledged**.

This is an important milestone:

- It confirms that the venue has the order and will try to match it according to its rules.
- It may carry additional information (for example, venue order ID, display status).

Latency in receiving an acknowledgment affects:

- How quickly your system can be confident that the order is live.
- How it handles client-side timeouts; if your own timeout is too short, you might cancel or resend an order that was actually fine, creating duplicates or over-trading.

A robust design:

- Clearly distinguishes between “sent but unacknowledged” and “acknowledged and live.”
- Avoids aggressive client-side resends without careful reconciliation.

- Logs timestamps for decision, send, and acknowledgment for later latency analysis.

**Resting**

Once acknowledged, the order may become **Resting** in the book:

- For a limit order that is not immediately marketable, it queues at its price level, waiting for opposite-side interest.
- For certain order types (for example, hidden or pegged), it may reside in specialized internal structures but still be logically resting.

While resting, the order is exposed to:

- **Fill opportunities:** Incoming market or marketable limit orders.
- **Adverse selection:** Informed traders hitting your quote when it is bad for you.
- **Market regime changes:** News or volatility spikes making your existing price obsolete.

Your system must monitor resting orders and react to:

- Market data changes (for example, mid-price moving away).
- Internal signals (for example, strategy no longer wants exposure).
- Risk limits (for example, position or P&L thresholds exceeded).

Latency in reacting to these can be as harmful as latency at entry. A stale quote that remains in the book for tens of milliseconds too long can be repeatedly picked off.

## Execution States: Partially Filled and Fully Filled

### Partially Filled

An order becomes **Partially Filled** when some, but not all, of its quantity trades. This state is more complex than it looks.

On each partial fill:

- The venue sends a trade execution message and an updated remaining quantity.
- Your OMS updates the order's filled quantity and average price.
- Your risk and position systems update exposure.

Latency in handling partial fills affects:

- **Hedging:** If your strategy hedges filled portions (for example, in a pairs trade or spread), slow processing can leave you temporarily unhedged.
- **Routing of the remainder:** You may wish to cancel the remaining quantity on this venue and re-route to another, especially if the remaining size is small or the queue position is poor.
- **Client feedback:** For agency trading, you may need to report partial fills back to clients quickly.

Software design tips:

- Treat each partial fill as a trigger for an event handler, not just a database update.
- Keep the logic in that handler as lean as possible; complex recalculations can be offloaded to slower, asynchronous processes.
- Ensure idempotency: duplicate fill messages (for example, from recoveries) should not double-count.

### Fully Filled

An order reaches **Fully Filled** when the executed quantity equals the original (or remaining) quantity. At this point:

- The order no longer has open quantity in the book.
- No further child actions (cancel, modify) should be sent for this order.
- Final execution price and fees can be computed, and P&L realized.

Latency after full fill may seem less critical, but two issues remain:

- **Hedge completion:** If the order is part of a larger strategy (for example, leg of a basket), the timing of full fill can trigger related actions.
- **State cleanup:** Delayed state cleanup can leave ghost exposure in risk systems, causing unnecessary limit breaches or blocking new trades.

A clean architecture clearly separates:

- The low-latency path: updating order state and risk exposure.
- The slower path: reporting, analytics, and archival.

## Ending Early: Cancelled, Rejected, Expired

### Cancelled

An order enters **Cancelled** when you decide to withdraw it from the market before it is fully filled. This involves two parts:

- You send a cancel request to the venue.
- The venue processes the request and confirms cancellation.

Between sending the cancel and receiving confirmation, the order is in a transient state:

- It may be filled in full or in part if an opposing order hits it before the cancel is processed.

- You must treat it as still live until the venue confirms otherwise.

Latency here is critical:

- Slow cancels increase the window during which stale quotes can be hit, especially around news or when your strategy suddenly reverses.
- High cancel latency in one venue, relative to others, should inform how aggressively you post there.

To manage this:

- Measure cancel round-trip times per venue.
- Incorporate those measurements into strategy logic (for example, cancel further away from the expected shock when dealing with slow venues).
- Avoid client-side assumptions like "once I send cancel, I am safe"; always wait for explicit confirmation or reconcile via exchange state.

### Rejected

**Rejected** may occur at several points:

- Internal pre-trade risk reject (never sent).
- Immediate exchange reject on receipt (for example, invalid price, symbol, or session state).
- Post-acknowledgment reject (for example, self-trade prevention, credit issues).

When a reject occurs:

- No further matching will take place for that order.
- The strategy may need to resubmit with corrected parameters or adjust its plan.

Latency to *learn* about rejection is important:

- If you assume an order is live when it is not, you may hedge phantom exposure or reduce risk unnecessarily.
- In a routing context, you might delay sending the order to alternative venues, missing liquidity that would have been available.

Good practice:

- Treat rejections as high-priority events in your event processing pipeline.
- Maintain detailed logs with reject reasons to detect configuration or connectivity issues quickly.

### Expired

An order becomes **Expired** when its time-in-force condition ends without full execution:

- **Day** orders expire at session close.
- **Good-till-time** orders expire at their specified timestamp.
- Some conditional orders (for example, certain stops) may expire if their trigger is not hit by a deadline.

Expiration is usually handled by the venue:

- The exchange cancels the order at the appropriate time.
- A cancel/expire message is sent back to your system.

Latency in receiving expiry notices affects:

- End-of-day reconciliation and reporting.
- Decisions on whether to re-enter similar orders in a new session.

From a risk standpoint, expiry is less dangerous than unexpected fills, but your systems must still keep state accurate: thinking an order is still live when it has expired could cause incorrect expectations about future fills.

## Race Conditions and Edge Cases

Real trading systems must handle more than the "happy path." Several race conditions are common:

### Cancel vs. Fill Races

A classic scenario:

- You send a cancel at time $t$.
- The exchange receives an incoming market order against your quote at roughly the same moment.
- Depending on precise timing and venue rules, the fill may be processed before or after the cancel.

Your system must:

- Accept that some fills after cancel request are legitimate.
- Reconcile final state based on exchange messages, not assumptions.

Design implications:

- Avoid triggering drastic strategy changes (for example, reversing positions) until you have clear, consolidated information about fills and cancels.
- Use sequence numbers and time stamps to order events correctly, especially after recovery from outages.

### Client-Side Timeouts vs. Exchange State

Another common issue:

- Your system sets a timeout: if no ack is received within, say, 500 milliseconds, it assumes failure.
- The exchange is slow but eventually acknowledges and even fills the order.

If your system has already decided the order "does not exist" and sends a replacement, you can end up with double exposure.

To avoid this:

- Timeouts should trigger *investigation and reconciliation*, not blind resubmission.
- Recovery logic should be able to query exchange state (where possible) to confirm whether an order is live.

## Why Explicit State Modeling Matters

The core message of this section is that you should not treat orders as static records with a few fields. They are dynamic processes with a life cycle. Modeling that life cycle explicitly has several benefits:

### Visibility into Latency

By tracking when each state transition occurs, you can:

- Measure latency between key points (for example, Created to Sent, Sent to Acknowledged, Resting to Cancelled).
- Detect drifts or anomalies (for example, cancel latency on one venue doubling).
- Tie performance degradation back to infrastructure or venue issues.

### Robust Risk Management

State-aware risk systems:

- Know which orders are live and which are not, reducing phantom exposure.
- Can distinguish between pending, partially filled, and fully filled states when enforcing limits.
- React appropriately to rejections and expiries, instead of treating them as generic "errors."

### Better Strategy Design

Strategies can make more nuanced decisions when they are aware of order state:

- Cancel or reprice if an order has been resting too long without fills.
- Route remaining quantity differently after partial fills, based on how much time is left in the schedule.
- Adjust aggression if cancel latencies are high, to reduce the chance of being picked off.

Across this chapter we have moved from order attributes, to matching rules, to venues, to routing. This final section brings the focus back to the individual order, but now as a sequence of states over time.

At each state transition:

- The exchange and your system both do work.
- Latency in either can improve or degrade your realized execution quality.

By treating the order life cycle as an explicit state machine, and by instrumenting each transition, you make latency visible and manageable. This is the foundation on which later chapters on architecture, monitoring, and optimization will build: you cannot improve what you do not see, and you cannot see latency without understanding where, in the order's life, time is actually being spent.

# Chapter 3

# Latency Definitions, Taxonomy & Measurement

*Latency is more than a single number on a slide-it is a full probability distribution shaped by clocks, code paths, and market microstructure. This chapter gives you the vocabulary to talk about latency rigorously, the tools to measure it without lying to yourself, and the statistical habits needed to see where your system is truly fast-and where it only looks fast on average.*

## 3.1 Latency Taxonomy and Nomenclature

In earlier chapters we treated "latency" informally: the time between a stimulus (a price move, an order book change) and a response (your order reaching the exchange, the strategy updating its state). That informal notion is enough to motivate why latency matters. It is not enough to design, debug, or improve a trading system.

As soon as you try to answer questions like

- "Did our new NIC driver reduce our wire time or just move delays elsewhere?"
- "Is this venue slow today, or is it our colo network?"
- "Why do cancels take longer than new orders during the open?"

you need a shared, precise vocabulary. This section builds that vocabulary. We will:

- Distinguish one-way and round-trip latency and tie them to concrete trading workflows.
- Decompose end-to-end latency into segments: application, OS, NIC, network, exchange gateway, and matching engine.
- Name common latency categories: network latency, gateway latency, exchange latency, and so on.
- Introduce jitter and explain why simple averages are often misleading.

The aim is not to be pedantic for its own sake. A consistent taxonomy lets engineering, quant, and trading teams talk about the same thing and identify where design effort and capital really move the needle.

## From "how long" to "which part"

Most traders start with an end-to-end intuition: "I sent an order at time A, the fill came back at time B, so my latency is B minus A." That value is important, but it hides structure.

Between A and B, many steps happen:

- Your strategy decides to act.
- Your application encodes and hands the order to the operating system.

- The NIC and network deliver it to the exchange.
- The exchange gateway and matching engine process it.
- The path back reverses those steps for the acknowledgment or fill.

When something slows down, you need to know *which* step. The taxonomy in this section is essentially a way of slicing the A-to-B interval into meaningful, named segments that can be measured and owned by specific teams or components.

## One-way vs. round-trip latency

We start with the two most common high-level measures.

**One-way latency.** In trading systems, we will use "one-way latency" to mean:

> The elapsed time for a single direction of travel along a defined path, from a clearly specified start event to a clearly specified end event.

Two very common examples are:

- **Order send (client-to-exchange) one-way latency:** From the instant your strategy decides to send an order (or hands it to the order gateway) until the instant the order is accepted by the exchange gateway or enqueued at the matching engine.
- **Market data one-way latency:** From the instant the exchange produces a market data event (for example, a trade or book update) until the instant your strategy consumes it and can act on it.

The crucial point is that one-way latency is always tied to a *specific path and event pair*. Without that, numbers from different teams or tools are not comparable.

**Round-trip latency.** "Round-trip latency" measures there-and-back:

The elapsed time between a request leaving a defined boundary and the corresponding response being observed again at that same boundary.

For trading, typical examples include:

- **Order round-trip latency:** From when your client sends an order to the exchange boundary (for example, when the packet leaves your NIC or a colo router) until when the corresponding acknowledgment or fill message returns to that same boundary.
- **Ping/pong style latency:** From when a synthetic test message is sent to a remote system until a test response returns.

Round-trip latency is often easier to measure reliably, because you only need one accurate clock at the observation point. It is also a more direct proxy for questions traders ask, like "how long until I know if I'm filled?"

**Why do we care about the distinction?**

- Strategy performance, such as queue position and hit rate, is more sensitive to *one-way* latencies on the path from information to action and from action to the book.
- Operational monitoring and many benchmarking tools produce *round-trip* measurements, because they are easier to instrument and less sensitive to clock synchronization.

Later sections on clock synchronization will show why measuring one-way latencies across multiple hosts is harder than it seems. For now, the main rule is: whenever you say "latency," specify whether you mean one-way or round-trip and which events define the endpoints.

## A canonical trading path

To make the taxonomy concrete, we will refer to a simplified but representative trading path. Imagine a single order leaving your strategy and making its way to the exchange:

- **Client application:** Strategy logic decides to send an order and passes it to an order gateway component.

- **Operating system (OS) and NIC:** The OS transmits the packet through the kernel networking stack to the NIC, which puts it on the wire.

- **Network:** The packet travels through switches, routers, and possibly a metro or long-haul link to reach the exchange's network edge.

- **Exchange gateway:** The exchange gateway receives the packet, validates protocol and risk rules, and forwards the order to the core.

- **Matching engine:** The matching engine enqueues the order, updates the order book, possibly trades, and emits acknowledgments and market data.

- **Return path:** Acknowledgment and fill messages traverse the exchange gateway, network, NIC, OS, and client application in reverse order.

We now introduce a visual schematic of this path and the main segments of latency along it.

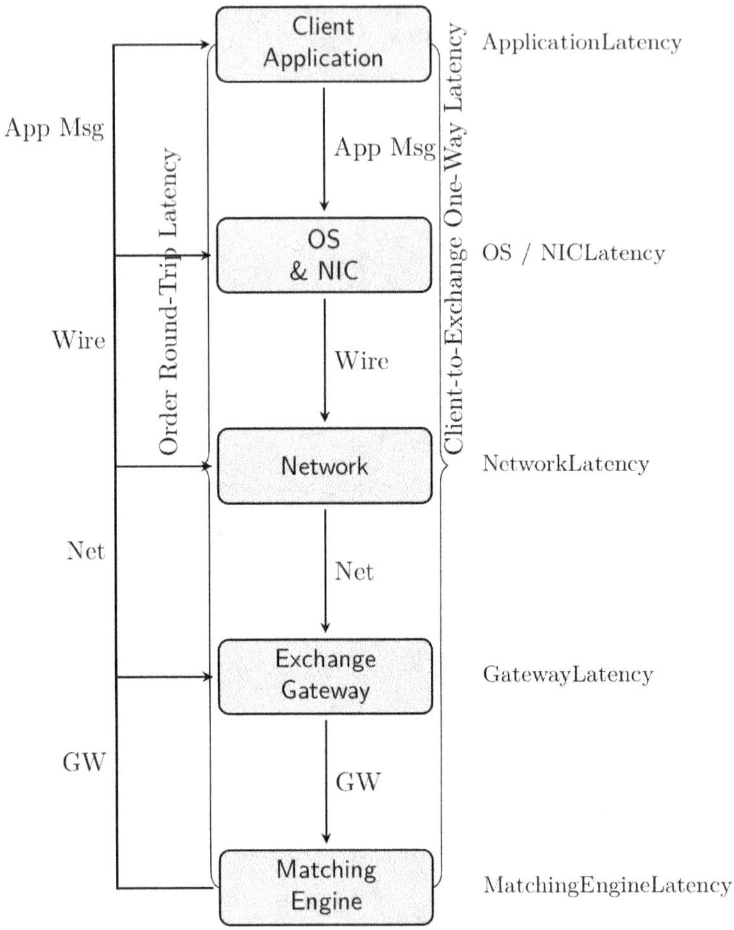


This simple diagram will serve as a reference as we define specific latency terms.

## Decomposing end-to-end latency

Using the canonical path, it is natural to talk about *end-to-end* latency as the total time across several segments. For example, one-way order latency from the client application to the matching engine can be verbally decomposed as:

Application time + OS/NIC time + network time + gateway time + matching engine time.

We now define these segments more formally.

**Application latency.**

Application latency is the time spent inside your own process before the operating system takes over. Examples include:

- Strategy decision time from receiving market data to deciding on an order.
- Time to build and encode the order message (for example, FIX or binary protocol encoding).
- Any queuing in your in-process pipelines (such as message queues between strategy and gateway threads).

You typically measure application latency with timestamps taken in user space, at the points where data enters and leaves your process or individual modules.

**OS and NIC latency.**

OS/NIC latency covers everything from when your application hands the message to the kernel until the NIC places the packet onto (or retrieves it from) the wire. This includes:

- Kernel networking stack processing.
- Driver overhead.
- NIC internal buffering and DMA.

In ultra-low-latency designs, this component is often reduced by bypassing parts of the kernel (for example, using user-space networking stacks) and by tuning NIC settings. Measuring it typically involves hardware timestamping or careful kernel-level instrumentation.

**Network latency.**

Network latency is the time the packet spends traveling between your NIC and the exchange gateway. It is largely a function of:

- Physical distance and medium (fiber, microwave, millimeter wave).
- Network device processing (switches, routers).
- Queuing at congested links.

In this book, when we say "network latency" we mean this *path latency between hosts*, not the latency of your internal application network queues.

**Gateway latency.**

Gateway latency is the time the order spends in the exchange gateway component from network ingress to handing off to the matching engine. Depending on the venue, this may include:

- Protocol parsing and validation.
- Risk checks (for example, fat-finger limits, credit limits).
- Internal routing to the appropriate matching engine instance.

Gateway latency is usually outside your direct control but can be characterized per venue and often varies with load.

**Matching engine latency.**

Matching engine latency is the time between the matching engine receiving your order and producing the corresponding book update and acknowledgments. It includes:

- Queueing behind other orders at the matching engine ingress.

- Order book updates and trade matching.
- Emission of execution reports and market data messages.

As with gateway latency, you cannot control this directly, but your order timing and behavior relative to the rest of the market affects how much queuing you experience.

## Naming common latency categories

Armed with the segment decomposition, we can now define several commonly used latency categories. Different firms sometimes overload these terms, so we are explicit about what they mean in this text.

**Client latency.**

We will use "client latency" to describe latencies that are fully under your control, primarily:

- Application latency.
- OS and NIC latency on your own hosts.

When a trader says "our stack is slow today," the engineering question is, "is client latency higher than normal, or is the venue/network slower?"

**Network latency.**

As defined previously, network latency is the path latency between your NIC and the exchange gateway. Because it depends on physical routes and load, you often split it further as:

- **Physical propagation latency:** The ideal speed-of-light component given the path and medium.
- **Device and queuing latency:** Additional delay from switches, routers, and congestion.

From an architecture point of view, you can reduce propagation latency only by changing geography or medium; you can improve device and queuing latency via better network design and capacity planning.

**Gateway latency.**

We will often group gateway and related pre-matching overhead under "gateway latency." In venue comparisons, teams often say things like, "Venue A has a faster gateway but a slower matching engine than Venue B." This shorthand refers to the average or percentile behavior of these internal segments.

**Exchange latency.**

"Exchange latency" or "venue latency" is sometimes used loosely. In this book we define it as:

> The latency contributed by the exchange's own systems from the moment a packet reaches the exchange network edge until all corresponding outputs (acknowledgments and market data) leave the exchange.

That includes gateway and matching engine latencies and any internal routing or processing in between. It *excludes* your own client and wide-area network latencies. Many venues provide some form of exchange-relative timing, such as timestamps in acknowledgments or market data, that help you estimate exchange latency components.

**End-to-end latency.**

End-to-end latency usually refers to:

- One-way: client application decision to matching engine book update (or vice versa for market data).
- Round-trip: client application sending a request to observing the corresponding response.

Because this combines multiple components, end-to-end latency is the most intuitive number for traders, but the least useful for diagnosis unless you also know how it is composed.

## Path-specific latencies in trading workflows

Different trading workflows traverse slightly different paths and, therefore, have different latency structures. Using the same taxonomy for each makes comparisons meaningful.

**New order latency.**

A new order typically follows the canonical path: client → OS/NIC → network → gateway → matching engine, then reverse for the acknowledgment and fill. New order latency is often the primary focus for aggressive strategies trying to capture fleeting opportunities.

**Cancel and replace latency.**

Cancel and replace messages may be handled differently inside the exchange:

- Some venues prioritize cancels in the gateway or matching engine queues.
- Others treat them similarly to new orders.

From your side, cancel messages traverse essentially the same client and network path. However, the matching engine component may be shorter (a cancel that finds your order in the book and removes it) or longer (a cancel that must search multiple queues or handle complex states). When measuring, always compare like with like: cancel path vs new-order path, not just raw turnaround numbers.

**Market data reaction latency.**

Market data reaction latency describes the path from an exchange event to your internal state change or order:

- Matching engine generates a trade or book update.
- Exchange disseminates this via its market data gateways.
- Network carries the feed packets to your NIC.
- OS and application receive, decode, and apply the event.
- Strategy logic reacts and, potentially, sends an order.

Here, the key segments are exchange market data latency, network latency, and your client processing latency. For many strategies, reducing reaction latency is as important as reducing order send latency, because it determines how stale your view of the book is when you act.

## Exchange-derived vs client-derived timing

A practical complication is that different parts of the path are observed with different clocks.

- **Client-derived timestamps** come from your systems: application logs, hardware timestamping NICs, network taps in your colo cage, and so on.
- **Exchange-derived timestamps** come from the venue: fields in market data messages, timestamps in order acknowledgments, or out-of-band timing feeds.

Because clocks are never perfectly synchronized, a rigorous vocabulary must also specify the *time basis* of any latency measurement. For example:

- "Client-observed order round-trip latency from NIC to NIC" uses only your own timestamps near the wire.
- "Exchange-relative gateway latency" might be defined as the difference between the timestamp when the packet arrived at the exchange edge and the timestamp when the order was enqueued at the matching engine, both measured by the exchange.

Later chapters will show how to combine client-derived and exchange-derived timings to reconstruct richer pictures of the path, but only if you keep careful track of which basis each number uses.

## Jitter and the limits of averages

So far we have spoken as if each latency component has a single value. In reality, every component varies over time and with load. This variation is called *jitter*. Formally:

> Jitter is the variability of latency around some central tendency (for example, median) for a given path and workload.

Two systems might both have an average one-way latency of 50 microseconds, but dramatically different jitter profiles:

- System A is almost always between 45 and 55 microseconds.
- System B is usually 20 microseconds but sometimes spikes to 500 microseconds.

From a trading perspective, System B may be much worse, even though its average is similar or better, because tail events lose races and miss fills. This is why a rigorous taxonomy goes hand in hand with robust statistical treatment, covered later in the chapter:

- Use percentiles (for example, median, 90th, 99th) to describe typical and tail behaviors.
- Track jitter separately for each segment (client, network, exchange) when possible.

Whenever someone reports a single latency value without specifying variance or percentiles, treat it as an incomplete description.

## Why precise nomenclature matters

To close this section, it is worth emphasizing how these definitions are used in practice.

**Design discussions.**

When proposing a new architecture, you might say:

> "This design trades a small increase in client application latency for a large reduction in network latency by moving the strategy into the exchange colo and using a shorter fiber route."

Everyone in the room should understand which segments move and by roughly how much.

**Performance debugging.**

When production alerts show elevated end-to-end round-trip latency, a precise vocabulary lets you quickly narrow down the suspects:

- If client-to-NIC timestamps are stable but NIC-to-exchange timestamps have grown, suspect the network.
- If exchange-derived timestamps for gateway processing have spiked, suspect venue load.
- If only your own application timestamps have shifted, suspect changes in your software or host.

**Venue and configuration comparisons.**

When comparing two venues or two configurations of the same venue, saying "Venue X is 20 microseconds faster" is ambiguous. Saying:

> "For small orders, Venue X has lower exchange gateway latency at the 99th percentile, while network and client latencies are comparable."

is informative and actionable.

The rest of this chapter will build on this taxonomy. We will examine how clock synchronization affects your ability to measure one-way and segment-specific latencies, how to instrument the tap points along this path, and how to analyze the resulting latency distributions in a way that reflects the economic impact on your trading.

## 3.2 Clock Synchronization & Time Sources

In the previous section we created a precise vocabulary for latency: one-way versus round-trip, client versus network versus exchange, and so on. All of those definitions quietly assume something fundamental: that we can trust the timestamps we use to measure them.

If your clocks are wrong, all of your carefully defined latencies are illusions. You may think the exchange is slow when, in fact, your local clock is drifting. You may "prove" that a new network path is faster when you are really just comparing two hosts whose clocks disagree by a few microseconds.

This section explains why time is the foundation of latency analysis and how trading firms build time-distribution systems that are accurate, stable, and observable. We will:

- Describe common time sources and their typical accuracy: GPS-disciplined oscillators, PTP grandmasters, NTP servers, and exchange timestamps.
- Show how these sources are distributed inside a trading firm (PTP domains, boundary and transparent clocks).
- Explain the impact of clock error on one-way latency and why round-trip and exchange-relative measurements are often safer.
- Discuss operational issues: monitoring skew and offset, handling leap seconds and failures, and meeting regulatory and audit expectations.

Throughout, the emphasis is practical: how good is "good enough," and how do you design a time system that supports the latency measurements you care about?

## Why time quality matters for latency

A timestamp is only as good as the clock behind it. In latency work we care about three basic properties of clocks:

- **Accuracy:** How close is the clock to "true" time, usually Coordinated Universal Time (UTC)?
- **Stability:** How smoothly does the clock run? Does it drift or jump?
- **Consistency:** How well do different clocks in the system agree with each other at any moment?

Different latency measurements stress these properties in different ways:

- **Round-trip measurements on a single host** (for example, packet leaves NIC, packet returns to NIC on the same machine) only need that host's clock to be internally consistent over the measurement window. Absolute accuracy versus UTC is less important.
- **One-way measurements across hosts** (for example, client send time on host A, receive time on host B) require that A and B share a common, accurate time base. Here, both accuracy and cross-host consistency are critical.
- **Exchange-relative measurements** (for example, comparing your timestamp to a timestamp embedded by the venue) require that your clocks agree with the exchange's clocks within a known bound.

If your clocks are off by 50 microseconds, any one-way latency number smaller than that is unreliable. If your clocks occasionally jump backwards, you can see "negative" latencies. Before we worry about micro-optimizing order encoding or NIC settings, we must ensure our time system is good enough to see the effects.

## Common time sources in trading

Modern trading environments draw time from a small set of primary sources and then distribute it to every host involved in trading, monitoring, and logging. The most important sources are GPS-disciplined oscillators, PTP grandmasters, NTP servers, and exchange-provided timestamps.

### GPS-disciplined oscillators (GPSDOs)

A GPS-disciplined oscillator is a local device that uses signals from Global Positioning System satellites to align an extremely stable local clock (for example, an oven-controlled crystal oscillator) with UTC.

Conceptually:

- The GPS receiver listens to satellites that broadcast precise time and orbit information.
- The device compares its local oscillator against the GPS time and gently corrects it.
- The result is a time reference that is both accurate (tied to GPS) and stable (thanks to the local oscillator).

A GPSDO in a data center environment typically provides sub-microsecond accuracy to UTC at its output. It can expose that time via:

- Electrical time signals such as pulse-per-second (PPS).
- Network time using the Precision Time Protocol (PTP).
- Sometimes the older Network Time Protocol (NTP).

GPSDOs are the usual starting point for building an in-house time infrastructure. They require roof access or other suitable antenna placement with clear sky view, and they are not infallible: antennas fail, local interference occurs, or GPS signals are intentionally jammed or spoofed. For that reason, serious setups often use multiple GPS receivers and supplementary sources.

### PTP grandmasters

The Precision Time Protocol (PTP), standardized as IEEE 1588, is designed to distribute highly accurate time over Ethernet networks. A PTP grandmaster is the authoritative clock in a PTP domain; it often draws its own reference from a GPSDO.

In a typical trading data center:

- One or more PTP grandmasters receive time from GPSDOs.
- The grandmasters act as the root of one or more PTP domains.

- Switches and servers run PTP clients (also called slaves) that adjust their local clocks to follow the grandmaster.

PTP can deliver sub-microsecond accuracy across a well-designed network, especially when combined with:

- **Transparent clocks:** Switches that measure and correct for the time packets spend inside the device, reducing the effect of switch latency on time distribution.
- **Boundary clocks:** Switches that act as PTP clients upstream and PTP masters downstream, isolating segments and improving scalability.

Because PTP operates at the Ethernet layer with hardware timestamping support in many NICs and switches, it is much better suited for high-frequency trading than older, software-only NTP on the same network.

### NTP servers

The Network Time Protocol (NTP) is an older, widely used protocol for synchronizing clocks over IP networks. NTP can be good enough for many IT systems (millisecond-level accuracy) but is usually not sufficient by itself for microsecond-level trading measurements.

However, NTP still plays roles in trading environments:

- As a backup or sanity check against a PTP/GPS infrastructure. If PTP says one thing and NTP says something wildly different, that is a red flag.
- For less latency-critical systems, such as back-office servers and user desktops.
- As a coarse initial sync for devices that later refine time via PTP or hardware timestamping.

A firm may run internal NTP servers that, in turn, synchronize to GPS-DOs, public time services, or both.

### Exchange-provided timestamps and time feeds

Many exchanges embed timestamps in messages or provide dedicated time services. These include:

- Timestamps in market data messages (for example, "matching engine time" for a trade).
- Timestamps in order acknowledgments or drop copies.
- Separate multicast or unicast time feeds designed to help members align to the venue's clock.

These timestamps are by definition on the exchange's time base, not yours. They are useful even if your own clocks are not perfect, because they allow you to measure certain intervals in the venue's frame of reference. For example:

- The time from when the exchange received your order to when it was matched and the book update was generated.
- The latency inside the exchange's market data dissemination path.

To combine these with your own timestamps, you still need to understand and manage clock offset between you and the venue, but exchange timestamps can significantly improve the quality and interpretability of your latency analysis.

## Time-distribution inside a trading firm

Once you have one or more good time sources, you must distribute that time reliably and consistently to every place you take latency measurements: trading hosts, monitoring systems, packet capture boxes, and so on. This is where PTP domains, boundary and transparent clocks, and good network design come in.

### PTP domains and hierarchy

A PTP domain is a logical group of devices that share a grandmaster. In a typical deployment:

- Each data center may have its own PTP domain, with redundant grandmasters.
- Devices in a domain discover the best grandmaster using a built-in election algorithm (the "best master clock" algorithm).
- If the primary grandmaster fails or loses its GPS reference, another eligible device can become the master.

Well-architected firms often separate PTP domains by function or geography to contain faults and simplify reasoning. For example:

- A domain for the exchange colocation facility.
- Another domain for a regional data center hosting risk systems and analytics.

They may then use higher-level processes to compare and monitor the relative offsets between domains.

### Boundary and transparent clocks

Without help from the network, PTP packets accumulate delay and jitter as they pass through switches and routers, degrading time accuracy. Boundary and transparent clocks mitigate this.

**Transparent clocks:** A switch configured as a transparent clock time-stamps each PTP event packet as it enters and exits the device, then adjusts a special field in the packet to record how long it spent inside the switch. This allows downstream clients to correct for that internal delay and improves end-to-end precision.

**Boundary clocks:** A boundary clock switch acts as a PTP client towards its upstream grandmaster, maintaining its own internal clock synchronized to that source. It then acts as a PTP master for downstream devices. Each boundary clock regenerates timing information, creating a tree of masters and clients that scales better and keeps local segments clean.

In practice, a trading firm's core switches in a colo rack may run as boundary clocks, with trading servers as PTP clients. Edge devices facing the exchange may also participate to ensure that packet capture boxes and latency probes share the same accurate time base.

### Host synchronization and tuning

On each trading host, PTP or NTP client software is responsible for adjusting the system clock to follow the chosen masters. Two aspects need attention:

- **Adjustment method:** Many systems use gradual adjustments (slewing) rather than sudden jumps (stepping) to avoid confusing applications. For latency work, jumps are especially dangerous, because they can make latencies appear negative or arbitrarily large.
- **Kernel and NIC support:** Modern kernels and NICs can timestamp packets in hardware and expose these timestamps to PTP and application software. Enabling and verifying this capability is crucial for achieving the expected time accuracy.

Engineers often maintain strict configuration baselines so that all latency-critical hosts use the same PTP client settings, kernel versions, and NIC firmware, reducing the risk of subtle timing differences across otherwise similar machines.

## Clock error and its impact on latency measurements

Even with excellent infrastructure, clocks are never perfect. To use latency metrics responsibly, you need an intuitive sense of how clock error translates into latency error.

### Offset between clocks

Consider two hosts, A and B, each synchronized to the same PTP domain. At a given instant, host A's clock may differ from host B's true time by some small amount, and vice versa. The **offset** between their clocks is the difference between what each clock reads for the same real-world moment.

For one-way latency measured as "send timestamp on A" to "receive timestamp on B," the error in the measurement can be as large as the offset between A and B. If A is 2 microseconds fast and B is 3 microseconds slow, then a real 10-microsecond network latency could appear as:

- As small as 5 microseconds (if errors happen to offset in one direction).
- As large as 15 microseconds (if they offset in the other direction).

If your offset bounds are, say, plus or minus 1 microsecond, this may be acceptable. If your offsets are tens or hundreds of microseconds, one-way latency numbers close to that scale are effectively noise.

### Stability and jitter in time

Clocks do not just sit still with a fixed offset; they wander. Temperature changes, oscillator quality, and network noise all introduce drift and jitter in the apparent time.

From a latency perspective, this means:

- Long-running averages may hide periods where time accuracy was much worse.
- Short measurement windows can be distorted if they fall during adjustments or transients.

Consequently, serious latency analysis always goes hand in hand with time-health monitoring. If you see a spike in reported latency, you must be able to check whether there was simultaneously a spike in clock offset or PTP error messages.

### When round-trip is safer than one-way

Because cross-host clock offsets are hard to control perfectly, many firms prefer to base their key latency metrics on round-trip measurements around a single, well-synchronized observation point. For example:

- Measuring "NIC-to-NIC round-trip" at the client side: time from packet leaving the NIC until response packet returns to that same NIC.
- Measuring "feed handler reaction time" on a single host: time from market data packet arrival (timestamped in hardware) to corresponding order send event, both on the same machine.

In both cases, a **single** clock defines both ends of the interval, so cross-host offset is irrelevant. This does not solve every problem—you still need that one clock to be stable—but it removes the hardest part of the synchronization story.

## Exchange-relative timing

Earlier, we described exchange-provided timestamps as another time source. Now we can be more precise about how to use them in latency work.

### Measuring internal venue latency

Suppose an exchange includes two timestamps in its order acknowledgment:

- A time when the order arrived at the gateway.
- A time when the matching engine processed the order.

By subtracting these (in the exchange's own time base), you obtain an estimate of the venue's internal processing latency, independent of your own clock. This is powerful, because it lets you:

- Compare gateway versus matching engine delays without worrying about your network or time accuracy.
- Observe how venue latency changes with market load or configuration.

You are still trusting the venue's time system, but for internal venue comparison that is usually acceptable.

### Aligning client and exchange time

Often you want to relate your time base to the exchange's: for example, to estimate true one-way network latency or to reconstruct the exact sequence of events across both sides.

There are several approaches:

- **Direct time feed:** Some venues provide a PTP or NTP service from their own time infrastructure. Your PTP clients can then synchronize directly to the exchange's grandmaster, reducing relative offset.
- **Message-based alignment:** If you receive frequent messages with exchange timestamps (for example, a dedicated time tick or heartbeat), you can estimate the difference between your clock and the exchange's by comparing when you observe those messages to the embedded times.

Whichever approach you use, it is important to record and monitor the estimated offset, because it directly bounds the accuracy of any cross-time-base latencies you compute.

## Operational considerations: monitoring and failure modes

Designing a time system is only half the job; running it reliably is the other half. For latency work, you must assume that:

- Clocks will occasionally misbehave.

- Time sources will be lost or degraded.
- Configuration changes will accidentally alter timing behavior.

Your architecture should therefore treat time as a first-class operational concern.

### Monitoring skew, offset, and quality metrics

At minimum, you should continuously monitor:

- **Offset to master:** The estimated difference between each client's clock and its PTP grandmaster or NTP server.
- **Jitter and delay:** How much variation there is in the timing messages themselves (for example, PTP path delay estimates).
- **Source quality:** Whether grandmasters still have a valid GPS lock or have fallen back to freerunning mode.

These metrics should be available both in real time (for operational dashboards) and historically (for forensic analysis). When analyzing a suspicious latency pattern, being able to overlay clock health metrics on your latency graphs is often the difference between a quick diagnosis and confusion.

### Handling leap seconds and time jumps

Occasionally, the global time standard introduces leap seconds or other adjustments. Time protocols and operating systems handle these events in different ways: some smear the adjustment over a window, others perform a discrete jump. Trading systems must be designed and tested to handle these situations gracefully.

Practical steps include:

- Agreeing on a firm-wide policy (for example, always using time-smearing distributions where available).

- Testing strategy and logging behavior through simulated time jumps.
- Ensuring that monitoring systems flag any sudden steps in system clocks.

Time jumps are particularly dangerous for latency analysis, because they can make any measurement that crosses the jump nonsensical. The safer approach is to treat such windows as unreliable and explicitly mark them in downstream analysis.

**Redundancy and failover**

A robust time system avoids single points of failure. For example:

- Multiple GPS antennas feeding separate GPSDOs.
- At least two PTP grandmasters per domain, ideally from different vendors or with different firmware baselines.
- Peer time sources (NTP or cross-domain checks) used only for monitoring, not automatic steering, unless carefully tested.

Failover logic should prefer degraded but monotonic time over abrupt jumps. From a trading perspective, a few extra microseconds of clock error for a short period may be acceptable; a sudden 100-millisecond backwards step is not.

## Regulatory and audit implications

Finally, time is not only an engineering concern; regulators and auditors care as well. Many jurisdictions now require:

- That order, trade, and market data events be timestamped to a certain precision (for example, microseconds).
- That these timestamps be traceable to UTC within a specified maximum error.

- That firms maintain records of time-source configuration, monitoring, and failures.

For a trading firm, the practical consequences are:

- You must be able to demonstrate, after the fact, that your clocks were within required bounds when a given event occurred.
- Your latency analysis may itself become part of regulatory reporting or investigations.
- Weak time infrastructure is a governance risk, not just a performance issue.

This reinforces the central message of the section: credible latency numbers depend on credible time. Investing in a solid time architecture—good sources, careful distribution, robust monitoring—underpins everything else in this chapter. Without it, the fine distinctions you learned in the latency taxonomy become academic, because the measurement errors swamp the values you care about.

In the next section we will move from time foundations to concrete instrumentation and tap points along the trading path, building on both our latency taxonomy and our understanding of time sources to design measurements that are precise, low-overhead, and operationally trustworthy.

## 3.3 Instrumentation & Tap Points

The previous sections gave us two essential ingredients for latency work:

- A shared *vocabulary* for different kinds of latency along the trading path.
- A *time system* capable of generating trustworthy timestamps.

We now turn to the third ingredient: *where* and *how* to take those timestamps so that latency measurements are accurate, low-overhead, and useful in day-to-day operations.

This is the problem of *instrumentation*. In practice, instrumentation comes down to three questions:

- At which boundaries in the trading stack do we place "tap points"?
- Do we measure in hardware, in software, or both?
- How do we record, correlate, and use these measurements without disturbing the system we are observing?

The goal of this section is to give you a structured way to answer those questions, and a concrete blueprint for a minimal yet powerful set of tap points that most latency-sensitive trading systems should maintain.

## From abstract segments to concrete tap points

In the latency taxonomy, we decomposed an order's journey into segments:

- Application
- OS & NIC
- Network
- Exchange gateway
- Matching engine

For instrumentation purposes, we refine that view slightly. Instead of thinking only in terms of "where time is spent," we think in terms of *boundaries where messages cross*:

- Between exchange and your network (edge of your colo).

- Between your network and your hosts (NIC boundary).
- Between the operating system and your process (socket or queue boundary).
- Between modules in your application (strategy, routing, risk, gateway).

A *tap point* is any place where you observe messages or events crossing such a boundary and attach a timestamp or counter. By choosing a small, well-designed set of tap points, you can:

- Measure end-to-end and per-segment latency.
- Detect where additional queuing or delays appear under load.
- Cross-check client and exchange views of the same traffic.

Before we introduce a recommended set of taps, we need to understand the types of instrumentation available.

## Hardware-level vs software-level instrumentation

Broadly, you can instrument your system at two levels:

- **Hardware-level taps:** Operate below or alongside the operating system, typically at the level of physical links or NICs.
- **Software-level taps:** Live inside the OS or your applications, using logs, counters, or tracing frameworks.

Each has strengths and weaknesses.

## Hardware-level instrumentation

Hardware-level instrumentation aims to observe packets as they move across physical links, with minimal interference and maximal timing precision.

Common examples include:

- **Optical or copper taps:** Passive devices inserted into a link that replicate traffic to a capture device without introducing meaningful latency or jitter.
- **SPAN or mirror ports on switches:** Configured to send a copy of selected traffic to a monitoring port. These are easier to deploy than physical taps but can add load to switches and may drop packets under stress.
- **Timestamping NICs and FPGA cards:** Network cards or FPGA-based appliances that can timestamp packets as close as possible to the physical layer, often with nanosecond resolution.

The major advantages of hardware-level taps are:

- *High precision:* Timestamps reflect the time a packet is actually on the wire.
- *Low observer effect:* Good taps add negligible delay and do not require changes to your trading software.
- *Unified view:* A single capture point can see traffic for multiple hosts, protocols, and applications.

Their downsides include:

- *Cost and complexity:* Specialized hardware, rack space, and capture infrastructure.
- *Limited semantic context:* You see packets and headers, but you may not know which strategy instance or order object generated them without additional correlation.
- *Deployment friction:* Inserting physical taps or reconfiguring core switches is operationally sensitive.

## Software-level instrumentation

Software-level instrumentation uses the tools already present in your operating systems and applications:

- **Kernel probes:** Hooks into the OS networking stack or system calls, placed via built-in tracing frameworks.
- **User-space timers:** High-resolution timers inside your processes, recording timestamps around key functions or message queues.
- **Application logging:** Structured logs with timestamps and identifiers, especially at module entry/exit points.

Advantages include:

- *Rich context:* You can tag timestamps with order IDs, strategy names, symbol, or any other metadata.
- *Flexibility:* You can add or adjust instrumentation as code evolves, without touching the network.
- *Lower cost of entry:* No specialized hardware is strictly required.

Disadvantages:

- *Potential overhead:* Poorly designed logging or tracing can add latency and jitter.
- *Less direct view of the wire:* You see when your process thinks it sent a message, not necessarily when the bits left the NIC.
- *Clock dependencies:* Measurements are limited by the accuracy and stability of the host's own clock.

In practice, robust latency analysis combines both approaches. Hardware-level taps anchor your understanding of what happens on the wire; software-level taps explain *why* and link measurements back to business logic.

## A taxonomy of tap locations along the trading path

We now return to the order and market data paths and identify archetypal places where taps can be placed. Think of this as a checklist rather than a prescription; your exact setup will vary, but the categories are broadly universal.

## External network edge

This is the boundary between your network and the rest of the world, often at a cross-connect to the exchange or a WAN router in your colo facility.

Possible taps:

- **Optical or copper taps** on the cross-connect to the exchange.
- **SPAN ports** on the last switch before traffic leaves your cage.

What you measure here:

- Time when orders actually leave your environment and when exchange responses enter.
- Time when market data packets reach your edge.

These taps are key to understanding *network latency* and for reconciling your view with the venue's.

## Host NIC ingress/egress

The next boundary is at each trading host's NIC: where packets enter and leave the server.

Possible taps:

- **Hardware timestamping** on the NIC, exposed via the OS.
- **Kernel-level packet capture** with timestamps as close to the driver as possible.

What you measure:

- Time when an outbound order packet hits the NIC (egress).
- Time when inbound acknowledgments or market data packets are received (ingress).

These taps let you separate *client host effects* from pure network behavior. The difference between NIC timestamps and external edge timestamps tells you how much latency is added by your internal network and edge devices.

## OS-to-application boundary

Within the host, the next important boundary is between the operating system and your application. For example:

- When your order gateway process calls into the kernel to send a packet.
- When your market data handler receives packets from the kernel via sockets or shared memory.

Possible taps:

- **System call tracing** around send/receive calls.
- **User-space timestamps** right before/after blocking I/O or queue operations.

What you measure:

- OS & NIC latency: the difference between user-space send time and NIC egress time.
- Receive-side handoff latency: the difference between NIC ingress time and application receive time.

These taps illuminate how much time is spent in kernel code paths, driver queues, and socket buffers versus your own application logic.

## Application module boundaries

Within your application stack, messages pass between modules:

- Market data parser $\rightarrow$ strategy engine.
- Strategy engine $\rightarrow$ risk checks.
- Risk checks $\rightarrow$ order gateway.

Possible taps:

- **Structured logs or in-memory traces** at module entry and exit points.
- **Message envelope fields** carrying timestamps through internal queues.

What you measure:

- Strategy decision time: from input market data to output order decision.
- Risk and routing overhead: time spent in risk modules and routing logic.
- Queueing inside your own process: time messages sit in internal queues.

These taps are essential for capacity planning and optimization. They tell you whether a performance problem is due to the strategy's computation, a particular risk check, or simple overload of an internal message queue.

## Exchange-side taps (when available)

Although you do not control the exchange's instrumentation, many venues provide their own tap points in the form of:

- Timestamps in acknowledgments and market data.
- Drop copy feeds reflecting post-trade events.
- Dedicated time or status feeds.

These, combined with your external edge taps, allow you to reverse-engineer segments such as:

- Gateway processing time.
- Matching engine queueing and processing time.

You do not need physical taps inside the exchange; instead, you treat exchange timestamps as if they were taps at the gateway and matching engine boundaries.

## A canonical tap layout

We now summarize these possibilities into a realistic, minimal set of tap points that many firms use. This layout aims to give you:

- One or two high-precision hardware views of the wire.
- Correlated software-level timestamps at key process boundaries.
- Enough information to decompose end-to-end latency into meaningful segments.

The recommended taps are:

- **External edge hardware tap** on the link to the exchange (nanosecond-scale hardware timestamps).
- **Host NIC hardware timestamps** on the main trading hosts (nanosecond to sub-microsecond).
- **Application ingress/egress timestamps** for market data handlers and order gateways (microsecond or better).
- **Strategy, risk, and routing module timestamps** at internal message boundaries (microsecond or better).
- **Correlation IDs** carried from strategy to exchange and back, allowing you to stitch hardware and software traces into coherent per-order stories.

Midway through the section, it is useful to visualize this layout in a single schematic.

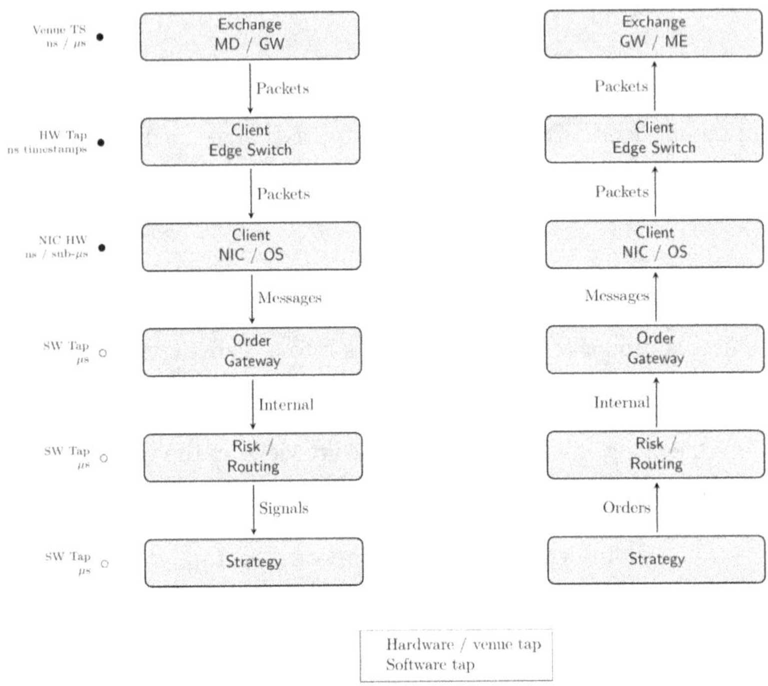


This figure is deliberately simplified, but it shows the core idea: a left-to-right pipeline with a small number of well-placed taps, some hardware-based, some software-based, each with a known resolution.

## Designing low-overhead instrumentation

A common failure mode in latency work is to instrument so heavily that the measurement itself changes the behavior you are trying to observe. This "observer effect" can be subtle: a few extra system calls in a hot path, synchronous logging to disk, or oversized trace messages can all add jitter.

To avoid this, follow a few design principles.

## Measure at boundaries, not everywhere

Rather than timestamping every function call, focus on boundaries:

- Where messages enter or leave a process or module.
- Where threads hand work to each other via queues.
- Where packets cross between OS and NIC.

These points give you a clean picture of each segment's behavior without polluting your inner loops. For example, instead of timing every step inside your strategy engine, you might timestamp:

- When a batch of market data updates enters the strategy.
- When the strategy outputs a batch of candidate orders.

You then use separate, focused profiling sessions to study internal computation when necessary.

## Prefer in-memory aggregation to synchronous logging

Writing logs synchronously to disk or over the network is expensive and variable in cost. For latency-critical code paths, it is safer to:

- Store timestamps and metadata in in-memory ring buffers.
- Periodically flush or sample them to persistent storage from a background thread.
- Allow tracing to be turned on and off at runtime, with clearly documented overheads.

Your goal is to make the presence or absence of instrumentation a small, measurable effect, not a dominant factor in latency.

## Sample intelligently

You rarely need a timestamp for every message. For many questions, sampling is sufficient:

- Record every $N_{iter}$-th event (for example, one in 1000).
- Record all events for a limited time window.
- Record only events matching certain criteria (for example, large orders, specific symbols).

Sampling reduces the volume of data to process and the overhead on the system, while still revealing the shape of latency distributions and their tails.

## Use consistent units and schemas

To correlate measurements across tap points and systems, you need a consistent schema:

- Define a standard timestamp field name, unit (for example, nanoseconds since epoch), and type.
- Define standard IDs used to join records (order ID, connection ID, session ID, etc.).
- Document which clock each timestamp uses (for example, host monotonic clock, PTP-synchronized system clock, exchange time).

Consistency here is as important as clock synchronization itself. Without it, you waste time writing brittle ad hoc transformations that introduce errors.

## Correlating hardware and software views

Hardware taps tell you when packets are on the wire; software taps tell you what your code was doing. To get full value from both, you must learn to correlate them.

## Correlation via IDs and packet content

The simplest approach is to associate each logical event (such as an order) with an identifier that appears both:

- In software-level traces (for example, internal logs keyed by order ID).
- In the on-the-wire messages (for example, FIX ClOrdID, binary order token).

You can then:

- Find the packet carrying that order in the hardware capture.
- Pair its wire timestamp with the software timestamps for the same ID.
- Compute segments such as "strategy to NIC," "NIC to edge," and "edge to exchange gateway."

For inbound flows (market data, acks), you can often map messages back to internal state changes via sequence numbers or other keys.

## Correlation via time windows

When explicit IDs are not available (for example, in anonymous multicast feeds), you can still correlate based on time and content pattern:

- Match packet timestamps at the edge with packet timestamps at the NIC by sliding a small time window and matching on sequence numbers or payload.
- Match NIC-level receive events to application-level receive events by similar time-windowing, assuming OS-to-application latency is small compared with network latency.

This is more fragile than ID-based correlation, but still useful for understanding aggregate behavior, especially if your clocks are well synchronized.

## Making measurements operationally useful

Finally, instrumentation is only valuable if it helps real people make better decisions. That means designing your tap points and data flows with operational use cases in mind.

## Real-time alerts and dashboards

From your tap points, derive a small set of key metrics suitable for live monitoring:

- NIC-to-exchange edge round-trip latency percentiles.
- Strategy reaction time distributions (market data in to order out).
- OS/NIC latency trends on critical hosts.

Feed these into dashboards that:

- Highlight deviations from normal behavior (for example, p99 latency doubling).
- Allow drilling down by venue, symbol group, or host.
- Overlay time-health information (PTP offsets, GPS status) with latency curves.

When something goes wrong in production, these are often the first tools engineers and traders reach for.

## Forensic analysis and post-mortems

For deeper investigations-such as unexplained misses, apparent arbitrage failures, or regulator inquiries-you need the ability to reconstruct individual event paths:

- For a specific order ID, retrieve all associated timestamps from strategy, risk, gateway, NIC, edge tap, and exchange messages.

- Rebuild a timeline showing who saw what, when, at each layer.
- Compare the path of a "slow" event with typical events under similar conditions.

This type of analysis depends critically on the discipline of your instrumentation: consistent IDs, clocks, and schemas enabling cross-system joins.

### Guiding design and capacity planning

Over longer horizons, aggregated measurements from your taps support architectural decisions:

- Whether to invest in lower-latency network routes or in optimizing application code.
- Whether to split a monolithic gateway into separate processes to avoid queueing.
- How to size hardware for peak load, based on how latency curves change as throughput increases.

Because your tap points are fixed and stable over time, you can compare before-and-after distributions fairly, confident that measurement methodology has not changed between configurations.

## 3.4 Statistical Analysis & Histograms

By this point in the chapter, you have three key ingredients:

- A clear *taxonomy* of latency: which segments exist and who controls them.
- A reliable *time base*: synchronized clocks and exchange timestamps.

- A concrete *instrumentation layout*: hardware and software tap points along the trading path.

These give you raw timestamp data. The next challenge is to turn those raw numbers into something you can reason about: latency distributions, percentiles, and tail metrics that link directly to trading outcomes.

This section explains how to move from "a pile of timestamps" to meaningful statistical summaries. We will:

- Show why averages are not enough in latency-sensitive trading.
- Introduce percentiles and tail-focused metrics.
- Explain how to construct and interpret latency histograms.
- Discuss practical issues: outliers, clock anomalies, censoring, and fair comparisons.
- End with a worked example comparing two system configurations with similar averages but very different tails.

The focus is deliberately intuitive: rather than formal proofs, we aim to build a practical feel for what each metric does and when it is useful.

## Why average latency misleads

The easiest summary of any dataset is its average (mean). For latency, this is often the first number people quote: "Our round-trip latency averages 120 microseconds."

In trading, this is rarely enough, for three main reasons.

**Latency distributions are usually skewed and heavy-tailed**

Latency rarely clusters neatly around a single value. Instead, you typically see many fast events and a long tail of slower ones:

- Most packets might traverse your network in 20–30 microseconds.

- A minority encounter queueing, garbage collection, interrupts, or contention and take 200–500 microseconds.

The average lies somewhere in between and does not tell you:

- How often you encounter those slow cases.
- How much worse the worst cases are than typical.

From a trading perspective, those tail events often matter most: they are exactly the ones where you lose queue position or miss a fleeting opportunity.

**Averages hide multimodality**

Many real systems have multiple "modes" of behavior:

- A fast path when everything is in cache and no locks are contended.
- A slower path under load, when work spills into extra queues or buffers.

If you plot the distribution of latencies, you may see two or more distinct peaks. The average sits in the middle of these peaks, corresponding to no real operating mode. Designing around an average that no event ever actually experiences is dangerous.

**Trading decisions depend on worst cases and percentiles**

Traders and strategists care less about how fast you are "on average" and more about questions like:

- "How often is my quote updated slower than my main competitor?"
- "On the 1% of worst days or worst bursts, how bad does latency get?"

These questions are inherently about *percentiles* and *tails*, not means. The rest of this section develops the tools to describe those features precisely.

# From raw timestamps to latency samples

Before introducing statistical measures, we should be explicit about what a "latency sample" is.

From your instrumentation, you typically have timestamps at two or more tap points for a single event (for example, an order, acknowledgment, or market-data update). A latency sample is simply the elapsed time between two chosen events, such as:

- Strategy output time and NIC egress time (client-side sending latency).
- NIC ingress time and strategy input time (client-side receive and processing latency).
- Exchange gateway receive timestamp and matching engine processing timestamp (venue internal latency).

For each path and segment you care about, you define:

- The start and end tap points (consistent with your latency taxonomy).
- The time basis (which clock).
- Any filters (for example, only orders over a certain size, or only a specific venue).

Evaluating these definitions across your data yields a collection of latency samples: one number per event. It is this collection that you will summarize statistically.

# Percentiles and tail-focused metrics

Percentiles give you a way to say, "what is a typical latency, and how bad do the slowest cases get?" in a way that is both rigorous and intuitive.

**Percentile basics**

If you sort all latency samples from smallest to largest:

- The median (50th percentile, often written p50) is the value that half of events are faster than and half are slower than.
- The 90th percentile (p90) is the value that 90% of events are faster than and 10% are slower than.
- Higher percentiles such as p99 and p99.9 focus on the slowest 1% or 0.1% of events.

For trading systems, at least three percentiles are usually tracked:

- p50: An indication of "typical" latency when things go well.
- p99: Captures rare slowdowns that traders often feel as missed opportunities.
- p99.9: Highlights extreme but still recurring tail events that might correspond to contention, garbage collection, page faults, or other sporadic issues.

A useful mental model is:

- p50 describes the experience of your "luckiest" interactions.
- p99 describes your "bad" moments that still happen regularly.
- p99.9 describes your "worst days" that, in aggregate, still matter a lot for P&L and risk.

### Maximums and conditional tail expectations

Alongside percentiles, several other tail-oriented metrics are informative:

- Maximum: The single largest latency observed. This can reveal extreme anomalies but is often too sensitive to rare glitches or measurement errors to use alone.
- Conditional tail average: The average latency of all events slower than a certain percentile (for example, the average latency of the slowest 1% of events). This gives you a sense of how bad "bad" really is.

Together, these metrics let you say things like:

> "Our p50 order send latency is 15 microseconds, p99 is 30 microseconds, and the average of the slowest 1% of sends is 60 microseconds."

This statement is far richer than "our average is 18 microseconds," and much closer to what traders actually experience.

## Histograms: seeing the shape of latency

Percentiles condense a distribution into a few numbers; histograms let you *see* the entire shape.

### What is a histogram?

A histogram groups samples into ranges or "buckets" and counts how many fall into each range. You then plot bucket ranges on the horizontal axis and counts (or proportions) on the vertical axis.

For latency:

- The horizontal axis might cover 0–1000 microseconds.
- Each bucket might represent, say, a 5-microsecond or 10-microsecond interval.

The resulting shape can reveal:

- A dominant peak at a fast latency (your normal operating mode).
- Secondary peaks corresponding to slower modes (for example, when the system is under load).
- A long right-hand tail of rare, slow events.

### Choosing bucket sizes and scales

Bucket sizing is a trade-off:

- *Too coarse* (for example, 100-microsecond buckets) and you smooth away important structure.
- *Too fine* (for example, 1-nanosecond buckets) and most buckets have zero or very few counts, making the plot noisy and memory-hungry.

A practical approach is:

- Use smaller buckets where data is dense (near the main peak).
- Use larger buckets further into the tail.

This idea underlies *logarithmic* and *HdrHistogram-style* bucket schemes.

**Logarithmic / Hdr-style buckets**

In these schemes, bucket widths grow as latency grows. For example:

- 1-microsecond buckets from 0–100 microseconds.
- 5-microsecond buckets from 100–500 microseconds.
- 25-microsecond buckets from 500 microseconds and above.

The details vary by implementation, but the goal is the same: high resolution around the fast, frequently observed latencies, and coarser resolution where events are sparse but large.

This lets you store and query millions of latency samples in a compact data structure, while still estimating percentiles with high accuracy and showing tails clearly.

**Linear vs logarithmic axes**

Histograms can be drawn with either linear or logarithmic axes:

- A **linear horizontal axis** (latency itself) is easiest to interpret for small, tight distributions but can compress the tail into a tiny area if a few events are vastly slower.

- A **logarithmic horizontal axis** spreads out the tail, making differences at higher latencies more visually apparent. This is useful when tail behavior is important for risk or design decisions.

Similarly, a logarithmic vertical axis can make small counts in the tail visible, though at the cost of interpretability for non-technical audiences.

For most day-to-day engineering work, a linear axis with Hdr-style buckets is a good compromise; tails remain visible without overcomplicating the picture.

## Data hygiene: keeping your distributions honest

Even with good bucket choices, several practical issues can distort your latency distributions if you ignore them.

### Outliers and measurement errors

Occasionally, you will see absurd values: negative latencies, latencies of seconds in a microsecond-scale system, or sudden jumps in what should be a stable metric. Common causes include:

- Clock adjustments or resynchronization events.
- Packet losses or mis-ordered correlations between requests and responses.
- Instrumentation bugs (for example, using the wrong clock or unit).

You should:

- Flag and investigate these events rather than automatically discarding them.
- For long-term statistical summaries, consider excluding data from periods where clocks were known to be unhealthy.

- When presenting results, be transparent about any filters you applied (for example, "excluded events during known PTP failures on this day").

### Censoring and timeouts

Sometimes you only observe that an event was "slow or failed" beyond a threshold, not its exact latency. For example:

- Orders that did not receive an acknowledgment within 500 milliseconds may be considered timed out.
- Monitoring systems may cap measured latencies at a maximum window.

This creates *censored* data: you know that latency was at least some value, but not exactly how large. Naively treating all such events as equal to the threshold underestimates tail severity.

In simple operational contexts, it is acceptable to:

- Report censored events in a separate category (for example, "timeouts", or "latency > 500 ms").
- Avoid overinterpreting the exact shape of the extreme tail if many events are censored.

For more formal analyses (for example, internal risk models), statisticians may apply methods specifically designed for censored data, but that is beyond our scope here.

### Sample size and representativeness

A distribution based on 100 samples is much less trustworthy than one based on 1,000,000. Be cautious when:

- Quoting p99 or p99.9 from tiny sample sets.
- Comparing distributions drawn from different traffic patterns or days.

As a rule of thumb:

- Focus on lower percentiles (p50, p90) when sample sizes are small.
- Collect enough data across representative trading conditions (busy times, quiet times, stress events) before drawing strong conclusions.

## Comparing two latency distributions fairly

One of the main uses of statistical analysis is to compare two configurations:

- Old vs new hardware.
- Two different network routes.
- Two versions of an application or NIC setting.

To compare fairly, keep the following principles in mind.

**Control for workload differences**

Latency depends heavily on workload:

- Message rate and burstiness.
- Mix of message types and sizes.
- Venue and symbol mix.

When comparing distributions:

- Use data from similar time periods (for example, same trading hours, same instrument set).
- Better yet, run A/B tests where old and new configurations handle similar traffic simultaneously.

If one configuration was measured during a calm market and the other during a volatile open, differences may reflect workload, not design.

**Align measurement definitions and tap points**

Ensure that both distributions:

- Use the same start and end tap points.
- Use the same time basis and units.
- Apply the same filters and sampling criteria.

If one setup measures strategy-to-NIC latency and another measures strategy-to-edge-switch latency, you are not comparing like for like. Similarly, if one uses hardware NIC timestamps and another uses application-level timestamps, apparent improvements or regressions may actually stem from differences in measurement methods.

**Look beyond a single metric**

When evaluating "is configuration B better than configuration A?" do not rely on a single number. Examine:

- p50, p90, p99, and perhaps p99.9.
- Histograms for shape differences (for example, extra peaks or heavier tails).
- Counts of timeouts or censored events.

A new configuration that improves p50 by a small amount but worsens p99 substantially might not be an upgrade in trading terms. Histograms and percentiles together make these trade-offs clear.

## Worked example: two systems with similar averages

We now illustrate these concepts with a simplified, synthetic example. Imagine two versions of your order gateway:

- **System A:** The existing, battle-tested version.
- **System B:** A new, supposedly optimized version.

Both systems show a similar average client-to-exchange one-way latency around 40 microseconds. If you stopped there, you might conclude that there is no meaningful difference.

However, when you plot full distributions and inspect percentiles, you see a different story: System B has a noticeably heavier tail. The following figure demonstrates how we might visualize this, using overlaid histograms and percentile curves.

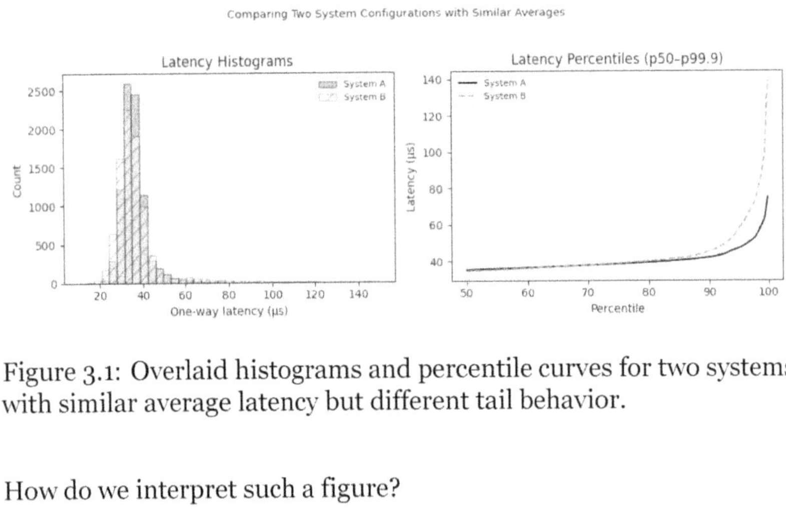


Figure 3.1: Overlaid histograms and percentile curves for two systems with similar average latency but different tail behavior.

How do we interpret such a figure?

- In the **histogram** (left), the main peaks around 30–40 microseconds are similar for both systems. However, System B shows more counts in the 60–120 microsecond range, indicating a heavier tail.
- In the **percentile plot** (right), the curves are close near p50 and p90 but diverge towards p99 and above. System B's p99.9 might be tens of microseconds slower than System A's.

From a trading standpoint, this suggests:

- Under normal conditions, the two systems feel similar.
- Under stress or during microbursts, System B suffers noticeably more slow events, which could hurt hit rates or P&L even though the average looks fine.

The decision to adopt System B should therefore weigh its potential benefits (perhaps lower CPU usage, new features, or cost savings) against the cost of worse tail latency. Without histograms and percentile analysis, you might never see that trade-off.

## From distributions to latency SLOs

Once you routinely compute and visualize latency distributions, you can begin to set explicit service-level objectives (SLOs) for your systems. For example:

- "For venue X, client-to-exchange one-way latency p99 must remain below 50 microseconds during continuous trading hours."
- "Strategy reaction time (market data to order) p99.9 must remain below 150 microseconds for symbols in our top liquidity tier."

These SLOs:

- Give engineers clear design targets.
- Provide early warning when the system drifts or when workloads change.
- Translate technical performance into language traders and risk managers can reason about.

SLOs grounded in distributions, not averages, are much more aligned with real trading outcomes. They recognize that in markets, the edge often lies in how you perform on your worst days and in your slowest moments, not just in how fast you are on average.

## 3.5 Benchmarking Methodologies

Up to this point in the chapter, we have focused on *understanding* latency: defining it precisely, measuring it with synchronized clocks, instrumenting the right tap points, and analyzing distributions with appropriate statistics. The natural next question is: how do we *use* these tools to evaluate changes to our systems?

In other words, how do we benchmark?

A good latency benchmark does two things:

- It generates traffic that is representative of the workloads your system will see in production.
- It produces measurements that can be fairly compared across different architectures, configurations, or code versions.

This section presents structured approaches to benchmarking trading systems, with special attention to latency. We will:

- Classify benchmark types: synthetic load tests, production replays, and live A/B or canary deployments.
- Discuss how to design realistic workloads: message sizes, burstiness, symbol and venue mix.
- Explain how to control for confounding factors so comparisons are fair.
- Outline reporting practices that tie benchmark results back to risk and expected trading benefit, not just microseconds.

The guiding principle is reproducibility: you should be able to re-run a benchmark months later and meaningfully compare it with past results.

### Benchmarking in the context of the latency stack

Everything covered so far in this chapter feeds into benchmarking:

- The *latency taxonomy* tells you which segments you might want to benchmark (for example, strategy reaction time vs network vs gateway).
- *Clock synchronization* ensures that benchmarks using different hosts and components can be compared.
- *Instrumentation and tap points* give you the raw data needed to characterize each benchmark.
- *Statistical tools* (percentiles, histograms) provide the language for comparing one scenario with another.

Benchmarking is not a separate activity; it is simply the systematic application of these tools to controlled experiments.

## Types of latency benchmarks

Broadly, there are three categories of latency benchmarking you will encounter in trading systems:

- Synthetic load tests (lab or staging).
- Production replays (lab or shadow environment).
- Live A/B and canary tests (in production).

Each has a role. Synthetic tests are easy to control but risk being unrealistic. Production replays capture real market structure without the financial risk of live trading. A/B and canary deployments give the most accurate picture of behavior under true conditions but must be designed carefully to avoid operational and trading risk.

## Synthetic load testing

Synthetic tests generate artificial traffic to exercise your system in a controlled environment. They are the natural starting point when you design a new architecture or tune a component.

### Closed-loop vs open-loop tests

It is useful to distinguish two high-level patterns:

- **Open-loop** You inject a predefined stream of messages into your system (for example, a feed of orders or market data) without reacting to the system's output during the test. The workload is fixed, and your system is a passive responder.
- **Closed-loop** The system's responses feed back into the workload generation in a simplified way, mimicking strategy behavior. For example, a test harness might send an order whenever it sees a certain market data pattern, creating a synthetic "strategy-in-the-loop."

Open-loop tests are simpler and more reproducible. Closed-loop tests are closer to real trading but more complex to specify and repeat.

### Components of a synthetic latency test

A good synthetic test specifies, at minimum:

- **Message types and protocols:** FIX, binary order entry, multicast market data, internal RPCs, and so forth.
- **Message size distribution:** Not just the average size, but how many small versus large messages occur.
- **Timing pattern:** Average rate, burstiness, diurnal pattern (for example, open vs midday).
- **Venue and symbol mix:** Different venues or symbols may trigger different code paths or risk checks.
- **Concurrency:** Number of connections, threads, or session instances active simultaneously.

The better these factors mirror production, the more meaningful your synthetic latency numbers will be.

### Workload realism and danger of "toy" tests

A common pitfall is designing a test that is too clean:

- Messages of uniform size.

- Constant-rate traffic without bursts.
- Single-threaded or single-connection workloads.

Under such conditions, latency can look excellent, only to degrade sharply in production under true market burstiness, lock contention, cache misses, or GC pauses.

To avoid this, base your synthetic workloads on measurements taken from production:

- Derive message size distributions from real logs.
- Reproduce burst patterns (for example, nanosecond or microsecond gaps between packets around the open).
- Emulate realistic concurrency: number of symbols, strategies, and sessions active at once.

When in doubt, err on the side of more stress rather than less. A design that only performs well in a toy environment is not robust.

**Capturing and analyzing synthetic test results**

For each synthetic test, you should:

- Collect latency samples at the same tap points you use in production.
- Compute percentiles, histograms, and other metrics as described earlier.
- Record resource usage (CPU, memory, NIC, disk) alongside latency, to see how performance scales under load.

Equally important is metadata:

- Hardware details: CPU model, core counts, RAM, NICs.
- Software details: versions of your code, OS, drivers, firmware.
- Configuration: kernel parameters, thread affinities, NIC settings.

Store this with the results so that later comparisons are meaningful. A benchmark without clear metadata is difficult to interpret or reproduce.

## Production replay

Synthetic tests are valuable, but they cannot capture the full richness of real markets. Production replay bridges this gap by using recorded real-world traffic to drive your system in a non-live environment.

### What is production replay?

Production replay means capturing live streams of:

- Market data packets (multicast or unicast).
- Order entry and acknowledgment traffic.
- Sometimes full pcap captures of the network interfaces.

and then playing them back later against:

- A copy of your trading system in a lab or staging environment.
- Potentially, an emulated exchange or "echo server" that responds deterministically.

During replay, you measure latency and system behavior just as you would in production, but without sending any real orders to exchanges or risking capital.

### Levels of fidelity in replay

Production replay can be as simple or complex as your needs and resources permit.

#### Packet-level replay.

At the highest fidelity, you:

- Capture full packets at the wire (for example, via a tap or SPAN port).

- Re-inject them into a test network interface at the same timing as originally observed.

This preserves real burst patterns, inter-packet gaps, and low-level protocol detail. It is ideal for testing feed handlers, gateways, and network behavior.

**Message-level replay.**

A simpler alternative is to:

- Extract higher-level messages (for example, decoded market data events or orders) from logs.
- Feed them into your system using an internal API or harness, approximating their original timing.

This is easier to implement but loses some details of the original network behavior (for example, loss, reordering, or exact packetization).

### Determinism and "echo" exchanges

For order flows, a common pattern is to pair replay with a simple "echo exchange":

- Your gateway sends orders to a harness that mimics the exchange protocol.
- The harness responds deterministically (for example, acknowledging all orders with fixed rules or simulated book logic).

You can then examine:

- Your internal latency distributions under realistic order loads.
- How resource usage and queuing behave under real peak volumes.

Because the reply behavior is deterministic, comparing two system versions under the same replay input is straightforward.

### Use cases for production replay

Production replay is especially useful when:

- You want to test changes under the exact market conditions that previously caused problems (for example, a volatile open or a known incident).
- You want to validate new architectures (for example, new threading models, new serialization libraries) before exposing them to live traffic.
- Regulatory or internal risk requirements demand pre-production testing with realistic data.

However, replay is not a complete substitute for live testing, because:

- It cannot fully capture peer behavior, such as other participants' reactions.
- It may not perfectly reproduce all network conditions (for example, live congestion on shared links).

It is best viewed as a powerful intermediate step between pure synthetic tests and live A/B experiments.

## Live A/B and canary deployments

Ultimately, you must test new systems under real market conditions. Live A/B and canary deployments are structured ways to do that while containing risk.

### A/B testing with parallel stacks

In a classic A/B latency test:

- You deploy two versions of the system (A and B) side-by-side, each handling a portion of the live traffic.
- The versions are as similar as possible except for the change under test (for example, new NIC driver, new risk module implementation).
- You compare latency distributions and trading outcomes between A and B over the same time window.

To do this safely:

- Ensure both stacks respect the same risk and position limits.
- Consider routing different symbol sets or strategy instances to A and B, rather than duplicating orders, to avoid self-competition.
- Monitor performance and risk closely, with the ability to quickly route all traffic back to the more stable version if needed.

From a measurement perspective, A/B testing is ideal because it naturally controls for:

- Market conditions (both see the same overall environment).
- Time-of-day and diurnal patterns.

Differences in distributions are therefore more likely to reflect the changes you made.

**Canary releases**

A canary release is a more cautious variant:

- You first roll out the new configuration (B) to a small fraction of traffic or to less critical symbols.
- You monitor latency, error rates, and trading outcomes.
- If metrics remain acceptable, you gradually increase the fraction of traffic routed to B.

Canarying is particularly useful for changes that are hard to fully exercise in lab environments, such as OS patches, kernel settings, or network reconfigurations.

Latency benchmarking in canary deployments should focus on:

- Comparing distributions between canary and baseline under similar workloads.
- Watching for new modes of failure or unexpected tail behavior.

If you see p99 or p99.9 latencies degrade significantly, even if averages remain similar, that is a warning sign.

## Controlling confounding variables

Whether you use synthetic tests, replays, or live A/B, one of the hardest parts of benchmarking is controlling for confounders—variables that change between runs and affect latency independently of your architectural change.

Key confounders include:

- **Market conditions:** Volatility, volume, and the presence of news events.
- **System load:** Number of strategies, symbols, and sessions active.
- **Environment drift:** Background OS tasks, other applications, or contention for network or storage.
- **Time synchronization health:** PTP or GPS problems can alter measured latencies.

To mitigate these:

- Prefer side-by-side comparisons (A/B, parallel replays) over before/after measurements separated by days or weeks.
- Record and, where possible, fix the environment: run benchmarks on dedicated hardware, minimize unrelated processes, and document kernel and driver versions.
- Correlate latency results with supporting metrics: CPU load, NIC statistics, time sync status. Strange latency shifts coinciding with time sync anomalies should be treated with caution.

If you cannot fully control confounders, at least document them, so that any comparison can be interpreted in context.

## Interpreting benchmarks in trading terms

Benchmarks often produce tidy tables of microseconds and percentiles. To be useful, these numbers must be translated into language that matters for trading: hit rates, queue position, slippage, and ultimately expected P&L.

### Linking microseconds to queue priority

Reducing latency by a few microseconds matters only if it improves your priority in the exchange's queues often enough to affect fills. This depends on:

- The distribution of other participants' latencies.
- The typical time between competing orders at the venue.
- The sensitivity of your strategy's edge to being first or early in the queue.

While you may not know competitors' internal latency distributions, you can:

- Empirically correlate changes in your own latency distributions with changes in fill probability and queue position.
- Use exchange-level data (for example, detailed order book updates) to estimate how often a small timing improvement would have altered the matching outcome.

In benchmark reports, it is valuable to present not just "p99 improved by 5 microseconds" but also:

> "Backtesting on replayed book data suggests this would increase our hit rate on a specific liquidity-taking strategy by X%, given the observed arrival patterns of competing orders."

### Balancing latency against other objectives

Architectural changes often trade latency against other qualities:

- Robustness and failover mechanisms.
- Code simplicity and maintainability.

- Resource consumption and cost.

Benchmarking should therefore include:

- Stability metrics: variance of latency, frequency of extreme outliers.
- Resource metrics: CPU, memory, network utilization at different loads.
- Failure behavior: how gracefully the system degrades under stress.

It may be rational to accept a small worsening of p50 latency if p99 becomes much better, or if failure behavior becomes more predictable. Clear benchmark data helps make such trade-offs explicit.

## Reporting and governance

Finally, good benchmarking is not just about running tests; it is also about documenting and communicating results in a way that stands up to internal scrutiny and, when relevant, regulatory review.

### Standardized benchmark descriptions

For each benchmark, maintain a concise but complete description covering:

- **Objective:** What question the benchmark tries to answer (for example, impact of new serialization library on feed-handler latency).
- **Setup:** Hardware, software versions, configuration, and any special environment constraints.
- **Workload:** Synthetic, replay, or live; message types, rates, burstiness, symbol and venue mix.
- **Measurement points:** Which tap points were used and what latencies were computed.

Attach key graphs (histograms, percentile curves) and summary tables (p50, p90, p99, p99.9, tail averages), plus any notable anomalies or caveats.

**Benchmark repositories and reproducibility**

Treat benchmarks as first-class artifacts:

- Store configurations, input data (or references to it), and analysis scripts under version control.
- Record hashes or identifiers for code versions and environment snapshots.
- Ensure that another engineer can re-run a benchmark, months later, and obtain similar distributions.

This discipline not only improves engineering rigor but also provides valuable evidence when explaining system performance to risk committees, auditors, or regulators.

This section has built on the measurement and analysis foundations of the chapter to show how to design meaningful latency benchmarks. We have:

- Classified benchmark types: synthetic tests, production replays, and live A/B or canary deployments.
- Emphasized workload realism, careful control of confounders, and the importance of shared tap points and time bases.
- Shown how to interpret benchmarks in trading terms and incorporate them into repeatable, documented processes.

Done well, benchmarking turns latency from a vague concern into a quantified, testable property of your trading system. It enables you to evolve architectures with confidence, knowing not only *how many* microseconds you gained or lost, but also what those changes mean for your strategies and your risk.

## 3.6 Visualizing Latency Distributions

The previous sections gave you two powerful capabilities:

- You know how to *measure* latency accurately at multiple tap points, using synchronized clocks and carefully placed instrumentation.
- You know how to *analyze* those measurements statistically: percentiles, histograms, and tail metrics.

What remains is to communicate these findings effectively. Engineering decisions, strategy design, and risk discussions are all made by humans with limited time and attention. A raw table of numbers or a dense CSV of timestamps is rarely enough to drive a decision.

In this section we focus on visualization: turning latency logs into clear graphics that help different audiences—engineers, quants, and traders—see the same reality. We will:

- Introduce time-series views that reveal how latency behaves across the trading day.
- Revisit distribution-oriented views (histograms, cumulative plots, violin plots) from a "how to use them" angle.
- Show how hop-by-hop visualizations (waterfall charts, heat maps) connect back to the tap points defined earlier.
- Discuss practical design choices: axis scaling, binning, color and patterns, and annotations.
- Conclude with a composite example that combines several views into a dashboard-style figure.

The emphasis is not on artistic perfection but on clarity: each plot should answer a concrete question better than text alone.

## Time-series views: latency over the trading day

Latency is not static. It changes with:

- Time of day (open, midday lull, close).
- Market events (news releases, auctions, halts).
- System events (deployments, failovers, network incidents).

Time-series plots show how latency metrics evolve across time, making such patterns visible at a glance.

### Rolling percentiles

A common and effective approach is to plot rolling percentiles (for example, p50, p90, p99) over the trading session:

- Choose a window (for example, one minute or five minutes).
- For each window, compute the percentile of interest for a given latency metric (for example, client-to-exchange one-way latency).
- Plot the resulting time series for each percentile.

This style of visualization answers questions like:

- "When did latency spike today, and how bad did it get?"
- "Is our p99 at the open consistently worse than during the rest of the day?"
- "Did a recent configuration change shift the entire curve or just the tails?"

Engineers can use such plots to correlate latency patterns with deployments or infrastructure incidents. Traders can correlate them with fills and P&L behavior.

### Diurnal patterns and seasonal comparisons

By overlaying or stacking time-series plots across days, you can observe recurring patterns:

- Daily rhythms: open auctions, scheduled news, futures roll days.
- Weekly or monthly patterns: option expirations, index rebalances.

For example, a plot of median and p99 latency at the same time of day across several weeks can reveal whether:

- Your system is stable.
- Latency is slowly creeping up.
- Certain events cause systematically worse tails.

This adds a temporal dimension to the statistical analysis in the previous section: distributions are no longer aggregated over an entire day but examined as functions of time.

## Distribution-oriented views: shape at a glance

Time-series plots tell you *when* latency changed; distribution-oriented plots tell you *how* it is distributed under given conditions.

### Histograms revisited

Histograms, introduced earlier, remain workhorses for latency visualization. A histogram for a well-defined segment and time window helps answer:

- "Is latency concentrated tightly around a single value, or spread out?"
- "Are there multiple peaks (fast and slow modes)?"
- "How heavy is the tail, and where exactly does it start?"

In visual comparisons (for example, old vs new configuration), overlaid histograms make it easy to see whether a change:

- Shifted the entire distribution left (faster) or right (slower).

- Reduced or increased the proportion of tail events.

When overplotting, use distinct patterns (solid vs hatched) and clear labels so that the figure remains legible in grayscale and when printed.

**Cumulative distribution plots**

A cumulative distribution function (CDF) or its complement (1 minus CDF) provides another way of visualizing percentiles as a smooth curve. On such a plot:

- The horizontal axis is latency.
- The vertical axis is "fraction of events completed within this latency" (CDF) or "fraction of events slower than this latency" (tail plot).

This allows you to read off percentiles visually. For example:

- The latency at which the CDF crosses 0.99 is p99.
- The latency at which it crosses 0.999 is p99.9.

Comparing two CDF curves on the same axes directly shows which configuration dominates: if one curve is consistently to the left (faster) at the same vertical levels, it is strictly better from a latency distribution point of view.

**Violin and box plots**

For audiences comfortable with more compact statistical graphics, violin or box plots can summarize distributions across multiple categories:

- Per-venue latency distributions.
- Per-symbol or per-strategy distributions.
- Per-host or per-region distributions.

Each "violin" shows the shape of the distribution for one category, often mirrored around a central axis, while box plots show median and quartiles with whiskers for tails.

These are particularly useful when you want to compare many categories side-by-side without overwhelming the reader with overlapping histograms.

## Hop-by-hop views: where latency accumulates

All the views so far consider one metric at a time (for example, end-to-end order latency). But the power of your instrumentation lies in having multiple tap points along the path. Visualization can help you compare these segments.

### Waterfall charts

A waterfall chart is a bar chart where each bar represents a segment of the path (for example, strategy processing, OS/NIC, network, gateway, matching engine), and bar heights are stacked to show their contribution to a total.

For a given percentile (say p99):

- Compute p99 latency for each segment separately, using your segment definitions.
- Arrange segments in order of the trading path along the horizontal axis.
- Use a stacked or side-by-side bar chart to visualize the contribution of each segment.

This makes it vivid where latency "lives":

- Is most of your p99 end-to-end latency coming from the network or from client processing?
- How does the mix change during volatile periods compared with calm periods?

From a design perspective, such charts guide where engineering effort is most profitably applied.

### Latency heat maps

Heat maps extend this idea into two dimensions. For example:

- Horizontal axis: time of day.
- Vertical axis: path segments (or venues, or hosts).
- Color: p99 latency or another percentile for that segment at that time.

Patterns jump out:

- Hot stripes (high latency) at the open for certain venues.
- Persistent hot bands for particular hosts indicating local issues.

Heat maps are powerful for operations teams looking for systemic problems: a misconfigured NIC or congested link may appear as a persistent, localized hotspot.

## Design choices: axes, binning, colors, annotations

Well-designed visuals depend as much on small presentation choices as on the underlying data. Here are key considerations.

### Axis scaling: linear vs logarithmic

For latency:

- A **linear horizontal axis** is intuitive and sufficient when most data lies within a narrow range and tails are not extreme.
- A **logarithmic horizontal axis** can be useful when you care about a wide range of latencies (for example, microseconds to milliseconds) and want to make detail in the tail more visible.

Always label axes clearly, including units, and avoid switching scales without explicit mention. When sharing plots with non-engineers, favor straightforward linear scales unless there is a compelling reason otherwise, and explain any log scaling in the caption.

### Binning and smoothing

For histograms:

- Choose bucket sizes that reflect the natural resolution of your measurements (for example, do not use 0.1-microsecond bins if your hardware timestamps are accurate only to 1 microsecond).
- When using variable-size or logarithmic buckets, mark where bucket boundaries change so the reader does not misinterpret bar widths.

Light smoothing (for example, connecting histogram midpoints with a line) can make plots easier to read without distorting interpretation, provided the underlying bins are still visible.

**Color, patterns, and grayscale**

In many trading firms, charts are printed or pasted into documents in grayscale. Regulatory submissions may also be printed. Therefore:

- Use different line styles (solid, dashed, dotted) and markers to distinguish series, not just different colors.
- For histograms or bars, use patterns (solid, hatched) and clear outlines.
- Reserve bright or saturated colors for projections on screens where color can be assumed.

Legends should be uncluttered and large enough to read after printing; captions should explain what each series or bar represents in plain language.

**Annotations and context**

Annotations turn a generic plot into a narrative:

- Vertical lines marking exchange opens, news releases, or configuration changes.
- Text labels noting incidents (for example, "NIC driver upgrade," "PTP grandmaster failover").
- Shaded regions indicating periods excluded from analysis due to clock issues or known outages.

These cues help connect latency behavior to real-world events, making plots more valuable to decision-makers.

## Tailoring views to different audiences

Engineers, quants, and traders each bring different mental models and priorities. Effective latency visualization speaks to all of them without dumbing down the content.

### Engineers

Engineers typically want detail:

- Hop-by-hop waterfall charts.
- Time-series plots of multiple percentiles, with overlays of resource metrics (CPU, NIC utilization).
- Correlations between latency and system events (deployments, GC cycles, network incidents).

Granular dashboards and diagnostic plots are appropriate here, as long as they are well organized and documented.

### Quants

Quants are interested in how latency affects model behavior and P&L. Useful views include:

- Latency distributions broken down by strategy, symbol type, or venue.
- Plots linking latency to hit rate or slippage (for example, a scatter or binned chart of p99 latency vs average fill price improvement).
- Scenario comparisons: before/after latency distributions overlaid with strategy performance metrics.

Visuals for quants should bridge system metrics and trading outcomes explicitly.

### Traders and risk managers

For traders and risk managers, the focus is on:

- High-level time-series of key percentiles (p50, p99) with simple thresholds: is latency within acceptable ranges?
- Clear, labeled comparisons of venues or configurations (for example, bar charts of p99 latency by venue).
- Annotated plots that tell a story (for example, "after moving to the new colo, our p99 latency to venue X decreased by 20 microseconds and remained stable during stress events").

Avoid overloading these views with too many lines or technical jargon. Instead, summarize the essence of the distributions in a small number of carefully chosen plots.

## Composite dashboards: combining views

In practice, teams often build dashboards that pull multiple views together. A well-designed dashboard allows a user to move from a broad picture into specifics in a few steps:

- Start with time-series p99 to see when latency is elevated.
- Drill into a histogram for a suspicious time window to examine distribution shape.
- Break latency down hop-by-hop with a waterfall chart to locate the segment responsible.

The following composite figure illustrates this idea: a time-series p99 latency plot, a histogram of latencies over a selected window, and a waterfall chart showing per-segment contributions for that same window.

This figure hints at how a real latency dashboard might operate:

- The time-series panel signals that something unusual happened around minute 60.
- The histogram for that window shows that the distribution became broader with a heavier tail.

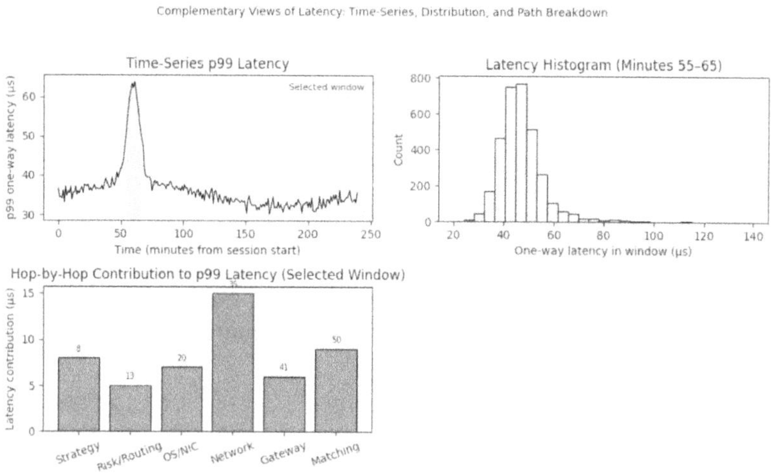


Figure 3.2: Composite dashboard-style view: time-series p99 latency over the session (top left), latency histogram for a selected high-latency window (top right), and hop-by-hop contribution to p99 latency in that window (bottom).

- The waterfall chart reveals that, during the spike, network and matching engine segments dominated p99 latency, while strategy and risk modules remained relatively stable.

In a live system, these views would be interactive, but even in static reports they provide a concise, multi-angle summary of latency behavior.

## From visuals to decisions

Visualizations are tools, not ends in themselves. Their purpose is to support decisions such as:

- Whether to invest engineering effort in optimizing a specific segment.
- Whether a new configuration is safe to roll out more broadly.

- Which venues or strategies are most constrained by latency.

A well-constructed set of latency visualizations:

- Helps engineers diagnose and fix performance problems quickly.
- Helps quants incorporate realistic latency assumptions into models and backtests.
- Helps traders and risk managers understand the capabilities and limitations of the platform in concrete, quantitative terms.

The techniques in this section, combined with the measurement and analysis foundations established earlier in the chapter, give you a complete toolkit for turning raw latency logs into shared, decision-ready insight.

# Chapter 4

# Trading System Architecture & Components

*Most trading shops run the same algorithms on paper-but what reaches the exchange is filtered through very different architectures. This chapter peels back the stack, from business logic to wire, to show how seemingly mundane design choices-where you put a queue, how you wire a state machine, whether two components live in the same address space-quietly add or remove microseconds. Rather than listing buzzword patterns, we'll trace the life of an order through a realistic system and highlight where latency hides, how complexity creeps in, and which boundaries you must get right if you care about both performance and survivability.*

## 4.1 Layered Architecture Overview

In earlier chapters we looked at the external world your trading system faces: markets that generate events, microstructure that defines what orders can do, and the basic idea of latency as the time between seeing something and reacting to it. In this section we turn inward and impose structure on the trading system itself.

A useful way to think about a modern electronic trading stack is as four main layers:

- **Strategy and signal generation**
- **Risk management and limits**
- **Session and exchange connectivity**
- **Infrastructure: operating system, hardware, and time**

Each layer has a distinct responsibility, a characteristic latency budget, and its own impact on safety and on how easily the system can evolve over time. Getting these boundaries right is one of the most important design decisions you will make.

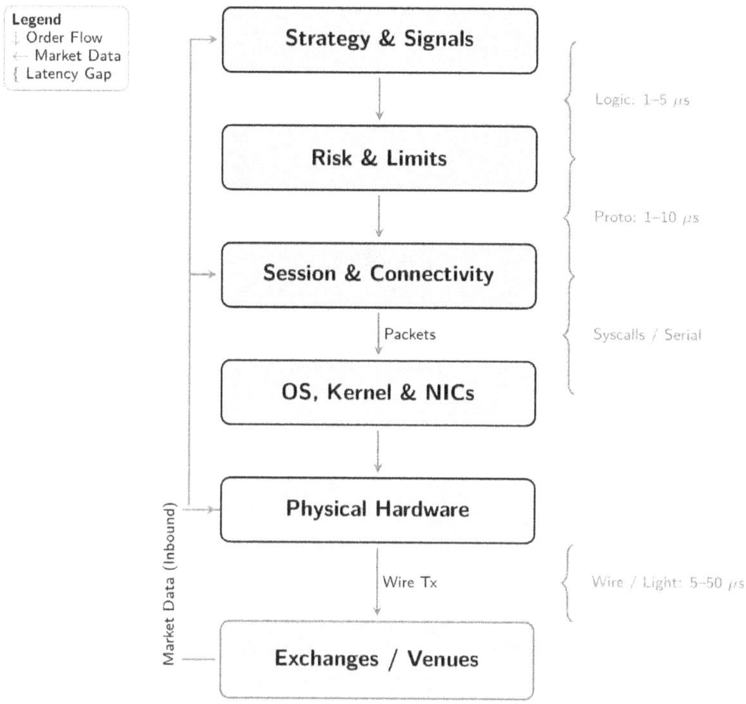


## Why layering matters

You can build a trading system as a single large program where everything talks to everything else. Many small shops do this at first. It can even be fast in the beginning, because there are no obvious boundaries to cross.

The trouble appears later:

- You want to change a strategy, but that change risks breaking connectivity.
- You add a new venue and suddenly strategy code is full of venue-specific quirks.

- A new pre-trade check is needed after a loss event, but its implementation drags latency all over the place.

Layering is not "corporate ceremony"; it is a tool to control three things:

- **Latency**: how much time each step can afford to spend.
- **Safety**: how reliably the system avoids doing catastrophic things.
- **Evolvability**: how easily you can change one part without breaking the others.

A good layered design makes these trade-offs visible and explicit. A poor one hides them until they bite you in production.

## The strategy layer: ideas meet the market

The **strategy layer** is where trading logic lives. It transforms observations about the market into trading intentions:

- Consumes: market data, internal signals, risk feedback.
- Produces: proposed orders, cancellations, parameter changes.
- Typical content: models, signal computation, order sizing, routing decisions.

From a latency perspective, strategy code lives under the tightest budget in most electronic trading systems. It often has only a few microseconds between receiving a key market event and deciding whether to trade.

From a safety perspective, the main risk here is *logic error*: the model is wrong, the order size is miscomputed, or the strategy behaves badly under a rare combination of events.

From an evolvability perspective, the strategy layer should be the thing you change most frequently: you add features, test variants, and retire old ideas.

These three facts suggest some design goals:

- **Keep the interface simple.** The strategy should talk to the rest of the system through a small, stable set of messages: "new order request," "cancel," "replace," and a clearly defined view of market data. It should not see details like TCP sessions or binary protocol fields.
- **Keep it stateless where possible.** Permanent state (positions, credit, exposure) is better handled in the risk layer. Strategy state should mostly be things like indicators and current working orders.
- **Keep venue knowledge out.** The strategy should not care whether an order ends up on Exchange A or B beyond high-level attributes (fees, latency, reliability). Venue-specific fields and peculiarities belong in the session layer.

If you violate these boundaries, you pay in:

- **Latency**, because strategies start doing work that belongs in other areas (for example, building protocol messages).
- **Safety**, because every strategy now has to understand risk and connectivity in detail.
- **Evolvability**, because changing a venue or a risk rule means touching every strategy.

## The risk layer: guardrails in the hot path

The **risk and limits layer** stands between strategies and the outside world. It decides whether a proposed order is acceptable given current limits and positions.

It typically performs:

- **Fast stateless checks**: maximum order size, price bands, symbol blocks, simple sanity checks.

- **Stateful checks**: position limits, exposure, credit usage, concentration limits.
- **Policy enforcement**: venue- or client-specific rules, regulatory requirements.

The risk layer is a *gatekeeper*. That role has strong implications for our three themes.

**Latency constraints.** Risk sits directly in the hot path from strategy to exchange. Every microsecond it consumes is directly visible in response time. Yet you cannot simply bypass it, because regulators, brokers, and your own risk appetite demand pre-trade controls.

This leads to two important design principles:

- **Order the checks by cost.** Do the cheapest, most selective checks first: simple value ranges, instrument blocks, or basic sanity tests. Only if those pass do you perform heavier computations that touch storage or large data structures.
- **Separate critical from non-critical checks.** Some checks must be executed for every order, others can be enforced at coarser time scales (for example, a monitoring system that alerts on aggregate exposure drift but does not block every single order).

**Safety constraints.** The risk layer is your main defense against runaway behavior:

- It must be *conservative*: in ambiguous situations, it should prefer to block rather than allow.
- It must be *deterministic*: given the same inputs, it should make the same decision; randomness in risk decisions is dangerous.
- It must be *auditable*: you should be able to explain after the fact why a particular order was allowed or rejected.

These requirements encourage clear data models: explicit limits per strategy, product, and account; clear ownership of who sets them; and logging of decisions.

**Evolvability constraints.** Markets, regulations, and your own business rules change. You will need to:

- Add new limits without editing strategy code.
- Tighten or loosen limits intraday.
- Apply emergency measures (for example, sweeping blocks on a product) without redeploying.

The risk layer therefore benefits from a configuration-driven design: most of its behavior (limits, thresholds) comes from dynamic configuration, not hard-coded constants scattered through strategies. The interface between strategy and risk should remain stable even as the set of checks grows.

If you push risk logic down into every strategy, you lose this flexibility and increase the chance that one forgotten strategy behaves differently from the rest during a crisis.

## The session layer: speaking the exchange's language

The **session and connectivity layer** is the part of the system that knows how to talk to exchanges and other venues. It has three main responsibilities:

- **Protocol handling**: building and parsing messages in the exchange's native protocol.
- **Session state**: logon, heartbeats, sequence numbers, reconnections, resend requests.
- **Translation**: mapping between internal order representations and what each venue expects.

On the "southbound" side, it works in terms of sockets, packets, and binary messages. On the "northbound" side, it presents a clean, venue-agnostic interface to strategies and risk: "order accepted," "order rejected," "order partially filled," with normalized fields.

**Latency constraints.** The session layer is also on the hot path, but its latency components look different:

- **Serialization and deserialization**: converting between internal data structures and wire formats.
- **Kernel crossings**: system calls for send and receive.
- **Session logic**: heartbeats, recovery logic, and maintaining in-memory state for thousands of orders.

A well-designed session layer minimizes copy operations and avoids heavy abstractions that allocate memory or trigger unpredictable behavior. It keeps the critical paths short and predictable, and moves heavier tasks (such as replay or gap filling) off the main thread where possible.

**Safety constraints.** The session layer is where many subtle problems emerge:

- **Mismatched state** between your view of an order and the exchange's view.
- **Session drops** that leave orders working on the exchange while your system thinks they are gone.
- **Protocol quirks** that, if misunderstood, result in rejected or misrouted orders.

To protect against these, the session layer must own exchange-specific knowledge. Strategies should not guess about session state or attempt to "help" with heartbeats or sequence numbers. This centralization makes it easier to fix and test protocol handling once, instead of repeating it in many places.

**Evolvability constraints.** New venues, protocol upgrades, and configuration changes (for example, new sessions, ports, or risk flags) primarily affect this layer.

If venue-specific concerns leak into strategy or risk code, every such change becomes a system-wide regression risk. Proper layering means you can:

- Add a new venue by implementing one more adapter in the session layer.
- Upgrade a protocol version with a bounded blast radius.
- Run the same strategy against multiple venues without code changes.

The key is a carefully designed internal representation of orders and executions that is rich enough to support all venues you care about, yet simple enough that strategies can reason about it.

## The infrastructure layer: the ground you stand on

Beneath the logical application layers sits the **infrastructure layer**: operating system, networking stack, network interface cards (NICs), CPU cores, caches, and time synchronization.

It is easy to think of this as “just hardware” or “just DevOps,” but for low-latency trading it is an integral part of the architecture:

- **OS and scheduling**: kernel settings, thread priorities, interrupt handling, and context switching.
- **Networking**: NIC configuration, offload settings, multicast handling, and queue mapping.
- **Time and clocks**: synchronization (for example, PTP), timestamping at various points in the path.

**Latency constraints.** Infrastructure defines your *floor* and your *jitter*:

- The best-case wire-to-wire time is limited by physical distance and NIC/OS performance.
- Jitter—variation in latency from one event to the next—comes from scheduling, interrupts, cache misses, and contention with other processes.

You cannot design a realistic strategy or session layer without understanding this floor. For example, if cross-datacenter latency adds dozens of microseconds, there is no point spending weeks shaving a microsecond in strategy code for that path.

**Safety constraints.** Infrastructure also constrains safety:

- If time synchronization is poor, your logs and measurements become misleading just when you need them during an incident.
- If NIC queues or kernel buffers overflow, you can lose or delay packets, affecting both market data and orders.
- If CPU isolation is poor, a background job can suddenly stall your hot path.

Risk and session layers often rely on infrastructure behaving within certain bounds (for example, packets delivered in order, time monotonicity). Violations of these assumptions, caused by misconfigured infrastructure, can undo careful safety logic elsewhere.

**Evolvability constraints.** Changes here are harder and riskier than in upper layers: moving to a new colocation facility, NIC model, or kernel version requires careful testing. This is another reason to keep the boundary between application code and infrastructure clean:

- Application code should depend on a small, well-understood set of infrastructure behaviors.
- Any infrastructure assumptions should be documented and, where possible, validated at startup.

If you intertwine application logic deeply with OS and NIC details, every infrastructure change becomes a refactoring project.

## Interfaces and data structures at the boundaries

Layering is defined as much by the *interfaces* between layers as by what happens inside each box. These boundaries are where latency and coupling tend to hide.

You can think of each boundary as a contract:

- **Strategy** $\leftrightarrow$ **Risk**: the contract is expressed in order request and decision messages.
- **Risk** $\leftrightarrow$ **Session**: the contract is expressed in "clean" order and execution models that are venue-agnostic.
- **Session** $\leftrightarrow$ **Infrastructure**: the contract is expressed in a small set of I/O primitives and timestamping points.

Two practical guidelines help keep these contracts healthy:

**1. Keep messages minimal but complete.** Each message crossing a boundary should contain exactly the information the other side needs—no more, no less.

Too little information forces the receiver to look elsewhere (adding hidden dependencies and latency). Too much information bloats messages, increases copy costs, and tempts the receiver to start depending on details it should ignore.

**2. Prefer simple, flat data.** Fancy object graphs and deep inheritance hierarchies are hard for both humans and processors to handle efficiently in hot paths. Simple, flat structures—with explicit IDs, timestamps, and basic fields—are easier to serialize, cache-friendly, and less error-prone.

When in doubt, imagine explaining the boundary to a new engineer on your team. If you can describe it clearly in a few sentences, you are probably on the right track. If you need to talk about many special cases and exceptions, the boundary is likely doing too much.

## Where latency is unavoidable, and where it is self-inflicted

Not all latency is equal. Some is *structural*: you cannot avoid it without changing the laws of physics or the rules of the exchange. Other latency is *self-inflicted*: the result of poor boundaries, unnecessary work, or over-engineering.

- Structural latency includes:
  - Speed of light between your server and the exchange.

  - Minimum time the exchange takes to process an order.
  - Kernel and NIC overhead for sending and receiving packets.

- Self-inflicted latency includes:
  - Extra serialization steps between layers that could share memory.
  - Duplicated risk checks in both strategy and risk layers.
  - Venue-specific logic in strategies that forces frequent rewrites and errors.
  - Logging and metrics done synchronously in the hot path.

A disciplined layered architecture helps you separate these categories:

- You can measure the latency budget of each layer and boundary.
- You can reason about which delays are inherent and which can be optimized.
- You can decide where to accept latency in exchange for safety or flexibility (for example, a slightly slower but much more robust risk check).

Without clear layers, everything blurs into a single "big ball of time," and it becomes much harder to locate and fix performance problems without breaking safety.

## Using layering to manage evolution

Finally, layering is your main defense against the fact that everything will change:

- Strategies will evolve as markets and ideas change.
- Risk rules will evolve as your risk appetite and regulations change.
- Sessions will evolve as venues upgrade and as you add or remove connectivity.

- Infrastructure will evolve as hardware, datacenters, and operating systems change.

The goal is *local change*: to be able to adjust one layer with minimal impact on others.

A practical test for your architecture is to imagine common change scenarios:

- "We need to add a new pre-trade limit." Should require changes only in the risk layer and perhaps configuration, not in each strategy.
- "We want to trial a new strategy on an existing venue." Should require changes only in the strategy layer and some risk configuration.
- "The exchange is rolling out a new protocol version." Should require changes only in the session layer, with strategies and risk unaware.
- "We are moving to a new server model and NIC." Should require changes only in infrastructure configuration and possibly some low-level tuning, not in strategy or risk code.

If you find that any of these scenarios imply touching many parts of the system, your layering is probably too weak or too leaky.

A clear layered architecture—strategy, risk, session, and infrastructure—is not optional decoration. It is the main tool you have to:

- Allocate and control latency across the stack.
- Enforce safety rules in a consistent, auditable way.
- Allow strategies, venues, and hardware to change at different speeds without breaking each other.

In the rest of this chapter we will build on this foundation, looking at how components inside and across these layers interact, and how design choices in those interactions create or eliminate latency, jitter, and fragility.

## 4.2 Component Interaction Models

In the previous section we imposed structure on the trading system by separating it into layers: strategy, risk, session, and infrastructure. That gave us a *static* picture of where responsibilities live. In this section we turn to the *dynamic* picture: how those components actually talk to each other at runtime.

Even with a clear layering, you still face crucial design choices:

- Does the strategy call the risk engine directly and wait for an answer?
- Does the strategy drop a request into a queue and continue, letting a separate worker process it?
- Should market data be pushed to everyone as it arrives, or should components pull what they need?

The way you connect components—their interaction model—is one of the main determinants of latency, jitter, and failure modes. Two systems with the same layers and the same algorithms can behave very differently depending solely on whether they use synchronous calls, asynchronous queues, or publish–subscribe buses.

### Three basic interaction styles

We will focus on three fundamental patterns:

- **Synchronous calls**: one component directly invokes another and waits for it to return a result.
- **Asynchronous queues**: one component posts a message to a queue; another component later consumes and processes it.
- **Publish–subscribe buses**: producers publish events to a bus; multiple subscribers receive the same stream, often independently.

These are building blocks. Real systems often combine all three in different parts of the stack. The key is to choose the right tool for each job rather than defaulting to a single style everywhere.

## Synchronous calls: simple and sharp

A **synchronous call** is conceptually the simplest way for components to interact:

> "I call you; you do your work; you give me an answer; only then do I continue."

Inside a single process, this can be as simple as one function calling another. Across processes or hosts, it might be a remote procedure call (RPC) that looks like a function call in code but actually sends a request over the network and blocks until a response comes back.

### Control flow and reasoning

The great advantage of synchronous calls is that they align with how we naturally think:

- **Linear reasoning**: you can read the flow top to bottom—"compute signal, call risk, call session, log result."
- **Obvious dependencies**: the caller knows exactly which actions depend on which other actions, because it waits for them.
- **Simple error handling**: if the callee fails, the caller sees an error immediately and can decide what to do.

This simplicity is enormously helpful for correctness, especially in core paths like order entry.

### Latency: low mean, potentially fragile tails

From a latency standpoint, in-process synchronous calls are hard to beat:

- A function call within the same process can complete in nanoseconds or tens of nanoseconds.
- There is no queuing, no context switch, no extra copy beyond what the function itself does.

If both caller and callee are within the same process and on the same thread, the added latency cost of the interaction itself is essentially zero; the only delay comes from the work performed.

However, synchronous calls have a built-in failure mode: **head-of-line blocking**. If the callee slows down or blocks, the caller is stuck:

- If the risk engine stalls on a slow database call, the strategy that synchronously asks for a risk decision will freeze.
- If an RPC call is synchronous and the network is congested, threads pile up waiting for replies.

This is where **jitter**—variation in latency from event to event—appears. Most of the time, calls are fast; occasionally, one is very slow, and everything behind it backs up.

### Synchronous calls in the trading stack

Synchronous calls are often the right choice for the *hottest* parts of the order path, especially inside a single process:

- Strategy calls a risk function that runs in the same address space.
- Risk calls into an in-process session adapter that prepares the wire message.

In this layout, the critical path from "decision to trade" to "packet ready to send" may be a chain of synchronous calls, all within one thread. Latency and jitter are minimized as long as each function adheres to strict performance discipline (no blocking I/O, no long loops, no heavy allocations).

Cross-process synchronous calls, by contrast, must be used carefully in latency-sensitive paths. An RPC from strategy to an out-of-process risk service adds:

- Serialization and deserialization cost.
- Kernel crossings to send and receive data.
- Possible queuing at the remote process.

The average cost might still be acceptable, but the tails can be dangerous: network blips or GC pauses in the remote service can create long stalls in the caller.

### When synchronous calls fail

The characteristic failure modes of synchronous interaction are:

- **Cascading delays**: one slow callee causes many callers to back up, which in turn delays their own dependents.
- **Reduced concurrency**: if a single-threaded component handles requests serially, everyone waits for their turn.
- **Deadlocks and timeouts**: if two components call each other synchronously or if calls never return under certain error conditions, the system can freeze.

Mitigations include:

- Timeouts and fallback decisions (for example, "if risk does not respond in $X$ microseconds, reject the order rather than waiting indefinitely").
- Explicit limits on concurrent calls.
- Using synchronous calls only where you control both sides and can enforce strict performance guarantees.

## Asynchronous queues: decoupling and buffering

An **asynchronous queue** introduces an explicit buffer between producer and consumer:

> "I put a message into the queue and immediately move on. You, perhaps on another thread or process, eventually take the message from the queue and handle it."

This changes the interaction in two key ways:

- The producer no longer blocks waiting for the consumer.
- Messages can accumulate in the queue when the consumer is slower than the producer.

### Control flow and reasoning

With queues, control flow becomes less linear:

- The producer does not know exactly when its message will be handled.
- If the producer needs a result, you need a second queue or callback path to send the response back.
- Error handling becomes more indirect; failures may be logged or retried inside the consumer rather than being raised directly to the producer.

For many people, this is harder to reason about. You lose the simple "call and return" mental model and must think in terms of independent components and eventual processing.

### Latency and jitter: smoothing vs. hiding problems

Queues change the latency profile in a more subtle way:

- When the system is lightly loaded and the consumer is fast, the extra delay introduced by the queue itself can be tiny (especially in-memory queues).
- Under load or when the consumer slows down, messages start to wait in the queue, adding variable delay before work even starts.

This means:

- Queues can **smooth** short bursts. If there is a brief spike in messages, the queue absorbs it and the consumer works through the backlog.
- Queues can also **hide** chronic slowness. If the consumer is consistently slower than the producer, the queue slowly fills up until it hits capacity or latency blows out.

In trading, this has direct implications:

- For non-critical tasks (logging, slow analytics, archiving), queues are ideal: you want to decouple them from the hot path and let them work at their own pace.
- For the main order path, adding a queue between strategy and risk, or between risk and session, must be justified very carefully. Every message now faces potential queuing delay, especially in busy markets when latency matters the most.

### Queues in the trading stack

There are several natural places to use queues:

- **From the hot path to background tasks**: for example, the session layer can push fills and order updates to a queue processed by a separate component that updates slower risk reports or back-office systems.
- **Between processes that are not strictly latency-critical**: a central position service, historical data loaders, or configuration management.

- **For bursty external inputs**: if you receive large, irregular bursts of market data for analytics that are not on the nanosecond path, a queue can absorb the burst.

Where you should *avoid* queues is in the tight loop from signal to order submission, unless you have a strong reason. Queues often become silent holders of "latent risk"—orders that exist in your system but not yet at the exchange.

### Failure modes of queues

Queues introduce their own characteristic problems:

- **Back-pressure and overload**: if the consumer cannot keep up, the queue grows. At some point you hit limits, and producers must either block or drop messages.
- **Reordering**: if multiple consumers pull from the queue, processing order may not match production order. This can be dangerous if messages must be processed in sequence.
- **Visibility**: slow buildup in queues can go unnoticed unless you monitor depth and latency.

Mitigations include:

- Explicit policies when the queue is near capacity: drop oldest, drop newest, push back on producers, or trigger a kill switch.
- Clear guarantees about ordering and delivery semantics: does the queue preserve order? Are messages ever dropped silently?
- Good observability: metrics on queue length, processing latency, and consumer health.

## Publish–subscribe buses: one-to-many distribution

A **publish–subscribe bus** (pub–sub) generalizes the queue idea. Instead of one producer and one consumer, you have:

> "Producers publish events to a topic; multiple subscribers receive copies of these events, each handling them independently."

Market data distribution is the classic example:

- A feed handler receives raw market data from an exchange.
- It normalizes and publishes updates to a bus.
- Multiple strategies, risk monitors, and recorders subscribe to that stream.

### Decoupling producers from consumers

Pub–sub has powerful benefits for evolvability:

- The producer (for example, the market data handler) does not need to know who is listening. You can add new strategies or monitoring tools without changing it.
- Subscribers can be started and stopped independently. They simply miss events while they are down, depending on the bus semantics.
- Different subscribers can process events at different speeds; one may be ultra-fast, another may be slow but thorough.

This allows the system to grow organically: new analytics, risk views, and experimental strategies can "tap into" existing data by subscribing to the appropriate topics.

### Latency and jitter in pub–sub

From a latency viewpoint, a good in-memory pub–sub bus can deliver events to multiple subscribers with only a small incremental cost per subscriber. However, you must pay attention to:

- **Copying cost**: naive implementations copy each message per subscriber, which can become expensive at high event rates.
- **Slow subscribers**: if a slow subscriber cannot keep up, you must decide whether to let it fall behind, drop its messages, or slow down everyone.
- **Delivery guarantees**: some buses provide "at-most-once" delivery (fast, but you can miss events), others offer "at-least-once" (more complex, potentially with duplicates).

For the most latency-sensitive strategies, you often want:

- A path that delivers market data directly from feed handler to strategy with minimal overhead, perhaps even bypassing a general-purpose bus.
- A bus used more heavily for secondary tasks: recording, slower strategies, monitoring.

In other words, pub–sub is excellent for *fan-out* but may introduce unnecessary overhead if you use it blindly for the hottest path without careful tuning.

### Failure modes in pub–sub systems

Pub–sub introduces new kinds of fragility:

- **Invisible subscribers**: a new subscriber with a bug can become a sink for resources, slowing down the bus or exhausting buffers.
- **Complex ordering**: if events flow through multiple topics and subscribers resubscribe or replay, it becomes harder to reason about the exact order in which they see events.
- **Recovery semantics**: if a subscriber crashes and restarts, what does it see? Only new events? A replay from some point? Who decides?

Designing a pub–sub system for trading requires clear answers to:

- Which topics are critical for real-time trading decisions?
- What happens to those topics under overload?
- Are trading strategies allowed to miss events, or must they see every one?

Many teams adopt a tiered approach: a very lean, strongly controlled path for critical data, and a more flexible bus for everything else.

## Comparing models along three dimensions

Let us step back and compare the three interaction styles along the three themes of this book: latency, jitter, and failure.

### Latency

- **Synchronous in-process calls**: lowest baseline latency; essentially just the work performed.
- **Asynchronous queues**: add at least some scheduling and queuing overhead; minimal when idle, higher when busy.
- **Pub–sub buses**: similar to queues but with extra overhead for distribution and, often, copying; baseline latency depends heavily on implementation.

For the tightest loops (e.g., signal $\rightarrow$ order), in-process synchronous often wins decisively.

### Jitter

- **Synchronous calls**: jitter comes mainly from variability in the callee's execution time and shared-resource contention.

- **Queues**: jitter includes both processing time variability and variable waiting time in the queue, which can fluctuate widely under load.
- **Pub–sub**: jitter is affected by bus design and subscriber behavior; slow subscribers or internal bus contention can cause occasional very long delays for some consumers.

Queues and buses tend to have more complex and fatter tail distributions of latency; they are good at averaging small variations but can hide build-ups until they suddenly explode.

### Failure modes

- **Synchronous calls**:
  - Fail fast and visibly when the callee is down.
  - Vulnerable to cascades if many callers depend on a single slow or failed callee.
- **Queues**:
  - Buffer errors: producers may not notice consumers failing until queues are full.
  - Overload can lead either to message loss or to global slowdowns if producers are forced to block.
- **Pub–sub**:
  - Introduce systemic risks if the bus becomes a single point of failure.
  - Optional subscribers can fail independently, but misbehaving ones can burden the shared infrastructure.

Understanding these patterns helps you design for graceful degradation: for example, allowing non-critical subscribers to drop messages while keeping core strategies fed in real time.

## Choosing interaction models for different paths

A practical way to apply these ideas is to classify your system's paths and match each class with a suitable interaction model.

### Ultra-critical, low-latency paths

Examples:

- Strategy deciding on and submitting an order.
- Risk checks that must be performed before any order can leave.
- Session logic that prepares and sends messages to the exchange.

Desired properties:

- Minimal latency and jitter.
- Predictable behavior under stress.
- Clear, synchronous error semantics (success or fail now).

**Recommended interaction style**:

- Synchronous, in-process calls between closely coupled components.
- Avoid queuing between steps unless queues are specifically engineered for extremely low overhead and you have a strong reason to introduce them.

### Medium-critical, real-time but not ultra-fast paths

Examples:

- Real-time risk dashboards.
- Intraday analytics that influence human decision-making but not every individual order.

- Distributing normalized market data to multiple listeners.

Desired properties:

- Reasonably low latency, but microseconds here are not existential.
- High flexibility: you will add and remove consumers over time.
- Tolerance for occasional small delays.

**Recommended interaction style**:

- Pub–sub buses for one-to-many distribution.
- Possibly queues between source and bus or between bus and consumers, depending on load patterns.
- Synchronous calls within each consumer, as needed, since they are not on the absolute hottest path.

### Slow, control-plane and batch paths

Examples:

- Configuration changes and strategy parameter updates.
- Back-office processing and reporting.
- End-of-day checks, reconciliations, and archiving.

Desired properties:

- Correctness and robustness outweigh raw speed.
- Ability to survive restarts and failures without data loss.

**Recommended interaction style**:

- Asynchronous queues and robust, possibly durable, messaging.

- Clear retry and error-handling semantics.
- Synchronous calls used sparingly, mainly for control interactions where blocking is acceptable.

## Avoiding over-engineering and under-engineering

A common anti-pattern is to treat every interaction as if it were a distributed system problem:

- Wrapping simple in-process calls in heavy RPC frameworks.
- Forcing all data through a general-purpose bus even when a direct call would be simpler and faster.
- Adding queues everywhere "for scalability" without a clear plan for how they will behave under stress.

This usually increases latency and complexity without adding meaningful robustness where you actually need it.

The opposite anti-pattern is to implement everything as synchronous calls in a monolith:

- Core trading and peripheral analytics share the same process and threads.
- A slow report or log writer can stall the hot path.
- There is no easy way to scale or isolate misbehaving components.

The right balance is guided by:

- **Path criticality**: is this interaction on the nanosecond path or the second-level path?
- **Change frequency**: will one side change more often than the other?
- **Failure impact**: what happens if this component is slow or down?

A small, high-performance core built on synchronous in-process calls, surrounded by asynchronous and pub–sub infrastructure for everything else, is a common and effective pattern.

Interaction models are as important as the components themselves. Synchronous calls offer simplicity and minimal latency but can cause sharp failures when a callee slows down. Asynchronous queues decouple producers and consumers and smooth bursts but introduce queuing delays and require careful back-pressure handling. Publish–subscribe buses make it easy to distribute data to many consumers and to evolve the system, but they add overhead and create subtle ordering and failure questions.

In a well-architected trading system, you do not pick one model and apply it everywhere. Instead, you:

- Use synchronous calls within the tightest loops where every microsecond matters and where you can strictly control performance.
- Use queues and buses to connect slower, more flexible, and more failure-tolerant parts of the system.
- Design with a clear understanding of how each interaction style shapes latency distributions, jitter, and how the system fails under stress.

In the next section we will look inside these interaction patterns at a finer granularity by modeling order behavior as explicit state machines, which provides another powerful tool for keeping complex, event-driven trading systems predictable and fast.

## 4.3 State Machines and Event-Driven Design

The previous sections gave us two complementary views of a trading system. First, we imposed a *layered architecture* (strategy, risk, session, infrastructure) so that responsibilities are clear. Then we examined *interaction models* (synchronous calls, queues, pub–sub) to understand how components communicate and how that shapes latency and failure modes.

We now zoom in further, to the level of individual orders and events. Even inside a well-layered, well-connected system, order handling logic can easily become a tangle of flags and special cases. This tangle is not just unpleasant to read; it creates unpredictable latency, subtle bugs, and behaviors that are almost impossible to reason about during a crisis.

The central idea of this section is simple but powerful:

> An order's lifecycle is best modeled as a *finite-state machine* (FSM), and the trading engine should be treated as an *event-driven loop* that advances these machines in response to well-defined events.

This approach:

- Tames logical complexity by making all possible order states and transitions explicit.
- Reduces unpredictable branching, which is good for modern CPUs and cache behavior.
- Makes testing and debugging much easier, because you can reason in terms of "from state A, on event B, we must go to state C."

## From ad hoc flags to explicit lifecycles

Consider how order handling often starts in a young codebase. Someone writes a function to send a new order. Later, they add a flag to indicate whether the order has been acknowledged. Then another flag for partial fills. Then a timestamp for a pending cancel. Soon you have code that looks like this conceptually:

- If the order is not yet acknowledged and not rejected and we have not requested a cancel, then ...

- Unless it is partially filled, in which case ...
- But if a reject has arrived while we are canceling, then ...

Each new corner case tends to add another condition. Over time, the number of possible combinations of flags explodes, and no one can be sure that all have been handled correctly.

Finite-state machines give you a disciplined alternative. Instead of many overlapping flags, each order is always in *exactly one* state, and only certain transitions between states are allowed. States are not brief conditions; they are named modes of existence for the order.

## The canonical order lifecycle

While details vary by venue and product, most electronic orders pass through a recognizably similar lifecycle. A simple but practical set of states might be:

- **New**: an order has been created in the strategy or order management system but not yet sent to the exchange.
- **PendingSend**: the order has been handed off to the session layer and is in the process of being transmitted; you have not yet received confirmation that the exchange has it.
- **Working**: the exchange has accepted the order and it is live in the market, capable of being filled.
- **PartiallyFilled**: some quantity has traded, but there is still remaining quantity working at the exchange.
- **Filled**: the order's full quantity has traded; there is nothing left working.
- **Canceled**: the remaining working quantity has been removed from the market, either at your request or due to some external condition (for example, the end of the trading session).
- **Rejected**: the exchange (or an internal risk check) has refused the order; it never became working.

You can think of these as the named "stations" through which an order can travel. Not every order visits every station, but an order should never be between stations or in two stations at once. At any moment, it has a single, well-defined state.

Events push orders along. Some typical events are:

- **NewOrder**: the strategy or client requests a new order.
- **SendToExchange**: the system sends the order to the session layer for transmission.
- **Ack**: the exchange acknowledges that it has received and accepted the order.
- **Fill**: all or part of the order trades.
- **CancelRequest**: the strategy or risk engine asks to cancel the remaining quantity.
- **CancelAck**: the exchange confirms that the order has been canceled.
- **Reject**: the order is rejected either pre-trade (risk) or by the exchange.

An FSM ties these together: from each state, certain events are allowed and lead to specific next states. Other event–state combinations are simply invalid and should be treated as errors or ignored.

## Event-driven loops: how orders actually move

A finite-state machine is a logical model. To make it operational, you need a mechanism that:

1. Receives events from the outside world (strategies, risk, venues, timers).
2. Locates the relevant order (or orders).
3. Applies the event to the order's current state, computing a new state.

4. Performs any side effects (for example, sending a message to the venue or to the strategy).

An **event-driven loop** is a natural fit. Conceptually it looks like this:

- There is a central loop that repeatedly takes the next event from an input queue (or from a set of input sources coordinated by the session layer).
- Each event has a type (e.g., NewOrder, Ack, Fill) and identifies which order it concerns.
- The engine looks up the order's current state, consults the FSM definition, and applies the transition.
- The transition updates the order's state and may enqueue new events (for example, sending a CancelRequest to the session layer).

You can treat the entire order management engine as a large collection of these per-order state machines, all being advanced by a single or small number of event-processing loops.

## Making states explicit and branching predictable

One of the biggest performance benefits of the FSM approach is that it turns complicated, nested conditionals into a simple, table-like structure:

- From state New, on event NewOrder: move to PendingSend.
- From state PendingSend, on event Ack: move to Working.
- From state Working, on event Fill with full quantity: move to Filled.
- From state Working, on event Fill with partial quantity: move to PartiallyFilled.
- From state PartiallyFilled, on event Fill for the remainder: move to Filled.

- From state Working or PartiallyFilled, on event CancelAck: move to Canceled.
- From state New or PendingSend, on event Reject: move to Rejected.

Instead of the CPU encountering a long chain of "if this flag and not that flag and not canceled," it quickly selects the correct transition based solely on the current state and the event type. This has several advantages:

- **Branch predictability**: modern CPUs are good at predicting simple, regular branches. A small, fixed set of states and events shallowly encoded is much easier to predict than arbitrary combinations of flags.
- **Cache friendliness**: the event loop touches a small, well-structured piece of memory (the order's state object) and a compact transition table, which tend to stay hot in cache.
- **Reduced code size**: the core logic can often be implemented as a simple dispatch based on state and event, rather than dozens of duplicated checks scattered throughout the codebase.

Even if you never look at a profiler, you will feel this in production: fewer mysterious latency spikes triggered by rare combinations of flags or untested paths.

## Handling rare and error paths cleanly

Not all events belong to the happy path. Exchanges can send out-of-order acknowledgements, network glitches can produce duplicates, and risk engines can reject orders at unexpected times.

With an explicit FSM, you model these as either:

- **Allowed but rare transitions**: for example, from Working to Rejected if the exchange cancels the order due to a halt, or from PendingSend to Canceled if the cancel overtakes the new order.

- **Invalid transitions**: for example, a Fill event arriving when the order is still in New locally and there is no record that it was ever sent.

Rare but allowed transitions can be given their own paths, often marked as "error handling" or "recovery" in comments and documentation. They remain first-class citizens in the state diagram, even if they are not part of the happy path.

Invalid transitions should be surfaced loudly: logged, counted, and often cause a local safety action (such as freezing the strategy or triggering a session reset) until you understand what happened. The point is that you can systematically define what "invalid" even means, because the FSM tells you which transitions are legal.

## Mapping the lifecycle to a state diagram

Once you have described the states and transitions in words, it is extremely helpful to draw them. A visual state diagram provides a shared language between traders, developers, and operations staff: everyone can point to the same picture when discussing order behavior.

Below we include a finite-state diagram that captures a typical order lifecycle in a low-latency trading engine. The main, expected path from New to Filled is emphasized, while less common error and cancellation paths are drawn more lightly.

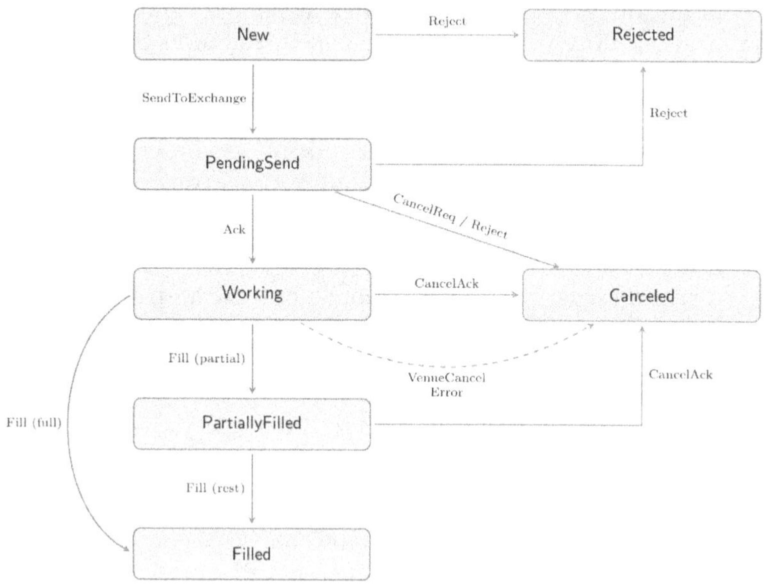


## Event-driven design in the wider engine

So far we have focused on the lifecycle of a *single* order. In practice, a trading engine handles thousands or millions of orders, all of which may be at different states and reacting to different events. Event-driven design scales naturally to this scenario.

Some key patterns emerge:

**Single-threaded hot loop with shared state.** In many ultra-low-latency engines, a single dedicated thread runs the event loop for the hottest path:

- All order state lives in memory owned by that thread.
- Events from sessions, strategies, and risk arrive into a queue or ring buffer that the loop reads.
- Processing each event advances exactly one or a small number of orders' FSMs.

The big advantage is that you can often avoid locks and complex synchronization entirely in the hot path. One thread owns the order book state, and all updates happen in a strictly serialized sequence of events. This dramatically reduces contention and jitter.

**Multi-threaded or sharded event loops.** As order volumes and symbol counts grow, you may need more concurrency. A common strategy is to shard:

- Partition orders by symbol, account, or some hash of an order ID.
- Assign each shard to a separate event loop and thread.
- Ensure that all events for a given order always reach the same loop.

Each event loop still runs a simple, predictable FSM per order, but now many such loops run in parallel on different CPU cores. The challenge is to maintain invariants that cross shards (for example, cross-symbol position limits), but the per-order logic remains clean.

**Integration with interaction models.** The interaction models from the previous section now fit naturally around the event loop:

- **Synchronous calls** are often used between small helpers within the same loop, such as pricing and risk subroutines.
- **Queues** may feed events into the loop from external processes (for example, a feed handler) or drain non-critical outputs to slower consumers.
- **Pub–sub buses** can distribute derived events (like aggregated fills or risk metrics) to downstream analytics without disturbing the main loop.

The key is that *within* the order engine itself, the primary abstraction is the event and the FSM, not a cloud of independent objects calling each other arbitrarily.

## Performance considerations: why CPUs like FSMs

The phrase "cache-friendly" can sound abstract. In this context, it largely means:

- The order state is stored in compact, contiguous memory structures.
- The event loop touches predictable locations: the next event, the corresponding order's state, and the transition logic.
- There are few unpredictable branches that would cause the CPU's branch predictor to misfire and stall.

Finite-state machines help achieve this by:

- **Reducing state sprawl**: instead of state being scattered across many objects and flags, each order's essential lifecycle state can be held in a small record (for example, current state, remaining quantity, last known price).
- **Concentrating logic**: instead of repeated conditionals, the core decision is often "switch on state, then switch on event type," which compilers and CPUs tend to handle efficiently.
- **Avoiding dynamic allocation on hot paths**: state transitions are usually simple field updates, not creations of new objects, which helps avoid garbage collection or allocator overhead.

The result is not necessarily the absolute shortest possible latency for a single order in isolation, but a much more stable latency profile across many orders and events—the tails shrink, and rare bugs stop producing wild stalls.

## Testing and observability of state transitions

An explicit FSM has a second major advantage beyond runtime performance: it is testable and observable in a structured way.

**Testing transitions.** For each allowed transition, you can write focused tests of the form:

> "Given an order in state X with attributes Y, when event Z arrives, we expect new state W and side effects S."

You can also generate negative tests:

> "Given state X, event Z is illegal; the engine should produce an error or ignore it, and the state should remain unchanged."

Over time, this gives you a comprehensive map of system behavior that is robust to refactorings. You no longer fear touching order logic, because tests will tell you if you accidentally removed or changed a valid transition.

**Logging and tracing.** For observability, the FSM encourages you to log at the right granularity:

- Each state transition can emit a small, structured log entry: order ID, old state, new state, event type, key fields (price, quantity), and perhaps a correlation ID that links back to strategy decisions.
- A sequence of these entries for a single order reconstructs its complete history.

During an incident, operations staff and developers can literally scroll through an order's transitions and see exactly how it moved from New to some terminal state, and which events drove that movement. This is much easier than piecing together ad hoc log messages sprinkled throughout unstructured code.

## Extending the FSM: partial fills, replaces, and more

The simplified diagram above captures the essence, but real-world lifecycles often add more nuance:

- **Replaces**: changing price or quantity of a working order can be modeled as transitions to intermediate states like PendingReplace, then back to Working or PartiallyFilled.

- **Time-in-force**: good-till-cancel, immediate-or-cancel, fill-or-kill orders can be modeled as states or as parameters that affect which transitions are legal.
- **Cross-venue routing**: parent orders split across child orders on multiple venues can be modeled as higher-level FSMs coordinating the states of many child orders.

The important point is not which exact set of states you choose, but that:

- All valid combinations have names and rules.
- All possible incoming events from strategies, risk, and venues are accounted for in each relevant state.
- You resist the temptation to squeeze edge cases into "temporary" flags that bypass the core FSM.

When complexity grows, you can introduce multiple cooperating FSMs (for example, one for each child order and one for the parent) rather than bloating a single giant machine.

Finite-state machines and event-driven loops give you a disciplined way to handle the rich, sometimes messy lifecycles of orders in an electronic trading system. Compared to scattered flags and ad hoc conditionals, they offer:

- **Clarity**: every order is always in one named state, and only certain events can move it.
- **Predictable performance**: transitions follow a small set of branches and touch compact state, which is friendly to CPU caches and branch predictors.
- **Robustness**: rare or invalid transitions are explicitly modeled, tested, and logged.
- **Observability**: a sequence of state transitions provides a precise, auditable narrative of an order's life.

When you combine the layered architecture from earlier, careful interaction models between components, and an event-driven FSM at the core of order handling, you get a trading system that is not only fast in benchmarks but also understandable and controllable in real markets, including on the worst days when conditions are most stressed.

In the next section, we will step from the logical design presented here to the question of *physical deployment*: how these event-driven components are arranged in processes and across machines, and how process boundaries and networks affect latency and reliability.

## 4.4 In-Process vs. Distributed Deployment

Up to this point we have treated your trading system mostly as a logical construct. We layered it into strategy, risk, session, and infrastructure, and we described how components talk to each other using synchronous calls, queues, and publish–subscribe. We then looked inside the order engine and saw how finite-state machines and event-driven loops keep order handling predictable.

In this section we move from logic to *placement*: where, physically, do these components run?

- Do strategy, risk, and session all live inside a single process (a monolith)?
- Are they separated into distinct services talking over the network (a microservice-style architecture)?
- Or are they split into many small, actor-like entities distributed across cores and machines?

These choices are not just about organizational fashion. They show up directly in latency, jitter, and failure behavior. In particular, they control how often your hot order path crosses:

- **Process boundaries**: entering and leaving the kernel, scheduling decisions, context switches.

- **Serialization layers**: translating in-memory objects into bytes and back.
- **Network hops**: traversing NICs, switches, and cable to reach other hosts.

Our goal is to understand the real cost of these boundaries so that you can choose a deployment style that fits your trading goals and constraints, rather than copying whatever is fashionable in general software engineering.

## What "deployment style" really means

When we say "monolith," "microservice," or "actor-style," we are really answering two questions:

- **Address space**: which components share memory and can talk via simple function calls?
- **Host**: which components share a physical machine, a rack, or a datacenter?

Every time you move from one address space to another (process to process) or from one host to another, you pay certain fixed costs and pick up certain risks:

- You must serialize and deserialize data (unless you use shared memory tricks).
- You rely on the operating system's scheduler and the network stack.
- You become vulnerable to partial failures: the remote piece might be slow or down.

In contrast, components that share an address space can:

- Share data structures directly through pointers or references.

- Communicate via function calls that complete in nanoseconds.
- Fail together (if the process dies, everyone dies), but not in strange, half-alive ways.

With that lens, let us look at the three deployment styles in turn.

## The in-process monolith: one engine, one address space

A **monolithic** trading engine places strategy, risk, and session logic in a single process, often as a single executable. Within that process, it might still be carefully layered and modularized; "monolith" here refers to deployment, not messy code.

## Latency: the baseline

For the hot order path, a well-designed in-process engine is very hard to beat:

- Strategy calls risk as a function.
- Risk calls the session adapter as a function.
- The session adapter writes directly into buffers that the network stack or NIC can send.

The only unavoidable costs on this path, once the decision to trade is made, are:

- The time to execute your own logic (risk checks, state updates).
- The time for the kernel and NIC to send a packet to the exchange.
- The exchange's own processing time.

There are no process boundaries or network hops inside your own stack. No serialization is needed between layers; they can share compact, in-memory representations of orders and positions. Tail latency is generally low and predictable, provided you control GC/allocators and avoid blocking operations.

## Jitter and contention

The main sources of jitter in a monolith are:

- **OS scheduling**: if other threads in the process (for example, logging, monitoring) compete with the hot thread for CPU.
- **Shared resources**: locking on shared data, or cache thrash caused by large working sets.
- **Runtime features**: garbage collection in managed runtimes, or expensive dynamic allocation and deallocation patterns.

The upside is that you can usually see and measure these within a single process; they are not obscured by network complexity. Techniques like pinning threads to cores, isolating the hot thread, and using simple allocators are easier to apply when everything is local.

## Failure modes

Failure behavior in a monolith tends to be *all-or-nothing*:

- If the process crashes, all functionality inside it disappears at once for that instance.
- Bugs in non-critical components (for example, a memory leak in a stats module) can bring the core engine down.

You can mitigate this with:

- Careful separation of critical and non-critical threads within the process.
- Defensive coding and resource limits for best-effort features.
- Multiple engine instances for redundancy (active/active or active/passive).

The key point is that in-process deployment trades some fault isolation for minimal latency and tight control.

## Evolvability and team structure

From an organizational perspective, monoliths are sometimes criticized for being hard to evolve. In trading, this is not always fair:

- You can still keep strategy code modular and isolated from session code.
- You can still version and deploy strategies separately as shared libraries or plugins loaded into the main engine.

However, large teams can find it harder when many unrelated changes need to be released together in a single binary, and when different groups want to own deploy schedules independently. That organizational concern often motivates a move toward services, even in performance-sensitive domains.

## Microservice-style deployment: many processes, many APIs

A **microservice** architecture splits functionality into separate processes or containers, each exposing an API (for example, over HTTP, gRPC, or a message bus). In trading, typical splits might be:

- A risk service that all strategies call for pre-trade checks.
- A separate order-routing service that manages exchange sessions.
- Strategy engines as their own processes calling into these services.

## Where latency shows up

Each service boundary introduces several concrete costs on the path from strategy to exchange:

- **Serialization and deserialization**: converting in-memory order objects into a wire format (JSON, Protobuf, custom binary) and back.
- **Kernel crossings**: system calls to send and receive over sockets or pipes.
- **Context switches**: the OS must schedule the service process to handle the request.
- **Network stack overhead**: even when client and server run on the same host, data still moves through the TCP/IP stack unless you use specialized IPC.

The average cost of a local RPC can be small in absolute terms on modern hardware, but in a low-latency trading engine you are living in a microsecond-scale budget. Even "only a few microseconds" per boundary accumulate quickly when chained, and the worst-case cost (tails) matters much more than the mean.

## Jitter and tail amplification

Microservices introduce several new sources of jitter:

- **Independent GC and scheduling**: each service has its own runtime and threads. A GC pause or CPU spike in the risk service delays all callers, regardless of how well-tuned the strategy process is.
- **Variable queuing**: if the risk service receives a burst of requests, it may queue them internally before processing, adding unpredictable delays.
- **Network variability**: even on the same rack, congested network paths or retransmissions can add spikes.

These effects combine multiplicatively when multiple services lie in series. A single slow or overloaded service can degrade end-to-end latency in ways that are hard to trace, because the slowness happens elsewhere.

## Failure modes and partial outages

Service boundaries do *improve* one kind of robustness: a bug in a non-critical service does not necessarily take down the entire stack. However, they introduce more complex failure modes:

- **Partial failures**: the strategy process is healthy but cannot reach the risk service, or gets timeouts.
- **Inconsistent states**: different services may have different views of positions or limits if updates are delayed or lost.
- **Cascading failures**: if one overloaded service starts timing out, upstream callers may retry aggressively, compounding the load.

To handle this, you need:

- Timeouts and fallback logic at every call site.
- Clear default behaviors when services are unavailable (for example, fail closed and stop trading, or use last-known limits).
- Careful capacity planning and back-pressure to prevent self-induced denial of service.

All of this is solvable, but it is not free. Every additional service boundary on the hot order path demands careful operational engineering.

## Why people still consider microservices

Given these latency and complexity costs, why are microservices attractive at all?

- **Independent deploys**: teams can update one service without rebuilding or redeploying others.
- **Technology heterogeneity**: different services can use different languages or frameworks.

- **Natural scaling**: you can allocate more instances to heavy services (for example, risk aggregation) without scaling everything else.

In trading, these benefits are often best applied to *control-plane* and *supporting* systems:

- Configuration management, historical data services, portfolio analytics.
- Real-time dashboards and user interfaces.
- Middle- and back-office workflows.

Putting microservices directly on the hottest path from strategy to exchange is much harder to justify unless your trading style is not especially latency-sensitive (for example, long-horizon strategies where a few milliseconds are irrelevant).

## Actor-style and sharded deployments: many small workers

An **actor-style** architecture splits work into many small, isolated entities (actors), each with its own mailbox (queue) and state. Actors communicate only by sending messages. This is conceptually similar to the event-driven FSMs we discussed earlier, but deployed at a broader scale.

In trading, you might see patterns like:

- One actor per symbol or per order book.
- One actor per client or strategy.
- One actor per exchange session or risk partition.

These actors can live in one process (using lightweight in-process mailboxes) or be spread across multiple processes and hosts.

## Latency in actor systems

If actors are all in the same process, sending a message can be very cheap: pushing a pointer into a lock-free queue that another thread reads from. The latency overhead compared to a direct function call is small, especially if you pin actors to specific cores.

However, actor systems often encourage more distribution:

- Actors may be moved from one process to another for load balancing.
- Actor frameworks may hide network hops behind the same messaging interface.

When that happens, the same costs as in microservices reappear:

- Serialization and deserialization per message.
- Kernel and network overhead per hop.
- Queuing and scheduling delays per mailbox.

The actor model tends to keep each unit of work small and localized, which is good for concurrency, but the path for a single order may touch more of these units.

## Jitter and message queues

Actor systems are essentially systems of queues:

- Each actor has an inbox that can grow under load.
- Slow actors accumulate backlogs; messages wait longer before being processed.
- Work-stealing or load balancing across actors and threads adds additional scheduling complexity.

This can offer nice properties at medium latencies: the system can gracefully survive bursts by letting queues grow, and can route around hot spots. But on ultra-critical paths where you care about the *distribution* of latency rather than just average throughput, each queue is another place where jitter can appear and propagate.

## Failure modes and resilience

Actor frameworks often provide convenient tools for resilience:

- Supervisors can restart failed actors.
- Messages can be persisted for durability in some implementations.
- Actors can be migrated away from failing nodes.

This can be very powerful for large, complex systems. However, the same caution applies: if your hot path relies on many hops across actors and nodes, the probability of encountering a slow or failed element along the way increases. You must be able to bound the number of hops for critical operations and understand exactly where those hops cross process or host boundaries.

## A comparative view: where do boundaries go?

We can now compare the three styles through the lens of the boundaries they introduce on the hot order path.

## Function-call boundaries (in-process)

- **Monolith**: strategy, risk, and session share memory; calls are simple function invocations.
- **Microservices**: only intra-service logic uses function calls; inter-service calls cross processes or hosts.

- **Actors**: intra-process actor messages may still be queued, but handler logic itself uses function calls and shared state within a thread.

Function-call boundaries are essentially free compared to everything else; their cost is the work you do, not the boundary itself.

## Process boundaries

- **Monolith**: none on the hot path, assuming a single process per engine instance.
- **Microservices**: at least one (strategy to risk, risk to session) if those are separate services.
- **Actors**: zero or more, depending on whether actors are co-located or spread across processes.

Each process boundary adds serialization, syscalls, context switches, and the potential for queues and timeouts. For ultra-low-latency trading, you usually want *zero* process boundaries between signal and packet for the main path.

## Network hops

- **Monolith**: only the unavoidable hop to the exchange.
- **Microservices**: additional hops for any remote services used on the hot path.
- **Actors**: similar to microservices if actors span hosts.

Each extra network hop adds microseconds or more, plus more variance. For high-frequency or latency-arbitrage strategies, this is almost always unacceptable on the core path.

## Hybrid architectures: a practical compromise

In practice, very few serious trading firms choose a pure form of any of these models. Instead, they adopt **hybrid** architectures that combine the strengths of each:

- **In-process core**: the hot loop—strategy evaluation, pre-trade risk, session logic—runs in a single process, sometimes even a single thread, to minimize latency and jitter.
- **Local sharding**: within that process, work may be sharded across cores or actors (for example, per symbol) while still avoiding process boundaries.
- **Out-of-process support services**: slower risk aggregation, monitoring, configuration, and reporting run as microservices or actor systems off the hot path.

Under this pattern:

- The *hottest* interactions use synchronous in-process calls.
- Queues and pub–sub buses are used to move data from the hot core to slower consumers, not inside the core itself.
- Microservices and distributed actors are used where their deployment and scaling advantages matter more than per-message microseconds.

For example:

- Fills and order updates are processed in the in-process engine and then also published to a message bus.
- A separate risk aggregation service consumes that bus and maintains longer-horizon exposures, feeding dashboards and alerts.
- The in-process engine performs only the essential checks needed for safe trading; more complex analytics happen off to the side.

This way, you keep the fast path lean and direct, while enjoying many of the flexibility benefits of distributed architectures elsewhere.

## Guidelines for choosing a deployment style

When deciding where to put process and network boundaries, it helps to ask a few concrete questions for each interaction or component:

### 1. Is this on the nanosecond or microsecond path?

If a component lies between "decide to trade" and "order leaves for the exchange," treat it as part of the nanosecond/microsecond path. For these:

- Prefer in-process, often single-process, deployment.
- Avoid crossing processes or hosts.
- Use synchronous calls and event-driven loops, not heavy IPC or general RPC frameworks.

### 2. How often does this component change?

If a component changes frequently (for example, strategies) but is latency-critical, you can still keep it in-process and load it as a plugin or module, with careful separation from the stable core.

If it changes frequently and is *not* latency-critical (for example, web dashboards), it is a good candidate for a microservice.

### 3. What happens if it fails or slows down?

If failure or slowness of a component must trigger a global stop to trading (for safety), then co-locating it in-process with clear fail-fast behavior may be acceptable or even desirable.

If you need it to fail independently while trading continues (for example, a reporting service), then put it out-of-process and use queues or buses to feed it.

### 4. Can we bound the number of hops?

For each order, you should be able to enumerate the exact sequence of components and boundaries it crosses. If this list includes many network calls, many queues, and many process boundaries, you likely have over-distributed your hot path.

Deployment architecture turns the abstract components we have discussed into a concrete, running system. The main trade-offs are:

- **Monolithic in-process engines** minimize latency and jitter on the hot path by avoiding process and network boundaries, at the cost of tighter coupling and less fault isolation.
- **Microservice architectures** offer independent deploys and scaling, but introduce serialization, kernel crossings, and extra hops that can dramatically enlarge latency tails if placed on the order path.
- **Actor-style and sharded systems** provide powerful tools for parallelism and resilience, but can also hide queuing and scheduling variability behind seemingly uniform message APIs.

For serious electronic trading, the most successful designs keep the critical order path as in-process and as simple as possible, while using distributed techniques where they bring clear benefits and do not threaten fill quality. By consciously choosing where to cross process and host boundaries, you control where latency hides, how it behaves in the tails, and how failures propagate through your system.

## 4.5 Risk Management & Kill Switches

So far, we have treated the trading engine largely as a performance machine: layered for clear responsibilities, wired together with appropriate interaction models, and internally structured as event-driven finite-state machines. In real markets, however, speed without control is dangerous. A single bug, misconfiguration, or runaway strategy can generate a flood of toxic orders in milliseconds.

This section focuses on how to embed *risk management* directly into the hot path in a way that is:

- **Fast**: adds as little latency and jitter as possible.
- **Deterministic**: behaves predictably, especially under stress.
- **Trustworthy**: traders, risk officers, and regulators can rely on it in a crisis.

We will look at two closely related topics:

- **Pre-trade checks and limits**: the everyday guardrails that ensure individual orders are sensible and aggregate exposure remains within bounds.
- **Kill switches**: emergency controls that reliably stop trading or a subset of trading when something goes badly wrong.

The challenge is to enforce meaningful safeguards without quietly eroding edge through excessive overhead or unpredictable blocking in your most latency-sensitive paths.

## Risk in the context of the architecture

Recall the layered architecture:

- The **strategy** layer proposes orders.
- The **risk** layer decides whether those orders are acceptable.
- The **session** layer translates accepted orders into venue messages.
- The **infrastructure** layer carries packets to and from the exchange.

We now zoom into the interface between *strategy* and *session* and treat the risk layer as a first-class component in between. From the event-driven perspective, risk decisions are just another kind of event processing: for each proposed order event, the risk engine emits either "allow" or "reject" (possibly with more detail).

The crucial twist is that risk is *not optional.* If the risk engine is slow or fails in an unpredictable way, you cannot simply push orders through; safe failure almost always means "stop trading." This makes risk one of the few components where a design that is slightly slower but extremely predictable may be superior to a design that is microseconds faster but fragile.

## Kinds of pre-trade checks

Before we discuss where and how to place risk checks, we need a clear view of what they typically are. They fall into several broad categories.

### Simple per-order sanity checks

These are stateless checks that look only at the order itself and maybe a small amount of static configuration:

- **Max order size**: is the requested quantity above a configured maximum for this instrument, account, or strategy?
- **Price bands / fat-finger bounds**: is the limit price far outside current market levels or pre-defined reference prices?
- **Order type filters**: is this strategy allowed to send this order type, time-in-force, or special instruction?
- **Symbol / venue blocks**: is this product or venue blocked for this client or account?

These checks are usually inexpensive: they are simple comparisons against numbers or membership in small sets.

### Exposure and position limits

These checks take into account historical and current state:

- **Net position limits**: will this order push the strategy or account beyond a maximum long or short position?
- **Gross notional or delta limits**: will the notional exposure or risk factor exposure exceed set thresholds?
- **Concentration limits**: will this order overly concentrate risk in a single instrument, sector, or venue?

These checks require fast access to current positions and exposures, which in turn must be updated as fills arrive. Their cost depends heavily on how you store and index that state.

### Credit and capital limits

These relate to the financial capacity of the participant:

- **Credit lines**: is there sufficient remaining credit with the broker or clearing counterparty?
- **Margin constraints**: will the position created by this order be adequately margined under current rules?

Often, these limits are enforced at coarser granularity and updated less frequently, but for some participants they must still be reflected in pre-trade checks.

### Regulatory and policy filters

These enforce specific rules beyond pure risk appetite:

- **Restricted lists**: instruments, issuers, or clients that cannot be traded due to internal or regulatory restrictions.
- **Pattern checks**: for example, wash trading or self-trade prevention rules.
- **Market-specific rules**: order-to-trade ratios, minimum resting times, or other venue policies.

Some of these are simple; others can become quite complex if you are not careful about scope and granularity.

## Ordering checks by cost and selectivity

Once you know what checks you need, the next design question is: *in what order should we apply them?* The answer has direct impact on latency.

Two principles guide the design:

- **Fastest, most selective checks first**. You want to reject obviously bad orders as quickly as possible, before investing effort in more expensive checks.
- **Shared computations and caching**. If multiple checks need the same derived quantity (for example, projected position after the trade), compute it once.

A typical order of evaluation might be:

- **Cheap sanity checks**: max order size, basic price bands, symbol and venue blocks.
- **Static policy filters**: order type, time-in-force, client entitlements.
- **Fast local exposure checks**: position and notional limits using in-memory state.
- **Heavier or less frequently binding checks**: more complex cross-portfolio or cross-venue limits, perhaps updated periodically and cached.

In an event-driven loop, this sequencing lives inside the handler for "NewOrderRequest" events. The handler either short-circuits early (on a rejection) or falls through to the next check.

The goal is that:

- Most orders pass quickly because they are well within all limits and never hit the heavier checks.
- Orders that should be rejected are blocked by the cheapest possible test, saving work and reducing load.

This is not only good for latency but also helps control the risk engine's own resource usage under stress.

## Placement options for risk checks

Where you place risk logic in the architecture matters as much as how you write it. There are four common patterns, often combined.

### In-strategy checks

Some simple constraints can live directly in strategy code:

- Maximum order size for a particular model.
- Prohibiting certain instruments or order types for that strategy.

Advantages:

- Zero extra latency; just logic in the same function that decides to trade.
- Strategy-specific knowledge can be used (for example, the model's own risk estimates).

Disadvantages:

- Inconsistent enforcement across strategies if not coordinated.
- Harder to audit and change centrally; risk officers must inspect many codebases.

This approach works best for *additional* safety, not as the only line of defense.

### Shared in-process risk engine

Here, all strategies running in a given engine send their proposed orders through a shared risk component in the *same* process, usually via synchronous calls or events on the same thread.

Advantages:

- Very low latency: no serialization or network hops.
- Consistent enforcement for all in-process strategies.
- Easier to manage and audit than per-strategy ad hoc rules.

Disadvantages:

- Limited to strategies running in that engine; cross-engine consistency still needs work.
- Bugs or load in the risk logic can directly affect the hot path (although this is an explicit and manageable risk).

For ultra-low-latency trading, this is often the preferred model for essential pre-trade checks.

### Out-of-process risk service

In this model, strategies (or engines) call a separate risk service, possibly shared across many machines or business units.

Advantages:

- Single point of truth for limits across systems.
- Independent deployment and scaling of risk vs. strategy code.
- Strong separation of duties: risk officers can manage the service, while quants focus on strategies.

Disadvantages:

- Additional process and often network boundaries on the hot path, with added latency and jitter.
- Complex failure handling: what do strategies do when the risk service times out?
- Potential bottleneck and single point of failure at high flow rates.

This design is more common where trading is not extremely latency-sensitive or where regulatory requirements strongly favor centralized enforcement, and in combination with lighter in-process checks.

### Venue-provided risk controls

Exchanges and brokers often offer built-in or configurable limits:

- Max order size per account or per symbol.
- Fat-finger price checks.
- Kill switches at the session or participant level.

Advantages:

- Provide a last-resort safety net even if your own systems misbehave.
- Managed by the venue or broker; may satisfy regulatory minima.

Disadvantages:

- Latency and behavior may be opaque or inflexible.
- Coarse-grained; cannot encode all of your internal risk policies.
- May not distinguish between different strategies or sub-accounts as finely as you need.

The right mindset is to treat venue limits as a *backstop*, not your primary risk management. Your own risk components should prevent you from ever hitting these outer walls in normal trading.

## Kill switches: emergency brakes for the engine

Pre-trade checks deal with "everyday" safety. **Kill switches** deal with emergencies: situations where you want to stop trading immediately and predictably.

There are several levels of kill switch:

- **Per-strategy**: stop a particular algorithm while others continue.

- **Per-session / per-venue**: stop sending orders to a given exchange or gateway.
- **Firm-wide**: stop all new trading activity from your systems.

A good kill-switch design separates two things:

- The **control plane**: how a human or automated monitor triggers a kill.
- The **data plane**: how the trading engine enforces that kill in the hot path.

### Control plane: triggering kills

Triggers can come from various places:

- Human risk officers, via a console.
- Automated monitors detecting anomalies (for example, too many rejects, P&L swings, message rates).
- External entities (brokers, exchanges) cutting you off.

The control plane needs:

- **Authentication and authorization**: only the right people or systems can trigger kills.
- **Auditability**: you can later see who did what and why.
- **Reasonably fast reaction**, but not necessarily microseconds; a second or two may be acceptable here as long as the data plane response is crisp once the command arrives.

Control messages travel through slower, more flexible channels: APIs, message buses, or admin connections, not through the same code paths as every order.

### Data plane: enforcing kills in the hot path

Once the engine receives a kill signal, enforcement must live in the same part of the system that processes orders. This typically means:

- A small piece of state in the hot path indicating whether a given strategy, session, or the firm as a whole is currently allowed to send orders.
- A very cheap check at the start of the order-processing logic: "is this context killed?" If yes, drop or reject the order immediately.

The design goals are:

- **Deterministic behavior**: once a kill is active, no new orders should be sent, with no exceptions or race conditions where some slip through.
- **Low overhead**: when kills are not active (99.9% of the time), the existence of this mechanism should cost you almost nothing per order.

A common pattern in an event-driven engine is:

- Treat "KillOn" and "KillOff" as events that update small flags in the relevant strategy or session state.
- For each NewOrderRequest event, the first lines of logic consult those flags; if any relevant flag is set, immediately route the order to a rejection path without performing further risk checks or session work.

This keeps both the hot path and the kill logic simple and explicit.

## Race conditions and edge cases in kill behavior

Designing kill switches is not just about adding a flag. You must reason about dynamic, real-time behavior:

### Orders already in flight

When a kill is triggered:

- Some orders may already be at the exchange.
- Some may be in your engine but not yet fully processed.
- Some may be in the network stack or on the wire.

Your design must decide:

- Do you allow existing working orders to continue trading ("no new orders"), or do you attempt to cancel them as part of the kill?
- If you send mass cancels, how do you track which orders were successfully canceled and which may still be live?

A robust approach often includes:

- Immediate stop to accepting *new* orders as soon as the kill flag is set.
- A systematic, perhaps slightly slower process to cancel or manage existing orders, with clear tracking and logging.
- Clear and documented semantics: everyone should know what "session kill" or "firm kill" means operationally.

### Consistency across layers and services

If you have multiple engine instances or out-of-process risk services, a kill signal must propagate consistently:

- All affected engines must receive and act on the kill in a bounded amount of time.
- Centralized risk or monitoring components should converge on the same view (killed or not).

This can be handled with:

- A central authority (for example, a risk control service) broadcasting kill state that all engines subscribe to.
- Or, in more decentralized setups, well-defined procedures for applying kills independently but with shared configuration.

Either way, engines should treat kill flags as local truths once received; they should not wait for further confirmation when deciding whether to accept an order.

## Balancing safety and latency

Risk management and kill switches inevitably add work to the order path. The art is to add only what is necessary, and to structure it in a way that does not create unpredictable tails.

Some practical guidelines:

**1. Avoid slow operations in the hot path.**

Pre-trade risk checks should not:

- Perform disk I/O or blocking network calls.
- Traverse large data structures that are not kept hot in memory.
- Depend on external services whose responsiveness you cannot tightly control.

If a particular check cannot be made fast enough, consider approximating it in the hot path (for example, using cached limits and conservative assumptions) and enforcing the precise version at a slower timescale, with alerts and possibly coarser throttling as backup.

**2. Accept conservative bias under uncertainty.**

When something goes wrong in the risk system itself–for example, data is missing or a state is inconsistent–the safer choice is almost always to:

- Reject the order and signal an error.
- Or, in extreme cases, trip a local kill for the affected strategy or session until the issue is understood.

This may cost you some good trades, but it protects against "unknown unknowns" becoming major loss events.

**3. Measure and monitor risk latency.**

Just as you measure strategy and session latency, you should:

- Track how long risk checks take per order, both on average and in the tails.
- Detect when risk latency suddenly increases (for example, due to configuration changes or data growth).
- Record decisions and reasons so that post-mortems can distinguish between correct rejections and system issues.

Risk that is too slow or too jittery can harm fills and P&L even if it is logically correct.

**4. Test kills as carefully as you test strategies.**

Kill switches are often used rarely in production, which means bugs can hide until a real emergency. To avoid this:

- Exercise kill paths in simulation or staging environments regularly.
- Verify that kills propagate and are enforced as expected.
- Include kill-trigger scenarios in incident drills and run-books.

A kill switch that does not work when needed is worse than none, because it creates dangerous false confidence.

Embedding risk management and kill switches into the hot path is not about bolting on a few extra checks or a red button. It is an architectural choice that must harmonize with the layered design, interaction models, and event-driven engine you already have.

Done well, it yields a system where:

- Each proposed order is screened quickly through a carefully ordered pipeline of pre-trade checks.
- Essential limits are enforced in-process, with predictable costs and clear behavior under stress.
- Kill switches can halt trading or portions of trading reliably, with minimal extra overhead when they are inactive.
- Risk policies can evolve without rewriting strategies or destabilizing connectivity.

The goal is not to eliminate all risk—that would mean not trading at all. The goal is to eliminate *uncontrolled* risk paths, especially those that combine high speed with low visibility. In the final section of this chapter, we will look at how observability—logging, metrics, tracing—completes this picture by making the performance and behavior of your risk and kill mechanisms visible before they fail in production.

## 4.6 Observability Hooks

In the previous sections we have focused on building a trading engine that is *structurally* sound: layers separated, interactions chosen carefully, order lifecycles modeled as finite-state machines, risk checks and kill switches embedded in the hot path. All of that effort, however, can be undermined if you cannot see what the system is actually doing in production.

Trading systems often fail silently at first. Latency drifts a little. One queue grows slightly. A new risk check adds a few microseconds. An exchange starts responding slower on a subset of symbols. None of these alone causes immediate disaster, but together they erode fill quality and profitability.

**Observability** is your defense against this slow decay. In this section we focus on how to instrument the trading stack with:

- **Metrics**: numeric summaries over time (e.g., latencies, rates, queue depths).

- **Logging**: structured records of important events and decisions.
- **Tracing**: end-to-end views of a single order or request across components.

Our aim is to place observability hooks so that:

- You can detect performance regressions and anomalies *before* they visibly hurt fills.
- You can reconstruct what happened to a specific order or strategy during an incident.
- The instrumentation itself does not become a major source of latency or jitter.

## Observability as part of the architecture

It is tempting to treat observability as something you "add later" once the system works. For low-latency trading this approach is risky:

- Retrofitted instrumentation tends to be ad hoc and uneven; hot paths may remain unmeasured because people are afraid to touch them.
- You may discover that key layers are impossible to instrument cleanly without disruptive changes.

Instead, think of observability as another dimension of your architecture, alongside layering and interaction models. For each component and boundary you design, you should also ask:

- What do we need to know about this component at runtime to be confident it is healthy?
- Where should we measure time and count events?
- How can we trace an individual order's journey across layers?

This mindset encourages you to create well-defined *observation points* just as you defined clear interfaces.

## What to measure: core signals

The set of possible metrics and logs is infinite; adding everything will slow your system and drown you in data. Instead, focus on a core set of signals that cover:

1. **Latency per stage**: how long each step in the order path and market data path takes.
2. **Volume and rate**: how many messages, orders, fills, and risk decisions you are processing.
3. **Capacity and back-pressure**: queue depths, buffer utilization, and rejection counts.
4. **Resource health**: CPU, memory allocator or GC behavior, NIC and kernel metrics.

Let us look at each in more detail.

## Per-stage latency

End-to-end latency (from market event to order at the exchange) is important, but it is not enough. To find and fix issues, you need to know how latency is distributed across stages:

- Strategy computation time.
- Risk decision time.
- Session adapter and serialization time.
- Time spent in queues, if any.
- Time from session send to exchange acknowledgment ("wire + venue" latency).

For each of these, you want not just an average, but a view of the distribution over time:

- Median and high percentiles (for example, 95th, 99th).
- How these percentiles change with market conditions (calm vs. busy).

The goal is to catch subtle regressions: a risk refactor that adds 3 microseconds at the 99th percentile, or a new logging statement that stretches the tail.

## Rates and volumes

Metrics on rates and volumes answer questions like:

- How many orders per second are we sending and receiving?
- How many market data updates per second are we processing?
- How many risk decisions per second (and how many are rejections)?

These metrics help you:

- Understand whether a latency degradation is due to heavier load or a code change.
- Detect runaway strategies (volumes much higher than expected).
- Size hardware and thread pools for peak conditions.

## Capacity, queues, and back-pressure

Wherever you have queues or buffers, you should track:

- Current depth.
- Maximum depth over a time interval.
- Number of dropped or rejected messages due to capacity.

For example:

- The input ring buffer feeding the event-driven order engine.
- Queues feeding out-of-process analytics or logging.
- NIC or kernel buffer utilization, if available.

Increasing queue depths are often the earliest sign of trouble: a consumer slowed down (perhaps due to a bug or a hidden dependency), and load is outpacing capacity. If you catch this early, you can act before queues overflow or latencies explode.

## Resource health and runtime behavior

Finally, you need visibility into broader runtime health:

- CPU utilization per core, especially for the threads running hot loops.
- Memory usage and allocator/GC behavior (frequency and duration of collections, allocation rates).
- NIC statistics: packet drops, errors, retransmissions, flow control.
- Kernel metrics: context switches, interrupt rates, softirq load on network cores.

Performance problems in trading systems are often caused not by explicit algorithmic slowness, but by interactions with the OS and runtime: a GC pause, a noisy neighbor process, a misrouted NIC interrupt. Without these metrics, such problems look like mysterious, random latency spikes.

## Where to hook into the stack

Now we connect these desired signals to the architecture we built earlier.

## Strategy layer

At the strategy level, instrument:

- Time between receiving a market event and deciding on an order action.
- Counts of generated orders, cancels, and modifies.
- Strategy-specific metrics (for example, spread, signal values, counters of unusual conditions).

Because strategies can be many and change frequently, keep instrumentation here lightweight and standardized. A shared helper or macro for "record strategy decision latency" prevents everyone from reinventing their own, possibly expensive, logging.

## Risk layer

For risk, focus on:

- Latency of pre-trade checks per order (with distribution).
- Counts of accepted vs. rejected orders by rejection reason.
- Current usage of key limits (for example, percent of position or notional limits used).

These metrics help you see:

- Whether risk checks are becoming a bottleneck.
- Whether a configuration change is causing many more rejections.
- Whether you are approaching critical limits, which may cause sudden behavior changes.

## Session layer

The session layer is the choke point between you and the exchange. Instrument:

- Time to serialize and send an order message.
- Time between send and exchange acknowledgment or reject.
- Counts of protocol errors, rejects by code, and reconnects.
- Heartbeat and sequence number metrics.

Per-session and per-venue metrics allow you to distinguish between:

- Internal problems (for example, your serialization got slower).
- External problems (for example, a venue's matching engine is lagging).

## Infrastructure and network

At the infrastructure layer, some metrics come from outside your code (OS tools, NIC counters), but you can still integrate them into your observability stack:

- Per-core CPU and interrupt usage.
- NIC queue depths, drops, and errors.
- Time synchronization status (for example, PTP offset and stability).

These provide crucial context for interpreting application-level metrics. For instance, if order latency spikes coincide with NIC queue bursts and softirq saturation, you know to look at network tuning, not risk code.

## Logging: structured, sparse, and meaningful

Metrics tell you *that* something is wrong; logs often tell you *what* and *why*. For trading systems, logs should be:

- **Structured**: key fields like timestamps, order IDs, states, and event types should be explicit fields, not buried in free text.
- **Sparse along the hot path**: you cannot log every micro-event synchronously; choose a few critical points.
- **Correlatable**: events relating to the same order, strategy, or session should be linkable by IDs.

Important log events include:

- Order lifecycle transitions (especially state changes such as New $\rightarrow$ Working, Working $\rightarrow$ Filled or Rejected).
- Risk decisions: reason codes for rejections, limit utilizations at decision time.
- Session anomalies: disconnects, recoveries, protocol-level errors.
- Kill switch activations and deactivations, with origin and scope.

Most of these can and should be logged asynchronously: the hot path enqueues log records into a buffer, and a separate thread or process handles formatting and I/O. The order engine should never block on disk or network I/O for logging.

## Tracing: reconstructing a single order's journey

Metrics and logs at component boundaries are powerful, but during complex incidents you often need to answer questions like:

> "For this particular order, where did we spend time, and what decisions were made?"

This is the role of **tracing**: recording enough information along the path so that you can reconstruct a per-order narrative.

A simple, practical tracing scheme for a trading engine includes:

- A unique **order ID** that is used consistently across layers (strategy, risk, session).
- Optional **correlation IDs** that tie together logical actions (for example, a parent order and its child orders, or an order and a kill event).
- Timestamps and state changes logged at major transitions.

You do not need heavy distributed tracing frameworks in the hot path. The key is that:

- Every major component, when it logs or emits metrics about an order, includes the order ID.
- Time is synchronized well enough across components and hosts to allow meaningful ordering of events.

With that in place, you can reconstruct:

- When the strategy decided to trade.
- When risk accepted (or rejected) the order.
- When the session sent it and when the exchange responded.
- Any cancellations or fills along the way.

Such end-to-end traces are invaluable in post-mortems and in debugging rare, path-dependent bugs (for example, races between cancels and fills).

## Synchronous vs. asynchronous telemetry

Every observability hook faces a design choice:

- **Synchronous**: measure or log directly within the hot path, blocking until done.
- **Asynchronous**: record minimal data locally, then hand off to a background worker.

For ultra-low-latency components, the default should be *asynchronous*, with synchronous operations reserved for:

- Essential timing that cannot be captured otherwise (for example, taking a timestamp just before and after a critical function).
- Rare, severe error conditions where you are willing to pay a performance cost to ensure something is recorded (for example, an invariant violation before triggering a kill).

Common patterns for asynchronous telemetry include:

- **Lock-free or low-lock ring buffers** for logs and metrics, consumed by dedicated threads.
- **Batching**: sending metrics and logs in batches at fixed intervals to reduce overhead.
- **Sampling**: only tracing a small percentage of orders in full detail during normal operation, with the ability to increase sampling during investigations.

The key is to ensure that telemetry itself does not introduce unpredictable delays. A logging queue filling up and blocking the hot path is a classic self-inflicted wound.

## Using observability to catch regressions early

Once you have observability hooks in place, the real value comes from how you use them to detect regressions *before* they damage trading performance.

Some practical habits:

### Baseline and compare

Treat performance and behavior metrics as you would P&L:

- Establish baselines for key latencies and rates under typical market conditions.
- After every meaningful change (code deploy, configuration update, infrastructure change), compare the new metrics to the baseline.
- Automate alerts for significant deviations, especially in tail latencies.

A small but persistent shift in, say, risk decision time may be invisible in one day's trading results, but over months it can erode edge.

### Correlate with market regimes

Latency, queue depths, and error rates depend on market conditions:

- Busy periods (open, close, macro news) naturally increase load.
- Some venues may degrade performance under stress.

By correlating your metrics with known market regimes (for example, volatility spikes), you can:

- Distinguish expected stress behavior from regressions.
- Size buffers and thread pools to withstand realistic peaks.
- Decide whether to adapt strategy behavior under stress (for example, temporarily widening limits or slowing certain activities).

## Build simple dashboards for key paths

You do not need flashy, complex dashboards to benefit from observability. A few focused views are often enough:

- Per-stage latency over time for a representative strategy and venue.
- Queue depths and drop counts for critical buffers.
- Counts of risk rejections by category.
- Kill switch state and recent activations.

The goal is for both developers and operations staff to be able to answer, quickly:

> "Is the system healthy right now? If not, where is the problem likely to be?"

## Design for incident analysis

Finally, observability should support disciplined incident response:

- When something goes wrong, you should be able to gather relevant metrics and traces from the affected period and reconstruct events.
- Post-mortems should link findings back to specific metrics (for example, "risk latency at the 99.9th percentile doubled after deploy X").
- Where possible, you should add or refine instrumentation based on each incident so that the same pattern is easier to detect next time.

Over time, this process turns your observability layer into a living, improving part of the architecture, not a static set of counters.

## Keeping instrumentation safe for latency

All instrumentation has a cost. The art is to keep that cost:

- Small compared to the budget of the component.
- Predictable, without long tails.

Some rules of thumb for hot paths:

- Record timestamps using the cheapest available clock that gives sufficient resolution and accuracy, and do not convert them to human-readable formats in the hot path.
- Prefer fixed-size, preallocated buffers for telemetry messages to avoid allocations.
- Ensure that any shared telemetry structures (like queues) are designed for the expected write rate under peak conditions.

For colder paths (for example, back-office integration, dashboards), you can afford richer logs and metrics, but you should still be mindful of not overwhelming storage or networks.

Observability hooks are the sensory organs of your trading system. They:

- Turn the architecture we have discussed—layers, interaction models, FSMs, risk controls—into something you can see and reason about while it runs.
- Allow you to detect performance regressions and anomalies early, before they manifest as lost opportunities or unexpected losses.
- Provide the raw material for incident analysis, tuning, and continuous improvement.

The key design principles are:

- Decide up front what to measure at each layer and boundary.

- Favor lightweight, asynchronous instrumentation in hot paths.
- Use structured logging and simple tracing based on shared IDs and synchronized time.
- Treat observability data as seriously as trading data: baselines, dashboards, and post-mortems.

When observability is designed alongside the rest of the system, you no longer have to choose between speed and insight. You can run fast and still know, with confidence, where latency hides, how design changes matter, and when your edge is at risk.

# Chapter 5

# Network Protocols & Physical Connectivity

*Every microsecond your strategy spends on the wire is shaped long before a single line of trading code runs. This chapter pulls back the data-center ceiling tiles and follows a packet's journey-from photons in fiber to headers in UDP-to show where latency really hides. By the end, you'll be able to look at a cage map, a cross-connect order form, or a multicast diagram and read them as directly as a P&L: hard constraints, trade-offs, and opportunities to win time that your competitors may not even realize exists.*

## 5.1 Optical Paths and Propagation Delay

Trading engineers spend a lot of time talking about nanoseconds in software, but the first and hardest limit in your system sits far below the application: nothing moves faster than the speed of light. Once you understand what that means in real cables and real routes, you gain a powerful sanity check. You can look at a data-center diagram or a proposed inter-city path and immediately translate "extra meters" into "extra nanoseconds," and judge whether a vendor's latency claim is even physically possible.

At this level, we are not yet worried about queues, operating systems, or TCP behavior. We are answering a simpler question: if I send a bit from point A to point B, and nothing else in the stack slows it down, how long does the journey through space and glass actually take?

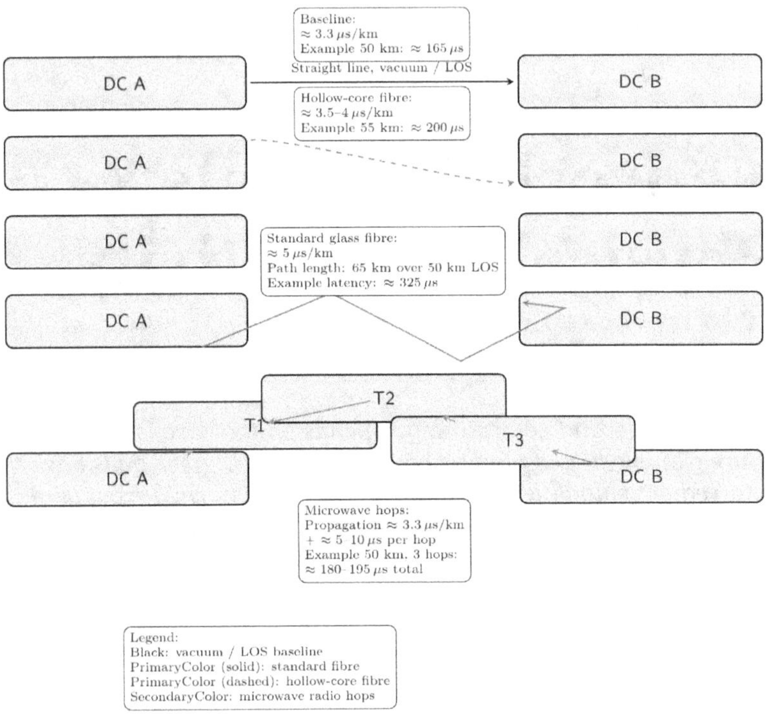


## From Physics to Rules of Thumb

In a vacuum, light travels about 300,000 kilometers in a second. What matters to you is the inverse: how long it takes to travel each kilometer. In round numbers, that is a little over 3 microseconds per kilometer in a straight line.

Signals in trading networks almost never get this best case. They travel through physical media that slow them down and through routes that are not straight. Instead of remembering the exact physics, traders and network engineers use simple rules of thumb:

- In standard glass fiber: think "about 5 microseconds per kilometer."
- In good hollow-core fiber: closer to 3.5–4 microseconds per kilometer.
- In line-of-sight microwave through air: around 3.3 microseconds per kilometer, similar to the vacuum baseline plus radio equipment overhead.

These numbers already tell you something profound: just choosing to put a link in glass instead of free space increases one-way latency per kilometer on the order of 50% or more. Over tens or hundreds of kilometers, this gap compounds into tens or hundreds of microseconds.

## Media Choices: Glass, Hollow-Core, and Air

Once you accept that you are always fighting the speed of light, the next step is to understand how each medium slows you down and what you get in return.

**Standard glass fiber.**

Most trading networks use standard single-mode optical fiber. It is cheap, robust, and carries enormous bandwidth. The downside is that light travels through glass significantly slower than it does through air or vacuum.

A simple mental model:

- For quick estimates, treat standard glass fiber as about 5 microseconds one way per kilometer.
- That means roughly 1 millisecond one way for 200 kilometers, ignoring all other delays.

If the straight-line distance between two data centers is 30 kilometers, and the measured one-way latency is 0.6 milliseconds, you already know something: your signal is not traveling just 30 kilometers of fiber. Either the route is significantly longer than the straight line, the fiber characteristics are unusually slow, or there are extra devices (repeaters, switches) adding forwarding delays.

**Hollow-core fiber.**

Hollow-core fiber is a specialized technology where light travels mostly through a hollow region (often air) guided by a surrounding structure, instead of moving entirely through solid glass. Because light in air is faster than light in glass, hollow-core fiber narrows the gap between fiber and microwave.

In practice:

- You can think of hollow-core fiber as shaving roughly 20–30% off the per-kilometer latency of standard fiber.
- For rough mental math, 3.5–4 microseconds per kilometer is a useful range.

Over 100 kilometers, that difference can be 150 microseconds or more one way compared to standard fiber. This is why you see hollow-core proposed for some ultra-low-latency financial routes, especially in metro or regional links where the economics can work.

**Microwave and millimeter wave.**

Microwave and millimeter-wave systems send radio waves through the air between towers. The propagation speed is close to the vacuum speed of light. Their latency advantages come from two factors:

- The medium itself: air is faster than glass.
- The geometry: microwave routes are typically engineered to be close to the geodesic straight line, whereas buried fiber must follow ducts, rights-of-way, and roads.

When you think about these systems, break the latency budget into two components:

1. Propagation through air: roughly 3.3 microseconds per kilometer.

2. Radio equipment processing at each hop: typically a few microseconds per tower, sometimes more depending on modulation and error correction.

A 60-kilometer line-of-sight path might have three or four radio hops. The propagation part is about 200 microseconds. The radios might add 20–40 microseconds total, leaving you with something still sharply better than an equivalent length of standard fiber.

The trade-offs are clear: microwave paths are faster but lower capacity and more weather-sensitive; fiber is slower but offers huge bandwidth and stability.

## From Straight Lines to Real Routes

So far we have pretended that your path is a straight line from data center A to data center B. Reality is more complicated.

In the field, actual fiber routes snake around obstacles, follow existing ducts, detour into intermediate facilities, and include deliberate slack loops for maintenance. Every meter of these detours converts directly into extra nanoseconds.

**Path stretch: when 50 kilometers becomes 70.**

Consider two exchange data centers in the same metropolitan area, 50 kilometers apart in a straight line. On a map, that looks simple. Underground, the carrier may run fiber along roads, across bridges, and through multiple intermediate points of presence.

It is common for the optical path length to be 20–40% longer than the geometric distance. In our 50-kilometer example, the actual fiber length might be 65–70 kilometers. What does that mean?

- Straight-line vacuum baseline: 50 km at about 3.3 microseconds/km gives roughly 165 microseconds.
- Standard fiber with 65 km of path: at 5 microseconds/km, about 325 microseconds.

The difference between 50 and 65 kilometers in glass is not an abstract number. It is around 75 microseconds in one direction, 150 microseconds round-trip. At latencies where matching engines respond in tens of microseconds, this is not a rounding error; it is a meaningful edge or disadvantage.

When evaluating a provider's route, you should always ask two questions:

1. What is the physical path length, not just the city-pair distance?

2. How much deliberate slack or detour is built into the route?

If the reported one-way latency materially exceeds what you would expect from the claimed length, suspect hidden path stretch or extra equipment.

**Slack loops and excess fiber.**

Carriers intentionally add "slack" to fiber runs: coils of extra fiber stored in vaults or cabinets. These allow technicians to repair or re-terminate fibers without pulling new cable. From an operations standpoint, slack is useful. From a latency standpoint, slack is dead weight.

A modest-looking coil holding 200 meters of spare fiber adds about 1 microsecond one way. Several such coils along a metro run can quietly cost you several microseconds. On long-haul links, extra kilometers might be introduced just to reach regeneration huts or to follow available ducts. Those extra kilometers behave no differently from the "main" kilometers: each one hits you for a few microseconds.

**Patch panels and cross-connect detours.**

Inside and between facilities, your optical signal often jumps through patch panels, meet-me rooms, and intermediate cages. Each detour has two separate latency impacts:

- Extra fiber distance: routes may go from your cage to a meet-me room, back to a main distribution frame, then onwards, rather than directly.

- Extra optical components: connectors, splitters, and transponders introduce tiny delays of their own and, more important, add opportunities for misconfiguration.

While the pure propagation delay of a connector is tiny compared to a kilometer of fiber, these detours typically involve additional tens of meters of fiber as cables route up and down racks and around rooms. Over a campus or co-location facility, that can become a few hundred meters, which is already in the sub-microsecond to microsecond range. In highly competitive co-location environments, a microsecond is a serious number.

## Metro vs. Long-Haul: Latency Budgets in Practice

It is helpful to mentally separate two regimes: metro distances (inside a city or region) and long-haul distances (between cities or countries). The physics is the same, but the way latency shows up in your architecture is different.

**Metro paths: every meter matters.**

Within a co-location campus or a metropolitan area, distances are typically tens of meters to tens of kilometers. Here, sub-microsecond and microsecond differences can dominate the race.

Typical situations include:

- The distance from your cage to the exchange's matching engine cage in the same building.
- The path from one data center to another across town.

A 20-meter difference in patching inside a building corresponds to roughly 0.1 microseconds in fiber. A 200-meter difference is about 1 microsecond. Once you start competing in environments where other firms fight for every microsecond, these numbers must be tracked and engineered, not treated as rounding errors.

On metro fiber rings, the non-straight nature of the route often dominates. Many metro carriers sell "ring" products where your traffic follows a loop that might be twice the minimal path length. In these cases, your one-way propagation budget is set less by the map distance and more by how many extra kilometers of ring you traverse.

**Long-haul paths: shape and medium dominate.**

Between cities, say New York and Chicago or London and Frankfurt, distances are hundreds to over a thousand kilometers. The basic propagation component alone is in the millisecond range. Over these distances, two factors set your baseline:

1. Whether your path is close to the great-circle straight line or significantly longer.
2. Whether you use fiber, hollow-core fiber, or microwave/millimeter wave.

On standard fiber, 1,000 kilometers immediately implies about 5 milliseconds one way in the best case, before counting any equipment delays. Any vendor claiming something dramatically lower in fiber must be offering either a shorter route than you think or a different medium.

Microwave long-haul routes, by contrast, might track the straight-line path more closely and operate closer to the speed-of-light baseline. The trade-off is that they require many towers, are weather-sensitive, and cannot match the bandwidth of fiber. From a pure latency perspective, however, the arithmetic is the same: count the kilometers, multiply by a per-kilometer figure, then add overheads for radios and regeneration.

## Technology Choices as Latency Design Decisions

With this understanding, you can now view connectivity decisions as explicit latency design choices rather than black-box services.

**Choosing fiber types and routes.**

When selecting a fiber provider or commissioning a custom route, you should be able to ask and answer:

- What is the physical length of the route, not just the city pair?
- What is the expected per-kilometer delay given the fiber type?
- How much slack and how many intermediate facilities are in the path?

Your mental arithmetic becomes:

1. Estimate per-kilometer delay: standard fiber, hollow-core, or a mix.

2. Multiply by the physical path length to get a baseline propagation budget.

3. Compare to measured latency and vendor guarantees to diagnose extra overhead.

If a vendor publishes a round-trip latency, you can invert the calculation: divide by two for one-way, divide by your assumed per-kilometer figure, and see what implied path length they must be using. If it is significantly longer or shorter than any realistic route between your endpoints, something does not add up.

**Microwave as a strategic overlay.**

Microwave and millimeter-wave systems are usually deployed as latency-optimized overlays on top of reliable fiber backbones. Their business case is literally the microseconds saved per kilometer.

To reason about them:

- Start from the straight-line map distance and multiply by about 3.3 microseconds per kilometer.

- Add a few microseconds for each hop (tower). The number of hops is set by terrain, line-of-sight constraints, and spectrum rules.

- Compare the result to the equivalent fiber path, which likely has both a slower medium and a longer physical distance.

In many real trading corridors, microwave reduces one-way propagation delay by hundreds of microseconds compared to commodity fiber. That margin is large enough to justify complex engineering, regulatory work, and operational risk for firms operating latency-sensitive strategies.

### Making Nanoseconds Intuitive

The goal of this section is not to turn you into a physicist, but to give you an instinct for how physical distance and media type show up as nanoseconds and microseconds in your trading system.

Some mental anchors:

- In glass, roughly every 200 meters costs you about 1 microsecond.
- In air, every kilometer costs you a little over 3 microseconds.
- A simple extra building-to-building detour of a few kilometers can quietly add tens of microseconds.
- Over inter-city distances, the choice between fiber, hollow-core, and microwave can shift your budget by hundreds of microseconds.

Armed with these rules, you can treat every data-center map, floor plan, and carrier marketing slide as a latency diagram. Later chapters will layer on queues, protocol behavior, and operating-system effects. Those all matter, but none of them can undo the fundamental rule: the shortest, straightest path in the fastest medium sets the lower bound on how quickly your orders and market data can possibly move.

## 5.2 Switch Architecture and Buffer Behavior

In the previous section we treated the network as a set of physical paths: glass, air, towers, and ducts. We built a "propagation budget" based on distance and medium. In a live trading system, however, your packets do not slide frictionlessly from one end of the fiber to the other. They are received, inspected, queued, and forwarded by switches and routers along the way.

At microsecond scales, the internal design of these switches matters as much as the length of the cable. Even if you have engineered a near-perfect physical route, a single congested switch can inject tens or hundreds of microseconds of queuing delay and jitter, or in the worst case, drop packets and trigger expensive retransmissions.

This section opens the switch chassis and looks at how architecture, buffering, and Quality of Service (QoS) policies shape the latency your trading applications actually see.

## Store-and-Forward vs. Cut-Through

Every Ethernet switch has the same basic job: accept packets on ingress ports and deliver them out the correct egress ports. The way it performs this job determines the minimum possible per-hop latency.

There are two main forwarding styles:

**Store-and-forward.**

In a store-and-forward switch, the device receives the entire packet into a buffer, checks its integrity (for example, by verifying a frame checksum), makes a forwarding decision, and only then begins transmitting the packet on the egress port.

This is simple and robust, but implies a minimum delay proportional to packet size and port speed. The switch cannot forward the packet until it has finished receiving it.

**Cut-through.**

In a cut-through switch, the device begins forwarding the packet as soon as it has received just enough of the header to know where it should go. The tail of the packet is still arriving at the ingress port while the head is already leaving the egress port.

Cut-through forwarding greatly reduces the fixed component of switching latency, especially for larger packets. However, it does not eliminate queuing delays when there is congestion. If multiple packets contend for the same egress port, they still line up in a queue.

To understand where delays really come from, we need a picture of the internal data path.

Diagrammatic representation:

This simplified block diagram highlights three places where latency ac-

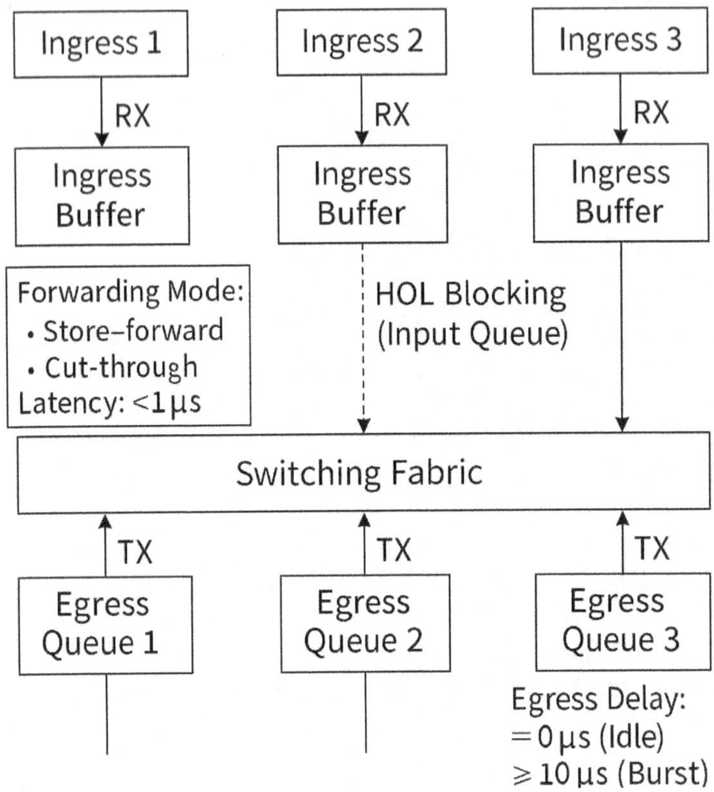


cumulates:

- Ingress buffers, where arriving packets are first stored.
- The switching fabric, where packets are routed internally.
- Egress queues, where packets wait for their turn on the outgoing port.

The fixed processing time in the fabric and the minimum time needed to inspect the packet are usually sub-microsecond to a few microseconds in modern low-latency switches. The variable part—the part that explodes under load—is queuing at ingress and especially at egress.

## Ingress and Egress Queues

At a high level, a switch is a set of queues with a decision engine in the middle. To reason about queuing delay, it helps to separate ingress and egress behavior.

**Ingress queues.**

Ingress buffering is used to absorb bursts that arrive faster than the switch fabric or internal buses can handle, or to deal with short-term speed mismatches between ports. In a well-designed, lightly loaded trading network, ingress queues are often shallow and short-lived.

However, if many high-rate sources send traffic into the same line card, ingress buffers can fill. When this happens, packets for different destinations may contend for the same internal resources, and backpressure may be applied to upstream devices. Even before any packet is dropped, the mere act of sitting in the ingress queue adds microseconds of delay.

**Egress queues.**

Egress queues are where most of the meaningful queuing delay is seen. All flows that leave the switch through the same port share a finite amount of bandwidth. When the combined incoming rate to that egress port briefly exceeds its capacity—for example, multiple market data feeds burst at once—packets line up.

Even with cut-through forwarding, an egress port that is already busy transmitting a long packet cannot start sending the next one until it finishes. Subsequent packets have to wait, and their waiting time is the queuing delay.

If an egress queue never builds up, the switch adds only its fixed processing time. If the queue periodically fills and drains—what we call *microbursts*—the latency spike experienced by unlucky packets can be an order of magnitude larger than the idle case.

In low-latency trading, you care less about the average time a packet spends in a queue and more about the worst-case or high-percentile times. A single 200-microsecond spike at the wrong moment can be the difference between a fill and a miss.

## Shared vs. Per-Port Buffers

How switches allocate buffer memory is just as important as how much memory they have. Two common designs are:

**Per-port buffers.**

Each physical port has its own dedicated pool of buffer memory. Traffic on Port 1 cannot directly consume buffer space assigned to Port 2.

This has a nice isolation property: one noisy neighbor cannot fully starve another port of buffers. But it also means that if Port 1 experiences a brief, intense burst, it can run out of buffer space and drop packets even though other ports sit mostly idle.

**Shared buffers.**

In shared-buffer designs, a common pool of memory is available to any port. When one egress port experiences a burst, it can temporarily consume a larger share of the buffer pool.

This improves burst absorption and can reduce packet loss during short congestion events. However, without careful limits, a few hot flows can consume most of the buffer pool and cause collateral damage elsewhere. Shared buffers also complicate reasoning: a port that looks lightly utilized may still see high latency if other ports are hammering the shared pool.

For trading networks, you typically want:

- Enough buffering to survive short microbursts without loss.
- Not so much buffering that a congested link builds up hundreds of microseconds of queued data.

Too little buffer produces loss and retransmissions; too much buffer produces “bufferbloat” and unpredictable latency. Low-latency switch lines often expose tuning knobs to cap queue depths and to partition shared buffers among classes of traffic.

## Head-of-Line Blocking

Head-of-line (HOL) blocking is a subtle but important effect. It occurs when one packet at the front of a queue prevents others behind it from being served, even if those trailing packets could otherwise proceed.

In a simple first-in, first-out egress queue, all traffic destined for a particular port sits in one line. Suppose three flows share an egress port:

- Flow A: continuous market data feed.
- Flow B: low-volume, latency-sensitive order traffic.
- Flow C: occasional bulk transfer (for example, log shipping).

If Flow C injects a few large packets, they enter the shared egress queue. Until those C packets are transmitted, the more time-critical order packets in Flow B are stuck behind them. From the perspective of Flow B, the presence of Flow C has increased its tail latency, even if the overall utilization of the link remains modest.

HOL blocking becomes even trickier in switches that use shared internal queues. A hot flow destined for one egress port can indirectly throttle traffic to another, because both are contending for the same internal resource. This is often invisible in simple per-port utilization graphs.

QoS mechanisms—priority queues, separate scheduling classes—are tools to mitigate head-of-line blocking. They allow you to say, in effect, "never let bulk traffic delay market data or orders." We will return to this after discussing microbursts themselves.

## Microbursts: Short Spikes, Large Effects

A *microburst* is a very short-lived spike of traffic that exceeds the capacity of a link or a queue, even if the longer-term average utilization is low. Microbursts are particularly common in trading networks because:

- Exchanges emit market data in bursts when many order book updates arrive at once.

- Many trading servers may react in the same direction at the same time, creating synchronized order bursts.
- Fan-out and fan-in patterns—one feed to many consumers, or many gateways to one uplink—naturally concentrate bursts on a few links.

Consider a 10 Gbps egress port feeding a set of trading servers. Under normal conditions, utilization averages 20–30%. During a major macro release or index rebalance, multiple upstream sources burst simultaneously. For a few hundred microseconds, the instantaneous arrival rate into that egress queue might effectively be 20–30 Gbps worth of packets. The queue fills, packets wait, and some may be dropped.

Two observations follow:

- Short microbursts may not show up in coarse monitoring. If you sample utilization every second, a path that is idle most of the time but hits 100% utilization for 300 microseconds will still appear only a fraction of a percent busy.
- The queuing delay seen by a packet caught in the middle of the burst is very real. It experiences the full depth of the queue at that instant, which might be tens of microseconds or more, even though the link is "lightly used" on average.

For latency-sensitive trading, this is dangerous. Your monitoring can tell you everything is fine while your strategy is quietly being delayed at the most important moments.

## QoS: Priority, Scheduling, and Trade-offs

Quality of Service (QoS) mechanisms in switches let you influence which packets wait in queues and which are served first. Used thoughtfully, QoS can protect trading-critical traffic from noisy neighbors and bulk flows. Used carelessly, it can create new forms of jitter and even self-inflicted loss.

Key concepts include:

### Classification and markings.

Packets can be tagged with priority markings, such as DSCP bits in the IP header or VLAN priority fields. Switches use these markings to map packets into different internal queues or scheduling classes.

In a trading environment, you might classify:

- Market data feeds as high-priority, latency-sensitive.
- Order entry and risk control messages as high-priority but often on separate logical paths.
- Heartbeats and control messages as medium priority (must not be starved).
- Bulk transfers (logs, database replication, file copies) as low priority.

### Priority queues.

Many switches support strict priority queues: a high-priority queue is always served before a lower-priority one, as long as it contains packets.

This can be beneficial: market data and orders are sent first, while log copies wait their turn. However, if you accidentally put too much traffic in the "high" class, lower-priority traffic can be starved. For example, if heartbeats or certain control messages are marked too low, they may experience long delays or even time out under heavy load, leading to disconnects or session resets.

### Weighted scheduling.

Weighted fair queuing and similar schedulers divide egress bandwidth among queues according to weights. For example, high-priority traffic might be guaranteed at least 50% of the bandwidth, but not allowed to take more than 80%, leaving room for important but less latency-sensitive traffic.

Weighted scheduling offers a more controlled compromise than strict priority. It lets you cap how much damage any single traffic class can inflict on others, at the cost of slightly more complex configuration and reasoning.

**Shaping and policing.**

Shaping slows traffic down by holding it in a buffer to conform to a specified rate. Policing drops or marks excess traffic. Both mechanisms can live at ingress, egress, or both.

In high-frequency trading, aggressive shaping on latency-critical paths is usually undesirable: you do not want your own switch deliberately introducing extra delay. However, carefully applied rate limits at the edge of your network can prevent your own bulk flows from overwhelming internal links.

The crucial design principle is simple: use QoS to reduce the chance that non-critical traffic causes contention and microbursts on paths that carry critical flows. Do not rely on QoS to "fix" fundamentally overloaded links or poor topology.

## Practical Guidelines for Low-Latency Switching

Putting these ideas together, we can outline some practical guidance for building and operating switching layers in trading networks.

**Interpret vendor latency numbers cautiously.**

Switch vendors advertise very low per-hop latencies, often sub-microsecond, for their cut-through low-latency product lines. These numbers are typically measured:

- With small packets.
- Under no load or very low load.
- With no queue buildup.

Treat these as the best-case fixed component of your per-hop budget. Your real-world latency under bursty trading conditions will be this number plus whatever queuing your traffic pattern induces. Always ask vendors for distribution data (for example, 99th and 99.9th percentile latency under realistic loads), not just averages or minima.

**Measure switch behavior in your own lab.**

To understand how a given switch model behaves under trading-like bursts, test it yourself:

- Generate synthetic market data bursts and measure end-to-end packet times across a single hop and a small cascade of switches.
- Vary packet sizes: exchanges do not send uniform frames.
- Measure latency distributions, not just averages. Look for outliers and long tails.
- Observe how latency changes as you approach line rate and as you introduce competing traffic classes.

These experiments will reveal not only microburst sensitivity but also how effective your QoS policies are at protecting critical flows.

**Engineer for worst-case bursts, not average load.**

Design switch fabrics and uplinks with awareness of correlated bursts:

- Avoid concentrating many noisy feeds or many gateways onto a single oversubscribed uplink if that uplink is on a latency-critical path.
- Favor designs where critical paths traverse only non-oversubscribed links and lightly loaded switches.
- Use QoS and traffic separation (for example, dedicated VLANs and physical interfaces) to keep bulk flows away from market-data and order-entry paths.

Your target is not "the average hop adds less than a microsecond." It is "even during extreme events, the hop rarely adds more than a few microseconds."

**Limit unnecessary buffering depth.**

Where your switch allows it, set reasonable maximum queue depths on latency-sensitive egress ports. A very deep buffer can hide problems by smoothing bursts but at the cost of unpredictable, large delays when it finally fills.

In low-latency segments, it is often better to accept a small, controlled amount of loss (which higher layers can detect and react to) than to silently accumulate hundreds of microseconds of delay in an oversized buffer.

**Separate roles: market data, orders, and bulk.**

Architecturally, the cleanest designs often create distinct paths for:

- Market data: multicast or unicast feeds, often one-way, tuned for minimal latency and jitter.
- Order entry and risk: request/response channels that must be fast but also reliable.
- Bulk and management traffic: everything else, which can tolerate more delay.

This separation can be logical (VLANs, QoS classes) or physical (separate switches and cables). The more you isolate latency-critical flows from the rest of your traffic, the easier it becomes to reason about and control queuing behavior.

## From Switches Back to the Whole Path

The physical propagation delay across a building or between cities gives you a hard lower bound on latency. Switches and their buffers determine how close you can get to that bound in the face of real-world traffic patterns.

When you combine these perspectives, a more complete picture emerges:

- The medium and distance set the best possible latency.
- The number of switching hops and their internal architectures set the best-case overhead above that.
- Traffic patterns, buffering schemes, and QoS policies determine how much extra delay you incur during bursts, and how variable that delay becomes.

As we move up the stack to IP and transport protocols in the next section, keep this in mind: many mysterious latency spikes attributed to "the network" are actually the result of very specific interactions between packet bursts, switch buffers, and protocol behavior. A trading architect who understands where and how switches add delay is far better equipped to build stable, predictable, and fast systems.

## 5.3 IP, UDP, TCP Trade-offs

By this point in the chapter, we have separated two fundamental pieces of "network latency":

- The *propagation and forwarding floor*, set by physical media and switches.
- The *queuing and contention overhead*, set by switch buffers, topology, and traffic patterns.

The next layer up is the protocol machinery that wraps your market data and orders into packets, moves them between hosts, and reacts when packets are lost or delayed. Even if your physical path and switching fabric are perfect, protocol choices can introduce extra delay, bursts, and dependencies that matter at microsecond scales.

In trading networks, the key players are IP at the network layer, and UDP and TCP at the transport layer. This section focuses on what they mean for latency, reliability, and behavior under congestion, and how to choose between them intentionally rather than by habit.

### IP as the Common Envelope

IP (Internet Protocol) provides the basic addressing and routing abstraction for your packets. Every IP packet has:

- Source and destination IP addresses, telling the network which hosts are talking.
- A protocol field indicating whether the payload is UDP, TCP, or something else.
- Additional fields used for fragmentation, checksums, and other housekeeping.

Three points are important for a trading architect:

**IP is unavoidable.**

Within a modern Ethernet network, IP is how you direct traffic between servers, gateways, and external venues. Whether your application uses UDP or TCP, IP is the wrapper the network sees. You do not "choose" IP in the way you choose UDP vs. TCP; you choose *on top of* IP.

**IP adds a modest but real overhead.**

IP headers increase packet size and give the switch or router more work to do per packet. On most trading paths, this overhead is small in absolute time, but it does matter when you are sending many small packets. Every extra byte of header is one more byte that must be serialized onto the wire, and every extra field is something that must be parsed and possibly inspected for ACLs, QoS, or routing.

**IP is best thought of as addressing, not reliability.**

IP by itself does not guarantee delivery, order, or timeliness. It will best-effort route packets; if they get dropped or delivered out of order, it is the job of the transport layer and the application to cope. That is where UDP and TCP come in.

## UDP: Minimalism and Application Responsibility

UDP (User Datagram Protocol) is sometimes described as "IP with ports." That captures its spirit: it adds just enough structure to let multiple applications share a host and talk to each other, and no more.

**What UDP provides.**

UDP adds:

- Source and destination ports, so many sockets on a host can receive independent streams of datagrams.
- A length field and a checksum, for basic integrity.

There is no notion of a "connection." Each UDP datagram is self-contained: it either arrives or it does not.

For trading, this has appealing properties:

- **Low overhead:** UDP headers are small, and processing logic inside the kernel is simple.
- **No built-in retransmissions:** If a packet is lost, the kernel does not stop and try to recover it. The application can detect and handle loss according to its own priorities.
- **No head-of-line blocking at the transport layer:** A late or lost datagram does not prevent later datagrams from being delivered, as long as they arrive.

### What UDP does *not* provide.

The flip side is that UDP offers almost no help with reliability or congestion:

- No guarantee that datagrams will arrive.
- No guarantee that they will arrive in order.
- No built-in flow control to stop a fast sender from overrunning a slow receiver.
- No built-in congestion control to slow down when the network is overloaded.

With UDP, the application is responsible for:

- Adding sequence numbers or timestamps so it can detect missing or out-of-order packets.
- Requesting or reconstructing missing data, if completeness is important.
- Being careful not to overwhelm the network or the peer.

For many trading use cases, this is exactly what you want. The application knows much more than the kernel about which data is important and how to repair it.

### UDP and market data.

This is why exchanges usually send market data over UDP, often using multicast:

- Many recipients need the same data at once. UDP multicast allows an exchange to send a single copy onto the network and let switches replicate it.
- Some loss is acceptable if it can be detected and quickly repaired, because new data is always arriving.
- The application (your feed handler) can implement recovery mechanisms tailored to the feed: gap requests, recovery channels, or fall-back to a secondary source.

From a latency perspective, UDP's main advantage is *absence*: it avoids the extra waiting and back-and-forth that TCP performs to guarantee reliability. A single lost packet does not block later packets at the transport layer; your feed handler can, for example, start using the newer book updates while it is still repairing a small gap in an older sequence.

**UDP and internal buses.**

Inside a trading firm, UDP is also a natural fit for internal event buses where:

- Messages are short-lived (for example, risk updates, quotes, or top-of-book snapshots).
- Consumers can tolerate small, constrained loss.
- The network is engineered to be very reliable, with modest fan-out.

In these settings, the combination of low overhead and application-level control over sequencing makes UDP attractive. But for orders and other transactional traffic, we typically want something stronger.

## TCP: Reliability, Ordering, and Hidden Delays

TCP (Transmission Control Protocol) was designed to provide a reliable byte stream over an unreliable packet network. It adds a relatively thick layer of logic above IP and UDP.

**What TCP provides.**

TCP offers:

- A connection abstraction: you establish a session between two endpoints, and within that session you read and write bytes.
- Guaranteed in-order delivery: the receiving application sees a contiguous stream of bytes in the order they were sent.
- Reliability: if packets are lost, TCP retransmits them until they get through or the connection fails.
- Flow control: TCP ensures a fast sender does not overrun a slow receiver's buffer.
- Congestion control: TCP adjusts its sending rate in response to perceived network congestion.

For many financial protocols—order entry sessions, clearing links, admin and control channels—these features match the business requirements:

- You must not silently lose an order.
- You need a clear, ordered history of messages.
- You are talking to a single well-defined peer, not a large fan-out.

**The latency cost of TCP.**

Reliability and ordering are not free. The mechanisms that make TCP robust also introduce latency, especially when the network is imperfect.

Some key effects:

- **Connection setup:** A full TCP connection involves a handshake. For long-lived sessions, this is a one-time startup cost, but if you establish and tear down connections frequently, handshake time can dominate.

- **Acknowledgements (ACKs):** The receiver sends ACKs to confirm successful receipt. These extra packets consume capacity and sometimes lead to delayed progression when ACKs are lost or delayed.
- **Head-of-line blocking:** If a packet in the middle of the stream is lost, TCP does not deliver later bytes to the application until the missing data is retransmitted and received. One lost packet can hold up an entire stream.
- **Congestion control reactions:** When TCP thinks the network is congested—because of drops or increased round-trip time—it reduces its sending rate. For an order session, this may translate into bursty delays when losses or microbursts occur elsewhere in the network.

At low loss rates, on a well-engineered path, TCP can provide excellent performance while giving you strong semantics. But under stress—precisely when markets are moving and volume is high—TCP's protective mechanisms can cause exactly the kind of unpredictable latency spikes traders fear.

**TCP, microbursts, and switches.**

Tie this back to the switch behavior from the previous section. Imagine a burst of packets from many sources overloads an egress queue for a short time:

- Some packets are delayed, increasing their effective round-trip times.
- Some packets are dropped, triggering TCP retransmissions.

TCP interprets this as congestion and backs off, shrinking its congestion window. The application sees this as a sudden increase in order turnaround times and lower effective throughput, just when it is trying to send more orders.

Moreover, because TCP enforces in-order delivery, even a single lost packet in a stream of small, latency-sensitive messages can block all subsequent messages behind it until recovery completes—a textbook example of head-of-line blocking at the transport layer, on top of any queuing in the network.

## Overhead and Packetization: Why a Few Bytes Matter

At first glance, the header overhead of IP, UDP, and TCP seems trivial. We are talking about tens of bytes in a world of gigabytes and terabits. But the high-frequency trading context is special:

- Messages are often small (e.g., tens of bytes of order instructions or book updates).
- The system may send or receive millions of packets per second.
- The cost of serializing each extra byte and parsing each extra field shows up both in line-rate and CPU-bound workloads.

Two main forms of overhead matter:

**On-the-wire size.**

Longer headers mean larger packets. Larger packets take slightly longer to transmit. On a fast link, the difference per packet is tiny, but over millions of packets per second it can aggregate into measurable delay and jitter, especially at congested points.

For example, an extra few dozen bytes per packet increase the amount of data that must pass through a switch egress queue during a burst. That can push the queue slightly deeper, adding extra microseconds to the worst cases.

**Per-packet processing.**

Each received packet must be parsed by the NIC and the host OS. TCP's richer state machines and options (for example, timestamps, selective acknowledgements) require more logic and memory accesses than UDP's simple datagrams.

Trading systems that operate close to the limits of a single core, or that process huge volumes of small messages, often find that per-packet processing overhead is critical. UDP's simplicity keeps the per-packet CPU cost down, which can translate into lower end-to-end latency from wire to application and back.

## Transport Semantics in Trading Scenarios

Armed with this understanding, we can examine common trading scenarios and see why the industry tends to prefer one transport over another.

**Order entry sessions.**

Order entry is transactional:

- Every order or cancel message matters.
- The exchange sends deterministic acknowledgements (ack, reject, partial fill, fill).
- Any ambiguity or silent loss is unacceptable from a compliance and risk standpoint.

For this reason, exchanges overwhelmingly use TCP (or TCP-like reliable streams) for order entry sessions. The costs—occasional head-of-line blocking, congestion reactions—are accepted in exchange for strong ordering and reliability. From a system design angle, you respond to this by:

- Engineering exceptionally clean, low-loss paths for these sessions.
- Isolating order traffic from noisy neighbors at both network and application levels.
- Monitoring round-trip times and retransmissions closely.

**Drop copy and post-trade feeds.**

Drop copy feeds (post-trade confirmations, fills) are often delivered over TCP, especially when they include a complete, auditable record of execution. Here, the latency requirement is usually looser than for order entry. A few extra milliseconds are often acceptable, while missing or corrupt records are not.

TCP's strengths—ordered, complete delivery—align with these needs. Optimizing these paths is still valuable, but they sit a tier below the absolute latency race.

**Market data and internal price buses.**

As noted, market data is typically UDP:

- It is one-to-many by nature.
- It values timeliness and continuity over perfect completeness.
- It can tolerate modest loss, as long as loss is detected and corrected quickly enough.

Internal price and signal distribution within a firm often follows the same model. Using UDP permits fan-out without per-receiver state in the transport layer and avoids TCP's head-of-line blocking. Applications build their own sequence checks, gap detectors, and repair strategies that are tuned to their domain.

**Internal control, admin, and management.**

For configuration, health checks, and other administrative traffic, the choice is usually guided by convenience and robustness rather than nanoseconds. TCP is often the default, because:

- Reliability matters more than raw latency.
- The volume is low, so overhead is unimportant.
- Existing libraries and tools expect a stream abstraction.

The key design principle is segregation: keep these channels logically or physically separated from latency-critical flows so they do not interfere or get caught up in the same queues.

## Avoiding Pathological Interactions

Certain combinations of protocol settings and exchange behaviors can produce ugly emergent effects. A few to watch for:

**Nagle's algorithm and delayed ACKs.**

Nagle's algorithm coalesces small TCP writes into larger packets to improve efficiency. Delayed acknowledgements let the peer avoid sending too many ACKs. In high-frequency trading, both can introduce unnecessary delay:

- An application that sends many tiny messages may find them batched.
- The peer may wait before sending an ACK, holding back progression of the stream.

Order entry libraries and gateways typically disable Nagle's algorithm and tune ACK behavior where possible. As an architect, you should verify that your stacks and middleware do so.

**Exchange throttling and TCP backoff.**

Exchanges often enforce rate limits. If you send too many messages, they may:

- Drop excess messages.
- Delay responses.
- Disconnect or penalize the session.

If these behaviors coincide with network-level drops, TCP may interpret them as congestion. The combination can yield sharp, nonlinear changes in effective throughput and latency. It is important to distinguish:

- Network congestion and losses, which your network engineers can address.
- Exchange throttling behavior, which must be handled by your trading logic and order throttles.

Instrument your system to see where delays actually originate: the network, the TCP stack, or the far-end application.

**UDP flood and invisible congestion.**

On the UDP side, the main risk is unregulated sending. Because UDP provides no built-in flow or congestion control, it is possible for an aggressive sender to saturate links or overwhelm receivers without any automatic brake.

In a trading environment, this can happen when:

- An internal publisher misbehaves and blasts messages faster than the network can carry them.
- A misconfigured replay tool or recovery channel floods traffic onto a shared path.

Switches respond with queuing and drops; receivers see gaps they must repair. From the outside, it may simply look like "market data is bad." Good design includes:

- Rate-limiting and sanity checks on internal publishers.
- Dedicated or bandwidth-reserved paths for critical UDP feeds.
- Monitoring of drop counters and queue depths at key aggregation points.

## Design Patterns: Choosing Transports Intentionally

Putting everything together, practitioners often adopt a simple rule of thumb:

> UDP for hot data; TCP for state and control.

"Hot data" means information that:

- Is time-sensitive and rapidly changing (quotes, books, certain risk metrics).
- Can be reconstructed or repaired from newer data if small pieces are lost.

"State and control" covers flows where:

- Every message must be accounted for (orders, cancels, trades).
- The stream represents a shared state machine that both sides must agree on.

This is not a rigid rule—there are exceptions and hybrid designs—but it is a useful starting point.

As you design your trading system's network architecture, ask explicitly for each channel:

1. What happens if one message is lost?
2. What happens if several are delayed?
3. Does the receiver need strict ordering?
4. Is it better to skip ahead to newer information, or must we wait?

If the answers emphasize timeliness and tolerance for occasional gaps, favor UDP with application-level recovery. If they emphasize completeness and consistency, favor TCP with careful tuning.

Finally, remember that protocol choice does not stand alone. The IP, UDP, or TCP headers ride on top of the physical paths and switches discussed earlier. Your real-world latency is the sum of:

- Propagation and serialization delay in the chosen medium.
- Switch processing and queuing behavior along the route.
- Transport-layer semantics—retransmissions, head-of-line blocking, congestion reactions.
- Application-level sequencing, recovery, and throttling logic.

Understanding the trade-offs between IP, UDP, and TCP gives you control over one of these layers. In the next sections, we will see how multicast distribution and co-location layouts interact with these protocol choices to further shape the latency profile of your trading system.

## 5.4 Multicast Market Data Distribution

So far in this chapter, we have treated packets mostly as point-to-point: an order message from your gateway to an exchange over TCP, or a

UDP datagram from one internal component to another. Market data behaves differently. An exchange publishes each update once, but hundreds of firms and thousands of servers may need to see it at nearly the same time. Sending a separate copy to each consumer would be wasteful and slow.

Multicast exists to solve this problem. It lets a single sender transmit one stream of packets that the network efficiently replicates only where needed. Used well, multicast is a powerful tool for low-latency market data; used poorly, it becomes a source of mysterious gaps, inconsistent books, and hard-to-diagnose performance issues.

This section follows a multicast packet from the exchange's publisher through routers and switches into your trading servers. Along the way we will see where latency and loss can creep in, and how design choices around subscription, routing, and recovery shape both timeliness (how fast you see the data) and consistency (whether your engines see the same data in the same order).

## Multicast Basics: One Stream, Many Subscribers

Recall from the previous section that most market data is carried over UDP. UDP does not maintain connections and does not guarantee delivery, but it offers low overhead and does not impose extra retransmission or ordering behavior. Multicast builds on UDP and IP by adding a group addressing model.

**Multicast groups.**

Instead of sending to a unicast IP address (one host) or broadcast address (everyone on a segment), the publisher sends to a *multicast* IP address, often in a special range reserved for this purpose. Each multicast address represents a *group*. Any host that "joins" the group will receive packets sent to that group, as long as the network between them is configured correctly.

For example, an exchange might define:

- Group G1: equity top-of-book feed.
- Group G2: equity depth-of-book A-M.

- Group G3: equity depth-of-book N-Z.

Your feed handlers subscribe only to the groups they care about; the network ensures that only those packets reach the relevant servers.

**Why multicast is a good fit for market data.**

This model aligns well with exchange feeds:

- **One-to-many by default:** The exchange emits a single packet; many firms receive it.
- **Bandwidth efficiency:** The network replicates packets only where paths diverge, rather than all the way from source to each destination.
- **Timeliness:** All receivers see the same packet nearly simultaneously, limited mainly by propagation and local switching.

However, achieving this in a real network requires coordination between endpoints and infrastructure. Two protocols are central: IGMP and PIM-SM.

## Joining the Group: IGMP on the Edge

IGMP (Internet Group Management Protocol) is how hosts tell local switches and routers, "I want to receive traffic for multicast group X." It operates on the edge of the network, between servers and their first-hop switches.

**How IGMP works in practice.**

At a high level:

- When a feed handler wants to subscribe to a multicast group, the OS sends an IGMP *join* message for that group out of its network interface.
- The directly attached switch or router receives this join and updates its state to say "on this port, there is at least one listener for group G."

- Periodically, IGMP *queries* and *reports* refresh this state so that the network can prune groups when no one is listening.

You rarely interact with IGMP directly; your market data software calls standard socket APIs to join a multicast group, and the OS does the rest. But understanding that IGMP is the "subscription signaling" is important when you configure your switches.

**IGMP snooping on switches.**

Layer-2 switches cannot run IP routing protocols, but they still need to know which ports should receive which multicast streams. Without multicast awareness, a switch might flood multicast packets out of all ports in a VLAN, wasting bandwidth and exposing unwanted traffic to hosts that do not care.

IGMP snooping solves this:

- The switch listens ("snoops") for IGMP join and leave messages from hosts.
- It builds a table mapping multicast groups to the specific ports that have subscribers.
- It forwards market data packets only to those interested ports, rather than flooding them everywhere.

For a trading floor, correctly configured IGMP snooping is critical. It reduces noise on non-trading servers, prevents accidental overload of links, and ensures that adding a new consumer does not suddenly change the behavior of unrelated ports.

## Building the Multicast Tree: PIM-SM in the Core

While IGMP runs between hosts and their first-hop devices, PIM (Protocol Independent Multicast) runs between routers in the wider network. In financial networks, the most commonly used mode is PIM Sparse Mode (PIM-SM).

**The idea of a multicast distribution tree.**

Imagine the path from an exchange's market data publisher to multiple trading firms:

- Near the exchange, a core router injects the multicast stream into the network.
- As packets flow outwards, routers replicate them only when necessary, feeding downstream routers that have listeners.
- The result is a *tree* rooted at the publisher and branching out to all subscribers.

PIM-SM is a control protocol that builds and maintains these trees:

- Routers that have downstream listeners (learned via IGMP or other mechanisms) send *join* messages upstream toward a designated rendezvous point or directly toward the source.
- As joins propagate, routers create state for the group, indicating on which interfaces to forward incoming packets.
- If all downstream listeners on a branch go away, routers send *prune* messages, trimming the tree.

In steady state, each multicast packet from the exchange follows a precomputed path through core routers, being copied only where needed.

**Sparse mode and why it matters.**

The "sparse" in PIM-SM reflects an assumption that only a small subset of the network wants any given multicast group. This fits market data well:

- Not every firm subscribes to every exchange or product.
- Within a firm, not every data center or subnet needs every feed.

Sparse mode avoids flooding the network with market data for which there are no listeners. It also makes the behavior more predictable: packets only traverse links that have been explicitly requested by joins.

# End-to-End Picture: Exchange to Engines

Diagrammatic representation:

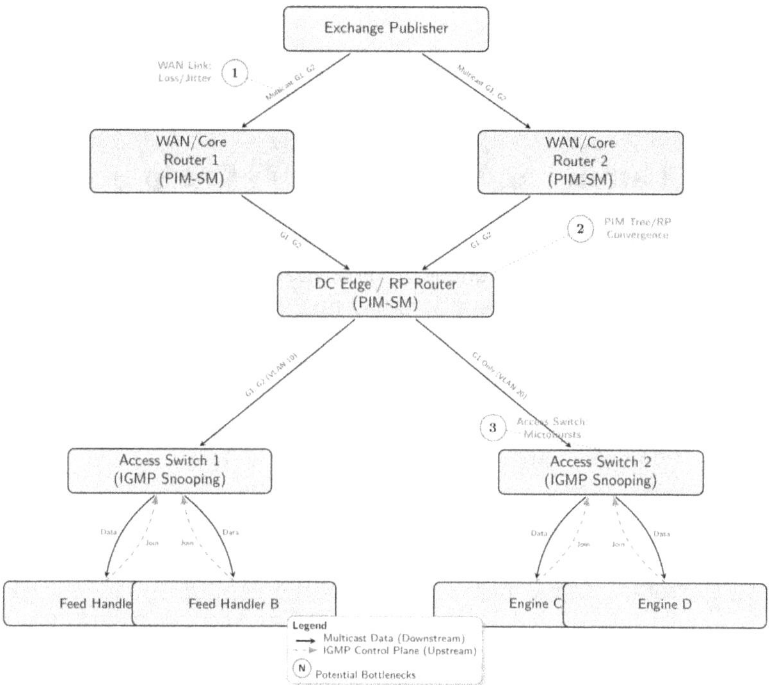


From left to right:

- The exchange publisher injects packets for groups G1 and G2 into its upstream router.
- Core routers run PIM-SM to form a multicast tree toward the data center edge router.
- The data center edge router feeds one or more "market data" VLANs on access switches.
- Access switches, using IGMP snooping, forward packets only to ports whose servers have joined those groups.

- Individual feed handlers and trading engines receive the packets, reconstruct order books, and drive strategies.

At each stage—WAN links, core routers, access switches—there are potential loss and latency points. Understanding where your tree runs and where replication happens helps you place monitoring and design redundancy.

## Where Latency and Inconsistency Creep In

Multicast itself does not guarantee that all receivers see packets at the same time, or at all. Differences in path length, queuing, and local configuration can create systematic skews and gaps.

**Path asymmetry and extra hops.**

Two servers in different data centers may subscribe to the same group, but their packets may travel through different sequences of routers and switches. One path might:

- Use a shorter, lower-congestion WAN route.
- Traverse fewer switches in the data center.

The result is a persistent latency skew: one engine systematically sees market data a few microseconds or tens of microseconds earlier than another, even though both are "subscribed to the same feed." In arbitrage strategies, this can be a significant competitive difference.

**Microbursts at fan-out points.**

As discussed in the switching section, points where a multicast stream fans out—such as access switches feeding many servers—are prone to microbursts. When the exchange emits a burst of updates, the access switch must replicate packets to many ports:

- Its internal fabric and egress queues may briefly saturate.
- Queuing delays and even drops occur on some egress ports but not others, depending on load and hierarchy.

Thus, two servers on different ports of the same switch may see slightly different loss patterns or latencies during stress events. Careful design (for example, spreading load, sizing buffers, and limiting oversubscription) is needed to keep this under control.

**Multicast tree changes and failovers.**

When a link or router fails, PIM-SM reroutes the multicast tree. Ideally, this happens quickly and cleanly, but in real networks, transient effects occur:

- Brief interruptions in packet flow while the tree reconverges.
- Short "loops" or duplication of packets as state changes.
- Temporary use of a longer or more congested path, increasing latency.

If you have redundant market data paths (for example, primary and secondary feeds), your architecture must decide how to arbitrate between them during such events. Without careful logic, you can end up with inconsistent views across engines or oscillations between feeds.

## Exchange Feed Topologies and Recovery Channels

Exchanges design their multicast feeds with both timeliness and recoverability in mind. Understanding these designs helps you build effective recovery and arbitration strategies.

**Primary and secondary feeds.**

A common pattern is:

- **Primary feed:** Main multicast stream, lowest latency under normal conditions.
- **Secondary feed:** Independent or partially independent stream carrying the same data, sometimes via a different physical path or data center.

Your systems can:

- Subscribe to both feeds.
- Prefer the primary under normal conditions.
- Fail over to the secondary if the primary degrades or fails.

The art lies in deciding what constitutes "degrades"—small, recoverable gaps versus sustained loss or outages—and how to avoid flip-flopping between feeds in marginal conditions.

**Gap-fill and replay channels.**

Because UDP multicast does not retransmit lost packets, exchanges often provide mechanisms to repair gaps:

- **Gap-fill channels:** Unicast or multicast streams that respond to explicit requests for missing sequence ranges.
- **Replay services:** Out-of-band channels that can replay a window of recent messages for a given instrument or feed.

Your feed handler typically:

- Tracks sequence numbers in the live multicast stream.
- Detects when a gap appears (for example, it jumps from sequence 100 to 103).
- Requests the missing packets via a gap-fill or replay channel.

There is an inherent trade-off:

- **Aggressive repair:** Immediately request and wait for gap-fill packets, ensuring a fully consistent book but accepting added latency while gaps are repaired.
- **Lenient repair:** Continue to process newer multicast packets while gaps are being repaired, accepting temporary inconsistency in favor of timeliness.

Different strategies may be appropriate for different business uses—ultra-low-latency strategies versus analytics and surveillance, for example.

**Forward error correction (FEC).**

Some feeds incorporate forward error correction, where redundancy is built into the stream so that certain patterns of packet loss can be corrected without explicit retransmissions. FEC:

- Reduces the need for separate gap-fill requests.
- Increases per-packet overhead (more bytes on the wire).
- Adds CPU cost in the receiver to reconstruct missing data.

For most firms, the choice to use a feed's FEC options is a balance between robustness and resource usage. From a latency standpoint, FEC can avoid the larger delays associated with out-of-band replay, but it does not eliminate the impact of severe burst loss.

## Local Distribution and In-House Architecture

Once market data enters your data center, you typically do not feed it directly from the border router to every trading engine. Instead, you construct an in-house distribution layer.

**Feed handlers and normalizers.**

Dedicated feed handler processes:

- Subscribe to the raw exchange multicast groups.
- Decode the binary protocols and normalize them into internal formats.
- Apply gap detection and recovery using exchange-provided channels.

These feed handlers then publish cleaned, normalized data onward—often using internal multicast (again over UDP) or specialized messaging buses. This splits responsibilities:

- The outer edge and feed handlers manage protocol quirks and loss recovery.
- Trading engines consume already coherent internal feeds, simplifying their logic.

**Internal multicast vs. unicast distribution.**

For distribution inside your firm, you can:

- **Use multicast again:** Feed handlers publish to internal multicast groups per asset class or venue. This preserves the bandwidth efficiency and simultaneous delivery properties of multicast.
- **Use unicast or a message bus:** Engines connect to a central hub or bus, which dispatches messages individually.

Multicast remains attractive when:

- Many engines in the same segment need the same data.
- You want to keep latency low and predictable.
- Your network team is comfortable managing IGMP and PIM inside the data center.

Buses or unicast distribution can be easier to reason about and debug, but may introduce extra hops, queueing, and per-subscriber load on the publisher.

**Sequence arbitration across paths.**

Many firms subscribe to multiple sources for the ”same” market data:

- Direct exchange multicast.
- A consolidated or normalized feed from a vendor.
- A backup path or physically diverse link.

An arbitration layer compares arriving messages, chooses the earliest reliable view, and fills gaps from slower or secondary sources. This layer must be designed with clear rules to avoid pathological behaviors like:

- Constantly flipping between feeds due to minor timing differences.
- Introducing re-ordering that confuses downstream engines.

Done well, arbitration can give you both low latency (using the fastest path) and robustness (falling back when that path falters).

## Design Patterns for Robust, Low-Latency Multicast

Putting all of this together, we can outline some practical design patterns.

**Dedicated market data VLANs and fabrics.**

Separate market data from other traffic:

- Use dedicated VLANs and, where justified, dedicated switches for multicast feeds.
- Avoid mixing heavy east-west bulk traffic with your feed VLANs.
- Apply QoS to prioritize market data on shared links.

This reduces the chance that unrelated traffic causes microbursts and drops on your market data paths.

**Careful IGMP configuration.**

On access switches:

- Enable IGMP snooping for the relevant VLANs.
- Configure IGMP queriers so that membership state is maintained even if the upstream router is quiet.

- Validate that only intended ports receive each multicast group.

Misconfigured IGMP can lead to flooding (wasting bandwidth and creating hidden load) or, worse, absence of data on ports that think they are subscribed.

**Monitoring at tree branch points.**

Instrument the key fan-out locations:

- WAN edges where exchange feeds enter your environment.
- Core-to-access links where multicast streams are replicated.
- Access switches with many subscribing servers.

Monitor:

- Packet and byte counters per group or per interface.
- Drop counters and buffer utilization.
- Latency and skew measurements between multiple feed handlers.

This lets you distinguish between exchange-side issues, WAN problems, and local switch overload.

**Well-defined recovery and failover policies.**

Clarify in design documents:

- When to trigger gap-fill requests, and how long to wait.
- When to fail over from primary to secondary feeds.
- How to arbitrate between multiple sources while preserving a consistent sequence view.

These rules should be tuned and tested using replayed historical stress events, not just calm days. The goal is to avoid improvisation during live market incidents.

**Testing under realistic burst conditions.**

Finally, remember that multicast behavior under stress is different from behavior at idle:

- Simulate exchange-like bursts into your environment.
- Observe how queues, drops, and recovery behave.
- Verify that all subscribing servers remain synchronized to within acceptable tolerances.

In doing so, you are not just checking raw throughput; you are ensuring that the delicate interplay of multicast routing, switching, and application-level recovery delivers both *timely* and *consistent* data to the engines that make trading decisions.

Multicast market data distribution is, in many ways, where all the themes of this chapter converge: physical paths, switch behavior, and transport semantics. A well-designed multicast architecture acknowledges the physics, respects the bottlenecks inside switches, and uses protocol mechanisms like IGMP and PIM-SM to build predictable trees. From there, the application layer takes on the final responsibility: turning a best-effort multicast stream into a coherent, low-latency view of the market.

## 5.5 Co-Location and Cross-Connects

The previous sections treated latency at the scale of cities and networks: how far light has to travel, how switches buffer packets, and how protocols deliver or delay them. Co-location brings the same questions into a much smaller space. Inside an exchange's data center, distance is measured not in kilometers but in racks and rows—yet those distances still translate directly into microseconds.

Co-location is often marketed as a flat commodity: "You are in the building, you are close." In reality, your exact cage location, the path your cross-connects take, and the way your patching is implemented can create stable, measurable differences in one-way latency between you and your competitors. This section examines those mechanisms and how to design for deterministic, repeatable performance.

## From Building to Rack: Shrinking the Scale, Not the Physics

Inside an exchange co-location facility, three physical elements matter most:

- **Cages and racks:** Where your servers sit relative to the exchange matching engines and meet-me rooms.
- **Cross-connects:** The dedicated cabling between your cage and the exchange or other providers.
- **Patching and jumpers:** The local cabling inside and between racks, patch panels, and distribution frames.

The same rule of thumb from earlier applies: in glass, every additional 200 meters of fiber costs you roughly one microsecond of latency. In a single building you will not see hundreds of meters in one hop, but a few tens of meters here and there add up. Because these distances are fixed, they create systematic, not random, advantages or penalties.

## Cage Placement and Raw Fiber Length

When you sign a co-location agreement with an exchange, you are assigned one or more cages—secure spaces where your racks will be installed. The exchange's own matching engine infrastructure also sits in cages, sometimes grouped in "primary" and "secondary" zones.

**Near vs. far cages.**

A simplified mental picture:

- Cages in the same row or adjacent row to the matching engines may require only a short run of fiber to reach the relevant cross-connect frame.

- Cages on the far side of the hall, or in a separate suite, may require a longer path via overhead trays or underfloor conduits, often zigzagging around other infrastructure.

The difference between a 20-meter and an 80-meter physical path is small in absolute terms but measurable:

- 20 meters of single-mode fiber costs you only a fraction of a microsecond.
- 80 meters costs you roughly four times as much—still submicrosecond, but no longer negligible against an ultra-tight budget.

Across an entire cross-connect path—including cage to meet-me room, meet-me room to exchange cage, and internal patching—these differences can easily grow to a few hundred meters. The result is stable latency differences on the order of one or several microseconds between firms.

**Multiple cages and internal topology.**

As your footprint grows, you may occupy multiple cages in the same facility. How you arrange your internal connectivity then matters:

- A "hub" cage that houses core switches and risk engines may be closer to the exchange cross-connect frames than remote "spoke" cages.
- Traffic from servers in spoke cages must travel extra fiber distance to reach the hub, then onward to the exchange.

If latency-critical strategies run in spoke cages, they inherit the additional distance; if they run in the hub, they stay closer to the matching engine. Placing the right workloads in the right cages is therefore an architectural decision, not just a capacity one.

## Cross-Connects: The Lifelines to the Exchange

A *cross-connect* is the physical link that ties your cage to the exchange's infrastructure or to another party (such as a carrier or vendor) inside the same building. It usually consists of:

- One or more strands of fiber (single-mode or multi-mode, depending on the handoff).
- Terminations on patch panels in your cage and at the meet-me room or exchange frame.
- Intermediate distribution frames or trays that route the fiber physically.

From a latency perspective, you care about both the type of fiber and the route it takes.

**Single-mode vs. multi-mode.**

Many modern exchange facilities standardize on single-mode fiber for cross-connects:

- Single-mode supports longer distances and higher bandwidths with lower dispersion.
- Latency per meter is slightly better and more stable than in some multi-mode deployments.

Multi-mode fiber may still appear in shorter intra-rack or intra-row connections, especially when using certain legacy optics. When you negotiate cross-connects, clarifying the media used and ensuring consistency across your critical paths avoids unnecessary variability.

**Number of paths and redundancy.**

Most firms order at least two cross-connects to an exchange:

- For redundancy: if one fiber is cut or one interface fails, the other can take over.
- For functional separation: market data on one, order entry on the other, for example.

These paths are not necessarily identical:

- They may run through different trays or physical routes to avoid common points of failure.
- The exchange may land them in different meet-me rooms or frames.

From a resilience standpoint this is desirable; from a latency standpoint, it means your "A" and "B" cross-connects can have slightly different propagation delays. Your architecture must know and account for this when measuring and comparing one-way times.

**The cross-connect lifecycle.**

Ordering and installing a cross-connect typically involves:

1. **Request:** You submit a cross-connect order specifying endpoints, media, and counts.
2. **Design:** The facility operator plans the route, assigns fibers, and updates records.
3. **Install:** Technicians pull and terminate the fiber, patching it into your cage and the remote frame.
4. **Test:** Basic continuity and power levels are checked; sometimes latency is measured.

For low-latency trading, you should go beyond basic tests:

- Ask for as-built documentation that describes the path length and intermediate points.
- Independently measure latency over the new cross-connect using test packets.
- Compare the observed latency to what you would expect from the claimed distance.

Discrepancies can reveal extra detours, mispatches, or inadvertent insertion of devices (for example, media converters or network taps) that were not in your plan.

## Patching, Jumpers, and Hidden Loops

Within your cage, and between cages and meet-me rooms, many short cable segments are used to connect servers, switches, and cross-connect panels. These are often treated as mere plumbing, but they, too, add distance and opportunities for error.

**Inside the cage.**

Typical elements include:

- Patch panels at the top or side of racks.
- Fiber patch cords from those panels down to individual server NICs or ToR switches.
- Cross-patching between racks to distribute feeds or interconnect switches.

Each patch cord may be only a few meters long, but routing can be indirect: up to a panel, across a horizontal manager, down to another device, and back. A conservative design minimizes:

- The number of intermediate panels a signal must traverse between server and cross-connect.
- The total length of patching needed to reach critical gear.

A single extra 10-meter jumper may not hurt, but dozens of such decisions across a complex cage add measurable propagation delay.

**Between cage and meet-me room.**

The path from your cage patch panel to the meet-me room usually involves:

- Horizontal or vertical trunk cables running in cable trays.
- Slack loops for maintainability.
- Intermediate consolidation points or splice enclosures.

From a generic facility point of view, all of this is standard practice. From a trading architect's perspective, it is part of the latency budget. Facilities sometimes use generous slack to simplify future moves, adds, and changes; you may be able to negotiate tighter slack practices on your critical cross-connects.

**Hidden loops and "shortcuts" that are not.**

Occasionally, operational convenience leads to surprising layouts:

- A cross-connect is temporarily patched through an intermediate panel during maintenance and never restored to the shorter route.
- A jump is added between two distribution frames rather than running a new direct link.

Each such "shortcut" can add tens of meters. Over time, these accumulate into routes that are materially longer than the original design. Regular audits—both of physical cabling and of measured latency—are essential to keep your co-location environment aligned with your latency goals.

## Measuring and Verifying Physical Paths

Good design starts on paper, but reality must be verified. Two families of tools help you understand and control actual physical paths: optical measurement and time-based measurement.

**Optical time-domain reflectometry (OTDR).**

An OTDR injects pulses of light into a fiber and measures reflections to build a profile of the fiber:

- It can estimate total fiber length with good precision.
- It can locate splices, connectors, and defects along the path.
- It can reveal unexpected extra distance or additional segments.

Using OTDR measurements on new or suspect cross-connects lets you compare claimed vs. actual length. For example, if a run was specified as 60 meters but the OTDR shows 120 meters, you know there is additional path you did not account for.

**Packet-based latency tests.**

Ultimately, what matters is how long it takes your packets to traverse the path. You can measure this by:

- Sending test traffic between two endpoints and timestamping at both ends using synchronized clocks.
- Measuring one-way latency and round-trip latency during quiet periods to approximate propagation and device delay.
- Repeating measurements over time to detect drift or step changes.

When you combine OTDR and packet measurements, you can isolate:

- Pure propagation delay due to fiber length.
- Additional device or queuing delays introduced by NICs, switches, or transponders.

This gives you a strong basis to push back if actual performance diverges from what a facility or vendor has sold you.

## Negotiating and Designing for Optimal Placement

Co-location layout is rarely under your complete control, but you often have more flexibility than you might think, especially when you are a significant customer or early tenant in a new facility.

**Cage location as a design variable.**

When selecting cage locations:

- Request maps that show where exchange matching engines, meet-me rooms, and core network gear are physically located.
- Prefer cages that minimize path length to the most critical counterparties, not just those that are convenient for power or cooling.

- Consider future growth: if you expect to add racks, can you expand in the same row rather than getting a distant second cage?

In competitive environments, some venues explicitly offer "latency tiers" based on distance. Even where they do not, de facto tiers can arise: early tenants get closer cages; later ones end up further away.

**Designing internal layouts for latency.**

Inside your cages, treat cabling layout as part of system architecture:

- Place latency-critical servers (for example, order gateways, key strategies) as close as possible, in terms of cabling, to the cross-connect landing points and ToR switches.
- Separate bulk or less time-sensitive servers to racks that can afford slightly longer paths.
- Document standard patching patterns and enforce them, avoiding ad-hoc solutions that increase distance and complexity.

Your internal topology should have clear "fast lanes" that minimize the number of hops and the length of cables between market data ingress, trading engines, and order egress.

## Repeatability and Determinism as Design Goals

A crucial distinction in co-location design is between random jitter and systematic skew:

- **Random jitter** comes from bursty queues, variable processor scheduling, and transient network conditions.
- **Systematic skew** comes from fixed differences in path length and device behavior.

By engineering cages, cross-connects, and patching carefully, you aim to:

- Minimize systematic skew against competitors: do not give away microseconds simply by being physically further without good reason.
- Make whatever skew remains deliberate and documented (for example, backup paths that are knowingly longer).
- Ensure that paths used for comparing signals (for example, across venues) are matched as closely as practical in length and device count.

Deterministic latency is not just about being fast; it is about being predictable. A trading strategy can adapt to a known, stable delay; it struggles with a delay that varies widely with each packet.

## Operational Practices to Preserve Latency Edges

Once you have designed an optimal co-location layout, you must maintain it over time. Day-to-day operations can quietly erode a carefully crafted latency edge.

**Change control for physical paths.**

Treat changes to cabling, patch panels, and cross-connects with the same discipline as changes to production code:

- Record every change in a structured inventory.
- Capture before/after diagrams and, where possible, before/after latency measurements.
- Avoid "temporary" workarounds that are left in place and gradually become permanent.

This reduces the risk that a late-night fix introduces an unnoticed extra 50 meters of cable on a critical path.

**Labeling and documentation.**

Good labeling:

- Helps technicians follow designed paths rather than invent new ones on the fly.
- Simplifies audits and troubleshooting when anomalies appear.
- Makes it possible to reason about which links are truly equivalent in length and behavior.

Your documentation should make it easy to answer questions like "Which fibers connect this specific server NIC to the exchange order entry port, and what is their total length?"

**Periodic audits and benchmarking.**

Over months and years, facilities evolve: new tenants arrive, new cross-connects are pulled, and infrastructure is rearranged. Periodic reviews help you stay ahead:

- Re-measure key path latencies and compare them to historical baselines.
- Spot-check OTDR measurements on selected cross-connects.
- Confirm that your cage layout and patching still match your documented design.

These practices catch gradual drift and protect the investments you have made in co-location.

## Co-Location as an Engineered Asset

Seen through this lens, co-location is not a binary attribute—"in" the exchange or not—but an engineered asset:

- The building provides an outer shell of proximity.
- Your cage location and cross-connect paths determine your baseline physical delay to the matching engine.
- Your internal patching and equipment placement determine how much of that baseline advantage is preserved or squandered.

Firms that treat these details as core architecture, rather than as facilities trivia, are able to achieve latency that is not only low but also documented, defendable, and repeatable. That, in turn, allows quantitative strategies to be calibrated against realistic assumptions and enables informed trade-offs when, later in the chapter, we introduce route diversity and disaster-recovery designs that add extra microseconds in exchange for resilience.

Physical placement inside an exchange data center is one of the few aspects of latency you can truly fix in place. Once you have secured and verified an optimal configuration of cages, cross-connects, and patching, that edge is baked into your infrastructure. The remaining challenge, addressed in the next section, is deciding when and how to deviate from the absolutely shortest path in order to survive failures and regional disruptions without losing your ability to trade.

## 5.6 Route Diversity and Disaster Scenarios

Up to this point, we have treated latency as something to be minimized: shorter fiber, faster media, fewer switches, smarter protocols, closer cages. In production trading systems, there is a second, equally important dimension: your ability to keep trading when the world misbehaves.

Fiber gets cut. Power grids fail. Exchange data centers evacuate. Microwave towers ice over. In those moments, the "best" single path—the absolutely shortest, cleanest route—may disappear or become unstable. A robust architecture accepts a small latency penalty *up front* in exchange for survivability *when* (not if) these events occur.

This section examines how to design redundant physical and logical paths—over fiber, microwave, and even satellite or Internet backbones—that jointly optimize two objectives:

- Ultra-low latency in the normal case.
- Graceful degradation, not sudden failure, in disaster scenarios.

## What Failure Looks Like on the Wire

Before designing for resilience, it is helpful to visualize what failures look like from the point of view of packets and trading engines.

**Fiber cuts and local infrastructure damage.**

Fiber routes can be disrupted by:

- Construction accidents (roadworks, digging).
- Fires or flooding in conduits or buildings.
- Equipment failures in intermediate huts or regeneration sites.

On your telemetry, this may appear as:

- A sudden jump from a stable low latency to no traffic at all.
- Rapid flapping (up/down) as devices attempt to fail over.
- Increased packet loss and error counts on specific interfaces.

If you have two "diverse" fiber paths that actually share the same physical conduit or bridge, both may fail simultaneously.

**Power events and data center outages.**

Regional power issues, cooling failures, or fires can:

- Knock out entire facilities, including your own cages and network equipment.
- Force exchanges to move matching engines to secondary sites.

From a packet point of view:

- Latency to the original site suddenly spikes or goes to zero.
- A new primary matching engine appears at a different physical location with different paths and latencies.

Your systems must recognize and adapt to these shifts without causing contradictory orders, stale quotes, or inconsistent risk views.

**Weather and line-of-sight media.**

Microwave and millimeter-wave links are sensitive to:

- Heavy rain and snow (rain fade).
- Fog and atmospheric conditions at certain frequencies.
- Ice accumulation or wind misaligning antennas.

Instead of hard failure, you may see:

- Gradual degradation of signal quality.
- Increased error correction overhead and jitter.
- Intermittent packet loss, leading to volatile effective latency.

These characteristics make microwave excellent for best-case latency but risky as your *only* path.

## Thinking in Path Portfolios, Not Single Links

A useful mental shift is to think of connectivity as a *portfolio of paths* instead of a single link. Much like in portfolio theory, you care about:

- Expected performance (latency, capacity).
- Correlation of failures between paths.
- Cost—in both capital and operational complexity.

Common path types include:

- **Primary low-latency fiber:** Shortest feasible glass route between two sites, often via a specialist provider.

- **Diverse fiber:** A second fiber path along genuinely different conduits, even if that route is longer.
- **Microwave / millimeter-wave:** Line-of-sight, near speed-of-light propagation, but weather-sensitive and lower bandwidth.
- **Satellite / Internet:** High-latency but widely available paths, usually last-resort for maintaining control and visibility.

The art is choosing which of these to combine, and how to orchestrate them, so that:

- Under normal conditions, you use the fastest path.
- When that path degrades, you can fail over to slower but stable alternatives.
- The failover process itself does not create chaos.

## Fiber Diversity: More Than a Different Provider Logo

Many firms assume they have "diverse" fiber simply because they buy from two different carriers. That is often an illusion. True diversity is physical, not contractual.

**Conduit and geography awareness.**

To assess fiber diversity between two locations:

- Obtain route diagrams and, where possible, right-of-way maps from providers.
- Look for shared infrastructure: same tunnels, bridges, river crossings, or utility ducts.
- Identify "choke points" where multiple providers must pass through the same narrow corridor.

Two fiber paths that both cross the same bridge over a river are not meaningfully diverse against a ship strike or bridge fire, even if they belong to different telecom brands.

**Operational independence.**

Consider also:

- Whether the paths share intermediate huts, power feeds, or regeneration sites.
- Whether field maintenance is contracted to the same crews, creating correlated human error risks.

The more independent the physical, electrical, and operational infrastructure, the more genuine the diversity.

**Latency vs. diversity trade-offs.**

Diverse routes are usually longer. For example:

- Primary fiber: near-geodesic path with aggressive slack minimization.
- Diverse fiber: more circuitous, using alternative highways or rights-of-way to avoid single points of failure.

This might add hundreds of microseconds one way over inter-city distances. The strategic question is:

> Is it worth accepting an extra half-millisecond on the backup path to survive a plausible regional cut that would destroy the primary?

For most serious trading operations, the answer is "yes"—as long as systems know which path is which and transition deliberately.

## Microwave and Fiber: Complementary Strengths

Microwave and millimeter-wave links have very different failure profiles from buried fiber, making them natural complements.

**Latency and path geometry.**

Microwave routes:

- Track close to the great-circle path between two sites, minimizing distance.
- Propagate at near the speed of light in air, faster than in glass.

This often yields hundreds of microseconds advantage over commodity fiber between major financial centers. However, capacity is lower, and error characteristics are burstier under bad weather.

**Failure correlation.**

Microwave failures are driven by:

- Weather conditions along the line of sight.
- Tower or radio equipment failures.

They are much less correlated with:

- Backhoe fiber cuts underground.
- Fires in cable conduits.

Conversely, fiber is unaffected by rain fade but may be vulnerable to construction incidents that leave microwave untouched. Combining the two therefore reduces overall correlation of outages.

**Design pattern: microwave primary, fiber secondary.**

One common pattern is:

- Use microwave for latency-sensitive arbitrage or hedging flows.
- Use fiber for bulk data (snapshots, historical data) and as a lower-latency-but-slower fallback when microwave degrades.

Decisions to switch from microwave to fiber might be triggered by:

- Packet loss or error rates exceeding thresholds.
- Latency jitter exceeding what your strategies can tolerate.

The key is to separate *transport choice* from *trading logic*: do not let individual strategies make conflicting decisions about which path to trust in real time. Instead, centralize link health assessment and expose a clear, consistent view to consuming systems.

## Satellite and Internet: Last-Resort Lifelines

Satellite links and generic Internet-based VPNs are not competitive for low latency. Their value lies elsewhere:

- Maintaining situational awareness when primary paths are gone.
- Keeping risk, compliance, and operations systems in sync across regions.
- Providing a communication channel for controlled, reduced trading activity in disaster modes.

**Satellite characteristics.**

Classic geostationary satellites introduce hundreds of milliseconds of latency. Even lower-earth-orbit constellations are still much slower end-to-end than direct terrestrial links. But:

- They traverse fundamentally different infrastructure: ground stations and space segments, not local ducts and bridges.
- They can remain available when regional terrestrial infrastructure is heavily damaged.

That makes them an attractive *out-of-band* control and monitoring channel, even if they are unsuitable for production order flow in normal conditions.

**Internet paths and VPNs.**

Encrypted tunnels over the public Internet are:

- Highly variable in latency and jitter.
- Dependent on shared carrier backbones and peering agreements.

They are poor choices for primary trading paths but can be valuable as:

- Emergency channels for order cancellation in extreme events.
- Temporary conduits for low-frequency trading strategies when dedicated links are unavailable.

The design principle remains: understand and document what traffic is allowed to use these paths, and under which clearly defined modes (for example, "disaster recovery only").

## Active/Active vs. Active/Passive Topologies

Once you have multiple paths, you must decide how to use them structurally. Two archetypes dominate: active/active and active/passive.

**Active/active.**

In an active/active design:

- Multiple paths are used simultaneously.
- Traffic is split or load-balanced across them, sometimes by function.
- Systems continually compare results across paths.

Pros:

- Continuous validation of all paths under real traffic.
- Potential capacity gains and some latency-hedging (for example, use whichever venue or path is momentarily faster).

Cons:

- Complexity in ensuring consistent state across paths.
- Higher risk of subtle race conditions or duplicate actions if ordering and idempotency are not designed carefully.

For example, sending identical hedging orders over two paths simultaneously without careful de-duplication can double your exposure.

**Active/passive.**

In an active/passive design:

- One path ("primary") carries all or most production traffic.
- Secondary paths are kept warm-synchronized but not heavily used.
- Failover logic promotes a secondary to primary when needed.

Pros:

- Simpler reasoning about state and ordering.
- Easier enforcement of "single source of truth" for a given flow.

Cons:

- Passive paths may not be exercised enough; hidden issues may only appear under real load.
- Failover events can be disruptive if not regularly rehearsed.

A hybrid approach is often used: secondary paths carry real but non-critical traffic (for example, analytics, backtesting data) so they are continuously exercised without directly controlling live risk.

## Failover Mechanisms and Transient Dangers

The mechanics of switching from one path to another can be more dangerous than steady-state operations on either path.

**Routing convergence and flapping.**

Dynamic routing protocols (for example, BGP or interior gateway protocols) can be used to redirect traffic when a path fails. During convergence:

- Some packets may be black-holed (dropped) as routes update.
- Some flows may transiently take longer, suboptimal paths.
- If conditions oscillate (for example, flapping links), routes may churn.

At the trading application layer, this can produce:

- Brief periods of high loss or latency.
- Out-of-order deliveries across sessions.

To mitigate, many trading networks:

- Prefer simple, deterministic failover mechanisms at the edge (for example, explicit interface priorities) over complex dynamic routing in the core for critical flows.
- Use hold-down timers and hysteresis to avoid oscillation between paths.

**Application-level failover and duplication.**

Beyond the network, trading applications must handle:

- Reconnecting order sessions to new endpoints when exchanges fail over to backup data centers.
- Ensuring that orders are not submitted twice over two paths.
- Maintaining a consistent view of open positions and risk across locations.

Robust design typically includes:

- Unique identifiers and idempotency keys for orders, so duplicated messages can be recognized and ignored.
- Clear ownership of "who can trade" in each mode (for example, only one site is active for a given instrument at a time).
- Synchronization mechanisms to hand over books and risk snapshots between primary and DR sites.

## Latency-Aware Resilience Planning

Balancing speed and survivability is not an ad-hoc exercise; it should be documented and rehearsed like any other risk process.

**Documenting path budgets and roles.**

For each significant connectivity pair (for example, Colo A to Colo B, Firm DC to Exchange DC), maintain:

- A list of all paths (fiber, microwave, satellite/Internet) with:
  - Expected one-way and round-trip latency under normal conditions.
  - Physical diversity notes (shared conduits, bridges, towers).
  - Capacity limits and typical utilization.
- A designation of primary vs. secondary roles for each flow type (orders, market data, admin).

This gives you a clear baseline against which to detect anomalies and decide on failovers.

**Defining failure modes and responses.**

Enumerate realistic disaster scenarios:

- Single fiber cut on the primary path.
- Loss of one microwave tower or heavy weather on the RF path.
- Exchange primary data center outage with DR activation.
- Regional power grid event affecting multiple facilities.

For each scenario, specify:

- Which paths are expected to remain available.
- How trading modes change (for example, from full HFT to reduced-rate or manual trading).

- Which systems or humans are authorized to trigger mode changes.

**Rehearsing and measuring.**

Planned failover drills are the only safe way to discover many failure-mode bugs:

- Intentionally withdraw primary routes or bring down primary links during controlled windows.
- Observe failover times, packet loss patterns, and impact on strategy performance.
- Validate that systems do not send duplicate orders or lose track of positions.

Crucially, measure latency shifts during these drills. If moving from a 1.5 ms path to a 3.0 ms path, your systems should be aware of the new baseline and, if necessary, adjust thresholds or behaviors.

## Accepting Microseconds for Macro Resilience

The core message of this section is that pursuing the absolute lowest possible latency at all costs is shortsighted. A trading business must also survive:

- Routine infrastructure failures (fiber cuts, equipment faults).
- Less frequent, but severe, disasters (regional outages, natural disasters).

Well-designed route diversity and disaster scenarios:

- Accept small, bounded added latency (for example, a few microseconds for diverse cross-connects in a building, hundreds of microseconds for a longer inter-city backup path).
- Dramatically reduce the risk of complete loss of trading capability.

- Provide predictable behaviors under stress, which can be priced into strategies and risk models.

When you view connectivity as an engineered portfolio of paths, you can place each medium—fiber, microwave, satellite, Internet—in a role that matches its strengths:

- Microwave: latency edge in fair weather; monitored carefully; backed by fiber.
- Primary fiber: reliable, fast baseline; engineered for minimal slack and hops.
- Diverse fiber: consciously slower, but physically distinct safety net.
- Satellite/Internet: control and visibility channel of last resort.

In combination with the co-location, switching, and protocol choices discussed earlier in the chapter, this perspective completes the picture: your trading system's latency is not a single number, but a distribution shaped by design decisions across physical, network, and application layers—under both sunny skies and in the middle of the storm.

# Chapter 6

# Operating System, Hardware & Runtime

*In a sub-microsecond trading stack, the operating system and hardware are not just a platform-they are part of your code path. This chapter shows where latency hides in cores, caches, NUMA topologies, and the kernel itself, and how deliberate runtime design can turn a 'fast' strategy into a genuinely deterministic one.*

## 6.1 CPU Microarchitecture for Trading

At this point we have treated the trading system largely as a set of processes, threads, and messages flowing across networks and through operating system services. To push latency into the single-digit microsecond range, we must now zoom in further, down to the level of the CPU core itself. In this regime, your "hardware" is no longer a black box. The shape of your code determines how well the core's pipeline, caches, and branch predictor can do their jobs, and that in turn determines whether a given market event is turned into an order in a few hundred nanoseconds or in several microseconds.

Modern CPUs are incredibly fast in terms of raw clock speed, but they are also fragile in the sense that small missteps in code structure can cause large stalls. An L3 cache miss, a mispredicted branch in the hot path, or a load that depends on a value not yet ready can easily dominate your tick-to-trade budget. The goal of this section is to explain, in trading terms, how the CPU actually executes your code and which coding patterns cooperate with the silicon rather than fight it.

## Pipelines and Execution at the Nanosecond Scale

A modern trading server core is a deeply pipelined, superscalar, out-of-order machine. These terms sound abstract, but they all relate to a simple question: how many useful instructions can the core retire every clock cycle, and how often does something interrupt that flow?

- **Pipeline** means that the core breaks instruction processing into stages (roughly: fetch, decode, execute, write back). Many instructions are in different stages of this pipeline at the same time, like cars on an assembly line.
- **Superscalar** means the core can work on several instructions per cycle, as long as they do not depend on one another.
- **Out-of-order** means the core can execute instructions in a different order than they appear in your program, when doing so hides latencies and keeps its functional units busy.

When you read that a core runs at, say, 3.5 GHz, that translates to about 0.3 nanoseconds per cycle. In an ideal world, your hot order-handling loop might retire three or four simple instructions every cycle. In reality, various forms of latency—waiting for data from cache or memory, waiting for the result of an earlier instruction, or backing up the pipeline after a mispredicted branch—create gaps. Those gaps accumulate directly into your tick-to-trade latency.

One way to think about the pipeline is as a conveyor belt that you cannot easily stop and restart. Flushing and refilling it is expensive because many partially processed instructions are thrown away and must be fetched and decoded again. This is exactly what happens on a mispredicted branch: you discover that the pipeline has been doing work along the wrong path and must back up.

Pipelines also interact tightly with the memory hierarchy. The core can only execute on data that is already present in its registers and small caches. Fetching data from further away—from larger caches or main memory—takes many cycles. The out-of-order engine tries to keep other work going while it waits, but if the stalled instruction is on the critical path of your trading logic, that delay becomes visible as extra microseconds on the wire.

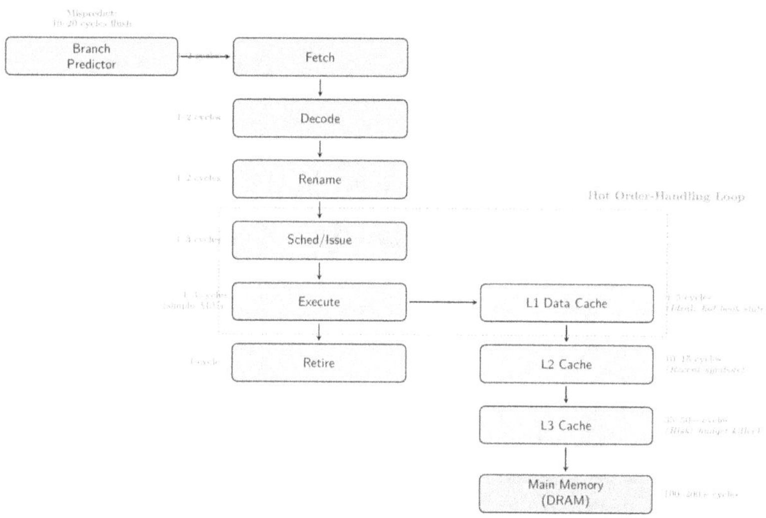


## Cache Hierarchies and Why Location Is Latency

To feed the pipeline, the core relies on several levels of cache. These are small, fast memories that sit between the registers and main RAM. The general structure on a trading server core is:

- A tiny **L1 cache** (data and instructions), very fast but only tens of kilobytes.
- A larger **L2 cache**, slower than L1 but still close to the core.
- A shared **L3 cache** (often called last-level cache) for the whole socket.

- Beyond that, **main memory** (DRAM), which is large but far away in latency terms.

From a latency perspective, each step down the hierarchy is a big jump. An L1 hit is a handful of cycles. L2 is perhaps a dozen cycles. L3 can be several dozen cycles. A trip to DRAM costs hundreds of cycles. At a few gigahertz, those hundreds of cycles are tens of nanoseconds to well over a hundred nanoseconds. Along a hot trading path that consists of only a few hundred instructions, even a single DRAM access can dominate total time.

A useful mental model is that of "rings of heat" around the core:

- Data you touch for almost every tick (order book state, current position, risk counters) should live in L1 if at all possible.
- Data you touch less often (per-symbol configuration, session state for less active markets) can spill into L2.
- Cold or rarely used data (config files, logs, rarely used error paths) should not sit in the caches you rely on for hot trading logic at all.

You cannot explicitly tell the CPU, "put this object in L1," but your data layout and access patterns strongly influence what naturally stays hot. Sequential access through arrays, tight structures without unnecessary padding, and stable access patterns encourage the hardware prefetchers to bring in the right cache lines before you need them.

In a trading context, this leads to several concrete guidelines:

- **Keep the hot working set small.** If your matching or routing logic needs to touch dozens of large objects to process one incoming tick, you are almost guaranteed to overflow L1 and L2. Strive to identify the few fields truly needed for the first trading decision and pack them together.
- **Prefer structures of arrays over arrays of structures when scanning.** If you frequently need one or two fields across many orders or symbols (for example, best bid/offer and last price), storing those fields contiguously allows the CPU to load many relevant values per cache line.

- **Avoid random pointer chasing in the hot path.** Following a chain of pointers (linked lists, tree nodes scattered across memory) often leads to one cache miss per step. A handful of such misses in sequence can add microseconds of delay under load.

Connecting this back to tick-to-trade: your effective latency is not only the sum of network and system delays; it is also the number of cache lines and memory locations you force the CPU to touch on the critical path. Every avoidable trip down the cache hierarchy is an opportunity to trim nanoseconds that add up across millions of ticks.

## Branch Prediction and Control Flow in Trading Code

The core's pipeline assumes it knows what you will do next. Branch instructions—"if this, do A, else do B"—break that flow. To keep the pipeline full, a dedicated branch predictor guesses which path you will take so that it can speculatively fetch and decode the next instructions ahead of time.

If the predictor guesses correctly, the pipeline continues smoothly. If it guesses wrong, the core must:

1. Throw away the speculative instructions it fetched along the wrong path.
2. Fetch and decode the correct path.
3. Refill the pipeline before it can retire useful work again.

This is the **branch misprediction penalty**, often on the order of ten to twenty cycles or more. A few mispredictions in an order-handling loop can turn a clean, sub-microsecond path into a noisy, multi-microsecond one, especially when combined with cache misses.

Trading code is full of branches:

- Message type dispatch: is this a quote update, a trade, an order acknowledgment?

- Symbol routing: which strategy instance or gateway should handle this symbol?
- Risk checks: is this order over the limit, out of band, or otherwise invalid?

The key is that not all branches are equally predictable.

Branches with a stable outcome (for example, a rare error condition that almost never triggers) are usually easy for the predictor. Branches that follow a regular pattern (for example, alternating in a simple periodic way) may also be handled well. But branches with outcomes that look random from the CPU's perspective—such as heavily interleaved symbols, fast-changing regimes, or dispatch on many message types—are much harder.

To cooperate with the branch predictor in your trading code:

- **Make common paths obvious and contiguous.** Arrange tests so that the most frequent case follows the fall-through path of the branch, and group related operations together. This reduces the number of instructions fetched on average and makes patterns more regular.
- **Replace branchy dispatch with table lookups where reasonable.** For example, instead of a long chain of "if message type is X," use an array or table indexed by message type that directly points to the handler. This often replaces several unpredictable branches with one index calculation and a predictable indirect load.
- **Avoid data-dependent deep nesting in the hot path.** Logic that branches multiple times on values that vary tick-to-tick can create a large, irregular decision tree. If possible, factor out rarely used branches into colder code or precompute certain decisions off the hot path.

In practice, one of the most effective exercises is to examine the control flow of your critical trading loop and ask: "If I were a branch predictor watching past behavior, would I be able to guess these outcomes?" When the answer is no, consider restructuring.

## Instruction-Level Parallelism: Doing More in the Same Time

Out-of-order cores extract **instruction-level parallelism** by executing independent instructions at the same time. For the trading engineer, this means that even if you cannot reduce the number of instructions, you can sometimes rearrange them or the data they operate on so that the core can overlap their execution.

Consider a simplified order handling sequence: parse message, look up symbol, check risk, build order, send. If each step strictly depends on the result of the previous one, the core must execute them nearly serially. But if parts of these tasks can proceed in parallel (for example, precomputing certain risk aggregates, or starting packet construction using fields already parsed while other fields are still loading), you create room for the out-of-order engine to hide latencies.

Some practical patterns that help:

- **Separate independent work.** If updating two independent pieces of state is required for each tick, try not to chain them through a single variable or lock. This allows the core to schedule them on different functional units.
- **Reduce long dependency chains.** A dependency chain is a sequence where each step uses the result of the previous one. Deep chains force the core to wait for a result before it can proceed. Sometimes, reordering calculations or precomputing partial results in a previous stage shortens these chains.
- **Exploit simple arithmetic and bit manipulations.** Operations like additions, subtractions, and simple bitwise checks are very fast and can often be scheduled around slower loads. If your hot path depends on complex operations (for example, expensive function calls) that could be simplified or approximated, doing so can free up parallel execution capacity.

Instruction-level parallelism does not change the logic of your trading algorithm; it changes how the hardware sees the scheduling opportunities inside that logic. Profiling tools that show pipeline stalls and issue width can help identify where the core is underutilized despite a busy thread.

## Coding Patterns That Respect the Silicon

Translating these microarchitectural concepts into day-to-day coding practice, several principles emerge for latency-sensitive trading paths.

### Design Data for the Cache, Not Just for the Programmer

The way you lay out data in memory is as important as the algorithms that operate on it.

- **Compact hot structures.** Identify the minimal subset of state required per symbol or per strategy instance to decide on an immediate reaction to a tick. Group those fields into a tight struct or array that fits comfortably within a few cache lines.
- **Align with cache lines.** While you should avoid thinking in terms of exact cache line addresses, it helps to know that cache lines are fixed-size blocks. Misaligned or scattered data can cause a single logical object to span multiple lines, increasing the number of loads required.
- **Avoid "object explosion" in the hot path.** Many small heap-allocated objects, especially when allocated and freed frequently, tend to be scattered in memory. This hurts both caches and TLBs (the address translation caches). Prefer contiguous storage (arrays, pools) where possible.

In a feed handler, for example, you might maintain a per-symbol structure that holds only the best bid/offer, last traded price, and a few flags. All richer analytics (full depth, derived indicators) can live elsewhere and be updated off the critical decision path.

### Flatten Control Flow Where It Matters Most

Deeply nested conditionals and large numbers of small functions in the hot path not only strain branch prediction but also create more instruction fetch pressure. While modular design is important, in the innermost trading loops you should aim for:

- **Few, well-understood branches.** Each branch should be either highly predictable or very important to take. For example, a single branch that checks whether the symbol is one of a small set of ultra-latency-sensitive instruments may be acceptable if its outcome is stable.
- **Inlined small helpers.** Common, tiny helper routines (such as simple parsers or encoders) are often better inlined so that the compiler can see and optimize the entire hot path, improving both pipeline scheduling and branch layout.
- **Early exits for unlikely paths.** Error and edge cases should, where possible, be handled via early exits to cold code, so that their instructions and data do not pollute caches needed by normal trading flow.

From a tick-to-trade perspective, you want the CPU to follow a short, straight, and predictable road for the majority of events, with rare detours for unusual conditions.

### Minimize Hidden Work in the Critical Path

Hidden work includes anything that the CPU must do implicitly before or after your visible code, often related to memory management or abstraction overhead.

- **Be cautious with abstractions that allocate.** Frequent dynamic allocations in the hot path (such as creating short-lived objects for each tick) can lead to allocator contention, cache churn, and unpredictable pause times.
- **Avoid unnecessary indirection.** Layers of virtual calls, callbacks, or generic wrappers can add branches and pointer dereferences that break cache locality and branch prediction. Some of this indirection may be worthwhile in colder layers of the system, but in the inner loops it is costly.
- **Understand your language runtime.** Garbage collection, JIT compilation, and other runtime services can introduce stops or background work. In truly latency-critical paths, prefer predictable, manual control over memory and execution timing,

even if that means using a more bare-bones subset of the language or a different language entirely for those components.

## Measuring When Microarchitecture Is the Bottleneck

Not every performance problem is microarchitectural. Sometimes the algorithm is simply doing too much work. Other times, the bottleneck is in the network or kernel. However, as your design matures and you isolate the trading hot path, microarchitecture often becomes the limiting factor.

To tell when this is the case, combine two perspectives:

- **Latency histograms at the application level.** Look at tick-to-trade distributions, especially the median versus the long tails. Sharp, discrete bumps often indicate particular stalls (for example, occasional trips to L3 or DRAM).
- **CPU performance counters.** Modern CPUs expose detailed counters for cache misses, branch mispredictions, pipeline bubbles, and more. Profiling tools can correlate these events with your code, showing you which lines or functions incur the most penalties.

If you see that your hot loop spends most cycles waiting on L3 or DRAM, then data layout and working set are likely culprits. If branch mispredictions spike in parts of the code that handle symbol dispatch or risk checks, you may need to redesign those decision trees. If the issue width is low and the core rarely executes more than one instruction per cycle despite low cache miss rates, instruction-level parallelism may be lacking.

A useful discipline for trading teams is to treat microbenchmarks of the core loop as first-class artifacts, much like unit tests. For each significant change in logic or data layout, validate how the change affects:

- cycles per tick in isolation,
- cache miss rates at each level,

- branch prediction accuracy,
- and the resulting impact on end-to-end tick-to-trade under realistic load.

By tying the behavior of the silicon back to familiar trading metrics, you build an intuition for how seemingly small code changes can promote or sabotage your latency goals.

## From Silicon Behavior to System Design Choices

While this section focused on a single core, the implications reach up into the broader trading system architecture described in earlier chapters. Decisions such as:

- how to partition symbols across processes,
- where to perform certain risk checks,
- how aggressively to precompute or cache results,
- and how to structure message formats

all influence how much data each core must touch per tick, how predictable the control flow is, and how often the hardware must recover from pipeline disruptions.

By understanding pipelines, caches, and branch predictors as concrete, measurable elements rather than mysterious internals, you can design trading systems that naturally align with the strengths of modern CPUs. Instead of constantly pushing against microarchitectural limits, your hot paths can flow with the grain of the hardware, turning nanosecond-scale advantages into meaningful improvements in real-world trading performance.

## 6.2 NUMA Awareness and Memory Bandwidth

In the previous section we looked inside a single core and saw how pipelines, caches, and branch predictors shape latency at the nanosecond scale. We treated the core as if it lived in isolation, with a private L1/L2/L3 hierarchy and a single pool of main memory. Real trading servers are more complex. They typically have multiple CPU sockets, each with its own set of cores and memory channels. From the operating system's point of view, there is one pool of RAM; from the hardware's point of view, that RAM is divided into regions that are "closer" to some cores than to others.

This non-uniform view of memory is called *NUMA*—Non-Uniform Memory Access. Understanding NUMA is essential once your trading system runs on multi-socket machines. If you ignore it, a hot trading thread can end up regularly fetching data from a remote socket's memory, silently injecting tens or hundreds of additional nanoseconds into every critical load. Over a tick-to-trade budget of only a few microseconds, that is a very expensive mistake.

### What NUMA Means in Practice

At a high level, a NUMA system works like this:

- Each CPU socket on the motherboard has its own local memory controllers and attached DIMMs. The physical RAM sticks are divided into *nodes*, typically one node per socket.
- All cores on a given socket can access the node's local memory through a short, wide path. This is the lowest-latency, highest-bandwidth route.
- Sockets are also connected to each other via interconnect links. A core on socket A can read or write memory physically attached to socket B, but that request has to travel across the interconnect, through socket B's memory controller, and back again.

- The operating system sees one combined memory space but internally tracks which pages belong to which node.

The key point is that a load from *local* memory is significantly faster than a load from *remote* memory. Similarly, the total bandwidth available to local memory is higher than what can be realistically sustained over the inter-socket links. For batch jobs this difference may be unimportant. For a latency-sensitive trading path, it is the difference between hitting your target and missing it.

When you allocate an object in your trading process, you normally do not think about where in physical memory it lives. On a NUMA system, the default is often "first touch": the memory page is allocated on the NUMA node of the core that first writes to it. This simple rule is helpful when your code is already well structured (threads mostly use data they initialize), but it can be disastrous when threads and data migrate across sockets.

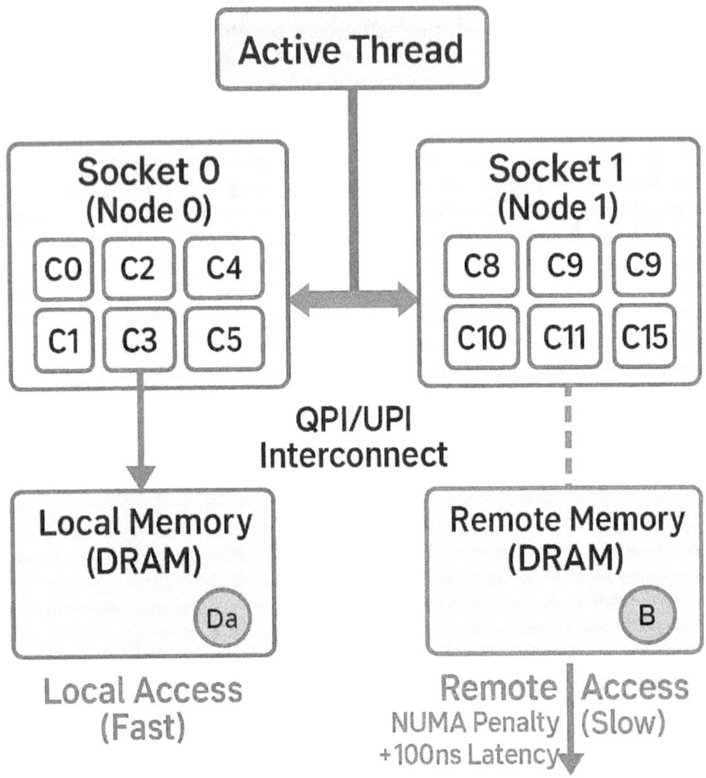


This simple picture already suggests the core design question for NUMA-aware trading systems: how do we make sure that each latency-critical thread mostly talks to "its own" memory and not to a distant bank across the interconnect?

## How Remote Memory Adds Microseconds

From the core's perspective, fetching data from main memory is already expensive compared with an L1 cache hit. On a multi-socket system, remote memory access adds an extra leg to that journey. The request must traverse:

1. The core's own internal caches (failing to find the data).
2. The socket's memory controller, which recognizes that the address belongs to another node.
3. The inter-socket link to the remote memory controller.
4. The remote node's DRAM and back.

Each step contributes additional latency. While the precise numbers vary by architecture and load, it is common for a remote memory access to be significantly slower than a local one. More importantly, the variability tends to be higher. If the inter-socket link is busy or the remote node is under memory pressure, the same load might be quick one moment and slow the next.

In a high-frequency trading system, this matters in two ways:

- **Single-event latency.** A single remote access in the hot path can add dozens of nanoseconds. If your code performs several such accesses per tick, you will see microsecond-scale penalties.
- **Jitter and tail behavior.** Remote accesses are more sensitive to other activity on the machine. As background processes or other trading strategies share the hardware, contention on inter-socket links and remote memory controllers can show up as fat tails in your tick-to-trade histogram.

The effect can be subtle. Your average latency might look acceptable, but as you start to examine the 99th percentile and beyond, you see sporadic spikes. Sometimes those spikes are not due to the network or the operating system scheduler; they are due to the memory subsystem taking a longer route for certain data.

## Discovering the NUMA Topology of Your Server

Before you can align threads and data with NUMA nodes, you must know how the hardware is laid out. On a typical Linux trading server, the relevant questions are:

- How many NUMA nodes are there?
- Which cores belong to which node?
- How much memory is attached to each node?
- What is the latency and bandwidth cost of local versus remote accesses?

System tools and documentation can answer these, but conceptually you should picture your server as several "islands" (nodes), each with its own cluster of cores and local memory. When we talk later about "keeping threads on their island," we mean keeping them on the same node as their data.

From a design viewpoint, this suggests that the unit of placement for latency-critical components should often be a NUMA node rather than the entire machine. For example, you might decide that one node is dedicated to a particular exchange feed and strategy combination, while another node handles a different venue.

## Pinning Threads to the Right Node

Once you know where your cores are, the next step is to ensure that latency-critical threads consistently run on a chosen subset of cores belonging to a specific node. This is often called *pinning* or setting CPU affinity.

Pinning on its own does two useful things:

- It keeps the operating system from moving the thread around the machine, which improves cache warmth and reduces unpredictable context switch overheads.
- It gives you a stable home for the thread, which you can then align with memory placement.

However, pinning is only half of the story. If the thread is pinned to node 0 but most of its hot data structures live on node 1, every tick will incur remote memory traffic. For NUMA awareness to pay off, threads and data need to be colocated.

A practical workflow for a trading team might look like this:

1. Decide which cores (on which node) will host the feed handlers and order gateways for a given venue.
2. Pin those processes or threads to those cores so they do not migrate.
3. Arrange for their primary data structures to be allocated on the same node, using appropriate allocation policies or first-touch patterns.
4. Verify, using profiling tools, that the majority of memory accesses from those threads are indeed local.

Pinning itself interacts with operating system scheduling, which we will discuss in more depth in a later section. For now, it is enough to recognize that NUMA alignment begins with making core placement a deliberate choice rather than leaving it entirely to the default scheduler.

## Placing Data on the Correct NUMA Node

Aligning memory placement with thread placement is where NUMA awareness becomes concrete. The goal is straightforward: the data structures a thread touches on its hot path should be physically located on the same NUMA node as the cores that run that thread.

There are three main levers:

- **First-touch allocation.** If a pinned thread initializes its own data structures (for example, filling in order book arrays or precomputing symbol state), the operating system will, on many systems, allocate the underlying pages on that thread's node. Ensuring that initialization runs on the same cores that will later use the data is a simple but powerful technique.
- **Node-aware allocators.** Some libraries and system calls allow you to request memory from a specific NUMA node. These are often used in multi-process or multi-threaded trading engines to ensure that each engine instance has its own local heap.

- **Process and service partitioning.** Instead of one giant process sharing data freely across sockets, you can choose to run separate instances of key components per node. Each instance allocates and uses its own local data, limiting cross-node traffic.

Consider a trading architecture where each process handles all symbols across multiple venues. Threads may roam freely and touch shared global structures. In a NUMA setting, this design naturally creates many remote memory accesses: any given core is likely processing symbols whose state was last touched (and whose memory pages were allocated) by a core on the other node.

A NUMA-aware redesign might instead:

- Partition symbols by node, such that each node is responsible for a subset of instruments.
- Ensure that market data for those symbols is parsed and stored by threads pinned to that node.
- Route orders for those symbols through order gateway threads also pinned to that node.

In effect, you carve the trading system into largely independent "mini-engines," each with its own local data and threads. Cross-node communication still happens—for example, for firm-wide risk aggregation—but the tick-to-trade hot paths remain mostly confined within a node.

## Memory Bandwidth Contention and Background Noise

NUMA is not just about latency. It is also about bandwidth: the rate at which each node can move data between memory and cores. Trading workloads, especially those that parse rich market data feeds or maintain detailed order books, can be surprisingly memory-bandwidth-hungry. At the same time, other activities on the machine—logging, monitoring, analytics, or unrelated batch jobs—also consume bandwidth.

Two aspects are important here:

- **Local bandwidth per node.** Each node has a finite number of memory channels. When many threads on that node perform large, streaming reads or writes (for example, writing extensive logs or handling bulk data), they can consume much of the available bandwidth, slowing down even small, latency-critical loads.

- **Shared inter-socket bandwidth.** Remote memory requests from one node travel over the same links as other inter-socket communication. Heavy cross-node traffic—whether from trading code or from unrelated processes—can congest these links and increase the cost of remote accesses.

Because of this, careful placement of background tasks is as important as careful placement of trading threads. Some guidelines:

- **Keep noisy neighbors off your trading node.** Assign logging daemons, backup processes, and batch analytics to cores on a different node from your most latency-sensitive threads. Let them compete for that node's bandwidth, not yours.

- **Separate heavy data processing from hot decision loops.** If you perform computationally or bandwidth-intensive analytics on the same node as feed handling and order sending, you risk throttling the very memory system the hot path relies on.

- **Be wary of large, shared data structures.** Global caches or shared queues that span nodes encourage remote accesses and bandwidth contention. Prefer per-node structures with occasional, intentional synchronization across nodes.

From an observability perspective, sudden degradations in p99 and p99.9 latency that coincide with backup runs or heavy report generation are often signs of bandwidth contention. NUMA-aware telemetry—where you track memory bandwidth and latency per node—can help you correlate these symptoms with their root cause.

## Design Patterns for NUMA-Friendly Trading Systems

Putting these concepts together, several architectural patterns emerge for trading systems that care about microseconds.

### Per-Socket Engine Instances

Instead of a single monolithic process, you run one engine instance per NUMA node. Each instance:

- is bound to the cores of that node,
- allocates its working set (order books, strategy state) locally,
- handles a defined subset of symbols or venues, and
- communicates with other instances only when necessary (for example, for global risk or cross-venue logic).

This model aligns well with both hardware and operational thinking. Each instance can be monitored and tuned independently. Failover and capacity planning can be done per node. Most importantly, each tick-to-trade path remains within a single node, minimizing remote memory traffic.

### Node-Local Queues and Services

Supporting services within the trading system—such as risk checks, position tracking, or internal market data distribution—can also be structured as per-node components. Rather than a single risk service used by all threads across nodes, you might have:

- A node-local fast path for risk state that is needed tick-by-tick.
- A slower, cross-node path for reconciling and aggregating risk at lower frequency.

Queues that connect stages of the pipeline (for example, from feed handler to strategy, or from strategy to gateway) should be placed in memory local to the consumers and producers on that node. If cross-node communication is required, treat it as an explicit design choice and budget for the additional latency.

**NUMA-Aware Testing and Profiling**

Finally, NUMA awareness should be part of your performance validation loop, not just an initial configuration step. Some practical habits include:

- Running microbenchmarks of your hot paths with threads pinned to specific nodes and measuring the difference between local and remote memory placement.
- Collecting latency histograms separately for each node's trading threads to detect asymmetries or interference.
- Monitoring per-node memory bandwidth, cache miss rates, and remote access counts using hardware performance counters.

When you see a node whose trading threads suffer from higher tail latencies or elevated remote access rates, you know to look for misplaced data, cross-node services, or noisy neighbors on that node.

## Connecting NUMA Back to Tick-to-Trade

It is easy to view NUMA and memory bandwidth as purely "infrastructure" concerns, separate from trading logic. In reality, they are inseparable from the tick-to-trade story. A beautifully optimized core loop, with carefully managed caches and branch prediction, will still underperform if half its loads arrive from the wrong side of the motherboard.

By understanding how socket topology and memory placement translate into concrete latency penalties, you gain a new set of levers:

- Decide *where* trading logic runs (which cores, which nodes).
- Decide *where* trading data lives (which node's memory).
- Shape your architecture so that the two stay together across the full life of a tick, from packet arrival to order transmission.

As the chapter continues into operating system scheduling, interrupt handling, and kernel bypass, this NUMA perspective will remain in the background. CPU isolation, interrupt mapping, and user-space networking all work best when applied per node, not just per machine. In a world where microseconds matter, trading system architecture is as much about placing computation and data in the right physical spot as it is about writing clever algorithms.

## 6.3 OS Scheduling and CPU Isolation

In the previous sections we treated the CPU mostly as a piece of hardware: pipelines, caches, branch predictors, sockets, and NUMA nodes. We assumed that once you pinned a thread to a core and aligned its data with the right NUMA node, the hardware would simply run that thread whenever it had work to do.

In reality, there is a powerful intermediary between your trading code and the core: the operating system scheduler. On Linux, this scheduler decides *which* thread runs on *which* core at *which* time slice. For general workloads this is a feature; the OS fairly shares cores among users and background services. For a latency-sensitive trading system, it is a source of uncertainty. Surprise preemptions, migrations between cores, and interference from noisy neighbors can all turn a carefully tuned microsecond-level pipeline into a jittery mess.

This section explains how the Linux scheduler thinks about threads, priorities, and cores, and then shows how to tame that behavior so that a small number of cores become dedicated "execution islands" for critical trading logic.

### How the Linux Scheduler Sees Your System

From the scheduler's point of view, the system consists of:

- A set of **CPUs** (cores), each with its own run queue.
- A set of **tasks** (processes and threads), each with:
- a scheduling *class* (normal, real-time, deadline, etc.),

- a *priority* within that class,
- and a record of how much CPU time it has used recently.

The scheduler's job is to pick, for each core, which runnable task should get the next slice of time. Its default goal is fairness and overall throughput, not low jitter on any particular thread.

For trading workloads, a few concepts are particularly important:

**Scheduling classes.**

Linux uses several classes, ordered by importance:

- **Real-time (RT) classes** such as *SCHED_FIFO* and *SCHED_RR*. These have fixed priorities and can preempt normal tasks. They are intended for applications that need strong timing guarantees.
- **Normal time-sharing class** (*SCHED_OTHER* or *CFS*, the Completely Fair Scheduler). This is the default class for most processes. It tries to give each task a fair share of CPU time relative to its weight (nice level).
- **Batch and idle classes** for very low-priority work.

Within each class, the scheduler maintains its own rules for which task runs next. Across classes, real-time tasks take precedence over normal tasks. This is both a tool and a danger for trading code: RT priorities can protect critical threads, but misconfiguration can also starve the rest of the system.

**Run queues and migrations.**

Each core has a run queue of tasks that are ready to run. The scheduler balances load by occasionally moving tasks between cores. From your thread's perspective, this can mean:

- Being moved to a different core (and thus a different cache and possibly a different NUMA node).
- Being preempted by another task on the same core when your time slice is up or when a higher-priority task wakes up.

These mechanisms are benign for web servers or batch jobs. For a trading loop that expects to run continuously on a particular core with warm caches and local memory, they are damaging.

## Why General-Purpose Policies Clash with Trading

The default Linux scheduling behavior is designed for a world where:

- Running many tasks concurrently is good.
- No single task is infinitely more important than the others.
- Average throughput is more important than the exact timing of individual events.

A latency-critical trading path violates all three assumptions. You typically have:

- A small number of hot threads (feed handlers, strategy engines, order gateways) that must run with extremely low jitter.
- A variety of support tasks (logging, monitoring, admin shells, backups) that matter, but not on the same timescale.
- A requirement that individual events—a particular market data packet, a particular order—be processed within predictable microsecond budgets.

Under default settings, even if you pin your hot thread to a core, the scheduler still believes that:

- Other tasks pinned or allowed on that core deserve time slices as well.
- Kernel threads (for interrupts, housekeeping, etc.) can run there too.
- Timer ticks and periodic accounting work should happen at regular intervals on all cores.

From the trading system's perspective, these are "noisy neighbors" and background chores intruding on the narrow, deterministic hot path you are trying to create.

To reconcile the two worlds, you need to *reconfigure* how some cores participate in scheduling, and how some threads are treated by the scheduler.

## Thread Affinity: Necessary but Not Sufficient

The first tool many developers reach for is *CPU affinity*: marking a thread or process as allowed to run only on a chosen set of cores. Affinity is crucial, but it has limits.

Affinity tells the scheduler, "this task may run only here," but it does *not* say, "nothing else may run here." Nor does it alter the scheduler's desire to balance load across cores; it simply constrains where this particular task can go.

Affinity helps in several ways:

- Keeps a critical thread from migrating between cores, preserving cache warmth and NUMA locality.
- Reduces interference between unrelated hot paths by assigning them to disjoint sets of cores.
- Provides a clear mapping between application components (feed handlers, strategies, gateways) and physical hardware resources.

But on its own, affinity does not block:

- Other user-space tasks whose affinity also includes those cores.
- Kernel threads (such as interrupt handlers or per-CPU daemons) that the OS schedules there.
- Periodic OS work such as scheduler ticks, resource accounting, and maintenance.

To get truly predictable behavior for trading threads, you need to go beyond affinity and alter the *role* those cores play in the system.

## CPU Isolation: Creating Execution Islands

*CPU isolation* is the practice of reserving one or more cores almost exclusively for specific purposes, such as running real-time trading threads, while the rest of the system does its work on other cores.

Conceptually, you divide the cores into two groups:

- **Isolated cores**: dedicated to latency-sensitive work. Only a carefully controlled set of threads may run here. OS noise is minimized.
- **General-purpose cores**: everything else. The kernel scheduler is free to balance normal tasks across these cores, and background services live here.

On Linux, achieving isolation involves a combination of:

- Boot-time parameters that change how the kernel schedules and where it runs periodic work.
- Affinity settings that control which threads may run on which cores.
- Real-time priorities and policies that give critical threads precedence within their isolated island.

While the exact mechanisms and names vary by distribution and kernel version, the design goal is stable: make a few cores behave as much like dedicated microcontrollers for your trading loop as the general-purpose OS will allow.

## Reducing Scheduler Noise on Isolated Cores

The largest sources of scheduler-induced jitter on a core are:

- Time-sharing with other user-space tasks.
- Time-sharing with kernel threads and interrupt handlers.

- Periodic timer ticks and maintenance work.

In a well-isolated setup, you address these as follows.

**Keep other user-space tasks off the isolated cores.**

This is the most straightforward rule. Any process that is not part of the critical trading path should have its affinity constrained to the general-purpose cores. That includes:

- Logging and monitoring agents.
- Automation scripts and maintenance jobs.
- Shell sessions and admin tools.

By default, the OS might happily schedule a short, innocent process on an isolated core just because that core looks idle. Affinity rules and system configuration must prevent this.

**Move interrupts and kernel threads away.**

Interrupts are small bursts of kernel work triggered by hardware events (for example, network packets, disk I/O, timers). Each interrupt can:

- Preempt the user thread currently running on that core.
- Run code that touches caches and TLBs, evicting useful trading data.
- Incur additional scheduling decisions (for example, waking tasks).

To protect isolated cores, you aim to:

- Steer most hardware interrupts (especially unrelated devices) to non-isolated cores.
- Minimize the number of kernel threads that may run on isolated cores.

Later sections will describe interrupt mapping and NIC configuration in more detail, but from the scheduler perspective, the point is simple: an isolated core used for trading logic should not also be the default home for disk or USB interrupts, for example.

**Limit periodic OS work.**

Traditional kernels wake each core at regular intervals (timer ticks) to perform accounting, scheduling, and maintenance. For busy servers this overhead is acceptable. For low-latency trading cores, each tick is a potential disturbance.

Modern Linux kernels offer modes that greatly reduce or eliminate periodic ticks on selected cores when they are running a single, well-behaved task. Configuring these modes for your isolated cores ensures that, once a trading thread begins its busy loop, the kernel largely stays out of the way.

## Real-Time Priorities for Trading Threads

Once cores are isolated, you still need a way to ensure that your trading threads outrank any remaining tasks that might run there (for example, necessary kernel work or a minimal set of support threads). This is where real-time scheduling policies come in.

By assigning critical threads to a real-time policy, you tell the scheduler:

- When this thread is runnable, it should run immediately, ahead of normal tasks.
- Its priority is fixed relative to other real-time threads; it is not subject to the fair-share adjustments used for normal tasks.

Used carefully, this allows you to arrange the trading workload on an isolated core as a small, clearly ranked set of loops:

- A feed-handler thread with the highest priority.
- A strategy thread with a slightly lower, but still real-time, priority.

- An order-sending or risk thread with another well-defined priority.

If any of these threads becomes runnable (for example, because a new packet arrives), the scheduler quickly hands the core to it, preempting lower-priority work if necessary.

However, real-time priorities must be used with discipline:

- A runaway real-time thread that never yields can starve even essential kernel work, potentially destabilizing the machine.
- Assigning too many threads high real-time priorities removes the meaningful ordering the scheduler relies on, leading to priority inversion and complex interactions.

In a trading context, the safest approach is to limit real-time scheduling to a thin layer of well-understood, carefully coded loops that are known not to block on slow operations (such as disk I/O or contended locks).

## Recognizing Scheduler-Induced Jitter

From the point of view of trading measurements, scheduler problems show up as:

- **Latency spikes** that are not explained by network conditions or obvious CPU saturation.
- **Multi-modal latency distributions**, where there are distinct clusters corresponding to "clean" and "noisy" execution.
- **Correlations with other system activity**, such as backups, cron jobs, or admin logins.

At the system level, you can investigate by:

- Examining per-core run queues: how many tasks are runnable on each core, and are isolated cores truly dedicated?

- Checking context switch rates: a high rate on a supposedly isolated core hints that other tasks or interrupts are still intruding.
- Monitoring migrations: frequent task movement between cores is a sign that affinity or isolation settings are insufficient.

When you fix scheduler issues, you often see the p50 latency remain roughly the same while the long tails (p99, p99.9) shrink dramatically. This is consistent with the idea that the core trading path was already efficient on average; what you are removing are the occasional, scheduler-driven disruptions.

## Incrementally Hardening the System

Turning a stock Linux distribution into a predictable trading platform is best done step by step. A reasonable progression is:

**Step 1: Map and pin.**

- Identify cores by NUMA node and decide which cores will be candidates for isolation.
- Pin trading processes and threads to these candidate cores and nodes.
- Verify that migrations are minimized and that caches behave as expected.

**Step 2: Separate noisy services.**

- Move non-trading services (logging, admin, monitoring) to other cores and, if possible, other NUMA nodes.
- Adjust affinity for system daemons so that they avoid candidate trading cores.

**Step 3: Isolate cores.**

- Configure the OS so that selected cores are treated as isolated execution islands.

- Confirm that default tasks, kernel threads, and interrupts no longer regularly appear on those cores.

**Step 4: Introduce real-time priorities.**

- Promote the most critical trading threads to real-time scheduling policies on the isolated cores.
- Ensure they do not perform operations that could block for long, which would undermine system stability.

**Step 5: Measure and iterate.**

- Re-measure end-to-end tick-to-trade latency, focusing on tail behavior.
- Use system-level metrics (context switches, run queue depths, interrupt counts) to verify that isolated cores are as quiet as expected.

This incremental approach helps avoid the two common failure modes:

- Making no changes at all and living with uncontrolled jitter.
- Applying aggressive real-time and isolation settings all at once, only to discover that something essential (for example, a watchdog or management agent) has been starved.

## How Scheduling, NUMA, and Microarchitecture Interact

OS scheduling and CPU isolation sit between the hardware-level considerations of earlier sections and the networking and kernel-bypass topics that follow. They mediate *when* your threads get to run on the cores and *with whom* they share those cores.

All three layers interact:

- **Microarchitecture**: Your code is tuned for specific cores and caches. Scheduler migrations break the assumptions you made about cache warmth and branch predictor history.
- **NUMA**: You place data on particular nodes to minimize remote memory access. Scheduler decisions that move threads to other nodes undo that careful placement.
- **Scheduling**: You isolate cores so that your tuned, node-local threads can run without interference, preserving the benefits of microarchitectural and NUMA optimizations.

When everything is aligned, a tick received on a specific NIC queue is handled by a feed thread on a particular isolated core, reading node-local data with warm caches, dispatching to a strategy on the same core, and sending an order out through a gateway thread that also lives in that isolated island. The scheduler's role, in this ideal, is mostly to stay out of the way.

As we move next into interrupt handling and polling modes, keep in mind that interrupts are themselves scheduled pieces of work. How you map them to cores and integrate them with isolated execution islands is just as important as how you configure user-space threads. Together, these choices determine whether your trading system experiences the operating system as a cooperative partner or as a source of unpredictable microsecond-scale noise.

## 6.4 Interrupt Handling and Polling Modes

So far in this chapter we have treated the CPU and OS as the place where your trading threads run: we optimized pipelines and caches, aligned threads and data across NUMA nodes, and carved out isolated cores so the scheduler stays out of the way. In this section we move one step earlier in the tick-to-trade path and ask a more basic question: *how does a packet actually reach your code in the first place?*

On a Linux trading server, there are two broad styles of receiving packets from the network interface card (NIC):

- **Interrupt-driven** receive: the NIC tells the CPU "I have work for you" by raising an interrupt.
- **Polling-based** receive: a core continuously checks the NIC (or a kernel queue) for new packets without waiting for interrupts.

Both approaches can deliver the same data to your application logic, but they behave very differently under load. They differ in jitter (how variable your latency is), CPU usage (how many cycles you burn waiting for packets), and tail latency (what happens at the 99th percentile and beyond). Trading teams routinely adjust this part of the system when pushing from "fast enough" to "competitive at the microsecond scale."

## From Wire to User Space: The Two Paths

At a conceptual level, the receive path from the wire to your strategy looks like this:

1. The NIC receives one or more packets from the exchange.
2. The NIC places packet data into a receive ring buffer in memory.
3. Some mechanism notifies the CPU that new packets are available.
4. Kernel or user-space code takes the packets from the ring, performs necessary processing, and ultimately delivers decoded messages to your trading logic.

The key distinction lies in step 3 and how that interacts with the OS scheduler and CPU microarchitecture:

- In an **interrupt-driven** model, the NIC raises an interrupt. The CPU stops whatever it is doing, runs an interrupt handler, which typically schedules further work in the kernel (for example, via NAPI), and eventually wakes your application.
- In a **polling** model, a dedicated thread on a core continuously checks the receive ring or a kernel-exposed queue for new packets. No external event is needed to "wake" it; it is already running.

Both models can coexist. Linux's NAPI framework, for example, uses interrupts to detect the presence of work and then switches to polling under load. Kernel-bypass frameworks push further, running dedicated poll loops in user space.

Understanding the trade-offs starts with how interrupts behave in a low-latency setting.

## Interrupt-Driven Receive: Efficient but Jittery

In an interrupt-driven system, the NIC is relatively passive until a packet arrives. When it has data:

- It raises an interrupt on a specific core (using MSI/MSI-X).
- The CPU's normal execution is temporarily suspended.
- The OS runs a short interrupt handler, which typically:
  - acknowledges the NIC,
  - schedules or performs the work to pull packets from the NIC's ring,
  - and may wake up any sleeping threads waiting for incoming data.

This has several advantages:

- **CPU-efficient at low traffic.** If there are long gaps between packets, the core can spend its time doing other useful work, or it can even enter deeper power states, because it does not have to constantly check for new data.
- **Simple to reason about.** The OS and NIC collaborate to wake your process when something interesting happens, using mature kernel mechanisms.

But there are important downsides for high-frequency trading:

- **Interrupt handling adds latency.** The trip through the interrupt handler, plus any scheduling decisions it triggers, adds extra steps between packet arrival and your trading code. Even if each step is small, the sum can be meaningful relative to microsecond budgets.

- **Interrupts cause preemption and cache disruption.** When an interrupt fires, the core's current task is paused, and its instruction and data caches may be perturbed. If your strategy is running on that core, it may be interrupted in the middle of a hot loop.

- **Jitter increases under load.** As traffic rises, the system spends more time handling interrupts and related work. The timing of when your thread is awakened and scheduled becomes less predictable, especially if multiple queues or devices share cores.

To reduce overhead, NICs and drivers support **interrupt moderation** or **coalescing**: they wait until multiple packets have arrived or a timer has elapsed before raising an interrupt. This can be highly beneficial for bulk throughput and CPU utilization, but it directly conflicts with low latency.

From a trading viewpoint:

- Coalescing reduces the number of interrupts (and thus CPU overhead) by batching packets.

- The batch introduces a built-in delay: the first packet of a burst must wait for the coalescing condition to be met.

- Packet ordering can become fuzzy inside the batch, complicating accurate time-ordering of market events.

With aggressive coalescing settings, your median latency may remain acceptable, but tail latency and jitter tend to worsen, and the exact arrival time of each packet becomes harder to control.

## Polling Receive: Burning Cycles for Consistency

Polling takes the opposite approach. Instead of letting the NIC wake the CPU, you dedicate a running thread to repeatedly check the RX ring (or a kernel queue) for new packets. This thread is typically:

- pinned to a specific isolated core,
- running at a high or real-time priority,
- and structured as a tight loop that reads from the NIC and hands messages to your trading logic.

The advantages are:

- **Low, stable latency.** When a packet arrives, there is no need for an interrupt to wake a sleeping thread. The polling loop is already running and can detect the new packet on its next iteration, often within a bounded, very small time.
- **Better cache locality.** Because the polling thread lives on its own core, the NIC's data path and your trading logic can share the same caches consistently. There are fewer surprise preemptions to disrupt the pipeline.
- **Predictable p99 and p99.9 tails.** With the OS and interrupts largely out of the hot path, long-tail outliers often shrink, even if the absolute median latency does not change dramatically.

The downsides are equally real:

- **High CPU usage.** A pure busy-polling loop can consume an entire core, even when no packets are arriving. From the OS's perspective, the core is 100% utilized whether the market is active or quiet.
- **Risk of starving other work.** If polling is not restricted to isolated cores, it can crowd out other tasks on the same core or node.

- **Operational complexity.** Designing and managing dedicated polling threads, and making sure they coexist cleanly with the rest of the system, requires more care than simply listening on a socket.

In practice, many high-frequency setups treat this as an explicit trade-off: they are willing to dedicate several cores to busy polling in exchange for lower jitter and tighter tail latencies, while leaving the rest of the machine to handle support and back-office tasks.

## Hybrid Approaches: NAPI and Controlled Polling

Linux's NAPI (New API) framework already blends interrupts and polling inside the kernel:

- At low loads, the NIC triggers interrupts to tell the kernel there is work to do.
- The kernel then polls the NIC for a bounded number of packets per interrupt, reducing interrupt overhead.
- At higher loads, the system may switch more heavily toward polling so that interrupts do not overwhelm the CPU.

User space can also adopt hybrid strategies:

- **Kernel busy polling**: the kernel provides options to have system calls such as receive operations busy-poll for a short period before sleeping, reducing wake-up latency while avoiding truly continuous polling.
- **User-space polling loops with back-off**: a receive loop may poll intensively under load but back off or sleep briefly during quiet periods to save CPU.

These hybrids aim to capture many of the latency benefits of polling while tempering CPU cost. They can be effective, especially for firms that cannot dedicate whole cores exclusively to busy polling at all times.

However, they reintroduce some variability: once back-off or sleep is involved, the wake-up timing again depends on scheduling and timer behavior.

For the most latency-sensitive parts of a trading system, especially on the path from market data to initial decision, most firms eventually move toward more aggressive polling on isolated cores. Hybrids are common on less critical paths, like internal fan-out or less time-sensitive venues.

## Tail Latency and Jitter: What Changes When You Switch

From a performance measurement perspective, the most important differences between interrupt-driven and polling-based paths show up in three areas:

**Median latency (p50).**

- Polling can modestly reduce median latency by eliminating interrupt and wake-up overhead.
- In many systems, however, median latency is already constrained mainly by decoding and strategy logic; the path from NIC to user space is only part of the story.

**Tail latency (p99, p99.9).**

- Interrupt-driven paths tend to have heavier tails, especially under bursty or high load, because interrupt storms, scheduling delays, and coalescing behavior all contribute variability.
- Polling flattens these tails by making the receive path less dependent on scheduler timing and interrupt behavior. With an isolated, busy-polling core, the time from packet arrival to detection becomes more consistent.

**Jitter and correlation with other activity.**

- In an interrupt-driven setup, latency spikes often correlate with unrelated system events: backup jobs, management logins, other processes becoming busy. These events affect the scheduler and interrupt handling.
- In a polling setup with proper isolation, these correlations weaken. External noise has less leverage on the hot path, because the polling thread neither sleeps nor shares its core with general-purpose tasks.

In other words, polling mainly buys you *consistency*. It is less about shaving every possible nanosecond from the fastest path and more about avoiding outliers that blow up your worst-case behavior.

## CPU Usage: Where the Cycles Go

It is tempting to look only at latency graphs when comparing interrupt and polling modes, but CPU usage is equally important.

**Interrupt-driven CPU profile.**

- At low market activity, the cores handling NIC interrupts may be mostly idle. They wake on demand, do some work, then go back to serving other tasks or idling.
- As activity increases, the cost of handling interrupts themselves, plus the overhead of waking and scheduling application threads, grows. You may see cores near saturation with interrupt handling and kernel work rather than application logic.
- Interrupt moderation can reduce CPU overhead at the cost of extra latency and batching.

**Polling-based CPU profile.**

- A polling core tends to show very high utilization all the time, because the polling thread is always running.
- The "wasted" cycles during quiet periods are the cost of guaranteeing immediate responsiveness when bursts arrive.

- With multi-queue NICs and RSS (receive-side scaling), you might dedicate multiple cores to polling, scaling up to match the feed's maximum burst rate.

If you view CPU as a scarce resource shared among many workloads, polling can look inefficient. If you view CPU cores near the exchange as an asset deployed to extract edge from the market, dedicating a handful of them to busy polling becomes easier to justify.

## Mapping Interrupts and Pollers to Cores

Regardless of whether you use interrupts, polling, or a mix, core placement is critical. This ties everything back to the earlier sections on NUMA and CPU isolation.

- **For interrupt-driven receive**, you want NIC interrupts (for specific queues) to be directed to cores on the same NUMA node as:
    - the NIC itself, and
    - the threads that handle the corresponding market data and trading logic.

  You also want those cores to be as free as possible from unrelated tasks, to minimize interference when interrupts fire.
- **For polling-based receive**, you typically:
    - dedicate one isolated core per hot queue to run a poll loop,
    - pin the trading logic that consumes those messages to the same core or to nearby cores on the same node,
    - and make sure that interrupts are either disabled for those queues or steered away, so they do not disturb the polling cores.

A common pattern for a single, very hot market data feed is:

- NIC queue 0 mapped to core A (isolated, same NUMA node).

- A polling thread on core A reads from queue 0 and decodes messages.
- The strategy and order generation logic either:
  - run in the same thread (for ultra-low latency), or
  - are fed via a lock-free queue to a strategy thread on core B, also on the same node and preferably also isolated.

In an interrupt-driven setup, you might instead have the interrupt for queue 0 routed to core A, where a handler wakes the feed handler thread, which then runs with high priority on that core.

The details differ, but the principles are consistent: keep data, interrupts or pollers, and trading logic tightly aligned on the same isolated hardware resources.

## Choosing a Strategy: Risk Appetite vs. Resource Budget

Given these trade-offs, how should a trading firm choose between interrupt-driven, polling, or hybrid approaches?

Several axes matter:

**Latency and jitter targets.**

- If you are competing in environments where *every* microsecond matters and where worst-case behavior is as important as median, you will typically favor polling on isolated cores, with interrupts minimized or disabled on those paths.
- If you operate strategies that tolerate somewhat higher latency and jitter—for example, many intraday or statistical-arbitrage styles—well-tuned interrupt-driven or hybrid paths may suffice.

**CPU budget near the exchange.**

- Polling assumes you can afford to dedicate cores to busy loops that are not always doing useful work.

- If rack space, power, or VM costs are tightly constrained, or if you must share hardware among multiple tenants, you may be forced to lean more on interrupts and moderation.

**Operational complexity.**

- Pure interrupt-driven models, especially when using standard kernel networking, are easier to set up and maintain. The OS does much of the work for you.

- Aggressive polling, especially combined with kernel bypass (discussed in the next section), pushes more responsibility into your code and operations team. Monitoring, failover, and capacity planning need to take dedicated polling cores into account.

Most sophisticated shops end up with a *portfolio* of approaches:

- The most latency-sensitive feeds and venues: polling on isolated cores, often with kernel-bypass frameworks.

- Less sensitive or backup paths: interrupt-driven or hybrid NAPI-based receive on less isolated cores.

- Internal services and post-trade systems: standard interrupt-driven networking with moderate coalescing for efficiency.

## Visualizing the Trade-Offs

To make the impact of these choices concrete, it is helpful to visualize how median and tail latencies change under different traffic levels for interrupt-driven and busy-polling receive paths.

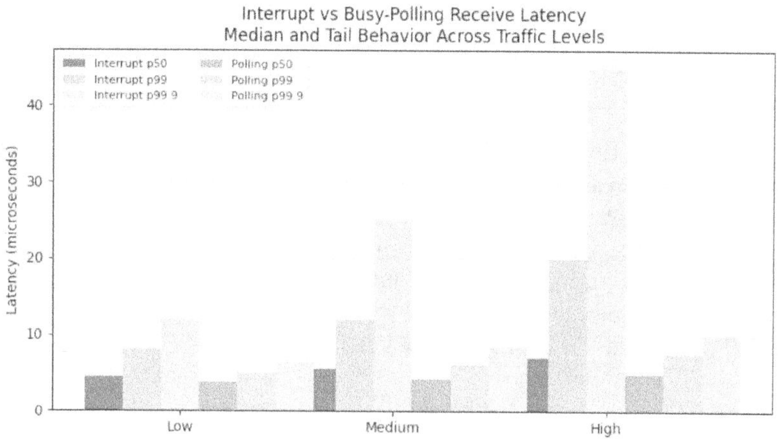


The exact numbers in such a chart depend on your hardware, kernel, and application, but the typical shape is robust:

- Interrupt-driven paths may have acceptable median latency at low traffic but see p99 and p99.9 degrade significantly as traffic increases.
- Busy-polling paths tend to keep p99 and p99.9 much closer to p50, at the expense of dedicating CPU resources.

## From Packets to Trading Decisions

Interrupt handling and polling modes sit at the junction between the network and everything else we have discussed in this chapter:

- The mode you choose affects how quickly and consistently packets enter the CPU's caches and how they interact with the scheduler.
- That, in turn, shapes how well your microarchitectural optimizations, NUMA placement, and CPU isolation can do their jobs.

If the receive path injects unpredictable delays or jitter, no amount of cache tuning or NUMA alignment in the subsequent trading logic can fully compensate. Conversely, when you adopt a polling strategy that delivers packets promptly and predictably into an isolated core with local memory, the rest of your optimizations can express their full benefit.

In the next section, we will push this idea even further by looking at kernel-bypass frameworks, where both interrupt handling and much of the kernel networking stack are removed from the hot path entirely. That step builds directly on the concepts here: once you understand how interrupts and polling shape latency through the kernel, you can make an informed decision about when it is worth taking on the additional complexity of bypassing the kernel altogether.

## 6.5 Kernel Bypass Frameworks

In the previous section we compared interrupt-driven and polling-based receive paths inside the Linux kernel. We saw that, by dedicating cores and using busy polling, you can greatly reduce jitter and tail latency, but you are still operating within the constraints of the kernel networking stack. Every packet still travels through multiple layers of kernel code, incurs system-call overhead, and is subject to kernel data structures and locking.

For many strategies this is acceptable. For the most latency-sensitive paths, however, teams look for further savings. This is where *kernel bypass* frameworks enter: user-space networking stacks such as DPDK, Onload, and AF_XDP that allow applications to interact with NICs more directly, shortening the path from wire to user code and reducing the number of times packet data is copied.

The goal of this section is not to teach every API detail of these frameworks, but to explain conceptually what changes when you bypass the kernel, how that affects latency and jitter, and when the additional complexity is worth taking on.

## The Traditional Kernel Networking Path

Before looking at bypass, it is helpful to spell out the "normal" path that a packet takes when you use standard sockets on Linux:

1. The NIC receives a packet and writes it into a DMA buffer in main memory.
2. The NIC signals the CPU, either via interrupt or through a polled mechanism such as NAPI.
3. The kernel's network driver pulls the packet from the NIC's ring and hands it to the kernel networking stack.
4. The networking stack processes protocol headers (Ethernet, IP, TCP/UDP, possibly higher-level helpers), performs routing and filtering, and locates the appropriate socket.
5. The packet payload, or part of it, is copied or referenced into kernel data structures associated with that socket.
6. Your application calls a system call (for example, a receive call) to read data from the socket. This triggers a transition from user space into the kernel, more checks and bookkeeping, and then finally a copy from kernel buffers into your user-space buffer.

Each step involves code, data structures, and often copies or transformations. The kernel stack is general-purpose: it supports many NICs, protocols, firewall rules, and applications. This flexibility is valuable for most workloads but comes at a cost:

- Multiple context switches between user and kernel space.
- Several layers of code, with associated branches and memory accesses.
- Buffer management that may not be tuned for your specific packet sizes and patterns.

Even if you use busy polling at the kernel level, you are still running through this general-purpose machinery. Kernel bypass frameworks ask a more radical question: can we move most of that machinery into user space, specialized for our trading application, and interact with the NIC as directly as possible?

## What Kernel Bypass Changes Conceptually

Kernel bypass frameworks vary in their design, but they share several key ideas:

- **User-space drivers or hooks.** Instead of relying solely on the kernel driver and network stack, the framework gives user space a more direct handle on the NIC's queues and buffers.

- **Dedicated RX/TX queues.** The NIC is configured with queues reserved for the application, often one or more per core. Packets for specific flows or MAC/VLANs are steered directly into these queues.

- **Zero-copy or fewer copies.** Packet data stays in pre-allocated buffers that are visible to user space, avoiding repeated copying between kernel and user buffers.

- **Poll-mode operation.** User-space threads run tight polling loops on these queues, similar to the busy polling discussed earlier, but now often bypassing large parts of the kernel's networking code.

In effect, the application takes ownership of a slice of the NIC and of the networking stack. The kernel still plays a role in control-plane operations (configuring the NIC, setting up queues, managing security and isolation), but the data plane—the path that each market packet takes—is largely under application control.

This side-by-side view highlights the main promise of kernel bypass: fewer layers and transitions on the hot path, combined with tighter control over queues and buffers.

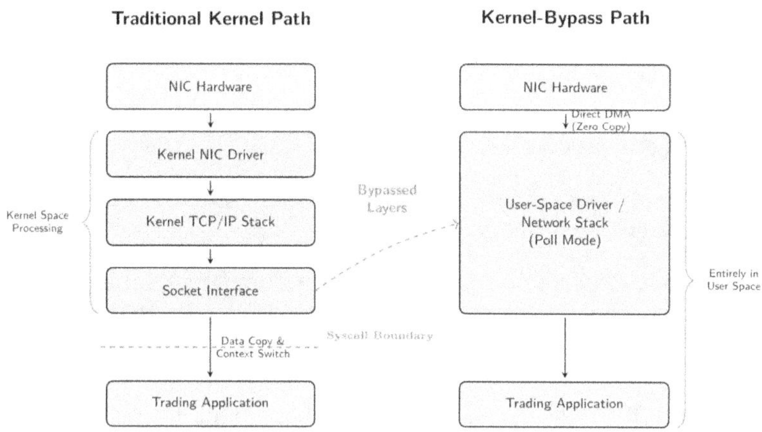


## Examples of Kernel Bypass Frameworks

Several concrete technologies implement these concepts in different ways. We will briefly describe three that are commonly encountered in trading systems.

### DPDK (Data Plane Development Kit)

DPDK is a set of libraries and drivers designed to allow high-speed packet processing in user space. Its defining characteristics include:

- **Poll-mode drivers.** User-space threads poll NIC queues directly, typically one or more queues per core. This meshes naturally with the CPU isolation and busy polling concepts covered earlier.
- **Pre-allocated buffer pools.** Packets are stored in fixed-size buffers (often called mbufs) drawn from pools that are visible to user space. Your code can process packets in place, reducing copying.
- **Fine-grained control.** You explicitly configure queues, buffer sizes, and core assignments in your application, rather than relying on kernel defaults.

Using DPDK, you can build a custom networking stack that does exactly what your trading system needs and nothing more. For example, a feed handler might:

- Bind one process per NUMA node.
- Dedicate several cores on that node to polling DPDK queues attached to a market data NIC.
- Parse and normalize packets directly from DPDK buffers into internal structures, then hand them to strategy code running on nearby cores.

The trade-off is that you also take on responsibility for tasks that the kernel stack previously handled: link configuration, certain error conditions, fragmentation handling if you use IP, and more. DPDK offers helpers for many of these, but the overall environment is lower level.

**Onload and Similar Socket Accelerators**

Solarflare's Onload (and similar technologies) take a different approach: they accelerate standard socket APIs rather than asking you to adopt an entirely new programming model. Conceptually, they:

- Intercept socket calls from your application.
- Handle data-plane traffic in user space using NIC-specific acceleration.
- Fall back to the kernel stack when acceleration is not possible or for control-plane operations.

From an application developer's perspective, this can be attractive:

- Much of your existing code that uses sockets continues to work with minor or no changes.
- You can gradually introduce acceleration to the hottest components without rewriting everything to use a new API.

However, you still need to think carefully about:

- Core placement and polling behavior inside the accelerated stack.
- Interaction with the kernel's view of networking, especially for non-accelerated flows.
- Vendor dependencies, since these solutions are closely tied to specific hardware.

### AF_XDP (Linux's XDP Sockets)

AF_XDP is a more recent Linux facility that provides a way to receive and send packets directly to user space via special sockets, combined with the eXpress Data Path (XDP) in the kernel. Conceptually:

- XDP runs very early in the kernel's networking pipeline, at or near the NIC driver, allowing packets to be redirected to custom paths before they enter the full kernel stack.
- AF_XDP sockets expose shared memory regions (umems) where packets land, which can be mapped into user space.
- User-space threads can then poll these buffers directly, similar to DPDK, but with tighter integration into the Linux kernel.

AF_XDP aims to provide many of the latency benefits of kernel bypass while remaining part of the mainline kernel, reducing the need for out-of-tree drivers and easing integration with other Linux features.

For trading teams already committed to Linux and looking for a middle ground between full DPDK adoption and plain sockets, AF_XDP can be an appealing option.

## Latency, Jitter, and Copy Count

From a performance perspective, kernel bypass frameworks primarily improve:

- **Context switch overhead.** Fewer transitions between user and kernel space on the critical path.

- **Copy count.** Fewer copies of packet data between buffers; in many designs, your code reads directly from NIC-backed buffers.
- **Control over timing.** With user-space poll loops on isolated cores, you largely control when packets are processed, rather than depending on kernel scheduling decisions.

As with pure polling modes inside the kernel, the most dramatic gains are often in the tails:

- Median latency from wire to application logic may improve, but sometimes only modestly, especially if your strategy logic is already a significant component of total latency.
- Tail latency and jitter improve as you remove sources of variability: kernel contention, generalized buffer management, and alignment with unrelated traffic.

One way to think about it is that each copy and each layer of indirection adds not just average cost but also variance. Kernel bypass frameworks smooth out these contributions by making the path shorter and more specialized.

## Costs and Risks of Bypassing the Kernel

The gains from kernel bypass come with non-trivial costs, which you must evaluate against your strategy's needs and your organization's capabilities.

**Increased complexity in your codebase.**

- You move closer to the hardware. Your team needs to understand NIC queues, buffer pools, and low-level networking details that were previously abstracted away.
- Debugging becomes more specialized. Tools and techniques aimed at the standard kernel stack may not apply or may require adaptation.

**Operational and deployment complexity.**

- Configuration of NICs, queues, and huge pages must be consistent across environments (development, staging, production).
- Monitoring must be extended to user-space networking. Metrics like queue depth, dropped packets in user space, and per-queue latency become part of your observability stack.
- Upgrades to kernels or NIC firmware need careful testing to ensure compatibility with your bypass framework.

**Interaction with the rest of the system.**

- Security and isolation: the kernel stack enforces many network-level policies. Bypassing it may require alternative controls or narrower scope (for example, only internal, trusted networks).
- Multi-tenant constraints: in environments where hardware is shared between teams or customers, dedicating queues and cores to bypass frameworks may be politically or technically difficult.
- Coexistence with normal traffic: you often need both bypass and standard networking on the same host, which makes configuration more intricate.

**Vendor and ecosystem lock-in.**

- Some frameworks (like Onload) are tightly bound to specific NIC vendors. Switching hardware or cloud providers can become harder.
- DPDK and AF_XDP are more general, but still require drivers and kernel features that must be supported by your platform of choice.

These costs do not make kernel bypass a bad choice; they simply mean it should be adopted deliberately, with clear expectations about the performance benefits and the engineering investment required.

## When Is Kernel Bypass Worth It?

Given these trade-offs, you can frame the decision to adopt kernel bypass around a few key questions.

**How tight are your latency and jitter requirements?**

- If your strategies compete at the very front of the queue in ultra-low-latency markets, and you are already using isolated cores, busy polling, and careful NUMA placement, kernel bypass is often the next logical step.
- If your edge depends more on model quality, cross-venue analytics, or longer-horizon signals, and your acceptable latency is in tens or hundreds of microseconds, the standard kernel stack—properly tuned—may be sufficient.

**Where is your current bottleneck?**

- Profiling should confirm that a meaningful share of your tick-to-trade time is spent in kernel networking code and context switches, not in your own logic.
- If your hot path is dominated by parsing, strategy computation, or risk checks, improving the networking stack may not move the needle as much as simplifying those components.

**What is your team's tolerance for complexity?**

- Organizations with strong systems-programming capabilities and dedicated performance engineering teams are better positioned to adopt and maintain kernel bypass frameworks.
- Smaller teams may choose to rely on more incremental optimizations—such as better NIC configuration, interrupt placement, AF_XDP, or socket accelerators—before committing to full user-space stacks like DPDK.

**What does your exchange connectivity pattern look like?**

- Environments with high packet rates, small messages, and simple protocols (for example, proprietary binary feeds) benefit most from bypass, because the relative overhead of the kernel stack is high.

- If your connectivity is dominated by heavier protocols (for example, full-fat TCP sessions with complex semantics) or if you rely on kernel features (such as TCP congestion control) as part of your risk management, bypassing the kernel may create more work than it saves.

Ultimately, kernel bypass is an economic decision: you trade engineering and operational effort for lower and more predictable latency. The higher the value of each microsecond to your strategy, the more attractive that trade becomes.

## Connecting Kernel Bypass to the Rest of the Architecture

Kernel bypass does not stand alone. It amplifies, and is amplified by, the other choices discussed in this chapter:

- **CPU microarchitecture.** Poll-mode drivers in user space benefit from the same pipeline and cache considerations as any other hot loop. Data structures backing user-space queues and buffers should be designed with cache friendliness in mind.

- **NUMA awareness.** User-space networking stacks give you explicit control over which queues and buffers live on which node. Aligning these with trading threads and NIC placement is essential to avoid remote memory penalties.

- **OS scheduling and CPU isolation.** Dedicated poll loops in user space assume isolated cores and well-managed scheduler behavior. Without that foundation, the benefits of bypass are quickly eroded by preemptions and interference.

- **Interrupt and polling strategy.** In many bypass setups, you disable or minimize interrupts for data-plane queues entirely, relying on pure polling. The conceptual groundwork from the previous section carries over directly.

Seen in this light, kernel bypass frameworks are not a magic bullet but the culmination of a series of architectural decisions. If you have already shaped your system so that hot paths run on dedicated cores, with local memory and minimal OS noise, kernel bypass offers a way to extend that control all the way down to the NIC. If you have not yet done that groundwork, bypass alone will not deliver its full potential.

For teams building and maintaining competitive trading platforms, understanding these frameworks—even if you do not adopt them immediately—is part of understanding where latency hides and how design choices at every layer, from network hardware to application logic, combine to determine your true tick-to-trade performance.

## 6.6 Compiler and Runtime Optimizations

By this point in the chapter we have worked our way up the stack from the silicon to the operating system and the network. We have seen how pipeline stalls, cache misses, NUMA placement, scheduler decisions, interrupts, and kernel-bypass paths can all add or remove microseconds from your tick-to-trade budget. In this section we turn to a different layer of control: your *toolchain* and *runtime*.

The compiler, linker, and language runtime sit between your source code and the machine instructions that actually run on the cores you have so carefully isolated. The way you build and configure your binaries can either reinforce the architectural work you have done so far, or undermine it. Two versions of "the same" code can differ noticeably in latency behavior purely because of build flags, linking choices, or runtime settings.

Our aim here is to show how to make the toolchain and runtime work for you rather than against you. We will move gradually from high-level concepts—what the compiler is actually doing—to concrete practices around targeted builds, profiling, and language features.

## What the Compiler Really Does for a Trading System

When you compile your trading engine, you are asking the compiler to make a series of decisions on your behalf:

- How to translate each statement into machine instructions.
- How to order and group those instructions to fit the microarchitecture.
- How to lay out functions and data in memory.
- How aggressively to inline functions, unroll loops, and reorder operations.

The compiler does not know your business goals or your tick-to-trade budget. It optimizes according to generic rules: "make the program fast on average," "shrink code size," or "respect strict language semantics." If you accept all the defaults, you may be leaving performance on the table, especially in hot paths that look different under real market load than they do in small test cases.

The first step is to recognize that compiling for low-latency trading is not a single decision, but a combination of choices:

- Optimization level and style.
- Target microarchitecture.
- How much link-time and profile information to feed back into the optimizer.
- Static versus dynamic linking.

We will look at each in turn, always with the same question in mind: how does this choice affect latency distributions, not just throughput?

## Optimization Levels and Trade-Offs

Modern compilers offer several "optimization levels" that control how much effort they spend reshaping your code. Higher levels typically mean more aggressive transformations, but also longer build times and sometimes more complex debugging.

For latency-sensitive trading code, two points matter:

- **Aggressive optimization is usually desirable for hot paths.** Inlining small functions, unrolling tight loops, and simplifying constant expressions all help the CPU's pipeline and caches. These optimizations tend to reduce the number of instructions on the critical path and improve instruction locality.
- **Not all code in your system is equally hot.** Compilation settings that are ideal for the innermost trading loops may be unnecessary or even counterproductive for auxiliary tools, admin utilities, or logging components.

A pragmatic approach is to:

- Identify the binaries or modules that contain your tick-to-trade hot paths (feed handlers, matching engines, strategies, gateways).
- Compile these with strong optimization settings appropriate to your compiler, while still enabling debugging symbols so that you can profile and analyze them.
- Allow less critical components to use simpler settings that ease debugging and reduce build complexity.

It is also useful to keep in mind that "faster" in compiler terms often means "higher average throughput," not "lower worst-case latency." Some optimizations (for example, vectorizing code or unrolling loops) can increase code size and use more registers, which might increase cache pressure in certain cases. This is why empirical measurement–microbenchmarks and profiling–is a necessary complement to any theoretical choice of optimization level.

## Targeting the Right Microarchitecture

Compilers can generate code that is compatible with a wide range of CPUs, or they can generate code tailored to a specific microarchitecture (for example, a particular generation of x86). Generic code runs anywhere but cannot assume the presence of recent instructions or microarchitectural features. Targeted code can make heavier use of specialized instructions and scheduling assumptions.

For trading engines that run on known, controlled hardware (for example, a specific line of servers in a colocated rack), you should take advantage of targeting:

- Enable the compiler to use instructions that are available on your deployed CPUs, such as modern vector or bit-manipulation instructions, when they help.
- Allow it to schedule instructions assuming a particular pipeline structure, port distribution, and cache behavior.

This does not replace the microarchitectural understanding we discussed earlier; rather, it allows the compiler to apply that understanding systematically. When you later upgrade hardware, you can revisit the target settings, rebuild your binaries, and re-profile under the new microarchitecture.

The key is to avoid the trap of building all binaries as if they might run on any CPU from the last decade. In a trading context you usually know exactly what hardware the critical binaries will use; your build should reflect that.

## Link-Time Optimization: Seeing the Whole Program

Traditional compilation happens one translation unit at a time: each source file is compiled in relative isolation, and the linker later stitches the pieces together. The compiler can only optimize locally; it does not know how other modules use a given function or how often.

*Link-Time Optimization* (LTO) changes this picture. With LTO:

- The compiler preserves additional information about each module's structure.
- At link time, a global optimizer analyzes the combined program, allowing:
  - inlining across module boundaries,
  - removal of unused functions and data,
  - better decisions about code layout.

For latency-critical code, LTO can yield:

- Tighter hot paths: small helper functions defined in separate files can be inlined into the core loop, removing call overhead and enabling further simplification.
- Improved instruction locality: the linker can place frequently interacting functions close together in memory, improving instruction cache performance.

The costs are mostly in build time and complexity. LTO builds are slower and sometimes trickier to debug, especially if your toolchain or build system is not accustomed to them. Nevertheless, for core trading binaries that change relatively infrequently, the benefits often justify the investment.

## Profile-Guided Optimization: Teaching the Compiler About the Market

Even with good optimization levels and LTO, the compiler still does not truly know which code paths are "hot" under real market conditions. It can guess based on heuristics (for example, loops are usually hot, error paths are usually cold), but those guesses may be wrong for your application.

*Profile-Guided Optimization* (PGO) closes this loop:

1. You build an instrumented version of your trading binary. This version records how often different branches are taken, which functions are called, and how loops behave.

2. You run this instrumented binary under a workload that resembles production: realistic market data, realistic strategy behavior, realistic bursts and quiet periods.
3. The profiler produces data files describing the observed behavior.
4. You rebuild the binary, feeding this profile to the compiler. The compiler uses it to:
    - lay out functions and branches so that hot paths are contiguous,
    - decide which functions to inline more aggressively,
    - optimize branch prediction hints and code generation.

For a trading system, PGO is particularly powerful because:

- Market data has structure: some message types, symbols, and time-of-day patterns are far more common than others. PGO lets the binary reflect these patterns explicitly.
- Strategy behavior can be highly asymmetric: a particular risk check might be tripped rarely but is very expensive when it happens. PGO helps mark that path as cold.
- Tick-to-trade hot paths tend to be stable over medium horizons, even as you tweak models. This stability makes profile investment worthwhile.

The challenge lies in capturing a representative profile. If the profiling run does not resemble real trading conditions—for example, if it uses synthetic data or only a narrow subset of venues—you risk over-optimizing for the wrong cases. A practical solution is to:

- Mirror production feeds into a staging environment.
- Run the instrumented binary there for a reasonable period (for example, several active market sessions).
- Refresh PGO profiles periodically as markets and strategies evolve.

PGO, when combined with LTO and good microarchitectural hygiene, can yield a binary whose instruction layout is closely aligned with the actual statistical structure of your trading workload.

## Static vs Dynamic Linking in a Latency Context

Another lever you control is how your binaries are linked:

- **Static linking** bundles most required libraries directly into the executable. At runtime, the OS loads a single large binary, with no need to resolve external symbols.
- **Dynamic linking** keeps libraries separate and resolves their symbols at load time, potentially with relocation and indirection at call sites.

From a latency perspective, main differences are:

- **Startup cost.** Dynamic linking involves extra work at process startup: loading shared libraries, resolving symbols, and applying relocations. For long-running trading engines, this cost is usually amortized, but it matters for components that restart frequently (for example, failover or per-session helpers).
- **Call overhead and code locality.** Static linking makes it easier for the linker and optimizer to inline library functions or to place them near your code in memory, improving cache behavior. Dynamic calls may involve extra indirection and less optimal layout.

Static linking also changes operational considerations:

- Deployments become more self-contained: the binary carries its dependencies, simplifying some aspects of version control and rollout.
- Updating shared components (for example, a common logging library) requires rebuilding all statically linked binaries that use them.

There is no universal rule here. Many low-latency systems statically link the innermost trading engine while allowing dynamic linking for auxiliary processes. The key is to make the choice consciously and to measure its impact on both latency and operational flexibility.

## Allocator Choice and Memory Behavior at Runtime

Beyond the compiler, the runtime behavior of your language's memory allocator can have a strong impact on latency. Allocators manage the heap: they respond to requests for dynamic memory and recycle unused blocks. In a trading engine, this happens when you create and destroy objects, grow data structures, or process variable-sized messages.

Potential problems include:

- **Contention between threads.** If many threads frequently allocate and free memory from a shared heap, they may contend on internal locks, causing stalls and cache invalidations.
- **Fragmentation and churn.** Allocating many differently sized objects and freeing them in complex patterns can fragment the heap, increasing cache misses and causing the allocator to perform more work per request.
- **Unexpected pauses.** Some allocators perform background work or cleaning that results in short pauses, which may show up as latency spikes.

To mitigate this:

- Prefer **per-thread or per-core arenas**, so that each hot trading thread uses its own allocation pool with minimal sharing. Many modern allocators support this directly.
- Avoid frequent allocation and deallocation on the critical path. Reuse objects when possible, use pools for fixed-size structures, and structure data so that most allocations occur at startup or during reconfiguration, not on every tick.

- Monitor allocator statistics and latency effect. If your latency histograms show spikes that correlate with allocation patterns, consider alternative allocators or custom pooling.

In some environments, teams adopt specialized allocators tuned explicitly for low latency. However, even with standard allocators, disciplined usage patterns—avoiding "object churn" in the hot path—can deliver most of the benefit.

## Managed Languages and Runtime Services

Many trading systems use a mix of languages: low-level components in C or C++, higher-level logic in Java, C#, or other managed languages. Managed runtimes bring their own sources of variability:

- **Garbage collection (GC).** Automatic memory management inevitably involves some form of reclamation. Even low-pause or concurrent collectors may introduce occasional delays, especially under allocation pressure.
- **Just-In-Time (JIT) compilation.** Many managed runtimes compile frequently used methods to optimized machine code at runtime. The first time a path becomes hot, the runtime may pause briefly to perform this compilation.
- **Background services.** JITs, JIT profilers, and other runtime services may run background threads that intermittently contend for CPU or memory bandwidth.

If you choose to place latency-critical components in a managed language, you must treat these runtime behaviors as part of your performance model, not as hidden details. Some guidelines:

- **Warm up** the runtime before markets open. Run representative traffic so that JIT compilation and class loading complete before you care about absolute latency.
- Prefer GC configurations that favor predictable, short pauses over higher average throughput. Measure with realistic workloads to ensure that worst-case pauses fit within your tolerance.

- Consider separating concerns: keep the absolute tick-to-trade hot path in a language with predictable, manual memory management; use managed languages for orchestration, configuration, analytics, and slower decision loops.

The core principle is the same regardless of language: avoid any runtime service that may decide, at a time of its choosing, to pause or interfere with your hottest loops.

## Language Features and Abstractions in the Hot Path

Even in low-level languages, certain language features and abstractions can introduce hidden costs:

- **Exception handling.** Unwinding stack frames and running handlers is expensive, especially if it triggers heap activity or logging. Exceptions should not be part of the normal control flow in a trading hot path.
- **Virtual dispatch and deep object hierarchies.** Indirect calls through virtual tables or function pointers introduce extra branches and can confuse branch prediction. They also tend to scatter related code and data in memory.
- **Heavy generic or reflective mechanisms.** Features that rely on runtime type inspection, dynamic allocation, or metadata tables can blow up the instruction footprint and allocation rate.

This does not mean you must write your entire system in a minimal subset of the language. Rather, you should:

- Keep the inner trading loops as simple and transparent as possible: straightforward control flow, explicit data structures, and minimal abstraction overhead.
- Use richer abstractions in code that runs off the hot path: configuration loading, backtesting, reporting, and so on.

- Make it easy to identify and review the set of functions that lie on the tick-to-trade critical path, and treat them as a performance-sensitive subset with stricter coding guidelines.

The compiler can only optimize what it can see and understand. Excessively complex abstractions in the hot path make it harder for the optimizer to simplify and arrange your code in a way that aligns with the microarchitecture.

## A Checklist for Latency-Sensitive Builds

Bringing these ideas together, it is useful to turn them into a concrete checklist that you can apply to any latency-sensitive trading binary:

- **Hardware targeting**
  - Are you compiling with settings appropriate to your actual server microarchitecture?
  - Have you validated that binaries run only on compatible hardware?
- **Optimization and linking**
  - Are critical modules built with strong optimization levels and, where appropriate, link-time optimization?
  - Have you decided explicitly between static and dynamic linking for hot binaries, based on latency and operational needs?
- **Profile awareness**
  - Have you collected representative runtime profiles under realistic market conditions?
  - Are you using these profiles to guide optimization and layout (PGO)?
- **Allocator and memory usage**
  - Is dynamic allocation minimized in the tick-to-trade hot path?

  - Are you using per-thread or per-core allocation strategies where possible?
  - Do latency measurements show any spikes correlated with allocation pressure?

- **Runtime services**
  - In managed environments, are GC and JIT behavior tuned and warmed up before the trading session?
  - Are background runtime threads segregated from isolated trading cores?

- **Language features**
  - Does the hot path avoid exceptions for normal control flow?
  - Are virtual calls, deep inheritance, or reflection used sparingly, with clear justification?

- **Continuous validation**
  - For each new build, do you re-run microbenchmarks of the hot loops and compare performance counters (cache misses, branch mispredictions, cycles per tick)?
  - Do you track changes in latency distributions (especially p99 and p99.9) across builds to catch regressions early?

## Closing the Loop: From Source to Silicon

Compiler and runtime optimizations form the last major link in the chain tying your source code to the physical behavior of the trading system. Earlier in the chapter we focused on infrastructure: CPU cores, caches, NUMA nodes, OS scheduling, interrupts, NICs, and kernel-bypass frameworks. Those layers define the environment in which your code runs.

The toolchain and runtime define what that code *is* in machine terms:

- Which instructions exist in the hot path.
- How those instructions are laid out in memory.

- What hidden work the runtime may perform behind the scenes.

By treating builds and runtime configuration as first-class design concerns, you ensure that the executable that lands on your trading servers behaves in line with the assumptions you made when analyzing pipelines, caches, and scheduling. When you change the source, you do not just ask, "is the algorithm correct?" but also, "how will this new code be compiled, optimized, and executed on our actual hardware and runtime?"

Trading performance at the microsecond scale is not the result of any single magic trick. It is the cumulative effect of many aligned decisions, from how you write loops and data structures to how you compile, link, and run them on carefully chosen cores and queues. Compiler and runtime optimizations are the final tuning knobs in that system, and when used thoughtfully, they can turn a merely fast design into one that is consistently, reliably ahead.

# Chapter 7

# Market Data Handling & Feed Handlers

*Every nanosecond your trading system spends mishandling market data quietly taxes your edge. This chapter opens the black box between the exchange and your strategies: we trace how ticks cross the NIC, get decoded from binary noise into structured events, survive packet loss and gaps, and finally fan out across your plant with predictable latency. By the end, you will see where latency actually hides in feed handlers, and how small design choices in buffers, protocols, and recovery logic determine whether your view of the market is merely fast-or reliably first.*

## 7.1 Feed Handler Design Patterns

In previous chapters we treated market data as a conceptual "event stream" that drives order books, risk, and strategies. In real systems, that stream starts life as raw packets on a network interface card (NIC). The job of the feed handler is to pull those packets off the wire, decode them into meaningful messages, and deliver those messages into trading processes at rates that can easily exceed several million updates per second during busy periods.

This section introduces the canonical architectures and concurrency patterns that make this possible. We will not focus on exotic micro-optimizations. Instead, we will show how a clear pipeline structure, the right queues, and disciplined use of threads and cores dominate performance and stability.

## The Feed Handler as a Pipeline

Almost all high-performance feed handlers can be described as a small number of stages connected in a pipeline:

- **NIC ingress**: the network card receives packets from the exchange.
- **Packet capture**: the operating system or user-space driver exposes those packets to your process.
- **Protocol parsing**: the raw bytes are parsed into protocol-specific messages.
- **Normalization**: protocol-specific messages are mapped into your internal, venue-agnostic schema.
- **Publication**: normalized events are pushed to strategy engines and other consumers.

Each stage transforms data and passes it to the next one. The design questions are: which stages share a thread, which run on separate cores, and how data moves between them. The answers determine whether you achieve both low *latency* (how quickly a single message moves through the pipeline) and high *throughput* (how many messages per second you can process steadily).

## Stages and Their Latency/Throughput Roles

Let us look more closely at each stage and why it exists.

**NIC ingress.** The NIC receives Ethernet frames from the exchange. Modern cards expose large hardware rings: circular buffers in which each entry points to a packet buffer. At this level you are not yet thinking about messages or order books; the job is simply to receive packets as fast and predictably as possible.

**Packet capture.** The capture stage reads packets from the NIC ring into user space. This can be done through the standard kernel network stack, but high-performance systems often use kernel-bypass frameworks or specialized drivers to reduce overhead and jitter. Conceptually, capture is still packet-oriented: you see network headers and protocol payloads, not yet individual trades or quotes.

**Protocol parsing.** The parsing stage walks the exchange's market data protocol and extracts individual messages. One packet might contain several market data messages, or one message might span multiple packets. The parser needs to reconstruct message boundaries and interpret the fields of each message. This is where you turn bytes into domain concepts such as "add order", "trade", or "book clear".

**Normalization.** Normalization maps protocol-specific messages into your internal schema. It translates exchange-specific symbols into your internal instrument identifiers, maps flags and enumerations into canonical values, and drops or passes through fields according to your firm's needs. Multiple downstream components should not need to know whether a message originally came from venue A or B, or whether it was encoded in protocol X or Y.

**Publication.** Finally, normalized events are published to strategy engines, risk modules, and other consumers. This involves fan-out: each event might need to go to many consumers, potentially on different threads or machines. How you handle this fan-out has a major impact on end-to-end latency and on how robust your system is to slow consumers.

At each stage you must balance two goals: avoid becoming the bottleneck (throughput) and avoid introducing unpredictable delays (latency jitter). The rest of this section will show how the architecture and queues between stages determine how well you achieve that balance.

## Queues as the Backbone of the Pipeline

The pipeline relies on *queues* between stages. The choice of queue type and size is not a low-level detail; it is central to the design.

**Single-producer/single-consumer ring buffers.** When exactly one thread produces data and exactly one thread consumes it, the most efficient structure is a ring buffer. Conceptually, this is just a fixed-size array with two indices:

- the producer index points to where the next item will be written;
- the consumer index points to where the next item will be read.

Because there is only one producer and one consumer, each index can be modified without locks: no two threads ever write the same index. Cache-friendly implementations ensure that the producer and consumer indices do not share a cache line, to avoid cache thrashing.

SP/SC ring buffers are ideal between capture and parsing when each of these tasks is single-threaded, or between a parser thread and a normalization thread.

**Lock-free queues for fan-in and fan-out.** When multiple threads need to push into or pull from the same queue, you need a multi-producer or multi-consumer design. Lock-free queues use atomic operations to coordinate access without coarse-grained locks. They are more complex and generally a bit slower than SP/SC rings under light load, but they scale across threads and cores.

Lock-free queues are commonly used:

- to combine messages from several parser threads into a single normalizer;
- to fan out from one normalizer into multiple downstream consumer queues.

**Bounded queues and backpressure.** All queues in a low-latency system should be bounded: they have a fixed capacity, and if they fill up, the producer must react. This is uncomfortable, because it forces you to make hard choices about what happens when the system is overloaded, but it is essential to avoid uncontrolled latency spikes.

Common reactions when a bounded queue is full include:

- *dropping* less-important messages, such as deep book levels that are unlikely to affect your decisions;
- *backing off* producers by briefly spinning or yielding, accepting a small increase in latency to avoid catastrophic build-up;
- *shedding load* by disconnecting from particularly noisy instruments or venues under extreme conditions.

What matters is that the tail latency (the worst-case delay) remains *bounded* and well understood. In a trading system, a rare 100-millisecond delay in seeing market data is often worse than dropping some updates and knowing exactly what your guarantees are.

## Threading Models: Who Owns Which Stage?

With stages and queues defined, the next design question is: how do you map stages to threads and cores? Three broad patterns show up in practice.

### Thread-per-core Pipelines

In a thread-per-core design, each major stage runs on its own dedicated core, often with a tight loop that busy-waits on its input queue.

For example:

- Core 0: capture thread reads from the NIC and writes raw packets into a ring.
- Core 1: parser thread reads packets, decodes messages, and writes protocol messages into the next ring.
- Core 2: normalizer thread reads protocol messages and writes normalized events.
- Core 3: publisher thread fans out normalized events to strategies.

The advantages are:

- predictable performance: each core has a single responsibility;
- minimal context-switching: each thread is always running and rarely blocked;
- good cache locality: a thread repeatedly touches similar data structures.

The main cost is the number of cores consumed and the additional end-to-end latency from having more hand-offs. Each hand-off adds at least one queue traversal and the time to move data between cores' caches.

**Event-Loop Models**

At the other extreme, an event-loop model uses one or a small number of threads that repeatedly poll several sources of work: NIC descriptors, queues, timers, and so on. A single event loop might perform capture, parsing, and normalization inline for each packet, then publish directly to downstream queues.

The advantages are:

- fewer hand-offs: capture, parse, and normalize can happen in one tight loop;
- improved latency for a single message, because it does not wait in multiple queues;
- better resource utilization on systems with fewer cores.

The risks are:

- a long or slow path (for example, a complex message type) can delay everything else in the loop;
- more complex code, because the event loop must handle many concerns.

Event-loop designs are popular when absolute minimum latency is required and the variety of work per message is tightly controlled.

**Hybrid Approaches**

Most production systems adopt some hybrid:

- A small event loop per NIC queue for capture and parsing, followed by separate threads for normalization and publication.
- Multiple parser threads feeding a single normalizer, with a separate thread (or process) owning dissemination to strategies.

Hybrids let you keep latency low where it matters most (often capture and parsing), while still decoupling heavier or more variable work (sometimes normalization and publication).

## Busy-Waiting vs. Blocking I/O

Another central design choice is how threads wait for work.

**Busy-waiting (polling).** A busy-waiting thread repeatedly checks its input source (a NIC descriptor ring or a queue) in a tight loop. When no work is available, it continues looping.

The benefits:

- extremely low wake-up latency; the thread usually notices new work within a few tens of nanoseconds;
- highly predictable behavior, because there are no system calls to wake or schedule the thread.

The costs:

- the core is effectively dedicated to that thread, continuously burning CPU;
- if the loop body becomes complex, you may waste significant energy and create thermal constraints.

Busy-waiting is commonly used in feed handlers between tightly coupled stages: for example, a parser thread that spins on a ring filled by a capture thread.

**Blocking I/O.** A blocking thread waits in a system call until work arrives, at which point the operating system wakes it. This is more resource-efficient but adds variability: wake-up latency depends on the scheduler and on other system activity.

Blocking designs are sometimes acceptable for publication stages or for consumers that are less latency-sensitive, but they are rarely used in the hottest part of the feed handler.

## Core Affinity and Minimizing Jitter

Once you assign stages to threads, you must also decide *where* those threads run. Modern CPUs have multiple cores, often arranged in clusters with different cache and memory relationships. The operating system scheduler is free to move threads between cores unless you tell it not to.

**Pinning threads to cores.** Core affinity is the practice of binding a thread to a specific core. Pinning the capture, parser, and normalizer threads to fixed cores avoids migration, which in turn avoids:

- cold caches after a migration to a new core;
- extra jitter as the scheduler balances threads across cores;
- interference from unrelated system processes.

In many trading systems, a set of cores is reserved exclusively for the trading application, and non-essential background services are either moved away or disabled on those cores.

**NUMA awareness.** On multi-socket systems, memory attached to one CPU socket is slower to access from another socket. Feed handlers should try to keep all threads that work on a particular data path on the same NUMA node, with queues and shared data structures allocated from memory local to that node. Otherwise, each message might cross socket boundaries multiple times, adding latency and jitter.

## Batching: Efficiency Without Head-of-Line Blocking

A recurring tension in feed-handler design is whether to process items one by one or in batches. Batching can improve throughput dramatically by amortizing fixed costs, but too much batching can increase latency and cause head-of-line blocking, where many later messages wait behind earlier ones in a batch.

**Packet coalescing.** At the NIC level, hardware and drivers may combine several small packets into a single larger packet before delivering them to your process. This reduces per-packet overhead, but it can delay early packets slightly while waiting for more to arrive.

For ultra-low-latency applications, you should tune these settings carefully, sometimes trading off a small increase in CPU usage to avoid extra buffering.

**Message batching across system calls.** Reading many packets at once from the NIC, or dequeuing several messages from a queue and processing them as a small batch, reduces the overhead of loop conditions and synchronization. For example, a parser might:

- read up to $N$ packets from the capture ring;
- decode all messages within those packets;
- then publish decoded messages to the next stage, possibly in small groups.

The key is to keep batches small relative to the arrival rate, so that each message does not wait long behind others in the same batch.

**Cache-line-aligned writes.** Batching also interacts with the CPU cache. Writing multiple events that are close together in memory can make better use of cache lines than writing one event per cache line scattered across memory. This is one reason why ring buffers with contiguous storage are favored over pointer-heavy linked structures.

However, if you try to accumulate very large batches before flushing them to the next stage, you increase latency and risk large bursts of work arriving downstream all at once. The guiding principle is: batch just enough to amortize obvious fixed costs (system calls, queue synchronization), but no more.

## Design Discipline vs. Micro-Optimization

It can be tempting to focus on low-level details such as individual CPU instructions or esoteric compiler flags. While these can matter in the final stages of tuning, experience shows that clear architecture and disciplined design are far more important.

**Separation of concerns.** Each stage should have a simple, well-defined responsibility. Capture should not be doing normalization. Publication should not be reconstructing protocol-level details. This makes it easier to reason about performance, test each stage in isolation, and adjust the pipeline as requirements change.

**Simple, predictable data flows.** Data should flow in one direction through the pipeline, with minimal cross-links or feedback. Complex graphs of queues and threads are hard to reason about under load and can hide subtle deadlocks or unbounded buffers.

**Explicit trade-offs.** Every time you introduce a new stage, a new queue, or a new batching point, you should ask:

- What is the benefit in throughput or modularity?
- What is the extra latency this might add in the worst case?
- How will this change the behavior under a burst at market open?

Teams that make these trade-offs explicit, document them, and periodically revisit them when markets or hardware change, build more robust systems than those that rely on ad-hoc tweaks.

## Putting It All Together

A well-designed feed handler for a single venue might therefore look like this:

- One capture thread pinned to a core, polling a NIC RX ring and writing packets into an SP/SC ring buffer.

- One parser thread pinned to another core, reading packets from that ring, decoding protocol messages, and writing them into a lock-free queue that can be consumed by multiple downstream components if needed.
- One normalizer thread pinned to a third core, reading protocol messages, applying symbol and field mappings, and emitting normalized events into bounded per-consumer queues.
- A publication layer that uses shared-memory queues for in-process strategies and possibly low-latency network transports for remote consumers, all while enforcing backpressure through bounded queues.

On top of this, the system applies:

- careful core affinity and NUMA-aware placement of threads and queues;
- limited, controlled batching that raises throughput without causing head-of-line blocking;
- monitoring of queue depths and latencies so that overload conditions are visible and can be managed.

With such an architecture, processing multi-million-message-per-second streams is no longer mysterious. It becomes the predictable outcome of good structural choices: the right stages, the right queues, and a disciplined approach to concurrency. Subsequent sections will build on this foundation to show how protocol decoding, gap detection, and normalization layers fit naturally into this pipeline and how they can be implemented without sacrificing the latency guarantees established here.

## 7.2 Protocol Decoding Techniques

In the previous section we treated the feed handler as a pipeline: packets flow in from the NIC, pass through capture and parsing stages, are normalized, and finally get published to strategies. We deliberately kept "parsing" abstract, treating it as a black box that turns bytes into messages.

We now open that black box.

This section explains how to convert raw binary feeds into structured market events at the rates and latencies that modern markets demand. We will focus on practical decoding techniques that are:

- *cache-friendly*: they work with, rather than against, the CPU's memory hierarchy; and
- *allocation-free*: they avoid dynamic memory allocation in the hot path.

The goal is simple to state but nontrivial to achieve: as packets arrive, you want to extract trades, quotes, and book updates as quickly as possible, without stalls, pauses, or unpredictable slow paths.

## From Packets to Messages

Recall the high-level flow:

1. The capture stage hands you a buffer of bytes, typically representing one or more network packets.
2. Within those bytes lies one or more market data *messages*, each following a protocol defined by the exchange.
3. Your decoder's job is to walk through the buffer, interpret the bytes according to that protocol, and populate in-memory representations of those messages.

Conceptually, think of a decoder as a strict, deterministic "script reader." The protocol specification tells you, byte by byte, what to expect:

- some bytes represent fixed-width integers or timestamps;

- some bits in a byte represent flags;
- other bytes encode lengths, field presence, or compression tokens.

The more regular and predictable this script is, the easier it is for the CPU to run it quickly. Irregularity, unpredictable branching, and scattered memory access all slow you down.

## A Taxonomy of Market Data Protocols

Most modern market data protocols fall into a few broad families. Understanding these will help you reason about their performance characteristics.

### Fixed-Width Binary Protocols

In fixed-width binary protocols, each message type has a fixed layout and size. For example:

- The first byte might be a message type code.
- The next four bytes might be a sequence number.
- The next eight bytes might be a price, and so on.

The key property is that, once you know the message type, you know exactly where each field sits relative to the start of the message. Many legacy equity and futures feeds, as well as some modern low-latency feeds, use this style because it is simple and fast to decode.

From a decoding standpoint, this is ideal: you can compute offsets once, then read fields directly at those offsets without additional parsing logic or branching.

### Tag-Length-Value (TLV) Encodings

In TLV-style protocols, data is sent as a sequence of tagged fields. Each field is usually:

- a tag identifying which logical field this is;

- a length specifying how many bytes follow; and
- a value containing the actual data.

This pattern is flexible and extensible: new tags can be introduced without breaking old parsers. However, it is also more work to decode, because you must:

- read the tag;
- decide how to interpret it; and
- skip over the appropriate number of bytes based on the length.

You cannot, in general, jump directly to "the price" or "the quantity" by offset alone. You must walk the TLV list and interpret each field.

### Field-Based Schemes: FAST and SBE

Many modern exchanges use more sophisticated field-based schemes to reduce bandwidth while retaining binary efficiency. Two common examples are FAST (FIX Adapted for Streaming) and SBE (Simple Binary Encoding).

**FAST.** FAST is designed to compress FIX-style messages by exploiting the fact that many fields change slowly or predictably. It uses:

- a static dictionary that describes all possible fields and their "operators" (copy, delta, default, etc.); and
- a stream of compressed bits and bytes that encode only the information that actually changed from the previous message.

Decoding FAST means reconstructing full messages from compressed representations using the dictionary and the state of previous messages.

**SBE.** SBE is a binary encoding designed for low latency and high throughput. It uses fixed offsets for most fields, like traditional binary protocols, but allows optional fields and evolving schemas. Messages are often wrapped in a simple frame that includes length and template (schema) identifiers.

SBE's design explicitly aims to be decoder-friendly: once you know the template, you mostly have fixed offsets and types.

## Performance Implications of Protocol Design

The protocol family determines what your decoder must do on each message. This, in turn, affects latency through three main channels.

**Branch predictability.** The CPU tries to guess which way each "if" or "switch" statement will go. Repeated, predictable branches become almost free; unpredictable branches cause pipeline flushes and stalls.

Fixed-width binary and SBE-style protocols keep branches predictable: once you know the message type, the decode path is almost always the same.

TLV and heavily compressed schemes like FAST introduce more variability in the per-message path, increasing the risk of mispredicted branches.

**Memory access patterns.** The CPU fetches memory in units of cache lines. When your decode path walks linearly through a buffer—reading bytes one after another—it benefits from streaming behavior: each cache line brings in bytes you will use next.

If your decoder jumps around in memory or follows pointers to scattered locations, it causes cache misses. Each miss forces the CPU to fetch data from slower levels of memory, adding delay.

Fixed-layout protocols allow nearly linear scans; more dynamic formats may involve more indirect access.

**State and dictionary management.** Protocols like FAST require maintaining per-field state across messages. Each decoded message typically updates the dictionary, which the next message's decoding depends on.

Maintaining this state can be fast if done carefully, but it increases the amount of data the decoder must touch per message and can reduce cache locality if the state is large or poorly organized.

## Design Principles for Fast Decoders

Regardless of the protocol, there are several common design principles for high-performance decoding.

### Pre-Allocating and Reusing Message Objects

A major source of latency spikes in naive decoders is dynamic memory allocation. If you allocate and free a fresh object for every decoded message, you:

- add overhead to every message; and
- risk occasional long pauses when the allocator's internal structures need to be reorganized.

Instead, most high-frequency decoders pre-allocate a pool of message objects and reuse them.

Conceptually, you can think of this as a conveyor belt of trays:

- Each tray represents a message object.
- The decoder fills a tray with fields from one message and passes the tray along to the next stage (normalization, book building, etc.).
- After the consumer is done with that tray, it is returned empty to the pool and used again for another message.

Because these trays are allocated once at start-up, there is no per-message allocation or deallocation in the hot path.

### Working Directly on the Input Buffer

Another performance pitfall is copying bytes unnecessarily. For example, a naive decoder might:

- copy the payload from the packet buffer into a temporary buffer;
- then copy individual fields into separate buffers or strings.

Each copy burns memory bandwidth and pollutes caches. Instead, efficient decoders treat the input buffer as read-only storage and use offsets or lightweight views into it.

Intuitively:

- Imagine the packet payload as a long ruler, marked in bytes.
- Rather than cutting the ruler into pieces (copies), the decoder remembers that "price starts at 30 cm and has length 8 cm," and "symbol starts at 50 cm and has length 8 cm," and so on.

When the next stage needs the price or symbol, it either reads it directly from those offsets or, if necessary, converts it into an internal representation at that point. This avoids intermediate copies and reduces memory traffic.

**Linear, Cache-Friendly Decode Paths**

Whenever possible, your decoder should walk through memory in a straight line. This means:

- start at the beginning of the message;
- read header fields in order;
- read body fields in order;
- stop when you reach the message length.

This "linear scan" style plays well with the CPU's caches and prefetcher. In many binary protocols, you can pre-compute the offset of each field, then read them in order without conditional jumps. Even in more dynamic protocols, you can often structure the code to avoid jumping backwards or repeatedly scanning the same region.

**Reducing Branches and Special Cases**

Every extra "if this field is present, do X; otherwise do Y" in the hot path has a cost. You cannot eliminate branches entirely, but you can:

- group similar message types together so that the decoder sees a stable pattern of branches;
- move rare, complex cases into separate, colder paths that are only executed when needed; and
- use simple, table-driven logic where appropriate, so that the decoder looks up behavior in precomputed tables rather than chaining conditionals.

Think of branches as road junctions in your decode path: a few, well-placed junctions are fine; a maze of intersections slows everything down and makes timing less predictable.

## Representative Decode Paths

Let us now sketch how these principles apply to specific protocol families. The goal is conceptual: we want you to visualize what the decoder does for each message.

### Decoding a Fixed-Width Binary Message

For a fixed-width protocol, the decoder's job is straightforward:

1. Read the message header from known offsets: message type, message length, sequence number.
2. Based on the message type, choose the appropriate decode routine. Each routine knows exactly where each field lives within the message.
3. Read each field by directly indexing into the buffer at precomputed offsets.
4. Populate a pre-allocated message object with the decoded values, referencing the original buffer if safe for fields like symbols.

Note what *does not* happen here:

- There is no scanning for delimiters or variable-length fields (except where explicitly designed).
- There is minimal branching: one branch to pick the decode routine, then straight-line code.
- There are no allocations: all storage is from pre-allocated objects.

As a result, per-message costs become extremely stable. This is the pattern many exchanges choose for their most latency-sensitive feeds.

### Decoding a FAST Message

FAST decoding is more involved but follows a regular pattern. Conceptually, the decoder maintains:

- a dictionary, which is an array of field states (the last seen value, default value, or other operator-specific state for each field); and
- a pointer into the compressed bit stream for the current message.

For each message:

1. Identify the message template (often with a small identifier in the stream).
2. For each field in that template, in order:
   (a) Consult the field's operator (copy, default, delta, etc.) and read any bits or bytes associated with this field.
   (b) Combine the operator, the new bits, and the previous state from the dictionary to produce the field's actual value for this message.
   (c) Update the dictionary entry for this field with the new value.
3. Populate the pre-allocated message object with the reconstructed field values.

This process is inherently more stateful than fixed-width decoding: each decoded message depends on prior messages via the dictionary. Performance depends heavily on:

- keeping the dictionary small and cache-friendly (for example, contiguous arrays rather than pointer-rich structures);
- reading the compressed bits in a linear fashion, minimizing back-tracking; and
- structuring the per-field logic to be as regular as possible, so the CPU learns the pattern of branches for common messages.

With careful implementation, FAST can still be decoded at very high rates, but its peak performance and predictability are usually below that of a well-designed fixed-width or SBE feed.

**Decoding an SBE Message**

SBE blends the advantages of fixed-width binary with schema evolution. A typical SBE message is:

- wrapped in a simple frame carrying length and template ID; and
- laid out in memory according to a template that defines field order, types, and offsets.

To decode:

1. Read the frame header: length, template ID, and possibly version.
2. Use the template ID to look up a pre-computed description of the message layout.
3. Read fields at predefined offsets, using types specified by the template.
4. For optional or variable-length fields (such as strings or repeating groups), use small control fields (like presence bits or counts) defined in the template to navigate the layout.

The key performance feature is that, once templates are loaded, your decode code can be highly regular. Many SBE implementations generate specialized decoders from templates ahead of time. These decoders are essentially hand-tuned fixed-width parsers for each message type.

## Error Handling Without Slow Paths

Real-world feeds are not always clean. Packets can be truncated, frames can be malformed, and exchanges occasionally send unexpected data. Your decoder must detect and handle these situations without turning every rare error into a slow path that punishes all messages.

**Detecting malformed data cheaply.** Whenever possible, use simple, local checks:

- Verify that declared message lengths fit within the packet buffer.
- Check that sequence numbers increase as expected.
- Validate that message type codes fall within known ranges.

These checks can often be expressed as inexpensive comparisons and bounds checks that the CPU can execute without disrupting the main decode flow.

**Separating hot and cold error handling.** When you detect an error:

- keep the main decode loop simple and non-blocking;
- record minimal diagnostic information (for example, a pointer to the buffer and an error code) in a side structure; and
- hand this off to a slower, separate component that logs or analyzes the issue.

The idea is analogous to a toll-road: most cars go through the fast lanes; only exceptional vehicles are diverted to the side for inspection. You do not want the entire highway to stop because of one misbehaving car.

**Avoiding heavy constructs in the hot path.** Exception mechanisms, complex logging, and string formatting are convenient but often expensive. In the hot path of a decoder, you should avoid them for the common case. Instead, rely on simple status codes and lightweight counters, escalating only when necessary.

## Observability: Knowing Where Time Is Spent

No matter how carefully you design your decoder, you will need to measure. Many performance problems only become visible under realistic load, with realistic data patterns.

Useful observability techniques include:

- **Per-stage timing**: measure how long it takes, on average and at the tail, to decode a message from buffer to structured object.
- **Per-message-type statistics**: track rates and latencies per message type. This reveals whether rare but heavy message types are causing spikes.
- **Cache and branch metrics**: using profiling tools, observe cache miss rates and branch misprediction rates on the decode path.
- **Error counters**: count malformed messages, unexpected lengths, or dictionary inconsistencies. A sudden increase often signals an upstream problem (for example, network corruption or a protocol change).

The aim is not to build a full-blown performance lab inside your decoder, but to have enough instrumentation to answer, with evidence, questions such as:

- "Why did latency spike at market open today?"
- "Which message types dominate CPU time?"
- "Did a protocol or schema change silently increase our per-message cost?"

## Putting Decoding in the Bigger Picture

It is useful to step back and see where decoding fits in the overall architecture:

- The *feed handler design patterns* section argued that good pipeline structure, with clear stages and queues, dominates performance.
- Within that pipeline, *protocol decoding* is often one of the primary latency hotspots, especially for compressed or complex feeds.

Your decoding techniques must therefore respect the broader architectural constraints:

- They should not allocate memory in the hot path, to avoid stalls that undermine the predictability of your ring buffers and queues.
- They should process messages in a streaming, linear fashion that matches the pipeline's event-driven nature.
- They should expose *structured* events that the normalization and aggregation layers can consume directly, without re-parsing or guessing at protocol details.

When designed this way, the decoder ceases to be a mysterious, opaque performance problem and instead becomes a well-understood mechanical stage: given a buffer of bytes, it emits a stream of structured events with known latency characteristics.

In the next section, we will build on this foundation to look at *gap detection and recovery*: how to detect when messages are missing or reordered, and how to repair the state of your order books so that strategies always see a trustworthy view of the market.

## 7.3 Gap Detection and Recovery

In the previous sections we treated market data as a continuous stream of decoded events flowing through a well-structured feed handler pipeline. We assumed, in effect, that every message sent by the exchange eventually arrives, in order, and is decoded correctly.

Real networks do not behave that politely.

Packets can be dropped, duplicated, or delayed. Messages can arrive out of order, especially on multicast feeds or when exchanges use multiple network paths. If you ignore these realities, your local order book will eventually diverge from the exchange's true state, sometimes in subtle ways that are hard to detect but easy to trade badly against.

This section explains how modern feed handlers detect missing data, repair their internal state, and demonstrate to the rest of the trading system that their view of the market is trustworthy again after loss or reordering.

## Why Gap Handling Matters as Much as Latency

From a trading perspective, latency only has value if your market view is *correct*. Acting quickly on a wrong book is worse than acting slightly later on a correct book. You may:

- hit liquidity that is no longer there;
- miss trades that would have been profitable; or
- violate risk and position limits because your internal state is behind or inconsistent.

Gaps in the data stream are the primary cause of book divergence. A single missing "delete order" or "trade" message can leave stale volume resting at a price level, or cause your notion of the best bid/offer to be wrong. Over time, errors accumulate unless you detect and correct them.

Gap detection and recovery therefore have two key goals:

1. **State correctness**: ensure that your internal representation of the book reflects all relevant exchange messages; and
2. **Trust signals**: provide clear, testable indications to strategy engines and risk systems about when the book is reliable and when it is being repaired.

## Sequence Numbers as the Backbone of Trust

Almost all modern feeds provide some form of sequence numbering. Sequence numbers are to market data what page numbers are to a book: without them you can still read, but it is hard to know if pages are missing or misordered.

## Per-channel and per-packet sequence numbers

Exchanges may assign sequence numbers at different levels:

- **Per packet**: each UDP packet in a multicast feed carries a sequence number. All messages inside that packet share the same number.
- **Per message**: each logical market data message carries its own sequence number.
- **Per channel or stream**: a given multicast group, TCP connection, or logical "book" has its own independent sequence space.

Your decoder should expose these sequence numbers to the gap detection logic as early as possible, ideally attached to the decoded message objects or at least to the packet container that carries them.

## Tracking expected sequence numbers

For each feed channel, the feed handler maintains:

- the *last seen* sequence number;
- the *expected next* sequence number; and
- counters of gaps detected, recovered, or unrecovered.

On each new message (or packet), the logic is simple in principle:

- If the incoming sequence equals the expected sequence, all is well; advance the expected sequence.
- If the incoming sequence is greater than the expected sequence, there is a *gap*: some numbers between expected and incoming are missing.
- If the incoming sequence is less than the expected sequence, the message is *late* or a duplicate; depending on the protocol, you may discard it or treat it as part of a recovery stream.

Sequence numbers are usually fixed-width integers that eventually wrap around. Gap logic must correctly handle this wrap-around by comparing in modulo arithmetic terms, not as simple signed or unsigned integers. Conceptually, you do not want the sequence to "go backwards" fatally just because a counter reached its maximum and restarted at zero.

## Distinguishing Reordering from True Loss

In practice, streams can exhibit *reordering*: message with sequence 101 may arrive before message 100. If you treat every instance of "incoming sequence > expected sequence" as hard loss, you will declare gaps too aggressively and trigger unnecessary recovery.

The challenge is to distinguish:

- transient reordering, where missing messages are likely to show up shortly; from
- true loss, where missing messages will never arrive and you must repair state.

## Reordering windows and timeouts

A common approach is to maintain a small "reordering window":

- When you see sequence 105 while expecting 100, you note that 100–104 are missing.
- Instead of immediately triggering recovery, you start a short timer or logical window for those missing numbers.
- If messages 100–104 arrive within that window, you apply them in the correct order and continue.
- If they do not arrive in time, you declare a genuine gap and start recovery.

How large should this window be? Too small, and you will treat harmless reordering as loss, causing frequent, expensive recovery cycles.

Too large, and your internal book will lag reality while you wait, undermining latency.

The right value depends on:

- the observed reordering behavior of the venue's feed;
- the physical and logical network paths; and
- your tolerance for short-term book inaccuracy vs. recovery overhead.

In very low-latency environments, the window may be expressed in microseconds; in more relaxed systems, in a handful of messages or milliseconds.

## Data structures for tracking pending sequences

Internally, you can think of gap tracking as keeping a small "to be filled" set of missing sequence numbers. When a new message arrives:

- if its sequence is the next expected, you apply it and bump expected;
- if its sequence is higher, you mark the intermediate sequences as pending;
- if its sequence corresponds to a pending value, you apply it and remove it from the pending set.

As long as all pending numbers are eventually filled before their timeout, no recovery is needed. Only when some remain unfilled beyond the window do you declare a gap.

For performance reasons, this pending set must be small and efficient. You do not want to maintain a large, general-purpose data structure; rather, you rely on the empirical observation that reordering depth is usually limited.

## What Goes Wrong When Gaps Persist

When missing messages do not show up in time, you have a true gap. To understand how to fix it, it is helpful to see what gaps do to your local state.

## Incremental updates and local state drift

Most modern feeds are *incremental*: they send you changes to the order book, not full snapshots on each update. You might receive messages such as:

- "add order at price 100, quantity 50";
- "reduce quantity on that order by 10";
- "delete that order";
- "trade against best bid 20 units"; and so on.

Your local book is a function of:

- the last full snapshot you applied; and
- *all* subsequent incremental messages, in correct order, with none missing.

If you miss even a single incremental update, your state drifts:

- Missing an add means you never create an order that should exist.
- Missing a delete leaves a ghost order.
- Missing a trade under-reports volume executed.

Critically, the drift is often *silent*: there is no obvious error in decoding or application, just a growing mismatch versus the true book at the exchange.

## When you can and cannot "patch around" a gap

It is tempting to ask whether you can sometimes ignore small gaps. For example, if you know an order was fully deleted later, does a missing intermediate "reduce" message matter?

In principle:

- For simple state variables (like a price that is always fully specified), you can sometimes reason that later updates render a missing step irrelevant.
- For rich order books and time-priority structures, this is rarely safe. Priority, queue position, and partial fills can all depend on the full history.

As a rule in production trading systems, you should treat any confirmed gap in an incremental feed as a reason to distrust your state until you have performed an explicit recovery.

## Core Recovery Tools

Once you accept that gaps require corrective action, the question becomes: what tools does the exchange give you to repair state? Typically, there are three:

1. incremental gap-fill mechanisms;
2. snapshot feeds or on-demand snapshots; and
3. replay or recovery channels.

## Incremental gap fills

Some exchanges provide dedicated gap-fill or retransmission services. Upon detecting a gap, your feed handler can request:

- "all messages from sequence X to sequence Y"; or

- "a retransmission of missing packets or messages on this channel."

These gap-fill messages are then sent, often over a separate unicast connection. Your handler applies them to its state as if they had arrived in the original stream, taking care to:

- apply them in correct sequence number order; and
- avoid double-applying updates if some missing messages arrive both via retransmission and late on the main feed.

Incremental gap fills are most effective when gaps are rare and narrow (few messages). For wider gaps or persistent loss, a fresh snapshot is often more efficient.

## Snapshots: starting from a known good state

A *snapshot* is a point-in-time, full picture of the order book (or a subset, such as top N levels). Feeds may offer:

- periodic multicast snapshots (for example, every few seconds);
- on-demand snapshots via a request/response protocol; or
- separate TCP-based snapshot services.

To repair state using a snapshot, you generally:

1. Pause or carefully stage application of live incremental updates.
2. Obtain a snapshot that includes a reference sequence number (or equivalent marker).
3. Apply the snapshot into a "shadow" copy of the book, not yet visible to strategies.
4. Apply all missing increments from the snapshot's reference sequence up to the latest known good sequence onto that shadow copy.

5. Atomically flip over, making the shadow copy the new active book.

This staging ensures that strategies never see a half-rebuilt book. Either they see the pre-recovery state (known to be compromised but typically flagged as such), or they see the fully repaired state after the flip.

### Rewind and replay of local state

In some designs, especially where you record all received messages to a local log, you can think in terms of rewinding and replaying:

- You maintain a durable or semi-durable log of all decoded, ordered messages.
- Upon gap detection and receipt of gap-fill data, you reconstruct the message sequence from some earlier safe point.
- You replay messages from that point into a fresh book builder, producing a corrected book.

This approach is conceptually clean and beneficial for offline analysis, but it can be more resource-intensive. In latency-sensitive paths you typically combine it with snapshots to avoid replaying huge histories during live trading hours.

## Integrating Recovery into an Event-Driven Model

Recovery logic must coexist with your main decode and book-building pipeline without blocking it. Otherwise, during recovery, your system might stop applying new messages, effectively creating self-inflicted gaps.

### Decoupling decode from recovery

A common pattern is:

- The decode loop continues to process incoming packets and messages, annotating them with gap-related metadata (for example, "this message arrived while we were recovering").
- A separate recovery controller monitors sequence tracking, initiates gap-fill or snapshot requests, and coordinates state transitions for the book.

You can visualize this as two parallel tracks:

1. a "hot" path that never stops decoding and queuing messages; and
2. a "control" path that occasionally pauses or redirects where those messages are applied (active book vs. shadow book) based on recovery state.

## Staging partial snapshots

During recovery, especially when using snapshots, you must be careful about partially applied state. Best practice is to use staging:

- Allocate a separate, shadow order book structure for each instrument or feed you are repairing.
- Apply the snapshot and subsequent missing increments into this shadow book while the active book continues to serve strategies, possibly with a degraded trust rating.
- Once the shadow book is fully caught up to the current sequence and validated, atomically replace the active book with the shadow.

Atomically here means that, from the perspective of downstream consumers, there is a single, well-defined instant at which the old book is replaced by the new, consistent one. This can be implemented with pointer swaps or similar techniques; the important point is that strategies never observe "half-rebuilt" state.

## Proving Trustworthiness to the Rest of the System

From the perspective of a strategy engine, what matters is not the internal cleverness of your gap handling, but whether it can trust the data it receives. The feed handler must therefore expose clear signals about its state.

## Book health indicators

For each instrument, book, or feed, you should maintain and publish simple health indicators, such as:

- **In-sync**: no unresolved gaps; all messages applied in sequence.
- **Recovering**: a gap has been detected; snapshot or gap-fill in progress; state may be stale or incomplete.
- **Out-of-sync**: recovery has failed or is taking too long; the book should not be used for trading decisions.

These states can be attached to the market data stream (for example, as side-band fields on book updates) or exposed through a separate status channel. Strategies can then:

- ignore or down-weight signals from books that are recovering or out-of-sync;
- adjust risk limits when too many venues are unhealthy; and
- log or alert when health transitions occur.

## Sequence number exposure

In addition to high-level health flags, exposing sequence numbers, or at least a monotonically increasing "book version" counter, allows downstream systems to:

- detect if they themselves have missed events from the feed handler;

- record which exact state they traded on, aiding later analysis; and
- correlate trades and risk decisions with specific points in the market data timeline.

This is especially helpful in post-trade investigations, where you may need to explain why a strategy behaved a certain way at a particular time.

## Operational Monitoring and Offline Analysis

Gap detection and recovery are not just coding problems; they are operational ones. Your system should provide enough hooks to monitor and analyze gap behavior in production.

## Monitoring gap rates and patterns

At minimum, you want to monitor:

- number and size of gaps per venue and per day;
- time to detect and time to recover each gap;
- frequency of reordering events that resolved without recovery; and
- time spent in recovering or out-of-sync states.

Patterns in these metrics can reveal:

- chronic loss on specific network paths or NICs;
- poorly tuned buffer sizes or queue depths; and
- exchange-side issues, such as bursts of packet loss on particular multicast groups.

## Replay facilities for incident analysis

When something goes badly wrong—a large, unrecovered gap, an unexpected book divergence, or a trading loss suspected to be data-driven—you need to replay and inspect the episode offline.

A replay facility typically:

- records the incoming packets or decoded messages to disk, with timestamps and sequence numbers;
- allows you to "rewind time" and feed this recorded data into a copy of your feed handler and book builder; and
- provides tools to visualize when gaps occurred, when recovery was triggered, and how the book state evolved.

This is invaluable both for debugging bugs in your gap logic and for holding external providers (venues, networks) accountable when data quality falls short of expectations.

## Design Principles: Correctness First, Then Speed

It is tempting, in a latency-obsessed environment, to treat gap handling as a secondary concern or to cut corners to save a few microseconds. This is a mistake.

The right order of priorities is:

1. **Correctness**: sequence tracking and gap detection must be unambiguous; recovery must lead to a book that truly matches the exchange.
2. **Transparency**: the health of each book must be visible and easy to reason about for strategies, risk, and operations.
3. **Efficiency**: only once correctness and transparency are in place do you optimize the performance of gap detection and recovery paths.

Fortunately, many of the performance techniques introduced earlier—cache-friendly data structures, allocation-free paths, clear separation of hot and cold logic—apply directly to gap handling as well. Sequence tracking can be done with simple counters; pending sets can be kept small and fixed-size; recovery controllers can be structured as straightforward state machines rather than sprawling, ad-hoc code.

With this discipline, your feed handler becomes more than a fast pipe. It is a trustworthy steward of market state, able to survive real-world packet loss and reordering, and to prove to the rest of the system exactly when its view of the market is reliable and when it is in the process of repairing itself.

## 7.4 Normalization & Aggregation

Up to this point, we have focused on a single feed: how packets are pulled off the wire, decoded into messages, and kept consistent even in the presence of gaps. Real trading systems rarely stop there. Most strategies look at many venues for the same instrument: different exchanges, dark pools, auction books, and perhaps internal crossing engines. Each has its own protocol, message types, and quirks.

For a strategy, however, it is not helpful to think "this is a NASDAQ add-order message in protocol X" or "this is a futures trade in protocol Y." What matters is a coherent view of *the market*: where can I trade, at what prices, in what sizes, and with which timing guarantees? That view must be consistent across venues and must preserve enough detail about where and when each piece of information originated.

In this section we explain how to transform heterogeneous exchange feeds into a unified, multi-venue view while preserving latency and *provenance*—the "who, where, and when" of each price level. We will:

- define what we mean by *normalization*;
- describe per-venue book construction on normalized data;
- show how those books are *aggregated* into consolidated views such as NBBO-style top-of-book or full depth across venues; and

- discuss how to track and expose provenance and timing so that strategies can make informed decisions about latency and data quality.

## Why Normalization and Aggregation Are Necessary

Imagine you subscribe to three exchanges, all trading the same equity. Each exchange:

- uses a different symbol (for example, one might include a suffix, another might pad with spaces);
- sends different message types and flags for the same concepts (for example, "add order" vs. "new order," different codes for auction states); and
- uses different timestamp conventions (exchange send time, nanosecond vs. microsecond, different epochs).

If you handed these raw feeds directly to a strategy, the code would quickly become unmanageable. Every branch would say "if venue A, interpret this way; if venue B, interpret that way," and so on. Worse, any change at a venue—a new message field, a different code for auction mode—would ripple through all strategies.

Normalization and aggregation solve this problem by introducing a set of shared representations:

- A *normalized event schema* that all venues map into.
- Per-venue order books built from those normalized events.
- Aggregated views (NBBO, consolidated book) built from the per-venue books.

The result is a clean separation of concerns:

- Feed handlers and normalizers take care of protocol details and venue-specific quirks.

- Strategies deal with logical concepts such as "best bid on venue X" or "consolidated best offer across all lit venues."

This separation makes the system easier to maintain and reason about, but it also has latency implications: normalization and aggregation must be done efficiently so they do not erase the gains achieved in the lower layers.

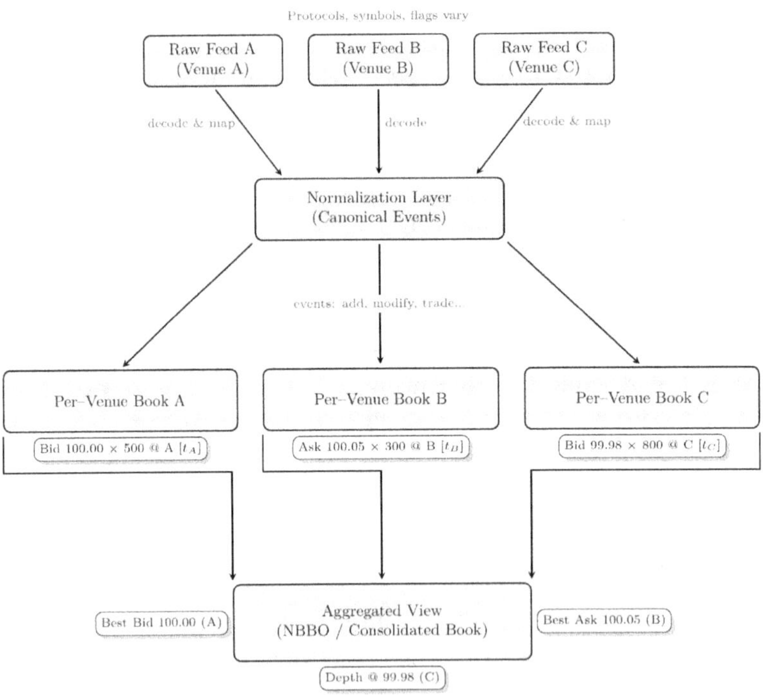


Aggregated price levels retain venue IDs (A,B,C) and timestamps ($t_A, t_B, t_C$) so strategies can reason about latency and source.

## What Exactly Is Normalization?

Normalization is the process of converting venue-specific events into a *canonical schema* used across your system. This involves several dimensions.

### Symbol and instrument mapping

Different venues identify the same financial instrument differently. Normalization maps these identifiers into a single internal key. For each incoming event, you translate:

- exchange-specific symbols or security IDs;
- series identifiers for derivatives; and
- corporate action-related codes or suffixes

into an internal instrument identifier that your strategy layer understands. Internally, you then say "instrument 12345" regardless of whether that is "AAPL", "AAPL.OQ", or "AAPL_20251219C00150000" externally.

This mapping is usually maintained in a reference data service and loaded into the normalizer at start-up, with updates as instruments are listed, delisted, or changed.

### Event type harmonization

Exchanges provide their own sets of message types: add order, modify, delete, trade, cross, auction state, and many others. Even when the concepts are similar, the exact semantics and flags often differ.

Normalization maps these into a consistent event vocabulary. For example:

- Venue A's "add order" and Venue B's "new order on book" both become a canonical *AddOrder* event with standardized fields.

- Venue-specific trade qualifiers (auction trade, dark-pool execution, opening cross) are mapped into a shared set of flags.
- Auction and halt messages are mapped into a canonical set of trading states (for example, *Trading*, *Auction*, *Halt*, *ClosingAuction*).

The goal is to let downstream code answer questions like "is this instrument currently in continuous trading?" or "is this a visible, on-book order?" without knowing which venue it came from.

### Field semantics and units

Even when fields look similar, there are subtle differences:

- Prices may be expressed in different units (ticks, decimals, implied multipliers).
- Sizes might be in shares, lots, or contracts, perhaps with venue-specific rounding rules.
- Side (buy vs. sell) might be coded differently.

Normalization standardizes these:

- All prices are converted into a canonical price representation, using stored tick sizes and multipliers per instrument.
- All quantities are expressed in canonical units (for example, shares or contracts), with clear rules for how partial lots are handled.
- Sides and other enumerations are mapped into a common set of values.

Done correctly, this means a strategy can safely compare bid and ask across venues, or evaluate total depth, without worrying about unit mismatches.

### Preserving venue-specific nuance

A vital point: normalization should not erase information that matters for trading. Many "minor" fields—like priority flags, special order conditions, or internal matching engine states—can be central to some strategies' edge.

A good canonical schema therefore has two layers:

- a core set of fields that all venues share (instrument, event type, side, price, size, timestamps); and
- an extension area where venue-specific nuance is preserved in a structured way (for example, per-venue flag fields or "extra attributes" keyed by venue and name).

This allows most strategies to live entirely in the core schema while more specialized ones can opt in to venue-specific details.

## Per-Venue Order Book Construction on Normalized Events

Once events are normalized, each venue still maintains its own order book. It is usually a mistake to merge venues too early at the event level; you first want to construct accurate, per-venue books, and only then aggregate.

### Why per-venue books?

Each venue has unique microstructure:

- different matching rules and priority models;
- different auction processes and states; and
- different visibility into hidden or iceberg orders.

A per-venue book captures this microstructure faithfully. For example, you might track:

- full depth of visible orders by price level;
- queue sizes and order counts per level;
- special states (auction imbalance, volatility halt) per venue.

Strategies may care deeply about which venue offers what, not just about the combined best bid and offer.

## Applying normalized events to books

Because events are now in a canonical format, the book builder can be written once and reused across venues. For each venue and instrument, the book builder:

- listens to the stream of normalized *AddOrder*, *ModifyOrder*, *DeleteOrder*, *Trade*, *TradingState* events, and so on;
- maintains an internal representation of the book (often price-level-based for speed); and
- emits derived events such as "top of book changed," "level 3 bid size changed," or "auction started."

Because this process is the same regardless of protocol, most bugs and performance optimizations in book handling are concentrated in one place rather than spread across venue-specific handlers.

## Handling iceberg and auction behavior

Normalization can also simplify complex behaviors such as:

- iceberg or hidden orders, where only part of the true size is visible;
- auction uncrossing events, where many orders trade at a single price; and
- mid-price order types, pegs, and other special instructions.

By translating each venue's representation of these behaviors into canonical flags and state transitions, you allow the per-venue book builder to expose consistent views like "total visible size," "auction indicative price," or "mid-price cross volume" with the same semantics across venues.

## Aggregation: From Many Books to One View

Once you have reliable per-venue books, aggregation is conceptually straightforward: you combine these books into one or more consolidated views that strategies can subscribe to.

### Simple NBBO-style aggregation

The simplest form of aggregation is NBBO-style top-of-book:

- For each instrument, track the best bid and best offer across all selected venues.
- When a per-venue top of book changes (for example, venue A improves its bid), update the aggregated best bid.

The aggregated view must carry not just the price and size, but also:

- which venue (or venues, in case of a tie) contributed that price; and
- the relevant timestamps (more on this below).

For some strategies, NBBO is enough; others need full-depth consolidated books.

### Full-depth consolidated books

A consolidated book includes depth across venues. Conceptually, you:

- take the price levels from each per-venue book;

- group them by price; and
- sum or otherwise combine the sizes to present a cross-venue view at each price level.

The aggregation rules must be explicit. For example:

- Do you sum sizes across venues at the same price to show total available size?
- Do you keep per-venue sizes separate but aligned by price?
- How do you handle venues with different tick sizes or odd-lot rules?

In practice, many systems expose both:

- a *summed* depth view for quick liquidity assessments; and
- a *venue-annotated* depth view where each price level carries a breakdown by venue.

### Aggregation latency and update policies

Every extra layer adds latency. Aggregation should therefore be lightweight and avoid unnecessary work. Common design choices include:

- Triggering aggregation only when per-venue top-of-book or specific depth levels change, rather than for every micro-update.
- Limiting aggregated depth to the levels that actually matter for your strategies (for example, top 5 or top 10), even if per-venue books track deeper levels.
- Using simple data structures that can update aggregated levels in constant or logarithmic time.

There is a trade-off between freshness and CPU usage. Aggregating every tiny change keeps the view perfectly up to date but consumes more resources. For many strategies, slight coarsening (for example, only emitting aggregated updates when price or size change by more than a threshold) is acceptable and can reduce load.

## Preserving Provenance: Venue IDs and Timestamps

Aggregation should never hide where and when information came from. At each consolidated price level, strategies often want to know:

- which venues contribute to that level;
- how fresh each venue's quote is; and
- whether any venue is delayed or degraded.

### Venue attribution

At minimum, each aggregated price level should retain a set of contributing venue IDs. For example, an aggregated best bid might say:

> Price 100.00, size 1,000, contributed by venues A (600) and C (400).

This allows strategies to:

- route orders intelligently (for example, preferring venues with better fill probabilities or rebates);
- avoid venues with known issues (for example, slow confirmations); and
- understand where slippage or missed fills might come from.

### Latency provenance: multiple timestamps

In earlier sections we discussed decode and capture times. At the normalized and aggregated levels, you often track three main timestamps for each event or price level:

- **Exchange send time**: when the exchange says it created or sent the message.
- **Receive time**: when your system's NIC or feed handler first saw the packet.
- **Aggregation time**: when your aggregated view incorporated the update.

By carrying these timestamps through normalization and aggregation, you can:

- estimate one-way latency from exchange to your system (receive minus exchange time);
- estimate internal processing and aggregation latency (aggregation minus receive time);
- compare freshness across venues at the same price.

For example, if two venues show the same best bid but one is consistently 200 microseconds "older" than the other, a latency-sensitive strategy might favor the fresher venue.

### Dealing with delayed or degraded venues

Sometimes, a venue will be slow or partially degraded. Its quotes may be stale, or its feed may be intermittently down. Aggregation logic should:

- detect when a venue's updates lag beyond a threshold;
- optionally exclude that venue from aggregated views or mark its contributions as "stale"; and

- expose this information to strategies, which may adjust routing and risk limits accordingly.

This is one reason why provenance and timing must be preserved: otherwise, an aggregated best bid could be dominated by an apparently attractive but actually stale quote.

## Early vs. Late Normalization

A recurring architectural question is: how early should you normalize?

### Early normalization

In early normalization, you convert protocol-specific events into canonical events as soon as they are decoded, before significant book building or other processing.

Advantages:

- A single, shared code path for book building and aggregation.
- Downstream components do not know about protocol details.
- Easier testing and reasoning about behavior, since most logic runs on normalized events.

Costs:

- Some work may be wasted if certain events are ultimately filtered out or not used.
- Normalization itself adds a small amount of latency to the hot path of every event.

### Late normalization

In late normalization, you keep protocol-specific representations longer, perhaps building per-venue books directly from them, and only normalize when you need to combine or export data.

Advantages:

- You can exploit protocol-specific efficiencies or fields more easily inside the venue-specific code.
- For niche or low-importance venues, you can avoid full normalization cost until needed.

Costs:

- More complex code paths: each venue may need a custom book builder.
- Harder to maintain and extend when venues or protocols change.
- Aggregation logic becomes entangled with protocol knowledge.

Most modern designs favor early normalization for major venues, because it centralizes complexity and keeps later stages simple. For very low-traffic or exotic feeds, late normalization is sometimes used pragmatically.

## Avoiding Double Work and Supporting Multiple Views

Different consumers need different views of market data:

- latency-sensitive strategies might want minimal, per-venue top-of-book data;
- analytics engines might want full depth, trade history, and auction metrics;
- risk systems might only need coarse, slower-moving summaries.

A naïve design would build separate pipelines for each view, duplicating normalization and aggregation work. A better design composes views from shared intermediate representations.

### Shared normalized event streams

Once you have a normalized event stream per venue and instrument, you can attach multiple consumers to it:

- a per-venue book builder for top-of-book only;
- another book builder tracking deeper depth and more statistics;
- a trade-only stream for analytics and VWAP calculations.

Because the normalization step is shared, you avoid re-decoding and re-mapping the same raw messages. This is one of the main performance wins of a normalized architecture.

### Multiple aggregated views from the same books

Similarly, once you have per-venue books, you can generate multiple aggregated views:

- an ultra-low-latency NBBO view that only cares about best bid and best offer;
- a full consolidated depth view built at slightly lower priority;
- specialized views (for example, consolidated auction imbalance across venues) for specific strategies.

Each of these reads from the same per-venue book representations, avoiding redundant work. The key is to design the per-venue book data structures so they can serve multiple consumers efficiently, often via read-only snapshots or shared-memory representations.

## Exposing Both Normalized and Raw Views

Normalization is powerful, but occasionally you need to see the raw feed. Examples include:

- debugging protocol issues or exchange-side anomalies;

- implementing a new strategy that exploits a subtle, venue-specific behavior not yet in the canonical schema; or
- validating that normalization has not introduced errors.

For these reasons, many systems expose both:

- a normalized view used by most production strategies; and
- a raw or lightly decoded view accessible to tools, research, and advanced components.

This can be done via:

- separate streams: one carrying normalized events, another carrying protocol-level messages;
- "side doors" in the book builder that allow inspection of underlying venue-specific fields when needed.

The important point is that production decision logic should not routinely depend on raw protocol quirks. If it does, those quirks should be brought into the normalized schema in a deliberate, well-documented way.

## Bringing It All Together

Normalization and aggregation sit at the point where engineering meets trading logic:

- Below them, feed handlers, decoders, and gap-handling mechanisms fight to deliver every message, in order, at microsecond-level latencies.
- Above them, strategies and risk engines consume logical events and books, ideally without caring which protocol or wire format they came from.

A well-designed normalization and aggregation layer:

- hides protocol and venue diversity behind a stable, well-documented schema;
- preserves provenance and timing so that strategies can reason about latency and data quality;
- supports multiple views (per-venue, consolidated, top-of-book, full depth) without duplicating work; and
- does all of this without becoming a latency bottleneck itself.

With this foundation in place, the final topic in this chapter—*dissemination to strategy engines*—can focus on how to move these normalized, aggregated views to consumers across processes and machines, preserving both latency and determinism, rather than on how to interpret dozens of incompatible feeds.

## 7.5 Dissemination to Strategy Engines

In the previous sections we followed market data from the wire through decoding, gap handling, and normalization and aggregation. At this point, you have a high-quality, normalized, possibly multi-venue view of the market. That view lives inside your market data subsystem: in memory on a set of machines and cores dedicated to feed handling and book building.

The final step is to deliver this information to the consumers that actually trade: strategy engines, risk checks, analytics, and monitoring tools. This step is deceptively simple to state—"send the data to the strategies"—but easy to get wrong in practice. An ill-designed dissemination layer can:

- add more latency than all the preceding stages combined;
- introduce jitter that makes strategy behavior hard to reason about; or
- collapse under bursty load when many consumers fall behind.

This section explains how to move normalized market events from feed handlers to strategies, both within a single process and across machines, while preserving the latency and determinism you worked so hard to achieve upstream.

## From Books to Buses: The Conceptual Model

By the end of normalization and aggregation, your system produces streams of structured events:

- per-venue book updates (top-of-book or full depth);
- consolidated views (NBBO, aggregated depth);
- trades, auction states, and other derived signals.

We will refer to the component that owns these streams as the *publisher* or *feed handler*, even if in practice it is a cluster of processes.

Dissemination adds an explicit *bus* between publishers and consumers. Conceptually:

- Publishers write normalized events into one or more channels on the bus.
- Consumers (strategies, risk, replay) subscribe to the channels they need.
- The bus guarantees certain properties about ordering, loss, and backpressure.

The central design task is to choose the right transport mechanisms and topology for this bus, given your latency and scale requirements.

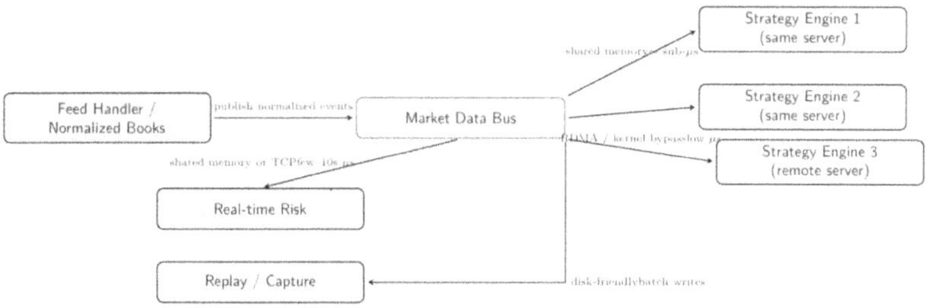


Central market data bus fans out normalized events to multiple consumers. Local strategies use ultra-low-latency shared memory; remote engines use RDMA or kernel-bypass transports; risk and replay tolerate higher latency.

## Dissemination Requirements

Before choosing mechanisms, it is helpful to enumerate what the dissemination layer must guarantee.

### Latency and jitter

Strategies are sensitive not only to average delay but also to *jitter*—variation in that delay. Two key metrics are:

- tick-to-strategy latency: time from exchange send (or NIC receive) to the strategy's first opportunity to react; and
- tail latency: the worst-case delay under realistic load, especially at bursts such as market open.

The dissemination layer must add as little as possible to both, and must not introduce rare but huge spikes that undermine confidence in the system.

### Ordering and loss semantics

Consumers need clear, testable answers to questions like:

- Will I see events in the same order as the feed handler applied them?

- Can I ever miss updates without being told?
- If I fall behind, will I be dropped, throttled, or allowed to catch up?

The dissemination design must make these semantics explicit and easy to verify in tests.

**Backpressure and isolation**

Different consumers run at different speeds. Some strategies process only top-of-book; others run heavy analytics. The bus must prevent slow consumers from:

- stalling the fastest strategies;
- causing unbounded buffer growth; or
- forcing the feed handler to slow down.

This calls for bounded queues and isolation between consumers.

## Dissemination Mechanisms: A Brief Tour

Three broad families of mechanisms cover most designs:

- in-process dissemination;
- shared-memory queues across processes on the same machine; and
- low-latency network transports across machines.

### In-process event buses

If your strategies run in the same process as the feed handler, dissemination can be as simple as passing pointers or references within the same address space. An *in-process event bus*:

- keeps events in shared memory buffers (for example, ring buffers);

- lets strategies subscribe by registering callbacks or polling queues; and
- avoids kernel calls entirely on the hot path.

The advantages are excellent latency and simplicity. The limitations are:

- everything is in one failure domain: a bug in a strategy can crash the feed handler;
- scaling across cores and NUMA nodes becomes complex; and
- you have limited isolation between unrelated strategies.

In-process buses are attractive for very small, highly optimized setups, but most larger trading platforms separate feed handling and strategy engines into at least different processes, if not different machines.

**Shared-memory queues across processes**

For strategies that run as separate processes on the same physical host, shared memory is the standard low-latency transport. In this model:

- The feed handler and strategies map a shared memory region into their address spaces.
- Within that region, they use ring buffers or similar queues to pass events.
- Synchronization relies on atomic operations, not the kernel scheduler.

Shared-memory dissemination can routinely add well under a microsecond of latency per hop when tuned well. It also provides a clean fault boundary: if a strategy process crashes, the feed handler can continue.

**Kernel-bypass and RDMA network transports**

When strategies run on different machines—perhaps in the same rack or across data centers—you need a network transport. Traditional TCP/UDP over the kernel network stack adds overhead and jitter. For latency-sensitive paths, trading systems often use:

- kernel-bypass user-space networking libraries to send and receive packets without context switches; or
- RDMA (Remote Direct Memory Access) transports that let one machine write directly into another's memory region.

Conceptually, you extend the same ring-buffer model used in shared memory across the network:

- The publisher writes events into a remote-visible buffer.
- The consumer polls or is notified when new data appears.

These mechanisms preserve the event-driven, allocation-free design of your local pipeline while spanning machines with single-digit microsecond costs, rather than tens or hundreds.

## Fan-Out Topologies: Matching Strategies to Channels

The next design choice is topology: how many channels you expose and how you connect publishers to subscribers.

**One-to-many buses for read-only consumers**

For consumers that only read data and do not need to coordinate with each other (for example, most strategies), a one-to-many bus works well:

- The feed handler publishes each event once into a central bus.
- The bus fans it out to multiple consumers via per-consumer queues.

Per-consumer queues are essential: they isolate consumers from each other. If Strategy A momentarily falls behind, its queue fills while Strategy B continues consuming at full speed from its own queue.

**Point-to-point channels for heavy analytics**

Some consumers perform heavy computation per event (for example, full re-pricing models, risk stress testing). It can make sense to isolate them on dedicated channels:

- A specialized analytics engine subscribes to a subset of events via its own queue or stream.
- The feed handler may publish a reduced or pre-aggregated view for this consumer, rather than the raw high-rate stream.

This prevents heavy consumers from wasting bandwidth and CPU on data they do not need, and lets you relax latency requirements for them without affecting core strategies.

**Replay taps and capture streams**

Replay and capture components need complete logs of events, often with additional metadata and compression. To avoid burdening real-time dissemination:

- You can attach a replay tap to the bus that reads the same events as strategies but writes them in a batch-friendly format to disk.
- Alternatively, the feed handler can write a compact, append-only event log as it publishes to the bus, decoupling replay capture from consumer behavior.

Importantly, replay taps are allowed more latency; they do not need to run on the same strict microsecond budget as strategies.

## Ordering Guarantees and Message Identity

Strategies often rely on clear ordering assumptions. The dissemination layer must therefore define what ordering it preserves.

**Global vs. per-instrument ordering**

Upstream, your feed handler and book builders process events in some order, often per-feed or per-instrument. Downstream, reasonable guarantees include:

- Within a single instrument and venue, events are delivered in the same order the book builder applied them.
- Across instruments or venues, no guarantees about relative timing are made (beyond timestamps).

Global total ordering across all events is rarely needed and often expensive; per-instrument (or per-book) ordering is usually enough.

**Monotonic sequence numbers or version counters**

To make ordering explicit and detectable by consumers:

- Each instrument-venue pair can carry a monotonically increasing book version or sequence number.
- Each consumer tracks the last seen version and can detect if it has missed updates (for example, by comparing expected vs. received version).

When a consumer detects a gap (for example, version jumps from 100 to 105), it can:

- request a replay or snapshot; or
- switch to a recovery state where it ignores signals until back in sync.

This mirrors the gap detection logic used earlier inside the feed handler, but at the dissemination boundary.

## Backpressure: Handling Slow Consumers Gracefully

No matter how carefully you tune your strategies, some will eventually fall behind—due to load spikes, garbage collection in managed-language components, or transient CPU contention. Backpressure is how the dissemination layer responds.

**Bounded per-consumer queues**

Every dissemination channel should be backed by a bounded queue. When that queue fills:

- the publisher must not block indefinitely (which would delay all other consumers);
- instead, it must take explicit action: drop messages, drop the consumer, or move it to a degraded feed.

A typical policy is:

- When a consumer's queue exceeds a soft threshold, mark it as "lagging" and start coarsening its updates (for example, only send summaries).
- If the queue hits a hard limit, disconnect the consumer or drop it to a slower, lower-fidelity channel.

The key is that slow consumers cannot stall the pipeline for everyone else.

**Loss semantics per consumer**

Backpressure decisions define each consumer's loss semantics. Examples:

- **Critical strategies**: either they stay within strict latency budgets and see every event, or they are disconnected and must explicitly recover.
- **Non-critical analytics**: they may receive coarser or sampled data under load.
- **Replay and logging**: they can tolerate brief stalls, but not data loss; the system may buffer more deeply or apply backpressure in the other direction by slowing publishing slightly when disk or network sinks are saturated.

These semantics must be documented and testable; strategies should not unknowingly run in a regime where they silently miss events.

## Instrumentation and Testing of Dissemination Latency

To ensure the dissemination layer behaves as intended, you need to measure it explicitly.

**Tick-to-strategy timing**

For a sample of messages, record:

- exchange send time (if available);
- NIC receive time;
- time after decoding and normalization;
- time when the event is written to the bus; and
- time when the strategy actually reads it.

From these, you can compute:

- network and exchange-side latency (receive minus exchange time);
- processing latency within feed handling and normalization (bus write minus receive);
- dissemination plus strategy-side wake-up latency (strategy read minus bus write).

The last component is what this section is about. You want its distribution (average, median, 99th percentile, worst) to be small and stable under realistic load.

**Synthetic load tests**

Lab tests with calm, low-volume data are misleading. Proper tests:

- replay realistic, high-burst days (for example, market open, news events) through your entire stack;

- run multiple strategies, including deliberately slow consumers; and
- monitor queue depths, disconnect events, and tick-to-strategy latencies.

The goal is to verify that:

- fast strategies continue to receive timely data even when others lag;
- backpressure policies trigger as designed; and
- overall system tail latency remains within your trading requirements.

### Schema evolution and compatibility testing

As your normalized event schema evolves, dissemination must remain robust:

- strategies compiled against older schemas may subscribe to a subset of fields;
- newer schemas may introduce optional fields or new event types.

Testing should include:

- ensuring older consumers continue to function when new fields are added;
- verifying that schema versioning information is propagated through the bus so consumers can adapt or reject incompatible updates.

This avoids surprises where a schema change causes silent misinterpretation of data.

## Putting Dissemination in the Overall Architecture

Seen in context, dissemination is the final leg of an end-to-end journey:

- Packets arrive at the NIC and are captured with minimal overhead.
- Protocol decoding turns bytes into structured events.
- Gap detection and recovery ensure those events form a complete, ordered stream.
- Normalization and aggregation present a coherent, multi-venue view.
- Dissemination moves that view into the hands of strategies and risk engines.

A well-designed dissemination layer:

- uses shared-memory and kernel-bypass techniques to keep latency low;
- provides explicit ordering and loss semantics per consumer;
- isolates consumers from each other via bounded queues and clear backpressure policies; and
- exposes enough instrumentation for you to confirm, in production, that strategies see timely and trustworthy data.

With all these pieces in place, your trading system has a solid architectural spine: from the wire to the strategy, every stage is designed with latency, correctness, and clarity of semantics in mind.

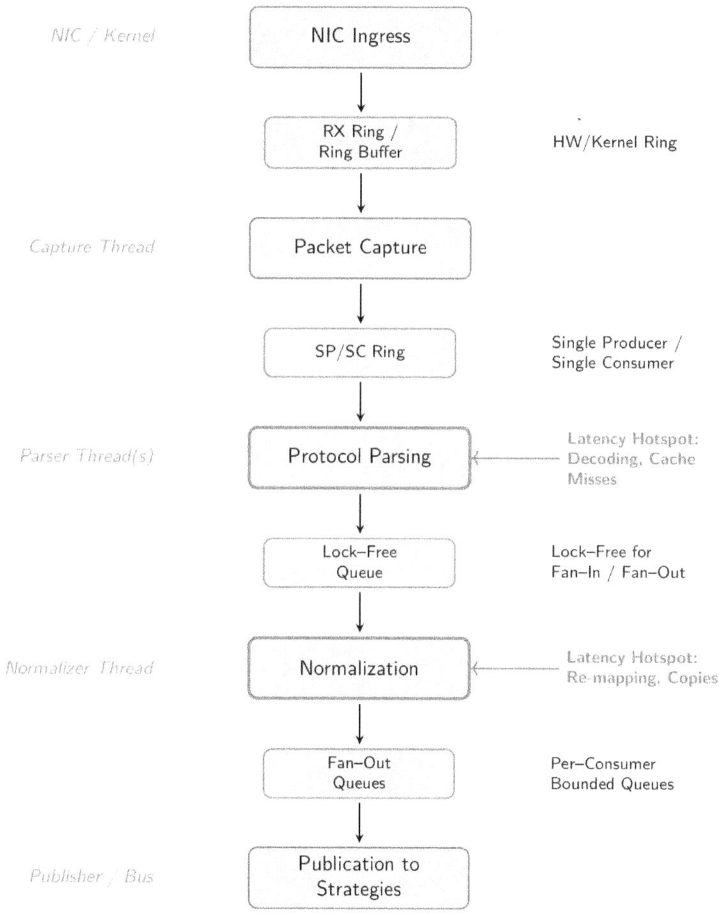
NIC / Kernel
NIC Ingress
RX Ring / Ring Buffer
HW/Kernel Ring
Capture Thread
Packet Capture
SP/SC Ring
Single Producer / Single Consumer
Parser Thread(s)
Protocol Parsing
Latency Hotspot: Decoding, Cache Misses
Lock–Free Queue
Lock–Free for Fan–In / Fan–Out
Normalizer Thread
Normalization
Latency Hotspot: Re-mapping, Copies
Fan–Out Queues
Per–Consumer Bounded Queues
Publisher / Bus
Publication to Strategies

# Chapter 8

# Order Gateways & Lifecycle Engineering

*Every trade you send lives or dies by the quality of its gateway. Before your strategy logic ever reaches an exchange matching engine, it must traverse a maze of sessions, serialisation layers, risk checks, and acknowledgements-each with its own microsecond tax and failure modes. This chapter pulls that maze apart. You'll see where latency really hides in order flows, how to engineer deterministic behaviour under stress, and what separates a merely fast gateway from one you can trust when markets are chaotic and every cancelled microsecond matters.*

## 8.1 Session Management and Heartbeats

In the previous chapter we treated the order gateway as a black box that takes trading intents from strategies, turns them into wire messages, and returns acknowledgements and fills. To open that box, we first need to understand the *sessions* that connect your gateway to each exchange: long-lived conversations that define how both sides log in, prove that they are still alive, keep their message streams in order, and recover when something is lost. Whether the protocol is text FIX, binary OUCH, or a proprietary variant, its session rules directly shape both latency and stability. A gateway that manages sessions carelessly may look fast in the median, but it will suffer from disconnects, retransmits, and pathological tail latencies at precisely the worst moments.

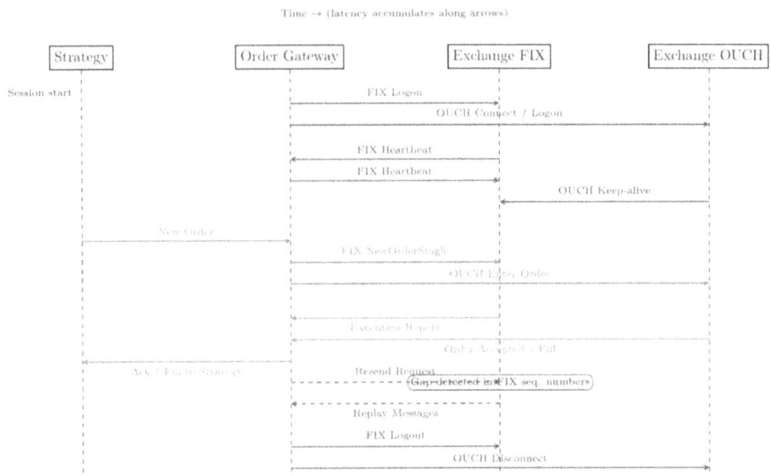


## What a Session Really Is

From the gateway's perspective, a session is not just a socket. It is a *stateful contract* between two peers about:

- **Connectivity**: how we establish and tear down the connection (logon, logout, disconnect).
- **Sequencing**: how we number messages so that gaps and duplicates can be detected.
- **Liveliness**: how we both confirm that the other side is still alive and that the network path is still passing traffic (heartbeats or keep-alive messages).
- **Recovery**: what happens if something is lost or delayed (resend requests, replays, resets).

Trading strategies tend to think in terms of *orders*; session protocols think in terms of *messages in sequence*. The order gateway stands between these two perspectives. It maps order state into protocol messages and vice versa, while staying within strict latency budgets. To do this well, you must design your session behaviour as deliberately as you design your alpha model.

We will focus on three families:

- **FIX**: text, tag-value, rich message catalogue, explicit sessions with sequence numbers and heartbeats.
- **OUCH**: compact binary, minimal message set, persistent connections but often simpler session rules.
- **Proprietary binaries**: exchange-specific variations that combine ideas from both.

## Step 1: Logon and Session Establishment

Every session begins with a handshake. Conceptually the handshake answers two questions:

- *Are you who you say you are?*
- *From which point should we continue our message stream?*

### FIX logon.

With FIX, the gateway sends an initial *logon* message. This contains identification information (sender and target IDs), authentication credentials, and often the sequence number from which the gateway intends to start. The exchange replies with its own logon, confirming the session and sometimes instructing the gateway to reset or adjust its sequence numbers.

At this point, the FIX session is not just a TCP connection. It is a *numbered conversation*. Every subsequent application message (orders, cancels, replaces) and every control message (heartbeats, test requests, resend requests) will carry an incrementing sequence number.

The latency impact here is twofold:

- If logon is slow or unreliable, your gateway may miss the opening of a trading session.
- If logon triggers sequence negotiation or resends, you may incur a burst of recovery traffic before you can send the first live order.

Good gateways minimize the work done during logon and pre-warm everything they can: sockets, TLS handshakes (if any), dedicated threads, and kernel state.

**OUCH and proprietary connect.**

By contrast, OUCH-style protocols generally favour a simpler sequence model. The client opens a TCP connection, sends a logon or "enter ordering" message with credentials and risk limits, and then starts sending orders. Some variants have simple per-message sequence numbers; others rely on a combination of order tokens and exchange-generated IDs to track state.

Even when the protocol does not emphasise sequences as strongly as FIX does, your gateway should *internally* treat the connection as a session:

- Track whether you are logged in and allowed to send orders.
- Track per-connection state such as available credit, configured symbols, and whether the exchange has flagged any issues.
- Decide where to store your own message sequence or order token counters so that reconnects are deterministic.

## Step 2: Sequence Numbers and Ordering Guarantees

Sequences are the backbone of reliable order state. Without them, you cannot say whether the fill that just arrived is the latest view of your order, or an old message replayed late.

**How FIX sequences work.**

In FIX, every message carries a sequence number that increments by one for each message you send on that session. The exchange maintains its own, independent incoming sequence counter for messages it receives from you, and you likewise maintain an incoming counter for messages from the exchange.

This gives us three important properties:

- **Gap detection**: if you are expecting sequence 105 and you receive 107, you know you have missed 105 and 106.
- **Duplicate detection**: if you receive the same sequence twice, you can treat the second as a duplicate and often ignore it.
- **Ordering**: you can reconstruct the precise sequence in which events happened, even if network delays or retransmissions reorder packets in transit.

The price you pay is *protocol overhead*. Every check for gaps or duplicates costs CPU cycles and branches. Every recovery action (such as a resend request) costs latency and bandwidth.

**Sequencing in OUCH and binary protocols.**

OUCH typically does not expose an explicit FIX-style sequence number in every message, but it still carries enough identity information (order tokens, timestamps, or short sequence fields) for your gateway to order and correlate events. Proprietary protocols sometimes add per-stream sequences similar to FIX, but in a smaller binary form, or provide a strict guarantee that messages are delivered in order on a given TCP stream.

For your gateway, the design goal is the same:

- Maintain a clear mapping from protocol identifiers to internal order state.
- Be able to tell if any message is missing or unexpectedly duplicated.
- Implement this in a way that has predictable per-message cost, not occasional spikes.

Well-designed gateways budget a few hundred nanoseconds to check and advance sequence state on each message, using simple integer increments and table lookups, rather than expensive dynamic structures.

## Step 3: Heartbeats and Liveliness

Once a session is live and sequences are in sync, the next question is: how do we know the peer is still with us? And how quickly will we discover a failure?

**The role of heartbeats.**

A heartbeat is simply a lightweight message that says: "I am still here, and the network path between us still carries traffic." FIX formalizes this as a heartbeat message at a negotiated interval (for example, every 30 seconds). OUCH and many proprietary protocols either have similar keep-alive messages or rely on TCP-level keep-alives or periodic application messages.

From a latency perspective, heartbeats and liveliness checks influence your system in several ways:

- **Failure detection time**: a shorter heartbeat interval usually means you will detect a dead connection sooner.
- **Background load**: heartbeats consume bandwidth and CPU even when the market is quiet.
- **Jitter**: if you send or process heartbeats in a way that interferes with order processing (for example, on a shared lock or queue), they can introduce timing noise into your measurements.

**Heartbeat configuration trade-offs.**

In practice, you must strike a balance:

- If your heartbeat interval is *too long* (say, 60 seconds), you may trade for a whole minute before noticing that the exchange has stopped sending updates or acknowledgements.
- If your interval is *too short* (say, 250 milliseconds) and your implementation is heavy-handed, you might spend a non-trivial fraction of your CPU budget sending, parsing, and logging heartbeats, or you might flood a stressed network path.

A common pattern is:

- Use a moderate heartbeat interval agreed with the venue.
- Monitor application-level traffic: if orders or fills are flowing, treat them as implicit proof of life and suppress additional heartbeats.
- Use very cheap timing checks (monotonic clocks, per-connection timers) so that testing whether to send a heartbeat does not itself create latency spikes.

**Detecting stalls, not just disconnects.**

Heartbeats are also your first defence against subtle *stalls*, where the TCP connection is technically up, but one direction of application traffic has stopped. For example:

- You continue to send orders, but receive no acknowledgements.
- Market data continues to flow, but the order entry channel is silent.

Well-engineered gateways track simple metrics per session: time since last outbound application message, time since last inbound application message, time since last control message. When any of these exceed defined thresholds, the gateway can escalate: raise alerts, consider a controlled disconnect and reconnect, or automatically back off sending new orders.

## Step 4: Resend Requests and Recovery Behaviour

No matter how well you engineer your network, at some point a message will be lost, delayed, or arrive out of order. Session protocols give you recovery tools; your job is to use them in a way that is both *correct* and *latency-aware*.

**Resend requests in FIX.**

When your gateway detects a gap in incoming FIX sequence numbers, it can issue a *resend request*: a control message asking the exchange to replay messages between two sequence numbers. The exchange replies by resending those messages, often with a flag marking them as possible duplicates.

This mechanism protects you against message loss, but it has two important latency side effects:

- **Burst traffic**: a large resend window can cause a burst of replayed messages, which can temporarily crowd out new acks and fills, and stress your processing pipeline.
- **State confusion**: until the resends are processed, your internal view of some orders may be incomplete, forcing you to take more conservative risk decisions.

A practical approach is to tune resend behaviour cautiously:

- Request the smallest possible window that covers the gap.
- Prioritize decoding and applying replayed messages because they directly affect your risk and position state.
- Limit how many resends you trigger in quick succession so you do not accidentally create a *self-inflicted denial of service* at the worst time.

**Recovery in OUCH and proprietary protocols.**

Many binary protocols handle recovery differently. Some:

- Offer no replay within the session; instead, you must reconcile from an external drop-copy or trade history feed after a disconnect.
- Offer a simple "start from sequence N" parameter when you reconnect, replaying all later messages.
- Require you to re-state your outstanding orders after a session reset, with the exchange cancelling any missing ones.

In all cases, the same latency and stability principles apply:

- Keep your recovery logic simple and deterministic. For any given sequence of events, the gateway should always rebuild the same final state.
- Plan for recovery in advance. Decide what happens if you lose a session mid-day: which orders will you assume are cancelled; which venues require explicit cancel-on-disconnect flags; how you will block new orders until reconciliation is complete.
- Budget time for recovery. If a reconnect and replay takes several seconds, build that expectation into your risk and strategy logic, rather than pretending it will never happen.

## Configuration Choices and Their Latency Impact

Session protocols come with many knobs: heartbeat intervals, maximum message rates, retransmission behaviours, timeouts. These are often treated as operational afterthoughts, but they are in fact part of your latency and stability design.

**Heartbeat interval and timeout.**

We have already discussed the basic trade-off. From a latency-engineering standpoint, you should also consider:

- Align heartbeat sending with lightweight timer ticks so that they do not coincide with heavy periodic tasks such as log rotation or batch risk updates.
- Separate heartbeat processing from the critical path of order sending where possible, for example by using dedicated threads or queues, so that a blocked heartbeat handler does not stall your strategy.

**Resend window size.**

For FIX venues that support replay, you can often configure how many messages to request at once or how aggressive your resend policy is.

- A large window simplifies coding but risks flooding your gateway with replays and pushing up p99 latency for live messages.

- A smaller, targeted window requires slightly more logic but keeps recovery traffic manageable and more predictable.

**Throttling and pacing.**

Many exchanges enforce message throttles: hard limits on orders per second, or softer pacing rules. The session layer is often where these limits are enforced, either by the venue or by your own risk controls.

From a latency perspective:

- If you burst orders until you hit the limit, the exchange may queue or reject excess messages, creating unpredictable delays.
- If your gateway has a local pacing mechanism (for example, token buckets or rate counters), the implementation must be low-overhead; otherwise the pacing check itself becomes a latency hotspot.

A well-designed gateway exposes these throttling parameters clearly and measures how often they are reached, so you can tune both strategy aggressiveness and session configuration together.

## Engineering for Stability Under Stress

Most of the time, markets are calm and your session logic is barely visible. The real test comes during stress: when volumes spike, when the exchange is under load, or when network paths are congested. Under those conditions, two failure patterns become common:

- **Chatter storms**: excessive heartbeats, resend requests, and other control messages crowd out useful application traffic.
- **Silent degradation**: heartbeats look fine, but in-order delivery and acknowledgements fall behind, leaving you trading blind or stuck.

To guard against these, design your session management with a few simple rules:

- **Control traffic should be cheap**. Heartbeats, test requests, and resend handling should use pre-allocated buffers, simple state machines, and minimal locking.
- **Application traffic comes first**. When the system is under load, give priority to decoding and acting on acknowledgements and fills over peripheral control chatter.
- **Measure, do not guess**. Instrument per-session latency: time from gateway send to exchange response, distributions of heartbeat arrival times, and frequency of resend events. Use this data to adjust intervals and thresholds.

Stability is often about predictability more than raw speed. A session configuration that is slightly slower in the median but produces tight, well-behaved tails can be far more valuable to a strategy than an ultra-aggressive setup that occasionally collapses or thrashes during a volatile open.

## Logout and Controlled Shutdown

Finally, every session ends. How you shut down matters, because it determines how much clean-up and reconciliation you must do before the next trading day.

**FIX logout.**

In FIX, a controlled shutdown uses explicit logout messages in both directions. The gateway tells the exchange that it wishes to end the session; the exchange confirms; both sides close the connection. If both implementations follow the protocol, they will agree on the final sequence numbers and on whether any messages remain outstanding.

A disciplined gateway will:

- Ensure that all outbound orders have corresponding responses, or explicitly mark any uncertain orders for reconciliation.
- Persist final sequence states so that the next logon can resume cleanly rather than forcing a reset and full replay.

### OUCH and binary disconnects.

For OUCH and similar protocols, logout may be as simple as sending a final "end of session" message or cleanly closing the socket. The same principles apply:

- Make the shutdown explicit and logged.
- Leave the session in a state where reconnecting is deterministic: you know which orders are still working, and you know from which point you should request any replay or reconciliation data.

## Putting It All Together

From the outside, session management and heartbeats can look like plumbing details. In reality, they define the *operating environment* in which your low-latency trading logic runs. FIX, OUCH, and proprietary protocols each offer different tools for managing connectivity, sequencing, and liveliness, but they all require you to make thoughtful configuration and design choices.

A well-engineered gateway:

- Establishes sessions quickly and predictably at logon.
- Maintains simple, fast sequence tracking that keeps order state consistent without heavy overhead.
- Uses heartbeats and liveliness checks to detect real problems quickly, without flooding the network or introducing jitter.
- Handles resends and recovery deterministically, with bounded latency and clear effects on state.
- Shuts down sessions cleanly, making the next start of day straightforward rather than a forensic exercise.

With these foundations in place, the remaining pieces of the order lifecycle—serialization, validation, risk checks, and cancel-replace workflows—have a stable base to build on. The next section will move from the session envelope to the contents of each message, showing how encoding and transport choices turn directly into CPU cycles and wire latency.

## 8.2 Low-Latency Serialization

In the previous section we treated the order gateway as a disciplined session peer: it logs on, maintains sequence numbers, sends heartbeats, and handles resends in a predictable way. That gave us a stable envelope for our traffic. We now turn to what actually flows inside that envelope: the bytes that represent each order, cancel, and fill.

From the strategy's point of view, an order is a neat in-memory object: instrument, side, price, quantity, time-in-force, and a few flags. The exchange, however, only sees a stream of bytes on a socket. *Serialization* is the act of turning that in-memory structure into bytes, and *deserialization* is the reverse step for incoming messages.

In a low-latency environment this translation is not a detail you can leave to a generic library. Every field you copy, every branch you take, every cache line you touch can show up directly in your wire latency. At the same time, those same bytes are what you will later use for debugging, replay, and regulatory reconstruction. Your goal is therefore twofold:

- Minimize per-message CPU cost and jitter.
- Keep the wire format and encoding rules simple enough that humans and tools can reason about them after the fact.

### From Objects to Bytes: The Basic Journey

The life of an outbound order message typically follows a simple conceptual path:

- The strategy creates or updates an in-process order object.
- The gateway's API layer translates that object into a protocol-specific representation (FIX, OUCH, or proprietary).

- A serializer walks over this representation and writes bytes into a buffer.
- The buffer is handed to the transport stack (usually TCP) and sent to the exchange.

On the way back, the steps are reversed: bytes arrive from the wire, are parsed into a protocol representation, and then mapped into internal order state updates and callbacks to the strategy.

Most of the latency you can directly control in the gateway lives in steps 2 and 3 (and the corresponding parsing). To engineer these steps well, it helps to break them into three aspects:

- **Encoding**: how fields and messages are represented conceptually (text vs binary, tag-value vs fixed layout).
- **Memory layout**: how those fields are arranged in memory for efficient reading and writing.
- **Transport interaction**: how buffers and system calls are used to hand bytes to the network stack.

We will discuss each in turn.

## Encoding Styles: Text vs Binary, Flexible vs Fixed

Different protocols embody different trade-offs in their wire encodings.

**Text FIX and tag-value encodings.**

Traditional FIX uses a simple human-readable tag-value format. Each field is written as:

- A numeric tag identifier (e.g., "55" for symbol).
- An equals sign.
- A textual representation of the value (e.g., "AAPL").
- A delimiter character.

Messages are sequences of such fields, often in a mostly fixed order. This format has attractive properties:

- Easy to inspect and debug with simple tools.
- Extensible: you can add new tags without changing existing parsers.
- Reasonably robust to missing or extra fields.

The downside is cost:

- Numeric fields must be converted to strings when sending, and parsed back to integers or decimals when receiving.
- Parsing involves scanning for delimiters, comparing tag numbers, and handling variable-length fields.
- Messages tend to be larger in bytes than equivalent binary representations, so they consume more bandwidth and can increase queuing and transport latency during busy periods.

For many buy-side and less latency-sensitive applications, this overhead is acceptable. For ultra-low-latency strategies, it is often too expensive in the critical path.

**Binary FIX and packed binary formats.**

To address performance concerns, many venues and firms have adopted binary variants of FIX or entirely custom binary formats. In a binary scheme:

- Numeric fields are stored directly in binary (for example, as 32-bit or 64-bit integers).
- Fields often occupy fixed-width slots, or are prefixed by short length indicators.
- The order of fields within the message is fixed and known ahead of time.

This buys you:

- Faster encode/decode, because the serializer knows exactly where each field lives.
- Fewer branches when parsing, because you no longer have to interpret tag numbers or skip unknown fields.
- Smaller messages, which reduces pressure on the network and on NIC and switch buffers.

The trade-off is less flexibility, especially if you adopt a strictly fixed layout: adding or changing fields may require version negotiation and careful migration logic.

**Custom flat binary structures.**

Some proprietary protocols go further and define messages as flat binary structures, conceptually similar to a well-defined record:

- The first byte or word is a message type.
- The remainder of the message is a fixed series of fields in an agreed format and endianness.

In the simplest case, serialization and deserialization are almost mechanical copies between in-memory structures and wire buffers, plus some byte-order conversions. This can be extremely fast, but it requires discipline:

- Alignment and padding must be explicitly controlled (we will discuss this shortly).
- You must be careful about differences between compilers, architectures, and languages so that your in-memory layout always matches the wire format.

For very tight latency budgets, a well-designed flat binary format is one of the most powerful tools available, provided you keep it simple and well-documented.

## Memory Layout, Alignment, and the CPU Cache

Even once you have chosen a wire encoding style, *how* you store data in memory can make a large difference to performance. Modern CPUs are very fast at doing simple, predictable work on data that is already in the cache, and surprisingly slow when forced to chase pointers and jump around memory.

**Alignment and padding.**

Most processors prefer that certain data types begin at specific byte boundaries in memory. For example, a 64-bit integer may be fastest to load when it starts on an address that is a multiple of 8 bytes. If your structures do not respect these preferences, the compiler may insert invisible padding bytes, or the CPU may need extra cycles to handle misaligned loads and stores.

From a serialization point of view:

- If you mirror your in-memory layout onto the wire naively, hidden padding can leak into your messages, making them larger and harder to parse.
- If you strictly pack everything on the wire with no padding, but your in-memory structures remain padded for alignment, you must pay a cost to copy fields into a separate packed buffer.

The usual solution is to design a *deliberate* layout:

- Decide on a fixed field order that naturally satisfies alignment requirements (for example, put wider fields first).
- Define your wire format explicitly in documentation, independent of any language-specific struct definition.
- Implement encoders and decoders that read and write fields in this order, with clear rules for any alignment padding that does appear on the wire.

This may look like extra work compared to relying on automatic layout, but it repays itself in clarity and performance.

**Cache friendliness and access patterns.**

The CPU cache rewards two patterns:

- **Spatial locality**: accessing data that is near other recently accessed data.
- **Temporal locality**: reusing data that you accessed recently.

In a high-throughput gateway, you will often be walking over arrays or queues of messages. How you organize these matters.

A common design decision is between:

- **Array of structures**: you keep an array where each element is a whole message or order object.
- **Structure of arrays**: you keep separate arrays for each field (e.g., one array of prices, one array of quantities, and so on).

For serialization, array-of-structures is often natural, because each order is self-contained. However, if certain fields are accessed much more frequently or in batches (for example, prices for risk checks), a structure-of-arrays layout may be more cache-friendly.

The key point is not to blindly apply one pattern, but to align your memory layout with the access patterns of your encode/decode and risk logic. Keeping frequently accessed hot fields together and avoiding unnecessary pointer chasing can cut a meaningful number of CPU cycles per message.

## Copy Avoidance and Buffer Management

Every time you copy bytes from one buffer to another, you pay in CPU time and memory bandwidth. In a system that may handle millions of messages per second at peak, these copies add up quickly.

**Zero-copy and low-copy design.**

There are several practical techniques to reduce copies:

- **Preallocated buffers**: Reuse fixed-size buffers for outbound messages instead of allocating new memory for each send.
- **In-place encoding**: Write fields directly from your internal objects into the network buffer, rather than into an intermediate representation.
- **Shared buffers for logging**: When possible, capture a reference to the same buffer for logging or replay, instead of making a deep copy.

You will rarely achieve truly zero copies across every boundary, because the operating system and NIC have their own buffering, but you can often reduce the number of application-level copies to one.

**Batching and system calls.**

Another hidden cost comes from *system calls* to send data on the network. Each call incurs overhead to transition from user space to the kernel and back. If your gateway sends many tiny messages one by one, this overhead can become a significant part of your latency budget.

Some common approaches to mitigate this are:

- **Small batching**: accumulate a few messages into a single buffer and send them in one system call, especially when strict single-message latency is not required.
- **Careful use of kernel options**: depending on the operating system and protocol, you may be able to control how aggressively the kernel coalesces small writes.
- **Alignment with protocol framing**: ensure that your batches respect message boundaries so that the receiver can parse them efficiently.

There is no one right answer: some strategies prioritize absolute minimum latency for each order and accept more system calls, while others accept slightly higher per-message latency in exchange for higher throughput and greater overall stability. The important thing is that you make this trade-off consciously.

## Transport Choices: UDP, TCP, and NIC Offloads

So far we have spoken as though everything rides on TCP, which is usually true for order entry. However, even within TCP there are choices that affect performance, and in some contexts you may encounter UDP-based protocols.

**TCP and its implications.**

TCP provides ordered, reliable byte streams, which is one reason it underlies FIX and OUCH connections. It also brings features like congestion control and retransmission, which add their own latency dynamics.

At the serialization level, this means:

- You do not need to implement your own packetization; you only need to frame messages inside the stream.
- You must be prepared for temporary stalls or bursts when the TCP stack retransmits or coalesces data under network stress.

Modern NICs and operating systems may offer offload features such as checksum offload or segmentation offload. These can reduce CPU overhead by letting the NIC handle some low-level details. However, they also interact with how your messages are grouped and timed on the wire, and can make fine-grained timestamping more complex. In a latency-sensitive gateway, it is worth testing offload configurations carefully, measuring both average and tail latency.

**UDP and custom transports.**

Some market data feeds, and a few specialized order protocols, use UDP. UDP does not guarantee delivery or ordering, so any recovery or reordering must be handled at the application level. From a serialization perspective, UDP's main implication is that you must ensure each message fits within a datagram and that your encoder is careful about maximum sizes.

While order entry over UDP is less common, you may still want to design your internal serialization path in a way that is transport-agnostic: messages are framed clearly, and the transport layer is responsible for how they are grouped or retransmitted.

## Design Patterns for Fast, Understandable Serialization

Bringing these threads together, what does a good low-latency serialization path look like in practice? Several patterns recur in robust gateways.

**Prebuilt message templates.**

For each message type (new order, cancel, replace), you can maintain a prebuilt template buffer:

- Static fields that rarely change (such as sender IDs, session IDs, or certain flags) are already filled in.
- Dynamic fields (price, quantity, client order ID) are left as placeholders.

When a new order arrives from the strategy, the serializer:

- Copies or references the template.
- Quickly overwrites just the dynamic fields.
- Appends any checksums or length fields at the end.

This cuts down on string building or repetitive formatting of constant fields, saving both CPU and branches. It also makes the encoded messages more uniform, which is helpful for debugging.

**Simple, explicit framing.**

Regardless of the encoding (text or binary), it is helpful to have clear message boundaries:

- For text protocols, this might be a unique delimiter character.
- For binary protocols, it is usually a length field and a type field at the start of each message.

Clear framing allows your receiver to scan a buffer and step from one message to the next without complex logic. This improves decode speed and makes it easier to recover from partial or corrupted data during troubleshooting.

**Clear separation of concerns.**

It is tempting to fold everything into a single monolithic encode/decode function. A better approach is to separate:

- Mapping between internal order objects and protocol field sets.
- The mechanics of turning those field sets into bytes.
- The handing off of fully encoded buffers to the transport layer.

This separation lets you adjust your internal data structures or transport behaviour without rewriting the core serialization logic. It also makes it easier to test encoders and decoders thoroughly using recorded fixtures.

## Making It Debuggable and Auditable

Performance is not the only goal. When something goes wrong—and it will—you will need to reconstruct exactly what was sent and received, sometimes months after the fact. Overly clever or opaque encodings make this painful.

Several practices help maintain debuggability:

**Stable, documented formats.**

Define your wire formats and field mappings in stable documents, not just in code comments. Include:

- Field names, types, and sizes.
- Byte offsets for binary layouts.
- Tag numbers and allowed values for text formats.

When you need to change the format, treat it as a versioned change with clear migration rules. This ensures that recorded traffic can still be parsed correctly even when the gateway evolves.

**Deterministic encoding.**

Given the same input order and configuration, your serializer should always produce exactly the same bytes. This might seem obvious, but it can be broken unintentionally by:

- Using data structures with non-deterministic iteration order.
- Including timestamps or variable IDs in places where they are not required.
- Depending on language or platform defaults for things like numeric formatting.

Determinism simplifies testing: you can store expected byte sequences in test fixtures and compare them directly to encoder output.

**Strategic logging hooks.**

Full per-message deep logging in the critical path is often too expensive for a low-latency gateway. However, you can still add low-impact hooks:

- Optionally mirror a small fraction of live traffic for detailed logging, sampling at a configured rate.
- Log message metadata (timestamps, lengths, sequence numbers) for all messages, while logging full payloads only under specific debug or incident modes.
- Use the same serialization routines for both live sending and logging, so that what you reconstruct offline matches what actually went on the wire.

A thoughtful logging strategy lets you turn up detail when needed without permanently carrying its full cost.

## Budgeting CPU Time per Message

Serialization decisions become much clearer when you translate them into an explicit time budget. For example, suppose your overall strategy-to-exchange latency budget is on the order of tens of microseconds. The gateway might allocate only a small fraction of that to encode/decode—perhaps a few microseconds total.

Within that envelope, you can reason about costs:

- How many branches does your encoder execute per message?
- How many cache lines does it touch?
- How many memory copies are performed?

You do not need detailed cycle counting to get value from this exercise. The goal is to avoid obvious waste: unnecessary conversions, repeated work, or complicated control flows that introduce jitter.

Once your basic design is in place, measurement completes the picture. Hardware-assisted timestamps, performance counters, and controlled benchmarks can show you:

- Median encode/decode times under typical load.
- Tail behaviour (for example, the slowest 1% of messages).
- How these metrics change when you adjust encoding, alignment, or transport settings.

Low-latency serialization sits at the intersection of protocol design, CPU architecture, and practical software engineering. Choices about encoding style, memory layout, and transport interaction all translate into concrete CPU cycles and wire latency. At the same time, these choices shape how easily you can debug, replay, and audit your trading activity.

A well-designed serialization path:

- Uses a wire format that is simple, deterministic, and well-documented.
- Aligns memory layout and access patterns with the CPU cache.
- Minimizes copies and system calls without sacrificing clarity.

- Exploits prebuilt templates and clear framing to keep per-message work predictable.
- Preserves sufficient structure and logging to support post-trade analysis and regulatory needs.

With both session management and serialization under control, we can now turn to what happens to an order *before* it leaves the gateway: the validation and risk checks that must complete within the remaining microseconds of our latency budget.

## 8.3 Order Validation and Risk Checks

So far, we have focused on getting messages to and from the exchange quickly and reliably. Sessions, heartbeats, and serialization gave us a fast and predictable conduit for orders. We now turn to what happens *inside* the gateway before an order is allowed onto that conduit: pre-trade validation and risk checks.

From the strategy's point of view, placing an order is a single action: "buy 1,000 shares at 25.10." From the firm's and regulator's point of view, that action must satisfy a wide range of rules:

- Is the order syntactically valid?
- Is the symbol tradable on this venue right now?
- Is the price reasonable, or obviously erroneous?
- Does the order fit within credit and position limits?
- Is the strategy behaving as configured, or has it gone out of control?

The challenge for a low-latency gateway is to answer all of these questions in a few microseconds, deterministically, under load. This section explains how to structure that work as a pipeline, how to keep each stage fast and predictable, and how to reconcile regulatory and firm-wide risk requirements with the realities of microsecond budgets.

## What Must Happen Before an Order Goes Out

Although implementations vary, most pre-trade pipelines contain the same types of checks. It is useful to name them clearly before we discuss performance.

Given a raw order request from a strategy, a typical gateway will apply:

1. **Syntactic validation**
    - All required fields present (symbol, side, price or market flag, quantity, time-in-force, account).
    - Fields in legal ranges (quantity $>$ 0, price non-negative where applicable).
    - Values conform to allowed sets (valid sides, order types, time-in-force codes).
2. **Symbol, instrument, and venue checks**
    - Symbol exists and is known to the gateway's instrument master.
    - Instrument is eligible for trading on this venue and in this session.
    - Any venue- or product-specific flags (short-sale rules, lot size constraints, trading phases).
3. **Basic price and size sanity checks ("fat-finger" checks)**
    - Maximum order notional or share quantity per order.
    - Price collars relative to recent market data (for example, no more than a certain percentage away from last trade or best bid/offer).
4. **Credit and exposure limits**
    - Per-account or per-strategy credit limits (max intraday loss, max capital deployed).
    - Firm-level aggregate limits across strategies.
5. **Position and concentration limits**

- Maximum long or short exposure in a given instrument, sector, or country.
- Limits on gross and net exposures.

6. **Strategy- or product-specific risk rules**

- Maximum order rate or message rate.
- Maximum participation rate in a symbol or venue.
- Custom constraints particular to the trading model (for example, spread bounds for market making).

7. **Final pass/fail decision**

- If all relevant checks pass: order is released to the serialization and session layers.
- If any check fails: order is rejected with a clear reason, and risk logs are updated.

This list may appear long, but each step can be engineered to be extremely cheap if we design data structures and access patterns carefully.

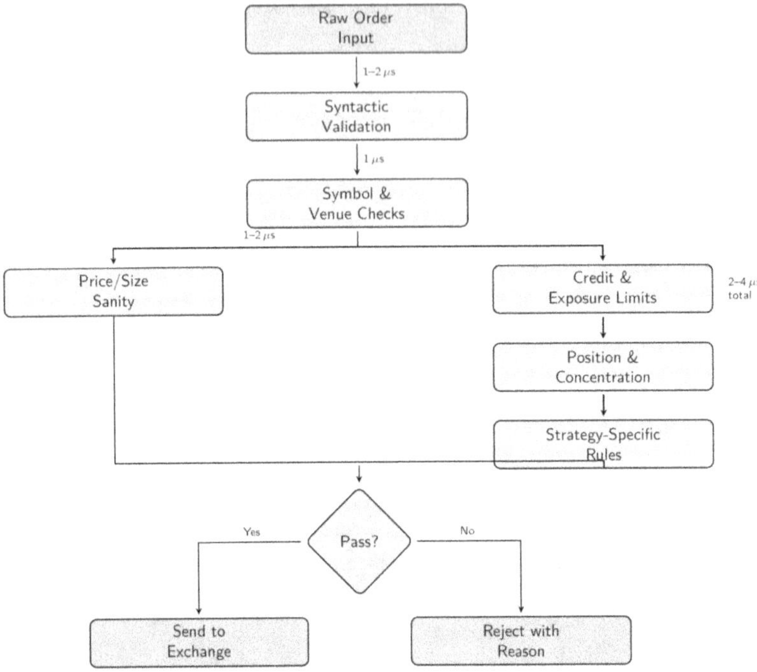


## Thinking in Pipelines and Budgets

A helpful way to reason about pre-trade checks is to imagine a literal assembly line. The order enters on the left and passes through a sequence of small stations. Each station performs one narrow task in constant or near-constant time and hands the order to the next.

In a low-latency gateway, each station must be:

- **Fast**: the work per order is bounded and small.
- **Predictable**: timings do not vary wildly between orders.
- **Independent**: changes in one station do not unintentionally slow down others.

Suppose you are targeting, say, 15 microseconds from strategy to the first byte leaving your server. You may decide that no more than one third of that budget (5 microseconds) will be spent on validation and risk. You can then roughly allocate:

- 2–3 microseconds for syntactic, symbol, and basic price/size checks.
- 2–3 microseconds for credit, exposure, position, and strategy-specific checks.

These numbers are illustrative, not prescriptive. The important step is to *make such a budget explicit*. Once you do, you immediately see why general-purpose database calls or complex dynamic logic are unacceptable in this path.

## Engineering Syntactic and Symbol Checks

The earliest stages in the pipeline are the easiest to keep fast, and they are your first line of defence against unnecessary work further downstream.

**Syntactic validation.**

Syntactic checks should be almost embarrassingly simple:

- Is each required field present?
- Is each value within a sensible numeric range?
- Does each field use an allowed code?

These questions can be answered with straightforward comparisons and table lookups. For example, mapping a textual side code to an internal enumeration can be done via a tiny precomputed table. Checking that order quantity is positive and below a configured maximum order size is a simple bound check.

The main performance rule at this stage is: *avoid complex control flow*. Syntactic validation should not branch on business rules or external state. It should be predictable enough that the CPU's branch predictor rarely mispredicts, which keeps this stage very cheap.

**Symbol and venue validation.**

Symbol checks are your bridge from raw orders to market-specific constraints. A naive implementation might query a database or remote service to find symbol metadata on demand, but that would be far too slow and unpredictable.

Instead, most gateways maintain an in-memory *instrument master*, a compact data structure keyed by symbol or internal instrument ID, holding:

- Basic attributes (tick size, lot size, currency).
- Venue eligibility flags.
- Short-sale or product-specific codes.
- Any static regulatory classifications.

Lookup should be constant time:

- Use arrays indexed by numeric instrument IDs wherever possible.
- Use hash tables or trees only where the key space is small and stable, and implementations are well-tuned.

The order of operations matters:

1. Resolve symbol to an internal instrument ID once.
2. Use that ID for all subsequent checks and risk calculations.

This avoids repeated string operations and ensures that later stages can use simple integer indexing.

## Fat-Finger Checks: Simple Rules With Big Impact

Fat-finger checks are designed to catch obviously wrong orders before they hit the market. They are often mandated by regulation and internal policy, but they also protect you from plain human error and system bugs.

Two common building blocks are:

**Maximum order size and notional.**

For each account or strategy (and sometimes for each symbol), configure:

- A maximum quantity per order.
- A maximum notional value per order (price times quantity).

At runtime, evaluating these is just:

- A few integer comparisons.
- A multiplication that is cheap on modern CPUs, especially if your price representation is a fixed-point integer.

**Price collars.**

Price collars limit how far away from a reference price an order may be placed. The reference can be:

- Last traded price.
- Best bid or offer.
- A more stable reference like a midpoint or theoretical price from the venue.

To keep collars fast:

- Cache the latest reference prices in an in-memory structure indexed by instrument ID.

- Update that cache as market data arrives, out of the order path.
- Store the collar thresholds (for example, "no more than 5% away") in precomputed numeric form.

When an order arrives, fetching the reference price is just an array lookup. Comparing the order price against allowed bounds is a handful of arithmetic operations and comparisons. This makes collars one of the cheapest and yet most powerful sanity checks in the pipeline.

## Credit and Exposure: Shared State Without Locks

Credit and exposure limits care about *what has already happened* today: fills, cancels, and working orders. Unlike syntactic and fat-finger checks, they cannot be evaluated purely from the order in isolation. This introduces the first real challenge: shared state.

**What you need to track.**

For each relevant dimension—often account, strategy, and firm—it is common to track at least:

- Realized profit and loss for the day.
- Unrealized profit and loss on open positions.
- Gross and net exposures.
- Outstanding notional in working orders.

Each incoming order proposes to change these quantities. Before you send the order, you should check whether the proposed new values would breach limits.

**Keeping it fast.**

The difficulty is not the arithmetic; it is safely reading and updating these aggregates on a hot path without heavy locking. Two general strategies are often combined:

- **Partitioning**: Assign strategies or accounts to specific threads or gateway instances, so that each thread updates only its own subset of limits, reducing contention.

- **Approximate global limits**: For firm-wide limits, maintain a central authoritative value that is updated less frequently, and use local approximations or guard bands in the per-thread checks.

Within a single thread or partition, credit checks can boil down to:

- Read the current aggregate.
- Add the proposed order's contribution (for example, its notional or risk weight).
- Compare against configured limit.

If your internal data structures are laid out as simple structs or arrays and updated in the same thread that performs the checks, this should consume only a small and predictable slice of your microsecond budget.

## Position and Concentration Limits

Position and concentration checks are similar in spirit to credit, but focus on *where* your exposures lie. You might want to prevent:

- Holding more than a certain number of shares in a single stock.
- Having too high a percentage of portfolio value in one sector.
- Shorting beyond regulatory or risk policy limits.

The key to speed here is precomputation and indexing.

**Per-instrument positions.**

At the simplest level, you track per-instrument positions:

- Maintain an array of positions, one entry per instrument ID.
- Update entries as fills occur, outside the order path.

At order time, checking that a proposed trade does not exceed the per-instrument limit is once again a matter of:

- One array read to fetch current position.
- A small arithmetic update to compute the hypothetical new position.
- A comparison against a limit.

**Buckets and aggregates.**

For sector, country, or other buckets:

- Map each instrument ID to one or more bucket IDs using static metadata in your instrument master.
- Maintain per-bucket exposure aggregates in arrays or compact tables.

When an order arrives, you:

- Fetch the instrument's bucket IDs.
- For each bucket, compute the impact of the order and compare with bucket-level limits.

If you limit the number of buckets per instrument (for example, one sector, one country, one region), this is still a small and bounded amount of work per order.

## Strategy-Specific Rules and Rate Limits

So far, checks have been mostly generic. Strategy-specific rules capture what is unique or particularly risky about a given trading approach.

**Message and order rates.**

Many firms and venues impose limits on:

- Orders per second per strategy.

- Cancels per second or cancel-to-trade ratios.

These can be tracked with lightweight counters and sliding windows:

- Keep per-strategy counters of messages in the last short interval.
- Update counters cheaply on each order or cancel.
- Compare against preconfigured thresholds.

Rate calculations that require complex time-window logic can be offloaded to slower monitoring systems, so long as the gateway's local checks remain simple enough for microsecond budgets.

**Model-specific constraints.**

Some strategies, such as market making or statistical arbitrage, have natural internal invariants: for example, never quoting a spread wider than a certain value, or never crossing one's own orders. You can enforce these by:

- Exposing a small configuration of constraints to the gateway (for instance, maximum spread, maximum skew).
- Passing a small amount of additional context along with each order (for example, a strategy ID or logical quote group).

The key is that evaluation at the gateway should remain a simple combination of table lookups and comparisons, not a rerun of the entire strategy logic.

## Hard Blocks vs Soft Flags

Not all risk information must be enforced synchronously. A useful distinction is between:

- **Hard blocks**: checks that prevent the order from being sent if they fail.
- **Soft flags**: checks that record a concern or a near-breach, but do not block the order.

From a latency perspective, hard blocks must live on the critical path; soft flags can be partially or entirely asynchronous.

For example:

- A firm-wide loss limit is often a hard block: once reached, you must restrict or stop trading immediately.
- A cancel-to-trade ratio approaching a regulatory threshold might be monitored via soft flags, with alerts or gradual throttling, but without blocking individual orders in the microsecond path.

A common pattern is:

- Keep a minimal set of hard-block checks in the gateway's synchronous path.
- Have a parallel process or thread analyze richer risk metrics more slowly, raising control signals (for example, "this strategy is misbehaving") that the gateway then enforces via a small number of additional, simple conditions.

This lets you satisfy complex firm-wide policies without turning your order gateway into a general-purpose risk engine.

## Dealing With Disputes and Conflicts

In practice, there will be times when strategy intent and firm-wide controls disagree. For example:

- A strategy wants to increase exposure in a stock precisely when the firm wants to reduce it.
- A limit update arrives (perhaps from risk management) while many orders are in flight.

Architecturally, the gateway should act as the final arbiter: it must have the authority to block orders even if the strategy disagrees. To make this robust:

- Treat limit configuration as data that can change at runtime, but only through controlled, logged channels.
- Apply updates atomically from the perspective of the validation pipeline, so that no order sees a half-updated state.
- Provide clear rejection reasons back to strategies so they can adapt or shut down gracefully.

This is as much an organizational discipline as a technical one. The more deterministic and transparent your pre-trade behaviour is, the easier it is to build trust between traders, quants, and risk managers.

## Micro-Budgeting and Measurement

After designing the pipeline conceptually, you should test whether it meets your microsecond targets in reality. The process mirrors what we discussed for serialization:

- Instrument the pipeline to record timestamps at key boundaries: before validation, after validation, after each major block if feasible.
- Run controlled test loads that exercise different paths—orders that pass, orders that fail early, orders that fail on credit, and so on.
- Examine not only average times but the distribution's tail: 99th and 99.9th percentiles.

If you see outliers, investigate whether they are caused by:

- Contention on shared data structures.
- Rare branches or exception paths that are slower.
- Interference from unrelated work on the same CPU cores.

The goal is not perfection, but stability: a risk pipeline whose timing is well behaved allows strategies to reason about end-to-end latency with confidence.

Pre-trade validation and risk checks are the guardian at the gate between your trading logic and the market. They must satisfy multiple masters: regulators, firm-wide risk management, operational robustness, and the trading strategies themselves. In a modern low-latency architecture, they must do all of this within a handful of microseconds.

The key design principles are:

- Break checks into a clear left-to-right pipeline, with simple responsibilities at each stage.
- Use precomputed lookup tables, in-memory instrument masters, and carefully managed shared state to keep per-order work small and predictable.
- Reserve the critical path for hard-block checks that truly require synchronous enforcement; push richer analytics and soft flags into parallel or slower paths.
- Treat limit configuration and risk outcomes as data with clear ownership, atomic updates, and explicit feedback to strategies.
- Continuously measure and tune the pipeline so that its latency is not only low but tightly controlled across different market conditions.

With a robust, microsecond-efficient risk pipeline in place, the gateway can confidently release orders to the exchange. The next section will examine what happens when those orders need to be modified or withdrawn at high speed: the cancel and cancel-replace workflows that dominate message traffic in many latency-sensitive strategies.

## 8.4 Cancel-Replace Workflows

In the previous section we treated an order as a single object flowing once through validation, risk checks, and serialization before being sent to the exchange. Real trading is rarely that simple. Latency-sensitive strategies-especially market making, arbitrage, and intraday alpha models-constantly adjust their orders as prices move. For every new order they send, they may send many cancels and cancel-replaces.

From the exchange's perspective, this activity is just a high-volume stream of messages. From your firm's perspective, it has deep implications:

- **Queue position**: how far back in the matching queue you sit after each modification.
- **Exposure**: whether you still have live orders in the market when you think you have cancelled.
- **Gateway complexity**: the data structures and state machines required to keep your internal view aligned with the exchange under stress.

This section explains how cancel and cancel-replace flows actually work, how they differ across venues, and how to design gateway logic that is both fast and deterministic even when the market gaps and acknowledgements arrive out of order.

## What Do We Mean by Cancel and Cancel-Replace?

Conceptually, there are three related actions:

- **Cancel**: Ask the exchange to remove a working order from the book.
- **Replace (amend)**: Ask the exchange to modify the terms of an existing order, such as price, size, or time-in-force.
- **Cancel-replace**: A combined operation where the original order is logically cancelled and a new order is created, often in a way that preserves or resets queue position depending on venue rules.

Different venues expose these in different ways:

- Some have explicit "replace" messages that take an existing order ID and a set of changes.
- Others require you to cancel the old order and then send a fresh new order.
- Some treat a replace as a full cancel followed by a new order behind the queue; others retain some or all of the original queue priority if certain fields (like side and price) remain unchanged.

Your gateway must hide this variation from strategies as much as possible, so that when a strategy says "cancel this order" or "move this quote up one tick," the effect is clear and consistent in the strategy's world view.

## Why Cancel-Replace Dominates Message Traffic

To see why cancel activity dominates, imagine a simple market-making strategy:

- It posts bids and offers around the mid price.
- Whenever the mid price moves, it wants to re-center its quotes.
- Whenever its inventory drifts too long or short, it wants to widen one side and tighten the other.

Each of these adjustments is implemented as:

- One or more cancel or cancel-replace messages to pull old quotes.
- One or more new orders to place updated quotes.

In a busy market, these adjustments may occur thousands of times per second. The number of cancels and replaces often exceeds the number of fills by an order of magnitude. This is why efficient cancel-handling is central to gateway performance and correctness.

## Thinking in Terms of Order States

To manage this complexity, it helps to have a clear mental model of an order's life as a finite set of states and transitions triggered by messages from you and from the exchange.

At a minimum, we need states such as:

- **New**: Order created locally but not yet acknowledged by the exchange.
- **Working**: Accepted by the exchange and resting on the book (possibly partially filled).
- **Partially Filled**: A special case of Working where some quantity has executed but some remains.
- **Cancel Pending**: A cancel has been sent, but we do not yet know if the exchange has removed the order or filled it first.
- **Replaced**: The order has been amended or rolled into a replacement order.
- **Filled**: Fully executed; no remaining quantity.
- **Cancelled**: Confirmed removed from the book with some remainder unfilled.

Each incoming or outgoing message moves the order from one state to another. Encoding these transitions explicitly in a state machine keeps behaviour deterministic under stress.

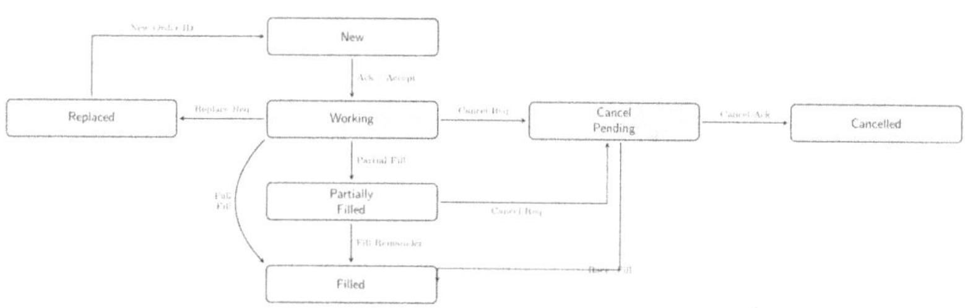

This diagram is not tied to any one protocol. FIX, OUCH, and proprietary binaries differ in how they label messages and order IDs, but the underlying lifecycle is the same.

## Queue Position: The Invisible Asset You Trade

When you post a limit order, you effectively buy a "ticket" in the queue at your price level. The earlier your order arrives relative to others at the same price, the closer you are to the front of the queue, and the more likely you are to be filled when contra-side volume appears.

Canceling and replacing may reset or preserve that ticket depending on venue rules:

- On some venues, any change to price or size moves you to the back of the queue.
- On others, reducing the size may keep your priority; increasing it may not.
- Some allow "non-price changes" (for example, client IDs or certain flags) that do not affect queue position.

For a latency-sensitive strategy, these rules have direct performance implications:

- If every tiny price improvement forces you to cancel and move to the back, you may trade off improved prices against lost queue priority.
- If certain types of replace preserve queue position, you may favour them explicitly in your workflow.

Your gateway should encapsulate these details in its venue adapter:

- For venues that support true in-place amend messages, the gateway can expose a "modify order" API that maintains the original ID and priority when allowed.

- For venues that require cancel-then-new, the gateway still offers the same API but internally sends two messages and models the queue impact appropriately.

Although the gateway cannot change the exchange's rules, it can ensure that strategies have a consistent conceptual model: when they ask for a replace, they know whether they are effectively rejoining the queue or not.

## Exposure and the Cancel Race

From a risk point of view, cancels are dangerous because they create races:

- You send a cancel for a working order.
- Before the cancel reaches the matching engine, a contra order trades against you.
- The exchange either fills you, cancels you, or partially both, depending on timing and volume.

During this race, three things are true:

- The strategy believes it is *in the process* of cancelling.
- The exchange is still free to fill any remaining quantity until it processes the cancel.
- The gateway's internal state must reflect both possibilities until the exchange's response arrives.

If your gateway mishandles this window, you can end up:

- Believing an order is cancelled when it was actually filled, understating your risk.
- Believing an order is working when it was actually cancelled, overstating your exposure and potentially over-hedging.

The "Cancel Pending" state in the state machine explicitly represents this uncertainty. When an order enters Cancel Pending:

- You should stop sending further replaces or cancels for it until you know the outcome.
- Your risk calculations should treat it as having *potential* fill exposure until the exchange confirms.

## Fast Lookup of Working Orders

To manage cancels and replaces at high speed, the gateway needs to locate the relevant order object quickly given different identifiers:

- A strategy-facing client order ID.
- An exchange-assigned order ID or token.
- Sometimes a composite of account, strategy, symbol, and side.

Under load, these lookups happen constantly. A typical cancel path is:

- Strategy sends a cancel referring to its own client order ID.
- Gateway finds the internal order object associated with that client ID.
- Gateway determines the corresponding exchange order ID and venue.
- Gateway constructs and sends the protocol-specific cancel message.

To keep this fast:

- Maintain direct maps from client IDs to internal order objects, and from internal orders to exchange IDs, using hash tables or arrays sized for your expected concurrency.

- Avoid scanning lists or performing complex searches in the hot path.
- Update these maps consistently as orders move through states (New, Working, Cancelled, etc.).

Ideally, finding an order should cost no more than a couple of pointer dereferences and simple hash operations, well within a microsecond on modern hardware.

## Handling Ambiguous or Late Acknowledgements

The exchange's responses do not always arrive in the neat order you would like. Consider a few scenarios:

- You send a cancel, then receive a fill, then receive a cancel acknowledgement.
- You send a replace, then receive an execution report against the *old* order ID followed by a replace acknowledgement.
- Network delays cause out-of-order arrival of acknowledgements relative to your sends.

Your state machine must be robust to these cases. Some key guidelines:

**Order of precedence of events.**

Your logic should define clearly:

- A fill always reduces remaining quantity, regardless of whether it arrives before or after a cancel or replace acknowledgement.
- A cancel acknowledgement moves the remaining quantity (if any) to Cancelled.
- A replace acknowledgement moves remaining quantity under the new order identity and state.

When messages arrive out of sequence, you reapply these rules consistently, rather than trying to second-guess the exchange's internal timing.

**Idempotency.**

Late or duplicated messages should not corrupt your state. For example:

- If you receive a second cancel acknowledgement for an order already in Cancelled, you should treat it as a harmless duplicate.
- If a fill arrives for an order you have already fully filled, you should verify that the total quantity remains within the limits and flag any discrepancy, but not double-count the execution.

Implementing this requires careful tracking of cumulative filled quantities and clear rules for when an order is considered "closed" for further changes.

## Venue Idiosyncrasies and Abstractions

Each exchange's protocol has its own quirks:

- Some treat any change to price or size as a full cancel and new order with a new ID.
- Others let you change size down without losing priority but size up only at the back of the queue.
- Some always return a new order ID for a replace; others keep the ID but mark the order as amended.

If you expose all of these differences directly to strategies, your trading logic becomes cluttered with venue-specific conditionals. Instead, a good gateway:

- Provides a small, uniform set of high-level operations: new, cancel, replace.

- Encapsulates venue rules in adapters that translate these operations into the correct protocol messages and internal state transitions.
- Documents the effective queue and exposure semantics per venue so that strategy designers can make informed decisions without coding to raw protocol details.

This abstraction layer is itself a source of complexity, but if designed carefully, it contains that complexity in one place rather than scattering it throughout your trading stack.

## Designing Deterministic Fast Paths

Under stress-high message rates, volatile markets-you want your cancel-replace logic to behave in a strictly deterministic way. That means:

- For any sequence of requests and exchange responses, your internal state machine should end up in a well-defined final state.
- Timing variations (earlier or later arrival of acknowledgements) should not change the ultimate interpretation of fills, cancels, and replacements.

To reach this goal:

**Separate hot and cold paths.**

Not all operations on orders are equally time-critical. For example:

- Moving an order from Working to Cancel Pending and constructing a cancel message is hot-path work; it must be very fast.
- Updating long-term audit logs or statistics about cancel ratios can be performed asynchronously.

Ensure that your hot path contains only the minimal steps:

- Lookup of the order object.

- State transition.
- Construction and dispatch of the protocol message.

All heavy logging, aggregation, and monitoring should be offloaded to other threads or systems.

**Avoid blocking on shared resources.**

Contention on shared locks or queues can cause severe and unpredictable latency spikes in cancel-heavy periods. Techniques to mitigate this include:

- Sharding orders by strategy or symbol across worker threads that do not share state.
- Using lock-free or low-contention data structures for global maps and journals where appropriate.
- Preallocating and reusing objects and buffers to avoid allocation overhead in the hot path.

**Explicit state transitions.**

Implement the state machine explicitly, with clearly enumerated states and transitions, rather than relying on ad hoc flags scattered across the codebase. This:

- Reduces the chance of contradictory flags (for example, an order simultaneously marked as both Cancel Pending and Filled).
- Makes it easier to reason about behaviour in rare edge cases.
- Simplifies unit testing: you can simulate sequences of messages and check that the final state matches expectations.

## Interaction With Risk and Limits

Cancel-replace workflows do not exist in isolation. They interact with your pre-trade risk and credit checks:

- When you cancel or reduce an order, you effectively release some reserved risk capacity (for example, open notional).
- When you replace with a higher quantity or more aggressive price, you consume more capacity.

If your risk engine lags behind your cancel/replace activity, it may either over-constrain you (by not releasing capacity soon enough) or underestimate your exposure (by releasing capacity prematurely).

To minimize these gaps:

- Tie risk updates closely to state transitions in the order state machine: for example, adjust open-notional aggregates when an order enters or leaves Working, not when the strategy sends a request.
- Treat Cancel Pending orders conservatively until you see the exchange's confirmation; assume they may still be filled.
- Ensure that both cancels and replaces flow through the same risk-aware gateway path, rather than taking shortcuts that bypass checks.

This integrated view ensures that high cancel activity under stress does not accidentally break the risk assumptions you built earlier in the chapter.

## Testing Under Stress and Failure

Because cancel-replace workflows are most critical when markets are moving fast, you should test them under realistic stress, including failure scenarios:

- Burst tests with very high cancel and replace rates.
- Simulated network delays and reordering of acknowledgements.
- Exchange-side scenarios such as partial system outages or halts that cause delayed or missing responses.

For each test, you should be able to answer:

- Does the internal order state machine end up in a consistent final state?
- Does exposure as seen by risk and the strategy match what the exchange would infer?
- Are latency distributions for cancels and replaces stable, or do you see pathological spikes?

Well-instrumented gateways often log key events in a compact journal-order creations, state transitions, and exchange responses-allowing offline replay and analysis. This journal becomes invaluable for both debugging and for demonstrating to regulators that your cancel-replace logic behaves as intended.

Cancel and cancel-replace workflows are where the neat, single-pass view of an order lifecycle meets the messy reality of active trading. They affect:

- **Queue position**, by determining how your orders move within the matching engine's queues whenever you amend them.
- **Exposure**, by introducing races and ambiguous windows where orders may be partially filled or cancelled.
- **Gateway complexity**, by requiring fast lookups, robust state machines, and careful coordination with risk and sessions.

A well-designed gateway:

- Represents each order as a finite-state machine with clear transitions for cancels, replaces, acknowledgements, and fills.
- Maintains efficient mappings between client and exchange IDs to support high cancel volumes.
- Encapsulates venue-specific rules so that strategies can use a simple, consistent cancel/replace interface.

- Keeps the hot path for cancels and replaces lean and deterministic, even at extreme message rates.
- Integrates cancel-related state changes cleanly with risk aggregates and exposure tracking.

With cancel-replace workflows understood and engineered, we are ready to look at the other half of the feedback loop: how acknowledgements, rejects, and fills return from the exchange and how to budget latency across the entire round trip from strategy to market and back.

## 8.5 Acknowledgement Handling and Latency Budgets

So far we have moved in one direction: from strategy to gateway, through validation and cancel-replace logic, out to the exchange. In live trading, however, the crucial signal is what comes back. Strategies adapt to acknowledgements, rejects, and fills; risk systems update exposures; operators watch response times and error rates. If the feedback loop is slow, noisy, or opaque, even the best outbound path will not rescue performance.

This section focuses on the *return journey* of an order:

- What kinds of responses the exchange sends (acks, rejects, cancels, fills, unsolicited updates).
- How the gateway should normalize, route, and record those events.
- How to think about and measure latency budgets across the entire round trip from strategy to exchange and back.
- How design choices in queuing, batching, and prioritization affect both median and tail response times.

We will treat latency not as a vague "be fast" requirement, but as a concrete, segmented budget: each segment of the round trip gets an allowance, and we design to meet it.

## The Return Path: Types of Exchange Responses

Once an order hits the exchange, a variety of messages may come back through the session:

- **New order acknowledgements** (often called "accepted," "live," or "resting"): confirm that the order is now working on the book.
- **Rejects**: indicate that the order was not accepted, usually with a specific reason (invalid price, symbol not eligible, limit breach, protocol error).
- **Cancel acknowledgements**: confirm that a cancel request has succeeded and the order is no longer working.
- **Replace acknowledgements**: confirm that a modification has been applied, sometimes with a new exchange order ID.
- **Partial and full fills**: report executed quantity, price, and possibly fees or flags (e.g., passive vs aggressive).
- **Out-of-sequence updates or busts**: late corrections, trade cancelations, or status changes initiated by the exchange.

The gateway's job is to turn this heterogeneous stream into something strategies and risk systems can rely on:

- A coherent *order state timeline* for each client order.
- A set of *events* (accepted, cancelled, filled, etc.) delivered with low and predictable latency.
- Logs and metrics that let you reconstruct behaviour and analyze performance.

This requires careful coordination with the state machines and data structures introduced in the cancel-replace section. Every incoming message is both a state transition and a timing data point.

## Breaking Down the Round Trip

To reason clearly about latency, it helps to decompose the end-to-end journey into segments. A simple but powerful breakdown is:

1. **Strategy → Gateway**: time from when the strategy decides to send an order to when the gateway receives it.

2. **Gateway (outbound processing)**: validation, risk checks, serialization, and session handling until the message leaves your server.

3. **Gateway → Exchange**: network and exchange ingress delay until the order reaches the matching engine and is processed.

4. **Exchange → Gateway**: processing at the exchange (including queueing, matching, and response creation) plus network delay back to your server.

5. **Gateway (inbound processing)**: parsing, state updates, and routing of the response back to the strategy and to risk/audit sinks.

6. **Gateway → Strategy**: time for the acknowledgement or fill to arrive and be handled by the strategy process.

In many firms, the last two segments are combined into a single "gateway-to-strategy" metric, and the middle network segments are sometimes estimated or treated as one "wire + exchange" bucket. Even so, thinking in segments forces you to ask: where exactly is time being spent, and which parts can we control?

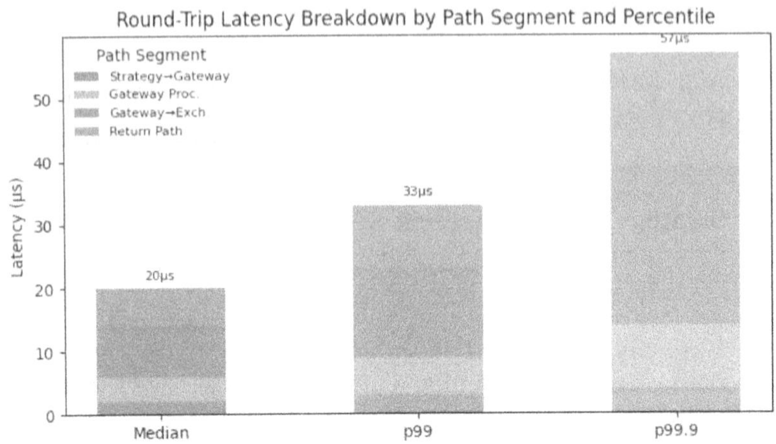


This sort of chart gives you an immediate visual intuition:

- Which segments dominate the median?
- Which ones bloat the tails at the 99th and 99.9th percentiles?

Your design work then targets the worst offenders first.

## Gateway Responsibilities on the Inbound Path

Just as we decomposed outbound work (validation, serialization, session logic), we should make the inbound responsibilities explicit. When a response arrives at the gateway:

1. **Decode**: parse the wire format (FIX text, OUCH binary, proprietary) into an internal representation.
2. **Correlate**: map exchange identifiers to internal order objects and client order IDs.
3. **Update state**: advance the order state machine (from New to Working, Working to Filled, Cancel Pending to Cancelled, etc.).

4. **Update risk**: adjust per-order and aggregate risk metrics (positions, exposures, P&L).

5. **Route**: deliver a normalized event to the strategy (and potentially to multiple subscribers such as risk dashboards or audit feeds).

6. **Record**: optionally log or journal the event for replay and compliance.

The main latency budget on this path is between ingress at the NIC and notification at the strategy. Risk and recording are also important, but they can often tolerate slightly more delay and jitter, or be partially decoupled.

## Normalizing Acks, Rejects, and Fills

Different protocols and venues encode similar ideas in different shapes. For example:

- Some splits acknowledgements into separate "accepted" and "booked" events; others combine them.
- Reason codes for rejects vary widely and may be cryptic.
- Fills may arrive either as incremental updates or as snapshots of cumulative executed quantity.

A gateway that forwards raw protocol messages directly to strategies forces every strategy to learn each venue's quirks. Instead, it is usually better to normalize:

- Map protocol-specific status fields to a small internal set (e.g., NEW_ACK, REJECTED, PARTIAL_FILL, FILLED, CANCELLED).
- Provide structured reject information (reason code, human-readable description, whether retry is likely to succeed).

- Present fills consistently as deltas (change in executed quantity and P&L) plus updated cumulative state.

Normalization costs a few CPU cycles but simplifies strategy code and makes it easier to collect uniform metrics across venues.

## Routing Responses Back to Strategies

Once a response is decoded and normalized, it must reach the relevant strategy instance quickly. Common patterns include:

- **Callback or event bus**: the gateway calls a registered handler or posts an event to a per-strategy queue.
- **Shared memory or IPC**: in colocated setups, responses may be written into shared memory ring buffers or similar mechanisms.
- **Networked strategy**: if the strategy itself is remote, acknowledgements are forwarded over an internal protocol (with its own latency profile).

For tail latency, two details matter:

- **Queueing**: if multiple strategies share a queue or thread, a burst of responses for one strategy can delay others.
- **Back-pressure**: if a strategy is slow to consume acknowledgements, the gateway must not allow its buffers to grow without bound or to block other critical work.

A robust design often gives each strategy (or small group of strategies) its own logical response channel, limiting interference. If a strategy falls behind, the gateway can apply local policies (for example, dropping low-priority updates or triggering protective throttles) without harming other flows.

## Engineering Explicit Latency Budgets

An explicit latency budget transforms vague aspirations into checkable constraints. A typical exercise might look like:

- Target median round-trip (decision to first ack/fill) of 30 microseconds.
- Target p99 round-trip under 70 microseconds.
- Assign nominal budgets:
  - Strategy → Gateway and back: 5–10 microseconds combined.
  - Gateway outbound + inbound processing: 10–15 microseconds.
  - Network + exchange: whatever remains; often the largest but also the hardest to control.

The gateway cannot dictate exchange matching times, but it can be precise about its own contribution. For example:

- Outbound (before send): validation, risk, serialization → 5–8 microseconds.
- Inbound (after receive): decode, correlate, state update, route → 3–6 microseconds.

Once you set these objectives:

- You can test them with synthetic traffic and real markets.
- You can monitor live performance and react when components drift out of spec.

It is important to focus on the *distribution*, not just the mean. A low average with a fat tail can be worse for many strategies than a slightly higher but tighter distribution: traders and algorithms need predictability.

## Measuring Latency: Timestamps and Telemetry

Good budgets are backed by good measurements. To attribute delay to each segment, you need timestamps at key points:

- When the strategy creates the order.
- When the gateway receives the order.
- When the gateway sends the encoded message (or hands it to the NIC).
- When the gateway receives the response from the exchange.
- When the gateway finishes processing the response.
- When the strategy processes the acknowledgement or fill.

In highly tuned environments:

- NIC hardware timestamps can give very accurate send/receive times at the network interface.
- The gateway can use a monotonic, high-resolution clock for internal stages.

Two practical cautions:

- **Overhead**: excessively heavy telemetry (for example, writing to disk synchronously on every event) can itself distort latency. Use lightweight counters in the hot path and batch detailed logs.
- **Clock consistency**: ensure that all components use properly synchronized and stable clocks (for instance via hardware time, not general-purpose NTP alone) so that subtracting timestamps across processes makes sense.

With these precautions, you can produce both real-time dashboards and historical reports:

- Median, p95, p99, p99.9 round-trip times per venue and per strategy.
- Breakdown of how much time was spent in each segment.
- Trends over days and weeks, revealing regressions or environmental changes.

## Queueing, Batching, and Prioritization

On the return path, your gateway faces the classic tension between throughput and latency:

- **Queueing**: responses arrive in bursts; processing them strictly in arrival order is simple but can disadvantage some strategies.
- **Batching**: grouping work (for example, decoding multiple messages from a buffer at once) improves CPU efficiency but can add small delays for individual messages.

There is no universal formula, but certain principles help:

**Keep critical events fast.**

Not all responses are equally urgent. For example:

- A new-order acknowledgement that unblocks further quoting is high priority.
- A supplemental status update that does not change risk or trading decisions may be lower priority.

You can reflect this by:

- Having separate internal queues for high- and normal-priority events.
- Ensuring that high-priority queues are drained first under load.

**Avoid head-of-line blocking.**

If many responses for one very active strategy are queued in front of a small number of responses for a slower strategy, the latter may experience unnecessary latency. To mitigate this:

- Allocate independent queues per strategy or per small group of strategies.
- Use a scheduling policy that gives each queue a chance to make progress, such as simple round-robin or weighted fair servicing.

**Use micro-batches judiciously.**

Reading from the NIC or sockets often yields buffers containing many messages. Decoding them in small batches (for example, up to a fixed number or a very tight time budget) can be more efficient than handling each message fully before moving to the next. The trade-off is:

- Better throughput and CPU cache locality.
- Slight additional delay between the arrival of the first message in a batch and its final delivery to the strategy.

By bounding batch size or processing time, you can limit the impact on tail latency.

## Fairness Across Strategies

Gateways often serve multiple strategies and desks with different latency sensitivities. A single, undifferentiated response pipeline may inadvertently let one flow starve others:

- A high-frequency strategy with huge volume can dominate queues.
- A slower strategy may see its own acknowledgements delayed behind those of its faster neighbour.

To address this, you can introduce explicit fairness and isolation:

- Reserve processing capacity or threads for latency-critical strategies.
- Rate-limit or deprioritize non-critical flows when the gateway is under stress.
- Instrument latency per strategy and set service-level objectives (SLOs) accordingly.

This is as much a governance decision as a technical one: the firm must decide which flows get priority and document those choices.

## Handling Rejects and Errors Transparently

Rejects and error responses require just as much discipline as positive acknowledgements. A common anti-pattern is to treat them as exceptional and route them through slower, less instrumented paths. This can lead to confusing behaviour under stress.

Better practice is to treat rejects as first-class events:

- Decode and correlate them with the same speed and care as a successful ack.
- Deliver them promptly to the strategy, including enough detail to allow automatic remediation where possible.
- Log them with structured data (reason codes, context) so that risk and compliance can analyze patterns.

From a latency-budget perspective, you want rejects to arrive quickly, so that faulty logic or configuration is detected early and does not continue to send bad orders. Slow, opaque rejection paths lead to large bursts of failures and messy post-mortems.

## Making Latency Behaviour Observable

A well-engineered gateway is not just fast; it is *observable*. That means:

- You can see, in near real time, how long acknowledgements and fills take per venue and strategy.
- You can relate performance anomalies to underlying causes (e.g., a spike in exchange processing, a network event, an overloaded risk component).
- You can reproduce and replay problematic sequences offline.

Practically, this involves:

- Lightweight metrics streams summarizing latencies and counts, suitable for dashboards.
- Moderately detailed logs of key transitions and events, sampled or rate-limited to avoid overload.
- High-fidelity journals for selected flows, used for debugging and compliance, recorded off the hot path as much as possible.

The measurement and telemetry infrastructure should itself respect latency budgets: collecting insights must not meaningfully slow down the trading path.

Acknowledgement handling is the other half of the order lifecycle: without fast, predictable feedback, sophisticated strategies cannot manage risk or adapt to the market effectively. By breaking the round trip into clear segments and assigning explicit latency budgets, you give yourself a framework to design, measure, and improve performance.

In a mature gateway:

- Exchange responses are decoded, normalized, and correlated to internal orders with very low and stable latency.
- Order state machines and risk aggregates are updated deterministically, even when messages arrive out of sequence.
- Responses are routed back to strategies in a way that minimizes head-of-line blocking and respects fairness and priority policies.

- Latency distributions are continuously measured and decomposed by path segment, venue, and strategy, so that regressions and anomalies can be caught early.
- Rejects and error conditions are handled as first-class events, with clear and timely feedback.

With both outbound and inbound paths under control and latency budgets made explicit, we are ready to address what happens when the environment is not well-behaved: disconnects, sequence gaps, exchange resets, and the replay logic that keeps the gateway's internal world in sync with the exchange under failure conditions.

## 8.6 Failure Modes and Replay Logic

Up to this point, we have worked in an idealized world. Sessions remain up, messages arrive in order, and acknowledgements and fills flow cleanly through the gateway with well-behaved latency. Real markets, and real systems, are not so polite. Links drop. Exchange gateways restart. Network devices briefly black-hole traffic. Messages are duplicated or delayed. If your order gateway is not designed for these realities, its internal view of the world will slowly drift away from the exchange's view—and that drift will show up as unexpected risk.

This section examines how things break and how to recover from those breaks in a deterministic, testable way. The aim is not to avoid all failures (that is impossible), but to make sure that:

- Failures are detected quickly and loudly, rather than silently.
- Recovery steps converge to a single, auditable order and position state.
- The logic is simple enough to test with realistic failure scenarios.

We will focus on four broad categories of failure:

- Session disconnects and network partitions.

- Sequence gaps and missing messages.
- Duplicates and out-of-order messages.
- Exchange resets and application-level restarts.

For each, we will connect back to the session, serialization, risk, and acknowledgement mechanisms introduced earlier, and show how replay logic ties them together.

## Failure as a Normal Operating Condition

The first conceptual shift is to stop treating failures as rare, catastrophic anomalies. In a modern electronic market:

- Minor connectivity glitches are routine.
- Exchange software is upgraded intraday.
- Network paths can briefly congest or reroute.

From the gateway's perspective, a **failure** is any event that calls into question the reliability of its current order and position state. That includes both hard events (socket disconnects) and softer signals (unexpected sequence gaps, unexplained latency spikes, unusually high reject rates).

Designing for failure, therefore, means:

- Having clear conditions under which you stop trusting the current state.
- Defining concrete recovery procedures for each condition.
- Ensuring those procedures are safe (they do not increase risk) and deterministic (they always lead to the same outcome given the same history).

## Session Disconnects and Network Partitions

A session disconnect is the most visible and, in some ways, simplest failure. The TCP connection drops, or the exchange sends a logout or termination message. A network partition is a subtler variant: the connection may technically remain open, but one direction of traffic is impaired or blocked.

The immediate impact is obvious:

- You cannot send new orders or cancels to the exchange on that session.
- You may or may not receive final acknowledgements or fills for messages already in flight.

Less obvious is the question: *what happened to the orders that were working at the time of the disconnect?*

Different venues handle this differently:

- Some support **cancel-on-disconnect**: they automatically cancel all working orders for that session when it drops.
- Others leave orders resting on the book until you explicitly cancel them after reconnecting.
- Some apply cancel-on-disconnect only if certain flags were set at logon or per-order.

A robust gateway therefore needs:

**A clear per-venue policy.**

For each session type and venue, know exactly what the exchange promises in disconnect situations. Capture this in configuration and code, not just in someone's memory or a PDF on a shared drive.

**An immediate protective reaction.**

Upon detecting a disconnect or a serious stall on the session:

- Block new outbound traffic for strategies that depend on that venue.

- Inform strategies and risk systems that the venue path is impaired.
- Start a controlled recovery procedure (which we will outline shortly).

Detection itself is driven by the heartbeats and liveliness checks discussed earlier. The crucial thing is that once you declare the session compromised, you adopt a conservative stance: assume the worst about orders until proven otherwise, not the other way around.

## Sequence Gaps and Missing Messages

Sequence numbers exist precisely so that you *notice* when you have missed something. When the gateway's incoming sequence counter discovers a gap (expected 105, received 107), it knows that at least one message is missing. That missing message might contain:

- A fill.
- A cancel acknowledgement.
- A replace acknowledgement or status change.
- A session-level instruction such as a reset.

Until that gap is resolved, the gateway's internal state is at best incomplete and at worst wrong.

**Gaps as triggers, not curiosities.**

Treat every sequence gap as a trigger for immediate action, not just a warning to be logged. Typical actions:

- Issue a resend or replay request for the missing range (in FIX and similar protocols).
- If the protocol offers no replay, escalate the severity: you may need to fall back to a full reconnect and external reconciliation.

**Minimizing the damage window.**

The longer the gap remains unresolved, the more downstream state becomes suspect. To minimize this window:

- Keep resend request logic simple and fast: the detection of a gap and dispatch of a request should be essentially immediate.
- Prioritize processing of replayed messages when they arrive, as they directly repair your state.
- Avoid queuing new application messages (acks and fills) behind large replay bursts; instead, interleave them in a way that maintains consistency without starving live traffic.

If your design treats resend handling as **slow-path maintenance work**, you will inevitably see long stretches where the gateway is trading on stale or partial information.

## Duplicates and Out-of-Order Messages

Network-level retransmissions, server restarts, and replay responses can produce duplicates and out-of-order messages. Without proper safeguards, these can corrupt your view of order and position state.

**Duplicates.**

A duplicate message is one whose sequence number and core content you have seen before. They can arise from:

- Exchange-side retransmissions in response to your resend requests.
- Network replays after transient failures.
- Exchange bugs or restarts.

Rather than trying to prevent duplicates entirely, your gateway should assume they can happen and make key operations idempotent:

- Applying a fill for sequence 120 when you have already processed sequence 120 must not double-count the execution.

- Receiving a second cancel acknowledgement for an order already marked Cancelled should not change any positions or aggregates.

This typically requires tracking:

- The highest sequence number processed.
- The cumulative filled quantity per order.
- Whether an order's final terminal state (Filled, Cancelled) has already been set.

**Out-of-order messages.**

Out-of-order messages present a more subtle problem. You may see:

- A cancel acknowledgement before the last fill for that order.
- A fill for an order you consider already replaced, due to internal exchange timing.
- Replay traffic interleaved with new live traffic.

To handle this, your state machine must not assume a strict temporal ordering beyond what the protocol guarantees. Some guiding principles:

- Fills always adjust remaining quantity, even if they arrive after a cancel or replace ack, as long as the timestamps and sequence numbers indicate they are legitimate.
- Terminal states should be set based on cumulative filled quantity and explicit cancel/replace outcomes, not on the order in which messages happened to arrive.
- When replay traffic is clearly marked (for example with a **possible duplicate** flag in FIX), you can choose to apply it only if it brings new information relative to your current state.

It is often helpful to think in terms of *event sourcing*: the order state is a function of the sequence of acknowledged events (new, partial fills, fills, cancels, replaces). If you apply the same events in any order consistent with the protocol's rules, you should reach the same final state.

## Exchange Resets and Application-Level Restarts

Sometimes the exchange itself restarts or initiates a protocol-level reset. You may receive a message that says, in effect:

- "Forget previous sequence numbers; start from here."
- "Your session has been reset; please log on again."

This is more than a networking hiccup; it is a potential discontinuity in the meaning of order IDs and status messages.

**Reset semantics.**

For each venue, you must understand:

- Whether a session reset implies that all prior orders have been cancelled, remain working, or require explicit restatement.
- Whether exchange order IDs may be reused or invalidated after a reset.
- Whether and how you can request a replay of missed events across the reset boundary.

A dangerous anti-pattern is to silently accept resets and continue updating internal order objects as if nothing unusual happened. Instead, a robust gateway:

- Treats a reset as a high-severity event that triggers reconciliation.
- Marks all affected orders as **state uncertain** until verification.
- Avoids sending new orders that depend on stale assumptions about working inventory.

## Durable Journals and Idempotency Keys

Replay logic depends on having a trustworthy record of what was actually sent and received. Relying solely on current in-memory state is not enough: if the gateway process itself crashes or is restarted, you risk losing the history needed to reconcile.

Two key tools address this: *durable journals* and *idempotency keys*.

**Durable journals.**

A durable journal is a persistent, append-only record of messages and state changes. At minimum, you want to capture:

- Outbound application messages to the exchange: new orders, cancels, replaces.
- Inbound responses: acknowledgements, rejects, partial and full fills, session events.

The journal should be:

- **Append-only**: new events are appended; old ones are never modified.
- **Ordered**: events appear in the order they were sent or received on each session.
- **Durable**: committed to disk or another reliable store frequently enough that a process crash will not erase recent history.

During normal operation, you will usually read from the journal only for monitoring or offline analysis. During recovery, it becomes your primary truth source: you can replay events to rebuild internal state after a crash or to compare with exchange-side logs.

**Idempotency keys.**

An idempotency key is a stable identifier that lets both you and the exchange recognize the same logical request across retries or replays. For example:

- A client order ID that you maintain uniquely per strategy and day.
- A composite of account, strategy, and a monotonic counter.

If a new-order message is retried after a disconnect, the gateway can reuse the same idempotency key, allowing:

- The exchange to recognize and ignore duplicate creations (if it supports such semantics).
- Your own systems to correlate events unambiguously even if sequence numbers or session IDs change.

When combined with durable journaling, idempotency keys make it much easier to reason about which requests actually took effect.

## Replay Mechanisms: From Lightweight Gap-Fill to Full Rebuild

Replay can mean several different things depending on scope:

- **Gap-fill replay**: requesting a small range of missing messages to close a sequence gap.
- **Session replay**: on reconnect, asking the exchange to resend all events from a given sequence number.
- **Internal state replay**: using your own journal to reconstruct order and position state after a process restart.

A well-designed gateway supports all three, in increasing order of disruption.

**Gap-fill replay.**

This is the least invasive: you detect a gap, request just the missing range, apply the replayed messages, and continue. Implementation tips:

- Keep requests narrow: ask exactly for what you are missing, not an overly large window.
- Process replayed messages in sequence, marking them as replays to avoid double-counting where appropriate.

- Ensure that live inbound messages can still be processed alongside replays without inconsistencies.

**Session replay on reconnect.**

After a disconnect, many protocols let you specify the last sequence number you saw and then replay from there. This is more disruptive, because:

- You may receive a large volume of old messages along with new ones.
- Some orders may no longer be relevant (e.g., fully filled and long since closed).

To handle this:

- Use sequence and timestamp filters to ignore replayed messages that provide no new information relative to your journal.
- For active orders, reconcile internal state with the replay: adjust cumulative fills, statuses, and positions as needed.

**Internal state replay after crash.**

If the gateway process itself restarts:

- It loads configuration and instrument data.
- It replays its own durable journal to rebuild in-memory order and risk state up to the last committed event.
- It reconnects to exchanges and, if supported, requests a session replay from the last known sequence.
- It cross-checks: any differences between internal reconstructed state and exchange replay are flagged and resolved explicitly.

This approach makes recovery a controlled, deterministic process, not a manual scramble of scripts and spreadsheet comparisons.

## Determinism and Testability

A central design goal throughout is determinism: given the same sequence of inputs (orders, responses, failures, replays), the gateway should always converge to the same final state. This property is invaluable for testing.

**Scenario-based testing.**

You can build test harnesses that:

- Feed in scripted sequences of outbound orders and inbound exchange messages, including gaps, duplicates, and resets.
- Inject simulated disconnects and reconnects at arbitrary points.
- Compare the final internal state (orders, fills, positions) against expected outcomes.

Because your state evolution is deterministic, failures in tests are reproducible and diagnostic. You can also compare behaviour across software versions: replay the same journal into old and new versions of the gateway and verify that they produce identical results, or understand and document any intentional differences.

**Simplifying the state space.**

Determinism is easier to achieve when your state model is simple. The tools we discussed earlier help:

- Finite state machines for orders with clearly enumerated states and transitions.
- Clear ownership of responsibilities between components (session, risk, strategy).
- Idempotent handlers for inbound messages.

If you find yourself relying on global, mutable flags or implicit assumptions about message ordering, you will have a hard time achieving reproducible recovery.

## Failing Loudly vs Failing Silently

Throughout this discussion, a recurring theme is that silent failure is worse than noisy failure. A gateway that continues trading while quietly out of sync with the exchange is far more dangerous than one that stops trading and demands attention.

**When in doubt, be conservative.**

When you encounter conditions that you have not explicitly modeled or fully understood:

- Prefer to stop or drastically limit order flow on the affected venue.
- Escalate alerts to human operators and risk managers.
- Enter a safe recovery mode that relies on explicit reconciliation before resuming normal activity.

This may mean missing some trades, but it preserves the one thing you cannot trade without: a trustworthy picture of your risk.

**Visible health indicators.**

To support this, gateways should expose clear health and synchronization indicators:

- Session status (up, degraded, down).
- Sequence alignment status (in sync, recovering, unknown).
- Replay activity (ongoing, completed, failed).

These indicators feed dashboards and alerts, but they also help strategies make informed decisions: for example, a strategy might automatically reduce or halt activity on venues whose gateways report degraded state.

Failure modes are not edge cases; they are an integral part of how an order gateway behaves in production. Disconnects, sequence gaps, duplicates, and exchange resets are all inevitable. What distinguishes robust systems from fragile ones is how they react and recover.

In a well-designed gateway:

- Session management and heartbeats detect connectivity problems quickly.
- Sequence numbers and gap detection trigger targeted replays, not quiet toleration of inconsistency.
- Idempotent state machines handle duplicates and out-of-order messages without corruption.
- Durable journals and idempotency keys provide the raw material for deterministic replay and reconciliation.
- Recovery procedures—from lightweight gap-fill to full state rebuild—are clearly defined, automated as far as possible, and routinely tested.
- Failures are surfaced loudly, and conservative defaults limit risk until synchronization is restored.

Taken together with the earlier sections on sessions, serialization, risk checks, cancel-replace workflows, and latency budgets, this completes our picture of the order gateway as not just a fast conduit, but as a resilient, observable, and auditable system. It is this combination of speed and determinism under stress that separates serious trading infrastructure from mere connectivity code.

# Chapter 9

# Optimization Patterns & Kernel-Bypass Techniques

*On a modern trading stack, the difference between 15μs and 5μs is rarely about algorithms and almost always about how you move bits. This chapter unpacks where the microseconds actually go-inside queues, caches, NICs, and the OS boundary-and shows how specific patterns of memory access, synchronization, and kernel-bypass networking can reclaim them without turning your codebase into an unmaintainable science project.*

## 9.1 Lock-Free Data Structures

In the previous chapter we treated latency mostly as a system-level phenomenon: packets traverse the NIC, the OS scheduler moves threads on and off cores, and your trading logic competes with everything else running on the machine. We now zoom in to a smaller scale: the data structures that connect components inside your process.

Queues sit on the hot path of almost every serious trading system. Market data flows from NIC-polling threads into strategy threads through queues. Orders flow in the opposite direction, through gateways and risk checks, again through queues. If these queues rely on kernel locks or heavy-weight synchronization, they can silently dominate your latency budget-even when the machine “looks idle”.

This section introduces the lock-free queues and supporting techniques that keep the hot path making forward progress without kernel locks, blocking mutexes, or scheduler interference. The goal is not to turn you into a lock-free algorithm researcher, but to give you enough intuition to recognize the right patterns, avoid the dangerous ones, and benchmark the rest.

## Why Traditional Locks Hurt in Low-Latency Paths

A mutex-based design is often “good enough” for business systems. For low-latency trading, it usually is not. The raw cost of taking and releasing a lock is rarely the problem; the variability it introduces is.

Concretely, when you take a mutex in a hot path:

- The lock state often lives in a shared cache line. Multiple cores spinning or updating that lock cause the cache line to bounce between cores, adding unpredictable stalls.
- Under contention, threads may block. Once blocked, they depend on the OS scheduler to wake them again, which introduces jitter on the order of microseconds or more.
- You are exposed to priority inversion: a low-priority thread can hold a lock that a high-priority thread urgently needs. The high-priority thread then stalls behind work that, in theory, should never have preempted it.

In a typical mutex-protected queue, both producer and consumer take the same lock. Imagine a market data handler pushing messages into such a queue and a strategy thread popping them off. Even if the queue is almost uncontended during a quiet market, the occasional burst creates a convoy: producers line up behind the lock, consumers line up behind producers, and a handful of unlucky messages experience large stalls. Median latency might look acceptable, but the tail percentiles inflate precisely when the market is busiest.

The alternative is to structure your data flow so that the hot path never blocks. If a producer cannot enqueue because the queue is full, it either drops work (for a best-effort stream like redundant market data) or applies backpressure in a controlled way (for critical paths like orders). Achieving that without locks is the domain of lock-free data structures.

## Single-Producer/Single-Consumer Ring Buffers

The simplest and most useful lock-free structure for trading workloads is the single-producer/single-consumer (SPSC) ring buffer. It is the canonical building block for:

- Feed handler → strategy handoff
- NIC polling thread → parser thread
- Strategy thread → single-threaded risk engine

The SPSC ring works because it deliberately constrains concurrency: exactly one thread writes (the producer), and exactly one reads (the consumer). That allows very simple rules about who is allowed to touch which pieces of state.

## Basic Layout and Discipline

Conceptually, an SPSC ring buffer consists of three elements:

- A fixed-size array of slots, each able to hold one message or pointer.
- A *head* index, owned by the producer, which points to the next free slot to be written.
- A *tail* index, owned by the consumer, which points to the next filled slot to be read.

The indices wrap around modulo the array size, which is why it is called a ring. The key ownership rule is:

- Only the producer modifies the head index.
- Only the consumer modifies the tail index.

Both sides may read both indices, but each side writes only its own. This means no variable is ever written by two cores at the same time, dramatically reducing the need for expensive coordination.

The enqueue (producer) logic, conceptually, is:

- Read the current tail index to see how much space is available.
- If the ring is full (head is about to overtake tail), decide how to handle backpressure.
- Otherwise, write the new item into the slot at *head*.
- Publish the new head value so the consumer can see that the item is available.

The dequeue (consumer) logic is symmetric:

- Read the current head index to see if there is anything to consume.
- If the ring is empty (head equals tail), decide whether to spin, yield, or sleep.
- Otherwise, read the item from the slot at *tail*.
- Advance tail to mark the slot as free for future producers.

There is no lock acquisition or release. Producers and consumers simply move their own pointers forward as work progresses.

## Why Fixed Size and Preallocation Matter

Most SPSC rings in trading systems are fixed size and preallocate all storage up front. This is not a stylistic preference; it serves several latency goals:

- **No runtime allocation:** Dynamic allocation can be surprisingly expensive and unpredictable under contention. Preallocating avoids allocator locks, page faults, and fragmentation-related cache misses.
- **Better cache locality:** A contiguous array means consecutive slots are near each other in memory. Sequential reads and writes map nicely onto cache lines and hardware prefetchers.
- **Predictable backpressure:** A fixed capacity makes it clear when producers are outrunning consumers. You can detect and handle this early instead of letting allocations grow unbounded.

You pay for this predictability by having to choose a capacity upfront and monitor for overflow. In practice, you size generously based on burst characteristics and instrument the system to detect when you are close to the limit.

## Memory Ordering and Visibility

So far, we have described the SPSC ring as if each load and store happens instantaneously and in order. On modern CPUs that is not literally true. Processors and compilers reorder operations internally when they can do so safely for single-threaded code. In concurrent code, this reordering can break your assumptions unless you use the correct memory ordering primitives.

The key requirement for an SPSC ring is simple to state:

> The consumer must never see a slot as “filled” before the producer has finished writing the item into that slot.

Translated into operations:

- When the producer enqueues an item, it must first write the item into the slot, and *only then* publish the updated head index to the consumer.
- When the consumer dequeues, it must first read the current head, and only read the slot contents if head indicates that the slot is filled.

On many platforms, this means:

- The producer's *store* to head must be marked as a "release" operation, which ensures that all prior writes (the item contents) become visible before the new head value is visible to other cores.
- The consumer's *load* of head must be a "consume" or "acquire" operation, which ensures it does not read the item contents before it has seen the head value.

You do not need to remember the jargon; what matters is the sequence: write the data, then publish the fact that the data is available, and do so in a way that other cores respect. Otherwise, rare race conditions can occur and be almost impossible to reproduce.

## Cache Lines and Padding

Even though only one thread writes each index, both threads read both indices. If head and tail live on the same cache line, then producer and consumer will keep invalidating each other's view of that line. This cache-line "ping-pong" introduces latency spikes that get worse with core distance (for example, across NUMA nodes).

The typical mitigation is to *pad* each index onto its own cache line:

- Place head in memory far enough from tail that they cannot share a cache line.
- Optionally pad the ring slots themselves so that hot fields do not collide with unrelated state.

This is an example of a theme that will recur in later sections: small layout decisions can have large performance implications when cores share mutable data.

## Mutex-Based Queue vs. SPSC Ring: A Visual Comparison

Before we move to more complex multi-producer/multi-consumer (MPMC) queues, it is useful to visualize the difference between a mutex-based queue and an SPSC ring in terms of timing, contention, and cache movement.

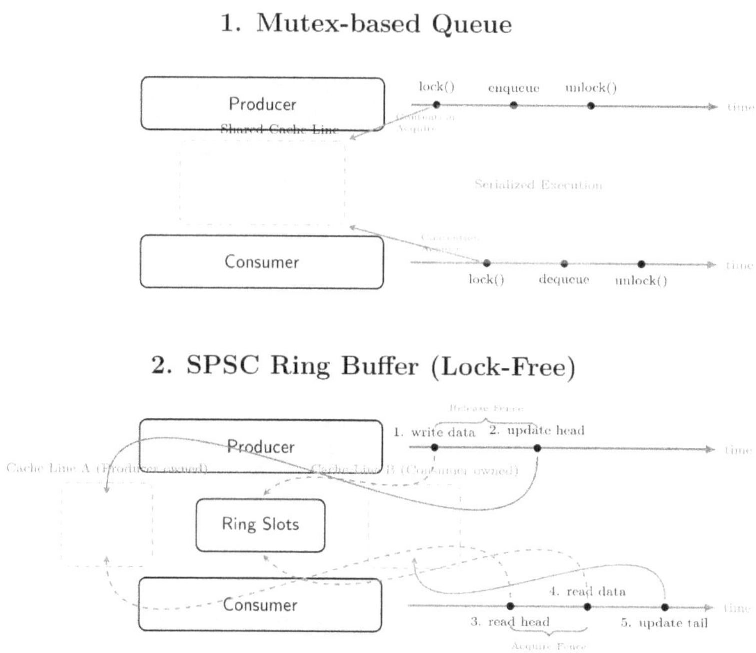


On the left, both threads compete for a shared mutex and repeatedly touch the same cache line. On the right, head and tail are disjoint; producer and consumer operate mostly independently, coordinating only through lightweight metadata updates with explicit memory ordering.

## Extending to Multi-Producer/Multi-Consumer Queues

Real systems are rarely limited to a single producer and a single consumer. You may have:

- Several feed handler threads producing into a shared normalization stage.
- Multiple strategies consuming from a shared market data bus.
- Many strategy threads producing orders into a common gateway.

The natural question is: can we build a single, global multi-producer/multi-consumer (MPMC) lock-free queue that works as smoothly as the SPSC ring?

The short answer is: *yes, but at a cost.* As you allow more threads to write and read the same structure, your coordination complexity and worst-case latency rise.

## Trade-offs in MPMC Designs

MPMC queues must ensure that:

- Multiple producers do not overwrite each other's entries.
- Multiple consumers do not pull the same entry twice or skip entries.
- All of this remains correct under arbitrary interleaving of operations.

To achieve this *without* locks, MPMC algorithms typically rely on:

- Atomic read-modify-write operations on shared indices or sequence numbers.
- Additional per-slot metadata to track whether a slot is empty, reserved, or filled.
- Careful use of memory ordering to ensure that reservations and publications are visible at the right times.

These structures can deliver very high throughput under load, but they tend to involve more cache-line sharing and more complex corner cases. As a result:

- Median latency can be good, but tail latency is often worse than a comparable SPSC topology.
- Debugging rare races, if the implementation is wrong, becomes challenging.
- Fairness between producers or consumers is not guaranteed; some threads may see more stalls than others.

In practice, many trading shops avoid a single global MPMC queue in the hottest paths. Instead, they prefer to shard the problem into multiple SPSC queues wherever possible.

## Sharding with SPSC Rings

Sharding means splitting your data flow so that each producer-consumer pair gets its own SPSC ring, or at least so that each core has a localized queue. Examples:

- Rather than having four feed handlers push into one global queue, assign each to a dedicated normalization thread with its own SPSC queue. A later stage can merge streams if necessary, possibly off the strict hot path.
- Instead of all strategies consuming from one massive bus, partition symbols or instruments by core, so each strategy instance reads only the subset it cares about.

- For outgoing orders, assign each strategy thread a dedicated SPSC ring to the gateway, and let the gateway multiplex them deterministically.

This approach has several advantages:

- Each ring behaves like the simple, predictable SPSC structure we already understand.
- Cache locality improves, because each thread repeatedly works with the same subset of queues and symbols.
- Worst-case latency is easier to bound, since contention is limited to well-defined edges (for example, at the final merge).

The downside is that your architecture must become more aware of partitioning: you need to design up front how work is divided across rings and cores, and how you handle skew (for instance, one symbol becoming extremely active).

## Safe Memory Reclamation in Lock-Free Designs

So far we focused on queues where all storage is fixed and preallocated. In such designs, memory reclamation is trivial: slots are reused in place as head and tail circulate. Once you move to more dynamic structures-trees, lists, hash tables-or even to queues holding pointers to dynamically allocated objects, you face a new question:

> How do you safely free memory that other threads might still be reading, without using locks?

In lock-based designs, you typically rely on the fact that a thread holding a lock cannot see a node after it has been freed, because the lock protects both the structure and the lifecycle of its nodes. In lock-free designs, readers may traverse a structure concurrently with writers that are deleting nodes. Simply freeing a node as soon as you unlink it risks use-after-free bugs.

Several techniques have emerged to manage this safely without regressing to global locks.

## Hazard Pointers

The hazard pointer idea is to let readers announce which objects they are currently accessing. The high-level process is:

- Each thread has a small set of "hazard pointer" slots.
- Before a reader accesses a pointer to a shared node, it publishes that pointer into one of its hazard slots.
- Writers that wish to delete a node first remove it from the shared structure, then add it to a "retire list" instead of freeing it immediately.
- Periodically, a writer scans all hazard pointers across threads. Any retire-list node that is not referenced by any hazard pointer is safe to free.

This introduces some overhead for publishing and scanning hazard pointers, but it ensures that no node is freed while a reader might still be using it. You retain lock-free progress: readers do not block writers, and writers do not block readers, beyond occasional lightweight coordination.

## Epoch-Based Reclamation

Epoch-based reclamation takes a slightly different approach, based on global "epochs" that represent broad time windows:

- All threads periodically announce which epoch they are currently operating in.
- When a writer removes a node, it associates the node with the current epoch and adds it to a per-thread retire list.
- A node can be safely freed once all threads have advanced past the epoch in which the node was retired.

If readers are well-behaved and move through epochs regularly (for example, once per batch of operations), then the system guarantees that no reader holds a reference to nodes from very old epochs.

Compared to hazard pointers:

- Epoch-based schemes can be cheaper per operation, because threads only occasionally update their epoch.
- They are less precise; you may hold on to retired nodes longer than strictly necessary, increasing memory use.

In many trading systems, where memory is plentiful relative to the small number of nodes on hot paths, this trade-off is acceptable. What matters is that reclamation does not introduce blocking or long pauses.

## Pre-Allocated Object Pools

For the hottest paths, especially queues, the safest and simplest "reclamation" strategy is to avoid frees entirely. Instead, you use pre-allocated pools:

- At startup, you allocate a pool of message objects or buffers.
- Producers take items from the pool when they need to enqueue new work.
- Consumers return items to the pool when done.

The pool itself must then be made concurrency-friendly, but because its operations are simple and repetitive, you can often design it around SPSC or sharded patterns.

The benefits are:

- No interaction with the general-purpose memory allocator on the hot path.
- Highly predictable allocation and deallocation costs.
- Easy to monitor pool exhaustion as a sign of overload.

The cost is that you must size the pool for peak usage and implement a fallback strategy when the pool is exhausted (drop, backpressure, or spill into a slower, possibly locking path).

## When Lock-Free Complexity is Justified

Lock-free data structures are not free. They increase code complexity, demand careful reasoning about memory ordering, and complicate debugging. Not every part of a trading system deserves this treatment.

A pragmatic guideline is:

- **Use lock-free SPSC rings** on the strictest hot paths: NIC polling to parsing, parsing to strategy, strategy to risk, risk to gateway. These are the paths where every microsecond counts and where you can usually enforce single-producer and single-consumer roles.
- **Consider sharded SPSC designs or carefully chosen MPMC queues** where multiple threads must exchange data at high rates, and where you can tolerate some complexity to avoid blocking.
- **Use plain mutexes** in configuration loading, admin APIs, logging control planes, and other cold paths where latency is not critical and simplicity matters more. A well-placed lock in a cold path is often "good enough" and far more maintainable.

Above all, measure. It is easy to speculate that replacing a mutex with a lock-free queue will help, but until you have latency histograms and benchmarks for your specific workload, you do not know where your bottlenecks truly are. In later sections we will discuss how to benchmark queue implementations, what to log when chasing rare races, and how to integrate these structures into a coherent, kernel-bypass architecture.

For now, remember the central theme: in ultra-low-latency trading systems, the hot path should be designed to *never wait unnecessarily*. Lock-free queues, used judiciously, are one of the most powerful tools you have to make that principle real.

## 9.2 Cache-Friendly Coding

In the previous section we focused on *coordination*: how to move data between threads without locks, and how the choice of queue structure shapes latency. In this section we move one level down, into the CPU itself. Even a perfectly designed lock-free pipeline will misbehave if its data structures fight the cache hierarchy.

You can think of the CPU as a very fast worker with a very small desk (the L1 cache) and several filing cabinets further away (L2, L3, and main memory). If the data the worker needs is already on the desk, work proceeds quickly and predictably. If the worker has to walk to a filing cabinet, or down the hall to another room, every trip shows up as extra latency.

Cache-friendly coding is about arranging your data and access patterns so that:

- The hot path mostly touches data already in the fastest caches.
- The CPU can guess your access patterns and prefetch data ahead of time.
- Different cores do not constantly fight over the same cache lines.

The payoff is not only lower average latency, but also much *tighter* latency distributions. For a trading system, this reduction in jitter is often more valuable than a small improvement in throughput.

### A Quick Tour of the Cache Hierarchy

Before we discuss layouts and access patterns, we need a basic mental model of the cache hierarchy. We will keep it simple and intuitive.

Modern CPUs have several layers of memory:

- **Registers** are the very small, very fast slots inside the core itself.
- **L1 cache** is like the core's private desk: tiny but extremely fast.

- **L2 cache** is another private cache per core, a bit larger and a bit slower.
- **L3 cache** (sometimes called "last-level cache") is typically shared among several cores on the same chip.
- **Main memory (RAM)** sits off-chip relative to the core and is much slower than any cache.

Data moves between these levels in fixed-size chunks called *cache lines*. A cache line is typically 64 bytes. The important consequences are:

- When you load a single byte, the CPU actually loads the entire cache line that contains that byte.
- If you store a value into an address, the entire line containing that address becomes "owned" or "dirty" in that core's cache and must eventually be shared or written back.

The CPU also has *prefetchers* that watch your access patterns. If they recognize a pattern like "this code walks forward through an array," they will quietly pull in future cache lines so they are already present in L1 or L2 when you need them.

When your code works *with* this machinery, accesses are fast and predictable. When it works against it—by touching data sparsely, randomly, or in a way that creates unnecessary sharing between cores—the result is more cache misses, more cache-line bouncing, and higher tail latency.

## Data Layout: Array-of-Structs vs Struct-of-Arrays

One of the most important layout choices in performance-critical trading code is how you organize related pieces of state. Two common patterns are:

- **Array-of-Structs (AoS):** You keep a collection of "records," each containing all fields for one entity. For example, an array where each element represents one symbol's quote, including bid, ask, last trade, statistics, and configuration.

- **Struct-of-Arrays (SoA):** You separate fields into their own arrays. For example, one array for all bids, another for all asks, another for last trades, and so on.

At first glance this may sound like an implementation detail. In practice, it can easily be the difference between cache hitting and cache missing throughout the hot path.

**Array-of-Structs: Convenient but Often Cache-Unfriendly**

Suppose you store per-symbol state as an array of structs, where each struct contains:

- hot fields like current bid price, ask price, and last trade time;
- warm fields like rolling statistics;
- cold fields like configuration flags, logging counters, or rarely used metadata.

Each struct may be quite large, perhaps spanning several cache lines. When your strategy loops over all symbols to, say, recompute risk on just the bid and ask, it must load at least part of each struct into cache. Because the hot fields are mixed with many cold fields, each access may pull in multiple cache lines, most of whose contents you do not need.

The consequences:

- You burn cache bandwidth and capacity on data that is not relevant to the fast path.
- Fewer hot entries fit in L1 and L2 at once, so you see more evictions and misses.
- The prefetcher has more difficulty, because the working set is effectively larger and noisier.

AoS can still be fine for small structures and cold paths, but when you combine large records with frequent scanning, it is a recipe for cache pressure.

**Struct-of-Arrays: Aligning Layout with Access Patterns**

In a struct-of-arrays design, you group fields by how they are accessed, rather than by which logical entity they belong to. For example:

- A "hot" array containing just the current bid and ask prices for each symbol.
- A separate array for warm statistics like moving averages.
- Another structure or table for cold metadata that is rarely touched during fast-path operations.

Now, when your strategy loops over all symbols to compute an action based solely on bid and ask, it walks a dense array of just those fields. The cache behavior improves sharply:

- Each cache line holds many consecutive entries of just the hot data, so every line brought into cache is useful.
- The hardware prefetcher can easily detect the pattern of stepping forward through a contiguous array and prefetch ahead.
- More hot entries fit in L1 and L2 at once, reducing the need to re-fetch lines from L3 or memory.

Conceptually, AoS optimizes for "give me everything about this one symbol," whereas SoA optimizes for "give me this one field for many symbols in a row." Trading strategies often behave like the latter, especially in scanning or cross-sectional computations.

## Splitting Hot and Cold Data

AoS vs SoA is one lever. Another is *hot/cold splitting*: separating frequently accessed fields from rarely accessed ones, even if you keep some AoS flavor.

Consider an order book representation. For each price level, you might store:

- Hot: price, total quantity, best order ID.

- Warm: per-order details.
- Cold: debugging flags, historical statistics, last time this level was updated.

If you group all of this into a single large record per level, every book update touches that large record, causing unnecessary cache traffic. Instead, you can design:

- A compact hot struct or array that holds exactly what the matching logic needs for each incoming message.
- A separate structure indexed by level or order ID that holds the rest, only consulted when needed (for example, for risk checks, reporting, or rare operations).

This design has several benefits:

- The hot path's working set shrinks dramatically, often fitting entirely in L1 or L2.
- Cold data can be paged out, compressed, or stored in more flexible structures without impacting latency.
- When you profile cache misses, you will see a clean separation between hot-path misses (which you strive to reduce) and cold-path misses (which often matter less).

Hot/cold splitting requires some discipline, because it fights the natural tendency to "put everything relevant in one nice struct." For low-latency systems, the right question is not "what belongs together logically," but "what is actually read or written together in time."

## Visualizing Caches and Layout Choices

To make these ideas more concrete, it helps to see the cache hierarchy next to contrasting AoS and SoA layouts, with arrows indicating how code typically walks through memory.

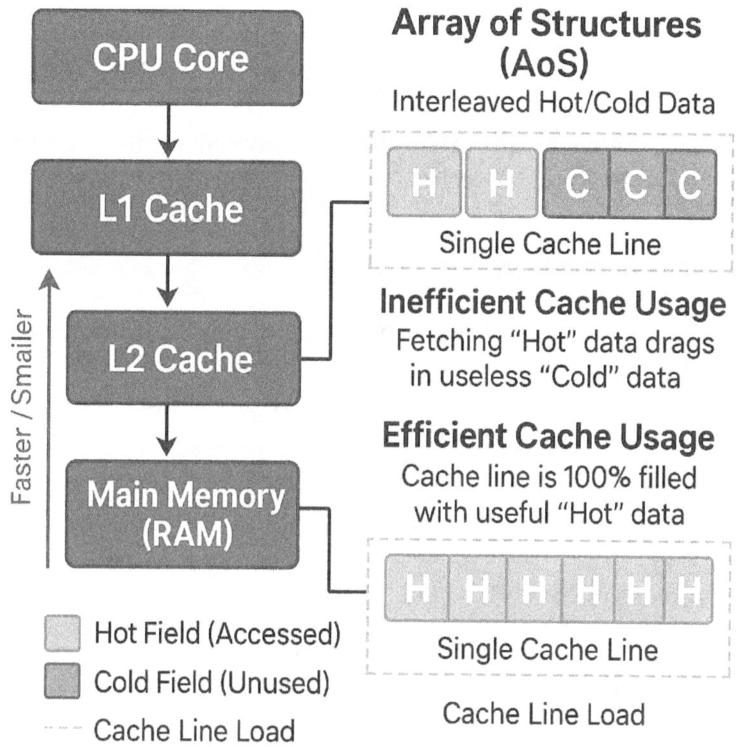


On the AoS side, each cache line brings in a mixture of hot and cold data. On the SoA side, hot fields are consecutively arranged and can be streamed through the caches efficiently, while cold metadata is segregated.

## False Sharing and Cache-Line Contention

So far we have focused on *one* core's view of its working set. In a trading system, multiple cores often update related state in parallel. If different cores write to distinct variables that happen to reside on the same cache line, you can encounter *false sharing*.

False sharing occurs when:

- Two or more threads update different fields.
- Those fields occupy the same 64-byte cache line.
- The cache coherence protocol must continuously move and invalidate that line between cores, even though no true data dependency exists.

Common trading examples include:

- Per-symbol counters or statistics laid out consecutively in an array, with different cores responsible for different symbols.
- Per-core latency or message counters stored in an array indexed by core ID.
- Sequence numbers or flags that are updated in separate threads but happen to be neighbors in memory.

The symptoms are often puzzling: a simple increment operation that should be trivial suddenly behaves as if it were a contended lock, introducing spikes and variability. Profilers may not clearly attribute the problem, because the root cause is the hardware's behavior, not any explicit synchronization.

### Avoiding False Sharing with Padding and Alignment

A straightforward way to avoid false sharing is to ensure that variables maintained by different threads do not share cache lines. Two common techniques are:

- **Padding:** Add unused bytes between fields or array elements so that each logical variable occupies a full cache line (or at least does not share one with another frequently written variable). For example, you might store each per-core counter in a struct that is explicitly sized and aligned to a cache line.
- **Alignment directives:** Ask the compiler or runtime to align frequently updated structures to cache-line boundaries, so that they are not accidentally placed at the end of one line and the beginning of the next.

Padding increases memory usage, but in critical hot-path structures the trade-off is almost always worth it. A few extra kilobytes or megabytes of RAM is cheap compared to the cost of persistent cache-line ping-pong between cores.

**Per-Core Sharding**

Another effective pattern is *per-core sharding*. Rather than sharing a single global counter or statistic, you give each core its own private copy and only aggregate them off the hot path.

For instance:

- Each strategy core keeps its own volume counters and latency statistics in local, cache-friendly structures.
- A background thread occasionally sums these per-core values to produce global metrics for monitoring or reporting.

From the cache's perspective, per-core sharding is powerful because:

- Each core updates data that is almost always resident in its local L1/L2.
- There is no need to move cache lines between cores for these updates.
- Aggregation can be scheduled at times and on cores where its cost is acceptable.

Of course, per-core sharding complicates logic that truly requires a single, strongly consistent value. But in many cases—counters, statistics, diagnostics—you do not need exact global synchronization on every update, only eventual consistency.

## Prefetching: When to Help the Hardware

Hardware prefetchers are surprisingly effective when your access patterns are simple: walking forwards through arrays, scanning tables, processing ring buffers. In those cases, "doing nothing" is often best; manual prefetching may only add noise.

However, some trading workloads can benefit from controlled prefetching:

- **Linked or tree structures:** Order books implemented as trees, or symbol maps that require pointer-chasing, present less predictable patterns to the hardware.
- **Scatter-gather access:** When processing a batch of updates that touch symbols in a non-sequential order, you may jump around in memory, defeating simple prefetch logic.
- **Producer-consumer distance:** In ring buffers or queues, there is often a small, known gap between the write and read positions that can be exploited.

The basic idea of software prefetching is to initiate the loading of a cache line *before* you need it, so that it has time to arrive in L1 or L2. Conceptually:

- While you are processing item $i$, you request the cache line for item $i + k$, where $k$ is chosen so the line arrives just in time for processing.

In practice, tuning $k$ is empirical. If it is too small, the prefetch arrives too late and you still miss. If it is too large, you bring data into cache long before you need it, risking eviction before use and polluting the cache with speculative loads.

The key points for low-latency systems are:

- Use software prefetching *sparingly* and only when profiling shows real benefit.
- Prefer to first improve layout (SoA, hot/cold splitting) and access patterns (sequential scans, batching) before turning to manual prefetch hints.
- Measure both median and tail latency with and without prefetching, as manual hints can sometimes reduce average time while harming predictability.

## Review and Micro-Benchmarks

Cache-friendly coding is as much about discipline as it is about clever tricks. Teams that succeed in this area usually adopt lightweight practices that catch regressions early.

A cache-oriented code review checklist might include questions like:

- Does this hot-path loop walk memory sequentially, or does it jump around?
- Are we mixing hot and cold fields in the same cache lines?
- Are different threads writing to fields that might share a cache line?
- Could we restructure this data from AoS to SoA, or split hot and cold parts?
- Is there any dynamic allocation or resizing that will disturb cache locality under load?

Micro-benchmarks complement reviews by measuring the real behavior of isolated components. For cache-related questions, useful micro-benchmarks include:

- Sequential scan of per-symbol state in AoS vs SoA layouts, comparing the time and variance per element.
- Update of per-core counters with and without false sharing, measuring stall cycles and jitter.
- Traversal of order book structures with different hot/cold splits, focusing on tail latency.

These benchmarks should be automated and run in a controlled environment, ideally on the same hardware and with similar compiler settings as production. When a code change modifies a key data structure, rerunning the benchmarks gives an early warning if cache behavior has degraded.

### Bringing It Back to Trading Latency

It is tempting to view cache-friendly coding as a low-level concern for specialists. In a modern electronic trading shop, it is central to meeting tight service-level agreements.

The message to keep in mind is simple:

> Every microsecond you save by structuring data and access patterns well is a microsecond you do not have to recover by more aggressive kernel-bypass tricks or riskier system tuning.

Lock-free queues reduce waiting between threads. Cache-friendly layouts reduce waiting inside each core. Together, they provide a foundation on which the more advanced techniques in this chapter—kernel-bypass networking, batching policies, and holistic system tuning—can be effective. Without this foundation, those higher-level optimizations will at best offer partial relief, and at worst simply shuffle latency from one part of the system to another.

In the next sections we will see how these principles apply to network I/O paths and batching strategies, and how to measure their impact end-to-end rather than in isolated micro-benchmarks.

## 9.3 Batching vs. Single-Shot Processing

The previous sections addressed how to move data between threads without blocking, and how to shape your data so that the CPU cache can work with you rather than against you. We now turn to a more subtle question: *how many messages should you process at once?*

Every hop in your trading system-NIC to parser, parser to strategy, strategy to risk, risk to gateway-has some fixed overhead per batch of work. You can either pay that cost for each individual message (*single-shot processing*) or amortize it across several messages at once (*micro-batching*). Neither approach is universally better. The right choice depends on where your service-level agreement (SLA) draws the line: at median latency, or at the worst one-in-a-thousand events.

This section analyzes when micro-batching is a latency win, when it quietly destroys tail behavior, and how to tune batching to your SLA instead of chasing generic throughput.

## Where the Per-Message Cost Comes From

To understand batching, it helps to list the kinds of costs that are roughly the same whether you process one message or ten:

- **Interface overhead:** Entering and exiting a subsystem, such as crossing from user space into the kernel (for example, a send or receive system call) or acquiring and releasing a lock around a shared data structure.
- **Descriptor and metadata handling:** Interacting with NIC queues, file descriptors, or internal queues: checking states, updating counters, performing checks that do not depend much on the number of messages inside the batch.
- **Code and cache footprint:** Loading a block of code and associated hot data into the instruction cache and data cache, which then stays hot for several similar operations.
- **Scheduling and wakeups:** Waking a thread, handling an interrupt, or making a thread runnable-all actions that cost similar time regardless of whether you then handle one message or several before going back to sleep.

If you pay these fixed costs for every single message, your per-message latency includes a lot of overhead that could, in theory, be shared. Micro-batching does exactly that: it pays once, then performs several operations while the relevant code and data are already "on the desk."

However, batching introduces a new component: *waiting time inside the batch.* A message that arrives just after you have processed a batch must wait until the batch window opens again. As we will see, this added waiting is what often damages tail latency.

## Single-Shot Processing: Minimal Waiting, Maximal Overhead

In a strict single-shot design, you process each incoming event as soon as you see it, without deliberately waiting to accumulate more work. Typical patterns include:

- A polling loop that, on each iteration, takes at most one message from a queue and immediately hands it to downstream logic.
- A network stack that calls into your application as soon as there is a single packet ready.
- A strategy that fires an order for every qualifying tick, without attempting to group orders.

The strengths of this approach are straightforward:

- **Best-case and tail latency are aligned:** A message rarely waits behind unrelated work. The time between "arrival" and "start of processing" is minimal and similar across messages.
- **Behavior is easy to reason about:** Each arrival triggers a small, bounded unit of work. Latency analysis can focus on the per-message processing time and queue depths, not on complex batching rules.
- **Jitter is mostly due to external factors:** Cache misses, OS noise, and shared-resource contention dominate; batching policies do not add their own noise.

The weaknesses are equally clear:

- Fixed overheads (syscalls, scheduling decisions, descriptor handling) are paid per message.
- You may miss out on natural opportunities to reuse cache state: code and data are loaded into cache, used for one message, and then dismissed before the next message arrives.

- In very high message-rate regimes, single-shot processing can become infeasible; the sheer number of calls overwhelms the system.

Single-shot processing is often the default in early prototypes: it is simple and tends to produce good p50 performance in modest load. The danger is that as traffic scales up, teams add ad hoc batching at various layers, without a clear view of the overall effect on tail behavior.

## Micro-Batching: Amortizing Overhead

Micro-batching deliberately groups several messages and processes them together as a unit. You encounter it at many layers of a trading system:

- NIC and kernel stacks frequently deliver packets in bursts (for example, a call that returns up to $N$ packets).
- User-space poll loops read multiple messages from a ring buffer before handing control back.
- Strategy logic may process a block of ticks before making a decision, or walk a batch of orders through the risk checks before sending them on.

The benefits of micro-batching are most visible when you look at the overall cost of processing a large number of messages during a busy interval:

- **Lower average per-message overhead:** If one syscall or wakeup handles ten messages, the direct per-message cost drops substantially.
- **Better cache locality:** Once the relevant code and data are hot in cache for the first message in the batch, subsequent messages may ride on those same cache lines, avoiding misses.
- **Higher throughput headroom:** Under peak loads, a batched design can often sustain higher message rates before saturating CPU, since it avoids repeated fixed overheads.

In latency terms, micro-batching can even improve median latency (p50) for messages arriving in the middle of the burst: they benefit from the warmed-up caches and reduced per-message work.

However, these gains come at a price: the introduction of *batching delay*, the time a message spends waiting to be grouped with others. This delay is the main reason why aggressive batching can quietly degrade your p99 and p99.9 performance, even as average and median metrics look fantastic.

## Where Batching Hurts Tail Latency

To see how batching hurts, consider a simple time-based batching policy:

- Every fixed interval (say, 50 microseconds), your component wakes up, collects all messages that arrived during that interval, and processes them together.

Messages that arrive near the *end* of the interval wait only a few microseconds before processing; messages that arrive just after a batch has been processed wait almost the full interval. Over many arrivals:

- Median latency may remain modest, because about half the messages arrive in the latter half of the interval and wait less.
- Worst-case latency within the batching window can approach the full interval length, *before* any additional processing or queuing delays.

Thus, if you configure a 50 microsecond batching window in an attempt to improve throughput, you have effectively added up to 50 microseconds of extra waiting time to some messages. If your end-to-end SLA is 100 microseconds, you have already spent half of your budget on batching delay alone.

Size-based batching has a similar effect:

- If you wait until you have, say, 32 messages before processing them, the unlucky 32nd message waits behind the previous 31, even if the system could have processed it earlier.

- Under low load, the time to accumulate a full batch can be long, so size-based batching interacts badly with quiet markets.

The crucial observation is this:

> Batching tends to tilt the distribution: it can keep the middle of the latency distribution tight while stretching the tail.

If you only look at averages or medians, you might conclude that batching "helped." Only when you plot p95, p99, and p99.9 do you see the full cost.

## Comparing Distributions: Single-Shot vs Micro-Batched

To build intuition, it is helpful to visualize how single-shot and batched processing affect latency distributions on the same workload.

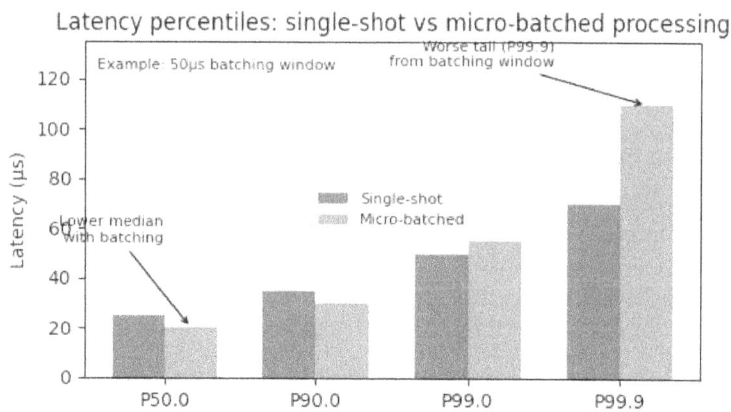


Figure 9.1: Illustrative latency percentiles for single-shot vs micro-batched processing. Batching can lower median latency while increasing extreme tail latency due to added batching delay.

In this stylized example:

- Micro-batching slightly improves p50 and p90 relative to single-shot processing, thanks to amortized overhead and better cache usage.
- p99 is roughly similar in both cases, suggesting that in most busy periods the system keeps up.
- p99.9 for the batched case is significantly worse, reflecting occasional messages that arrive just after a batch cut and occupy the worst possible position in the queueing pattern.

The exact numbers will differ on your system, but the shape of the distributions often follows this pattern. The question is: *which distribution is acceptable for your trading strategy and risk appetite?*

## Designing Tunable Batching Policies

Since neither pure single-shot nor uncontrolled batching is ideal, you need *tunable* batching policies. In other words, you want clear knobs that let you adjust the balance between throughput and tail latency. We can categorize batching policies into three broad families.

## Time-Based Batching

Time-based batching collects messages that arrive within a fixed time window and processes them together.

Key parameters:

- **Window length:** The maximum time a message is allowed to wait for the batch; this directly bounds batching delay.
- **Wakeup behavior:** Whether the system wakes exactly on the window boundaries or is allowed to process early if a certain condition is met (for example, queue not empty).

This approach offers predictable worst-case batching delay (equal to the window length), which is useful when reasoning about p99 and p99.9. It is especially common in network I/O, where poll loops wake up at regular intervals.

## Size-Based Batching

Size-based batching processes messages once a certain batch size is reached.

Key parameters:

- **Batch size:** The target number of messages to process together.
- **Timeout:** A maximum waiting time to prevent long stalls under low traffic if the batch size is not reached.

Size-based batching is attractive when you know the "sweet spot" batch size that maximizes throughput or cache benefits. The timeout acts as a safety valve to limit latency inflation in quiet periods.

## Adaptive Batching

Adaptive policies adjust batch sizes dynamically based on runtime observations, such as:

- Queue depth.
- Recent inter-arrival times.
- Observed latency against a target SLA.

Examples include:

- Increasing batch size when the queue is persistently full, to avoid overload and collapse.
- Shrinking batch size when tail latency metrics approach their thresholds.
- Using small batches in normal operation and only increasing batch size under clear overload conditions.

Adaptive batching is harder to reason about analytically, but it can offer a better compromise in real-world, bursty markets. To be safe, it must be *well-instrumented*: you need visibility into when and why the batch size changes, and how that correlates with SLA compliance.

## Tuning for Your SLA, Not Generic Throughput

Your goal is not to maximize "messages per second" in an abstract benchmark. Your goal is to satisfy a concrete trading SLA, which often includes statements like:

- "At least 99% of acknowledgements from this venue must be processed within 200 microseconds."
- "We must respond to top-of-book changes for this symbol set within 150 microseconds at the 99.9% level."

These are *tail-focused* constraints. To tune batching for such SLAs:

1. **Define acceptable percentiles:** Decide which percentiles matter (p95, p99, p99.9) and what thresholds they must meet for each major path (market data, strategy decision, order send, risk rejection).
2. **Measure the baseline without batching:** Start with either pure single-shot or the minimum batch size, and record latency distributions under realistic load and replayed market patterns.
3. **Introduce small batches and re-measure:** Gradually increase time windows or batch sizes and observe how each percentile moves. It is common to see p50 improve first, then p90, with p99 and p99.9 eventually worsening beyond acceptable thresholds.
4. **Stop when you hit the SLA boundary:** The moment any critical percentile crosses its SLA limit, treat that configuration as unusable, even if throughput still has headroom.
5. **Prefer configurations where the kernel and application agree:** For example, align NIC interrupt coalescing or user-space poll intervals with your application's own batching choices, so you do not accidentally introduce redundant layers of batching.

In other words, batching knobs should be tuned *backwards* from your latency targets, not forwards from raw throughput benchmarks.

## A Practical Evaluation Methodology

To evaluate batching strategies in a way that survives production traffic, you need more than a single "messages per second" metric. A practical methodology includes:

### Representative Workloads

Use workloads that resemble real markets:

- Include quiet periods, normal activity, and extreme bursts.
- Reproduce common intra-day patterns (for example, open auction, news releases).
- Capture symbol distributions that reflect your strategies' actual focus.

Synthetic uniform traffic can hide queueing dynamics that only appear in bursty, correlated flows.

### Detailed Latency Instrumentation

Instrument key points:

- Timestamp when a message enters a component's queue.
- Timestamp when processing actually begins.
- Timestamp when output (for example, an order) leaves the component.

From these, you can break latency down into:

- *Queueing time:* How long messages wait before being processed.
- *Processing time:* How long they spend in the component's logic.

Batching primarily affects queueing time; instrumenting both helps you see whether increased tails come from waiting or from CPU saturation.

## Distribution-Focused Analysis

Plot and compare:

- Cumulative distributions (CDFs) for each batch configuration.
- Percentile tables (p50, p90, p95, p99, p99.9).
- Histograms of queue depth over time.

Look for patterns such as:

- "Stair-step" effects in the latency distribution that align with batching windows.
- Periods where queue depth grows monotonically, indicating that the system cannot keep up under certain market regimes.
- Discrepancies between components-for example, a tight distribution in the strategy but a heavy tail in the gateway, pointing to over-aggressive batching at the gateway only.

## Putting It All Together

Batching and single-shot processing are not opposing religions; they are tools on a spectrum. Effective low-latency trading systems usually combine them along these lines:

- **Single-shot or minimal batching** on the strictest hot paths where every microsecond matters and traffic volumes are manageable-often at the last-hop order send or the earliest inbound market data processing.
- **Carefully tuned micro-batching** at stages where fixed overheads are large and predictable, and where small amounts of extra waiting time are acceptable in exchange for higher overall throughput-for example, in some user-space networking APIs or risk aggregation tasks.

- **Aggressive batching** only in clearly off-critical paths, such as logging, analytics feeds, or post-trade reporting, where even millisecond-level batches are acceptable.

Above all, align batching decisions with clearly stated SLAs and validate them with distribution-aware measurements. When used this way, batching becomes a precision instrument: you know exactly how much latency you are trading for how much throughput, and you can adjust your system confidently as markets and strategies evolve.

## 9.4 User-Space Networking Deep Dive

So far in this chapter we have focused on optimizations *inside* your process: lock-free queues, cache-friendly layouts, and batching policies. All of those assume that messages have already arrived in your address space. In practice, a large fraction of your latency budget is often spent earlier, on the journey from the wire to your user-level code.

Traditional kernel networking stacks are designed for generality and safety, not for microsecond-level determinism. Kernel-bypass stacks offer an alternative: they let user-space code interact with the NIC almost directly, avoiding many layers of overhead. This section breaks down how such stacks move packets from the wire to user code, what constraints this model introduces, and how to design around them.

### The Core Idea: Polling NIC Queues in User Space

In a conventional design, packets arrive at the NIC, trigger interrupts, and are handled by kernel threads that eventually copy data into your process. Every step—interrupt handling, context switches, traversing protocol stacks—adds latency and variability.

Kernel-bypass frameworks such as DPDK and Onload flip this model:

- They allocate NIC queues and buffers so that user-space can access them directly.
- They dedicate one or more cores to continuously polling these queues, instead of relying on interrupts.

- They move the core networking logic into a user-space library linked with your application.

Conceptually, the NIC becomes a very fast "packet queue provider," and your process becomes responsible for taking packets out of the queue, interpreting them, and eventually returning buffers for reuse. The operating system still configures the NIC and enforces some protection, but it is largely out of the hot path.

This design dovetails naturally with the lock-free and cache-friendly techniques we have already discussed: a polling thread sits in a tight loop reading from NIC rings (which are themselves ring buffers) and handing packets off to internal queues and state machines that live entirely in user space.

## From Wire to User Code: The Data Path

To reason effectively about kernel-bypass networking, you need a clear mental picture of the stages between "packet hits the wire" and "strategy sees a decoded message." We will step through the main stages and then show a schematic diagram.

### 1. Packet Arrival and NIC RX Queue Placement

When a packet arrives on the wire:

- The NIC hardware parses basic headers and classifies the packet into one of its receive (RX) queues. Modern NICs can maintain many RX queues, often one per CPU core or per traffic class.
- This classification uses mechanisms such as RSS (Receive Side Scaling) or flow director rules: hashes over source/destination addresses and ports, or explicit filters for certain multicast groups or TCP connections.
- The NIC writes the packet into a pre-configured buffer, typically in memory that your user-space process can also access. This write happens via DMA (Direct Memory Access), so the CPU is not involved.

The key point is that, unlike the traditional stack, the NIC is not waking the kernel up on every packet. It is simply filling in a queue of packet descriptors.

### 2. DMA into User-Space Buffers

Before any packets arrive, your application (or the kernel-bypass library on its behalf) has done some setup:

- It has allocated a pool of buffers in memory, often using huge pages for efficiency.
- It has registered those buffers with the NIC and IOMMU so that the NIC is allowed to DMA directly into them.
- It has configured the RX queues to point into this pool of buffers, arranged as rings of descriptors.

When the NIC receives a packet destined for a given RX queue, it:

- Picks the next free buffer from the ring.
- DMAs the packet payload directly into that buffer in RAM.
- Updates a descriptor in the RX ring to indicate that this buffer now holds a valid packet.

At this point, the packet's bytes are sitting in a user-space-accessible buffer; no system call has been made, and no data copy has taken place.

### 3. User-Space Polling and Packet Retrieval

A dedicated user-space thread, pinned to a specific core, continuously polls the NIC's RX queue. In a tight loop, it:

- Reads descriptors from the RX ring to see which ones are marked as "packet ready."

- For each ready descriptor, reads packet metadata such as size, checksum status, and buffer address.
- Hands the buffer pointer off to the next stage in your application: parsing, protocol handling, and eventual conversion into internal message objects.

This polling loop usually runs with minimal branching and no blocking calls. Because it only touches a small, predictable region of memory (the RX ring and a few hot fields in the buffers), it can be heavily cache-optimized.

### 4. Application Handoff and Internal Queues

Once the poller has identified a batch of received packets, it must hand them off to the rest of your trading system. Common patterns include:

- Enqueuing buffer pointers into SPSC ring buffers feeding parser or strategy threads.
- Parsing and decoding protocol headers in-line on the polling core, and only enqueuing higher-level messages.
- Applying early filtering or routing based on session, symbol, or message type to different downstream queues.

Here your lock-free queue knowledge becomes directly relevant. You want these handoffs to be non-blocking and cache-friendly so that the high-frequency path from NIC to strategy involves no kernel calls and no mutexes.

### 5. Buffer Recycling via Mempools

After a packet has been fully processed and no longer needed, its buffer must be returned to the pool so the NIC can reuse it. Kernel-bypass stacks typically use mempools for this purpose:

- A mempool is a pre-allocated, fixed-size pool of packet buffers.

- The NIC's RX ring draws from this pool; when the poller or downstream code is finished with a buffer, it returns it to the mempool.

- The pool is designed to be fast, often using per-core caches to avoid contention.

Done well, this design avoids dynamic allocation and free operations on the hot path. Done poorly, it becomes a new source of contention or memory leaks.

## Visualizing the User-Space Data Path

The data path from NIC to user code in a kernel-bypass setup is best understood as a horizontal pipeline, with queues and buffers connecting the stages.

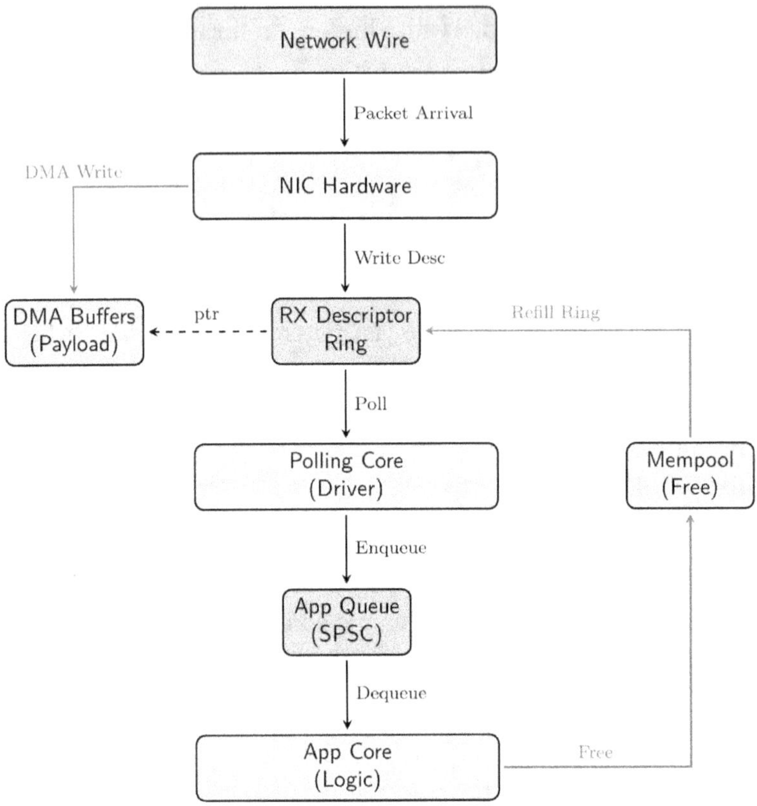


The diagram emphasizes three key properties of kernel-bypass stacks:

- Packets are DMA'd directly into user-space memory, avoiding extra copies.
- A dedicated polling core drives progress, instead of interrupts and context switches.
- Buffer lifecycles are managed explicitly via mempools, not hidden inside the kernel.

With this pipeline in mind, we can examine the design choices and constraints that matter in trading workloads.

## Mempool and Buffer Management

Mempools are central to the predictability of kernel-bypass networking. They determine how packet buffers are allocated, recycled, and shared between cores.

### Why Fixed-Size, Pre-Allocated Buffers?

Most kernel-bypass stacks use fixed-size packet buffers organized in pools for several reasons:

- **No hot-path allocation:** Allocation is done once at startup. The hot path only pops and pushes buffers from the pool.
- **Simpler DMA setup:** The NIC can be configured with a fixed mapping of buffer addresses, reducing IOMMU bookkeeping.
- **Predictable cache behavior:** Buffers are laid out in contiguous memory, and their size is known, making caching and prefetching more effective.

In trading, typical message sizes are small (market data ticks, order messages), so one fixed size per protocol stream is usually sufficient. For larger messages, you may chain multiple buffers, but that is less common on strict hot paths.

### Per-Core vs Shared Mempools

A shared global mempool is simple but can become a contention point if many cores are frequently allocating and freeing buffers. A common optimization is:

- Give each core its own small local cache of buffers, backed by a shared pool.

- Let hot paths allocate and free from the local cache without touching shared data structures.
- Refill or drain local caches in larger chunks, which can be coordinated more easily and less often.

This design echoes the per-core sharding principles from the cache-friendly coding section: keep the most frequent operations local to each core and only occasionally interact with shared global state.

### Avoiding Lifecycle Bugs

Direct control over buffer lifecycles is powerful but dangerous. Common pitfalls include:

- **Use-after-free:** Returning a buffer to the pool while some thread still holds a reference to it.
- **Leaks:** Losing track of buffers and slowly exhausting the pool under specific error conditions.
- **Double-free:** Returning the same buffer twice, causing the pool's internal structures to become inconsistent.

Defensive design patterns help:

- Keep buffer ownership transfers as simple and linear as possible: once a buffer leaves the poller, it should have a clearly documented owner.
- Avoid complex shared ownership schemes (for example, reference counting) on the hot path; these often reintroduce contention.
- Use assertions and debug counters in non-production builds to track pool occupancy and invariants.

## Flow Steering and Multi-Queue Design

The NIC's ability to steer different flows to different RX queues is a key enabler of scalable, low-latency designs. It lets you partition traffic over cores in a controlled way.

### Receive Side Scaling (RSS)

RSS is a hardware feature that hashes packet header fields (IP addresses, ports) to select an RX queue. For example:

- All packets for a given TCP connection will hash to the same queue.
- Different connections will tend to be spread among queues.

For trading, RSS is particularly useful for TCP-based market feeds or order gateways. You can:

- Map each connection or a small group of connections to a dedicated RX queue.
- Pin a user-space polling thread to the core associated with that queue.
- Avoid cross-core sharing of per-connection state, improving cache locality.

### Flow Director and Custom Rules

For multicast market data or more specialized routing, NICs often support "flow director" or similar programmable filters:

- You can specify that packets matching a certain multicast group and port go to RX queue 3, while others go to queue 5.
- You can partition symbol ranges or venue feeds across queues, aligning them with your application's internal sharding.

This is where architecture and microstructure knowledge meet: you can design the mapping from symbols and venues to cores based on how your strategies operate and how you want to share or isolate state.

### Balancing Load and Locality

The art lies in balancing two goals:

- **Load balancing:** Ensure that no single queue or core is overwhelmed while others are idle.
- **State locality:** Keep all packets that touch the same piece of state (for example, a given symbol's order book) on the same core to avoid cross-core cache traffic.

Simple approaches include:

- Start with a static mapping (for example, hash of symbol name or group ID) and adjust after observing imbalances.
- For critical symbols with very high activity, dedicate entire queues and cores, while batching less active symbols together.

Dynamic load balancing is possible but harder, because migrating flows between queues can disrupt cache locality and increase complexity.

## Zero-Copy vs Copy: Locality Trade-Offs

A common selling point of kernel-bypass stacks is "zero-copy" networking: the idea that packets can be processed in place where the NIC wrote them, without extra memory copies.

In practice, the trade-off is subtler:

- Processing directly in the DMA buffer is fastest in terms of memory bandwidth, since you avoid copying.

- However, those buffers may not be laid out in the way your application prefers for long-lived state. They are optimized for the NIC's access pattern, not your order book or risk engine's layout.

A pragmatic strategy is:

- For short-lived data (for example, transient market data snapshots used once for a strategy decision), process directly in the DMA buffer and discard.
- For data that must be integrated into rich internal structures (for example, updating a book or a risk state), copy from the DMA buffer into your own, carefully designed, cache-friendly data structures.

You then gain:

- A single, explicit copy at a well-chosen boundary.
- The ability to optimize internal structures for your access patterns, without being constrained by NIC buffer layout.
- Clear separation between "I/O buffers" and "application state," which aids reasoning and debugging.

It is worth measuring: a carefully implemented copy into a compact SoA layout may cost less, in end-to-end latency, than repeatedly traversing a strange layout in DMA buffers.

## NUMA, Huge Pages, and IOMMU Considerations

Kernel-bypass networking makes low-level hardware details more visible. Three topics matter particularly in trading systems: NUMA, huge pages, and the IOMMU.

### NUMA-Aware NIC Placement

On multi-socket systems, each socket has its own local memory and a group of cores. This is a Non-Uniform Memory Access (NUMA) architecture:

- Accessing memory local to a core's socket is faster and more predictable.
- Accessing memory attached to another socket requires going over an interconnect, adding latency and potential contention.

For kernel-bypass:

- Place NICs so that their PCIe buses are attached to the socket whose cores will poll and process the traffic.
- Allocate DMA buffers and mempools from memory local to that socket.
- Pin polling and strategy cores to that same NUMA node.

Ignoring NUMA can easily add tens of nanoseconds to every memory access along the path, which accumulates over many touches per packet.

### Huge Pages

Huge pages (for example, 2 MB instead of 4 KB) reduce the number of page table entries needed for a given memory region. This has two benefits:

- **Fewer TLB misses:** The Translation Lookaside Buffer (TLB) caches page table entries. With huge pages, a small TLB can cover a large region of memory, reducing misses.
- **Simpler DMA mapping:** The NIC and IOMMU need fewer entries to map the DMA region, which can simplify hardware behavior and reduce overhead.

For kernel-bypass stacks, allocating mempools and rings on huge pages is a common optimization. It costs a bit of setup complexity but can improve both throughput and tail latency.

### IOMMU Trade-Offs

The IOMMU controls which memory regions devices (like NICs) may access via DMA. It is an important security and isolation tool. From a performance standpoint:

- Enabling the IOMMU adds a layer of address translation on DMA operations.
- Depending on hardware and configuration, this can add some overhead and variability.

Trading shops often:

- Use permissive but still bounded IOMMU mappings for NICs that serve critical trading workloads.
- Carefully benchmark with and without certain IOMMU features to quantify any performance impact before making configuration decisions.

You should not disable safety features blindly for speed; instead, understand their impact and choose configurations that balance security with latency requirements.

## Monitoring and Operating Kernel-Bypass Paths

A kernel-bypass stack is powerful but also more exposed: your application is now responsible for activities that used to be hidden inside the kernel. Monitoring and operational practices must adapt.

Important metrics include:

- **RX queue fill levels:** How many descriptors are in use vs capacity. Persistent high occupancy suggests that your polling core or downstream processing cannot keep up.
- **Packet drop counters:** At the NIC and in the user-space stack. Drops may indicate buffer exhaustion, mis-sized mempools, or misconfigured flow steering.

- **Per-core CPU usage and latency:** Polling threads should generally be pegged near 100% user CPU (they are always running), but their per-packet latency should remain stable.
- **Mempool occupancy:** Trends in free-buffer counts, which can reveal leaks or abnormal bursts.

Correlating these metrics with end-to-end latency distributions is essential. For example:

- A spike in RX queue occupancy right before a burst of high p99 latencies suggests under-provisioned polling or parsing capacity.
- Sudden mempool depletion followed by drops may point to a bug in buffer reclamation.

Operationally, kernel-bypass stacks also require:

- Careful version control of NIC firmware and drivers.
- Repeatable configuration of huge pages, NUMA settings, and IOMMU mappings across hosts.
- Runbooks for safely restarting or rolling out changes to pollers and strategies, since a misstep can bring down a NIC's queues.

## Designing Around Constraints, Not Fighting Them

Kernel-bypass networking removes entire classes of overhead—interrupts, context switches, generic kernel stacks—but introduces new constraints:

- You must dedicate cores to polling, which cannot be used for other work.
- You must manage memory pools and buffer lifecycles carefully.
- You must design flow steering and sharding policies that balance load and locality.

Rather than viewing these as limitations, it is helpful to see them as *design levers*:

- Dedicating cores turns networking from a variable background service into a predictable, always-on engine that your latency model can trust.
- Explicit mempool and buffer management lets you avoid hidden allocations and unpredictable pauses, at the cost of some upfront complexity.
- Flow steering and multi-queue design give you fine-grained control over how market microstructure maps onto your hardware topology.

If you combine these capabilities with the lock-free queues, cache-friendly coding, and batching strategies from earlier sections, you can construct a data path where most variability has been deliberately designed away. The end result is not “zero latency”—the laws of physics and silicon still apply—but a system whose latency behavior is understandable, tunable, and robust under the traffic patterns that matter for your trading business.

## 9.5 Latency Anti-Patterns

By this point in the chapter we have assembled a toolkit of effective patterns: lock-free queues instead of blocking locks, cache-friendly layouts instead of scattered structs, controlled batching instead of ad hoc bursts, and kernel-bypass networking instead of generic OS stacks. Unfortunately, many real trading systems still exhibit unstable latency because they quietly undo these gains elsewhere in the code base.

This section catalogs the most common design mistakes that inject jitter and tail spikes into otherwise competent low-latency systems. You can treat it as a “do not do this in the hot path” checklist. Each anti-pattern appears frequently in production systems; none of them is exotic.

Our focus will be on understanding *why* each practice hurts latency, what signatures it leaves in measurements, and how to migrate away from it without rewriting your entire system.

## Dynamic Allocation and Unbounded Object Creation

One of the strongest themes in earlier sections was preallocation and reuse: fixed-size ring buffers, mempools, and carefully managed lifecycles. The mirror image of that good practice is a hot path that freely allocates and frees memory as it goes.

### Why Allocation Hurts Latency

Modern allocators are fast on average, but they are not designed with microsecond-level jitter in mind. Several issues arise:

- **Lock contention:** Many allocators use internal locks or atomic operations on shared structures. Under bursty load, multiple threads calling into the allocator at the same time can queue behind those locks.
- **Background work:** Allocators sometimes perform maintenance work—coalescing free blocks, returning memory to the OS—at unpredictable times, causing occasional stalls.
- **Fragmentation and cache misses:** As objects of varying sizes are created and destroyed, memory becomes fragmented. New allocations are more likely to land in cold cache regions, increasing miss rates.

These behaviors do not show up clearly in average metrics, but they cause precisely the "once in a while we see a 50 microsecond spike for no apparent reason" anecdotes that are common in trading teams.

### Typical Offenders

Examples of dynamic allocation anti-patterns on hot paths include:

- Creating new message or event objects for every incoming packet or outgoing order.

- Using standard containers (vectors, maps, hash maps) in a way that triggers frequent growth or rehashing.
- Building strings and temporaries in logging or metrics code invoked directly from the trading loop.

Because these calls are often hidden behind abstractions, developers may not realize that a simple push into a container or string concatenation can allocate.

### Mitigations

Moving away from dynamic allocation does not require perfection everywhere. Instead:

- **Preallocate and reuse** objects that appear in hot loops: messages, buffers, small structs.
- **Reserve capacity** in vectors and maps before the trading day so they do not grow unpredictably during trading.
- **Separate allocation-heavy code paths** (e.g., configuration or admin commands) from the fast path, and ensure they do not share allocator arenas with trading threads if possible.
- **Instrument the allocator** (or use tools) to identify which code paths are responsible for allocations during peak trading hours.

You are aiming not for zero allocations in the entire process, but for *no allocations on the hot path during peak activity*.

## Synchronous Logging and Metrics in the Hot Path

Every team knows they should not log too much. Yet in practice, logging and metrics are among the most frequent sources of latency spikes.

### Why Logging is Dangerous for Latency

Synchronous logging commonly involves:

- Formatting strings (often with allocations and complex formatting logic).
- Taking locks to serialize writes to log files or standard output.
- Performing blocking I/O to disks or network destinations.

Even a single slow disk write or a brief stall on a logging mutex can cause a cascade: trading threads block while logging, buffers back up, and suddenly p99.9 latency jumps.

Metrics pipelines share similar risks when they:

- Use shared counters protected by locks.
- Send metrics over the network synchronously, waiting on sockets.
- Create rich, structured metrics objects per event.

### Safer Alternatives

Good low-latency systems treat logging and metrics as background tasks:

- **Asynchronous logging:** Hot-path code writes simple, fixed-size records into a lock-free logging ring buffer. A separate thread drains that buffer and performs the heavy formatting and I/O.
- **Sampling:** Only a fraction of events—say, one in a few thousand—are logged in detail. The rest are either summarized or not logged at all.
- **Per-core metrics aggregation:** Each core updates its own counters (avoiding locks and false sharing). A background task periodically aggregates and publishes metrics.

For rare, critical errors where immediate logging is essential, it may be acceptable to pay the price of synchronous logging, but this should be explicit and very rare. Routine events, even important trading events, should use lightweight, non-blocking logging mechanisms.

## Excessive Abstraction and Indirection

High-quality software design often emphasizes abstraction, modularity, and reuse: virtual interfaces, dependency injection, and flexible class hierarchies. Those same techniques, when applied indiscriminately to hot paths, can undermine performance.

### How Abstraction Becomes a Latency Anti-Pattern

Several mechanisms are at play:

- **Virtual function dispatch:** Indirect calls via vtables can increase branch misprediction and disrupt instruction caching, especially in tight loops that process packets or messages.
- **Pointer chasing:** Deep object graphs and layers of indirection (objects containing pointers to other objects, and so on) scatter data across memory, hurting cache locality.
- **Increased instruction footprint:** Generic frameworks, templates, and complex layers of logic inflate the hot code path, causing more instruction cache misses and reducing the CPU's ability to optimize execution.

Individually, these costs may seem small. Combined—especially under bursty loads—they can add measurable jitter.

### Recognizing Over-Abstracted Hot Paths

Red flags include:

- The main message-processing loop is expressed in highly abstract terms, such as "for each handler in the chain, call handle(event)."
- The call stack for a simple tick-to-order decision spans many layers of helper functions and interfaces.
- You find it difficult to explain, step by step, what the CPU actually does when a packet arrives.

If it takes several minutes to trace the hot path through the code base, it is likely that the CPU is also "working hard" on that path.

### Balancing Clarity and Performance

The goal is not to abandon abstraction, but to use it judiciously:

- **Flatten critical loops:** For the few tight loops that define your critical latency paths, favor straightforward, explicit code over clever layers of abstraction.
- **Specialize hot components:** Allow yourself to write specialized implementations for performance-critical cases, leaving generic frameworks for the slower, less critical paths.
- **Avoid deep hierarchies** in objects touched on every tick; prefer simple structs or small, well-defined types.

A pragmatic pattern is to maintain a "slow and flexible" path (for back-office tools, rare message types, or debugging) alongside a "fast and specialized" path protected by clear boundaries and tests.

## Hidden Work in Standard Library Containers

Standard containers and utilities are immensely useful, but they hide internal behaviors that can become anti-patterns when used casually in hot paths.

### Common Pitfalls

Some examples:

- **Unbounded growth of vectors or hash maps:** Pushing into a vector or inserting into a hash map can suddenly trigger a large reallocation or rehash, pausing the thread while memory is moved and caches are disturbed.
- **Map lookups on the hot path:** Associative containers with pointer-heavy internal structures (like balanced trees) can cause repeated cache misses during per-message lookups.
- **Container copying:** Passing containers by value, or returning them by value, silently copies potentially large structures.

Because these operations are wrapped in familiar interfaces, they often escape careful scrutiny.

### Mitigations

Mitigation strategies follow the same themes as before:

- **Reserve capacities** for containers that will be used in hot paths before markets open, to avoid runtime growth.
- **Replace map lookups** with direct indexing when possible—using arrays or precomputed indexes for symbols, sessions, or other frequently looked-up keys.
- **Avoid modifying container shapes** (inserting or erasing elements) inside the critical loops; instead, update them in slower control paths or in batch maintenance windows.
- **Audit copies:** Make it explicit when containers are copied. In hot paths, use references or pointers, and make immutable data truly immutable to avoid accidental copying.

The underlying principle is that your hot path should operate on stable, pre-shaped data structures, not continuously reshaping them.

## Exceptions and Error Handling on the Fast Path

Exceptions are a powerful error-handling mechanism, but throwing and catching them is expensive and unpredictable in time. Even setting up for exceptions (e.g., stack unwinding metadata) can affect code generation.

### Why Exceptions Are Problematic

When an exception is thrown:

- The program must unwind the stack, running cleanup code along the way.
- Control flow becomes irregular, confusing branch predictors and instruction pipelines.

- The latency of the affected operation becomes unbounded relative to normal execution.

Although exceptions may be rare, their occurrence almost always creates extreme tail events in latency distributions—the very p99.9 or worse events you are trying to avoid.

**Safer Patterns**

In low-latency code:

- Reserve exceptions, if used at all, for initialization and configuration code, not for the per-message hot path.
- Prefer explicit error codes or status flags, checked in-line in a predictable way.
- In truly exceptional conditions on the hot path (e.g., corrupted data), consider failing fast and clearly, rather than attempting elaborate recovery that continues trading with compromised state.

The guiding idea is that "error handling" on the hot path should aim for *predictable* behavior, even in failure, not for maximum generality.

## Accidental Contention on Shared Atomics and Reference Counts

Lock-free programming emphasizes atomic operations as building blocks. However, indiscriminate use of atomics and reference counting can reintroduce contention and cache-line bouncing.

**How Atomics Become a Bottleneck**

Consider:

- A global atomic counter incremented on every message for statistics.
- Shared reference-counted objects updated by many threads.

- A "simple" flag used by multiple threads for coordination.

Each atomic update often implies:

- A read-modify-write on a cache line that must be owned by the updating core.
- Cache-coherence traffic as that cache line moves between cores.
- Potential serialization if many cores try to touch the same atomic in quick succession.

The effect is similar to a contended lock: threads stall waiting for ownership of the cache line that holds the atomic.

**Mitigations**

To avoid turning atomics into hidden locks:

- **Shard counters per core or per shard** and aggregate infrequently, as discussed in the cache-friendly section.
- **Avoid shared reference counting** in hot paths; prefer clear ownership transfers or preallocated, fixed graphs of objects.
- **Minimize the scope of atomics:** Use them at well-defined boundaries (for example, between modules) rather than throughout the core logic.

When you do need atomics, be explicit about their purpose and measure their impact with profiling tools that can attribute stalls to coherence traffic.

## Inconsistent or Over-Aggressive Power Management

This anti-pattern sits at the boundary between software and hardware configuration, but its effects are felt in code: unpredictable changes in core frequency or sleep states.

**How Power Settings Affect Latency**

Modern CPUs manage power through various states:

- **C-states** control how deeply a core can sleep when idle.
- **P-states and turbo** control how fast a core can run when busy.

If power management is left in a default, general-purpose configuration:

- Cores may enter deeper sleep states during quiet periods, taking longer to wake when a packet arrives.
- Turbo boost may cause core frequencies to fluctuate based on load and thermal conditions, changing the execution speed of your code over time.

The result is latency distributions that depend not only on your code and traffic, but also on what else the machine has been doing recently.

**Mitigations**

Although full power-tuning is covered later in the chapter, key guidelines are:

- Set consistent, predictable power policies for cores dedicated to trading: limit deep sleep states and stabilize frequency behavior.
- Isolate noisy, non-critical workloads onto different cores or machines to avoid triggering unpredictable power management responses on trading cores.

In other words, remove "hidden" dynamic behavior at the hardware level in the same way you remove hidden dynamism in your memory allocation or logging.

## A Checklist for Design and Code Reviews

To make this catalog actionable, teams often adopt a short checklist for design and code reviews of latency-sensitive components. Questions might include:

- Does any hot-path code allocate or free memory under expected trading load?

- Are logging or metrics calls synchronous, or can they block on I/O or locks?
- How many layers of abstraction does a single tick or packet traverse? Can we flatten the most performance-critical ones?
- Are we using standard containers in ways that can trigger reallocation or rehashing during trading?
- Could any exceptions be thrown on the per-message path? If so, what is their cost?
- Do we have global atomics or reference counts updated by many threads on every event?
- Are our power and CPU isolation settings consistent with the expectations of this code?

The goal is not to eliminate every imperfection, but to ensure that no major latency landmine survives review by accident. If you combine this discipline with the positive patterns from earlier sections—lock-free handoffs, cache-aware layouts, tuned batching, and kernel-bypass networking—you greatly increase the odds that your system's latency behavior in production will resemble what you saw in the lab, even on the busiest trading days.

## 9.6 Holistic System Tuning

The preceding sections have been deliberately local in scope. We optimized individual queues, refactored data layouts for cache locality, tuned batching policies, and examined user-space networking paths. In practice, however, the latency you see in production is the *result* of all these decisions interacting with hardware, the operating system, and live market traffic.

This section steps back and treats the trading system as a whole. The goal is to integrate CPU, OS, NIC, and runtime tweaks into a coherent tuning methodology rather than a grab bag of folklore settings. We will focus on three ideas:

- Latency behavior emerges from interactions; you must tune with a system-level mindset.
- Tuning should follow a structured workflow: baseline, isolate, change, validate.
- The most effective tweaks are those whose impact you can *see* in your measurements, not just those that "should help" in theory.

## Latency as a System Property

It is tempting to attribute latency problems to a single culprit: "the queue is slow," "the NIC is overloaded," or "the kernel is noisy." Reality is rarely that clean. Consider a tick's journey:

1. The NIC receives a packet, possibly batching it with others.
2. A user-space poller reads descriptors, maybe in bursts depending on batching and core load.
3. Parsed messages flow through lock-free queues into strategy cores.
4. Strategy logic touches various data structures in cache, sometimes generating misses to L3 or RAM.
5. Orders are sent out, potentially contending on shared queues or kernel interfaces.

Your p99.9 latency reflects all of these stages plus the variance added by CPU frequency changes, OS scheduling, and NIC configuration. Small changes in one part can amplify or cancel behaviors elsewhere. For example:

- Increasing NIC interrupt coalescing might reduce CPU load but quietly add microseconds before packets reach user space.
- Tightening batching in the application might remove some queueing, but expose the system to more overhead per message, raising CPU utilization and eventually causing scheduler-induced jitter.

A holistic tuning approach accepts that you cannot "fix latency" in only one layer. Instead, you design an end-to-end path and then adjust CPU, OS, NIC, and application settings so that they reinforce, rather than contradict, your intended behavior.

## A Structured Tuning Workflow

Ad hoc tweaks are alluring: change one BIOS setting here, one kernel flag there, retune a queue size, and declare victory. This rarely yields repeatable results. A more robust approach follows a workflow:

1. Establish a clean baseline.
2. Lock down variables.
3. Set explicit latency and jitter targets.
4. Tune one group of parameters at a time.
5. Validate using consistent, distribution-focused measurements.

### Step 1: Establish a Clean Baseline

Before tuning, you need a reference configuration that is:

- **Stable:** No ongoing changes to hardware, firmware, or kernel parameters.
- **Instrumented:** You can measure end-to-end latency, as well as key internal metrics (queue depths, CPU usage, packet drops).
- **Representative:** It uses realistic traffic patterns and covers your typical trading scenarios.

The baseline does not have to be fully optimized; it just has to be well understood. Document:

- BIOS versions and settings.
- Kernel version and configuration.

- NIC firmware versions and key parameters (queue counts, offload settings, coalescing).
- Application versions and critical configuration (batch sizes, core assignments).

This documentation becomes the anchor against which you will compare all later changes.

### Step 2: Lock Down Variables

Tuning is nearly impossible if the environment keeps shifting under you. Lock down:

- Hardware revisions and firmware: avoid silent updates in the middle of a tuning cycle.
- OS updates: schedule them explicitly and re-validate after each.
- Background workloads: ensure test or production machines are not running unrelated jobs that skew results.

Think of your trading platform as lab equipment: you want controlled experiments, not a moving target.

### Step 3: Define Latency and Jitter Targets

Before you touch any knobs, decide what success means. For each critical path—market data ingest, strategy decision, order send, and perhaps risk rejection—define:

- Which percentiles matter (for example, p95, p99, p99.9).
- Acceptable thresholds at those percentiles.
- How much jitter you can tolerate day-to-day.

These targets drive all subsequent decisions. A change that improves throughput or median latency but violates p99.9 for a key SLA is not a win, no matter how impressive the throughput chart looks.

### Step 4: Tune in Logical Layers

With a baseline and targets in hand, you can tune in layers:

1. CPU core pinning and isolation.
2. Power and frequency management.
3. NIC configuration (queues, coalescing, offloads).
4. Application-level batching, queue sizes, and thread scheduling.

Within each layer, make small, deliberate changes and re-measure. Resist the urge to change many unrelated settings at once; otherwise, you will not know which one mattered.

### Step 5: Validate and Iterate

After each change:

- Re-run the same workload used for the baseline.
- Compare latency distributions, CPU usage, queue depths, and error rates.
- Decide whether the change moves you closer to or farther from your targets.

Tuning then becomes an iterative process, with a clear record of which settings improved which metrics.

## CPU Pinning and Isolation

Assigning threads to cores is central to latency behavior. The general aim is to:

- Dedicate specific cores to critical threads.
- Reduce interference from other threads and the OS scheduler.
- Align application threads with NIC queues and memory locations.

### Pinning Pollers and Strategies

Key principles include:

- **One polling thread per RX queue, pinned:** Each NIC RX queue should be served by a poller thread fixed to a specific core. This keeps cache usage local and prevents scheduler-induced gaps in polling.
- **Strategy threads on nearby cores:** Strategy cores that consume from these pollers' queues should ideally sit on the same socket and as close in core topology as possible to minimize cross-core traffic.
- **Dedicated cores for hot threads:** Do not share these cores with other tasks, including background daemons, logging workers, or OS housekeeping.

Pinning reduces the scheduler's freedom. That is precisely the point: you are trading flexibility for predictability.

### CPU Isolation and Affinity

Beyond pinning individual threads, you can:

- **Isolate cores** so the OS does not schedule general-purpose workloads on them.
- **Configure IRQ affinity** so that any remaining interrupts are delivered to non-critical cores, or at least not to the cores handling your most sensitive paths.

The result is that critical cores spend nearly all their time executing your code, not being preempted to service other work. Combined with kernel-bypass networking, this can drastically reduce jitter in packet-processing times.

## Power Management and Frequency Scaling

Power management settings are an often-overlooked source of latency variability. Modern CPUs dynamically alter both clock frequency and sleep depth based on load and thermal conditions.

### C-States: Sleep Depth

C-states control how deeply a core can sleep when idle:

- Shallow states (light sleep) wake quickly but save less power.
- Deep states save more power but take longer to wake, adding wake-up latency.

For dedicated trading cores that are almost always busy-polling NIC queues, processing messages—it is often best to:

- Restrict or disable deep C-states so that cores remain ready with minimal wake-up cost.
- Keep at least one thread runnable on those cores to discourage the OS from idling them deeply.

You do not need to eliminate all power management; you just need to ensure that power-saving features do not introduce microsecond-scale wake-up penalties into your hot paths.

### P-States and Turbo: Clock Speed

P-states and turbo features control how fast each core runs:

- Turbo boost can raise core frequency under certain conditions, potentially improving best-case latency.
- But dynamic frequency changes can make latencies depend on recent history (for example, how hot the CPU is, how many cores are active).

Some shops prefer to:

- Set trading cores to a fixed, stable frequency (possibly modestly below the absolute maximum) to ensure consistent timing.
- Allow turbo only on non-critical cores, or monitor its effects carefully.

Here again, the trade-off is between maximum headline performance and predictable, repeatable behavior under load.

## NIC Configuration: Queues, Coalescing, and Offloads

Network interface cards offer numerous tuning knobs. The challenge is to configure them in a way that supports the end-to-end behavior you want, rather than conflicting with application-level decisions.

### Queue Configuration and Mapping

We saw earlier how RX queues and flow steering enable sharding by core. Tuning at this layer includes:

- Choosing the number of RX (and TX) queues to match your core budget.
- Ensuring each queue is consistently mapped to a specific core's poller.
- Avoiding over-allocation of queues that will never be properly serviced, which only adds complexity.

Balanced queue mapping reduces both contention and queue build-up. An under-serviced queue will show rising occupancy and eventually drops; an over-serviced one wastes CPU.

### Interrupt Coalescing vs Polling

In interrupt-driven networking, NICs often group packets before raising an interrupt, a process called interrupt coalescing. Kernel-bypass designs typically rely on polling instead of interrupts, but coalescing parameters can still be relevant, depending on the mode.

Trade-offs:

- More coalescing reduces interrupts (good for CPU load), but increases the time between packet arrival and handling (bad for latency).
- Less coalescing lowers delay but may increase overhead if you are still using interrupts in any part of the path.

If you are fully committed to polling on critical queues, you generally want:

- Coalescing minimized or disabled for those queues, so that hardware behavior aligns with your fast polling cadence.
- Any remaining interrupt-driven paths confined to less critical traffic (e.g., administration, slow feeds).

### Offloads and Checksums

NICs can offload work like checksum calculation, segmentation, or even partial protocol processing. These can be beneficial, but:

- Offloads may change the shape and timing of packet delivery (larger bursts, slightly different header handling).
- Some offloads interact poorly with kernel-bypass modes or with specific protocol stacks.

A pragmatic approach is:

- Enable only offloads that are well-understood and demonstrably helpful in your workload.

- Benchmark with and without each major offload feature rather than assuming the default is ideal.

## Runtime and Application-Level Tuning

With CPU, power, and NIC settings aligned, you next tune the runtime behavior of your own application: batching, queue sizes, thread counts, and timeouts.

### Aligning Batching Across Layers

As discussed earlier, batching can improve throughput and median latency but hurt tails. A holistic approach:

- Align NIC-level batching (for example, how many packets per poll) with application-level batching (for example, how many messages you process per loop).
- Avoid "stacking" multiple batching layers unknowingly—for instance, NIC coalescing, plus kernel buffering, plus user-space batching—each adding its own delay.
- Define a maximum allowed batching delay consistent with your SLAs, and ensure all layers respect that bound collectively.

This prevents the situation where each layer adds "just a little" batching, but the total delay becomes unacceptable.

### Queue Sizes and Backpressure

Internal queues buffer transient bursts. But over-large queues can:

- Hide problems (for example, a slow consumer) by accumulating work silently.
- Increase queueing time for outlier messages, damaging p99 and p99.9 latency.

A more disciplined strategy is:

- Size queues to accommodate realistic bursts, not worst-case fantasies.
- Implement backpressure or shedding policies when queues approach capacity (for example, temporarily dropping less critical data, or signaling upstream to slow down).
- Monitor queue depths in production; sustained growth is a sign of mis-tuned capacity or an overloaded component.

### Thread Counts and Work Distribution

More threads do not always mean lower latency. Too many threads:

- Increase scheduling complexity and cache contention.
- Can lead to harmful sharing of data and atomics.

Effective designs:

- Start from the hardware: count cores and NUMA nodes; decide how many can be dedicated to trading.
- Assign clear roles: NIC pollers, strategy workers, gateway threads, and background maintenance.
- Keep the number of hot-path threads per core to one; avoid hyper-threading your fast-path threads unless you have strong evidence it helps.

A smaller number of well-understood threads is easier to reason about and tune than a tangled web of workers.

## Observability and Validation

Holistic tuning is only as good as your ability to observe the system. You need instrumentation that connects high-level latency outcomes back to CPU, OS, and NIC behavior.

### What to Measure

Key measurements include:

- **End-to-end latency distributions** for critical paths, broken down by stage when possible.
- **Per-core CPU utilization and run-queue lengths,** to detect contention or unexpected background activity.
- **Queue depths** at key handoff points: NIC RX queues, internal message queues, and gateway queues.
- **Hardware counters,** such as cache misses, branch mispredictions, and memory bandwidth usage on hot cores.
- **NIC statistics:** RX/TX errors, drops, and queue overflows.

Together, these form a picture of where time is actually spent and where variability enters.

### Relating Changes to Effects

After each tuning step, ask:

- Did the expected metric move in the expected direction?
- Did any unexpected metric degrade (for example, CPU utilization spiking on a supposedly "cool" core)?
- Did the overall latency distribution for our SLAs improve or deteriorate?

If the results are ambiguous, consider rolling back the change and designing a more targeted experiment. Over time, you build a map: "this BIOS change shifts p99 by a few microseconds," "that NIC queue rebalancing cuts drops but increases CPU usage by X%," and so on.

## A Practical Tuning Playbook

To make these ideas concrete, here is a simplified playbook that many trading teams follow when bringing up a new platform or host:

1. **Baseline:** Install known-good BIOS, kernel, NIC firmware. Configure minimal kernel-bypass setup. Instrument end-to-end latency under replayed market loads.
2. **CPU layout:** Pin NIC pollers and strategy threads to specific cores. Isolate those cores from other workloads. Re-measure.
3. **Power tuning:** Adjust C-state and P-state policies for trading cores to favor consistency. Re-measure; ensure no regressions in tails.
4. **NIC tuning:** Configure RX/TX queues, flow steering, and coalescing to match core layout. Enable only essential offloads. Re-measure latency and drop rates.
5. **Application tuning:** Adjust batching, queue sizes, and thread counts to meet SLAs, guided by p95–p99.9 results. Verify that changes do not trigger new bottlenecks or contention.
6. **Stress tests:** Run high-load and worst-case market scenarios, observing behavior under strain (queue saturation, drops, CPU saturation, latency spikes).
7. **Rollout and monitor:** Deploy to production gradually, with dashboards tracking the same metrics and alerts tuned to deviations from lab baselines.

Each step is small and testable. If something goes wrong, you can trace it back to a specific change. Over time, this playbook evolves into your firm's own "operational doctrine" for low-latency tuning.

## From Folklore to Engineering Discipline

In many organizations, low-latency "tuning" begins as folklore: a handful of engineers remember that disabling some kernel feature "once helped" or that "this BIOS option is faster." Without measurement and structure, those stories harden into superstition.

The aim of holistic system tuning is to replace superstition with engineering discipline. You:

- Understand the roles of CPU, OS, NIC, and application in shaping latency.
- Apply changes in a controlled workflow.
- Use clear SLAs and measurements to judge success.
- Document your environment so improvements are reproducible.

Combined with the concrete techniques from earlier sections—lock-free data structures, cache-friendly coding, thoughtful batching, and kernel-bypass networking—this discipline lets you build trading systems whose latency profile is not an accident, but a designed property that can be explained, defended, and evolved as markets change.

# Chapter 10

# Reliability, Safety & Production Operations

*Low latency only matters if your system is still alive when the market gets weird. This chapter pulls back the curtain on the operational machinery-redundancy, monitoring, chaos testing, compliance plumbing, and disciplined post-mortems-that lets a trading engine stay fast on its best day and safe on its worst.*

## 10.1 Redundancy and Failover Architectures

Low latency is worthless if the system is not available when the market is moving. In the preceding chapters we treated the trading path as if it were always present: packets flowed, prices updated, decisions were made, and orders reached the exchange. In production, hardware fails, processes crash, switches reboot, links flap, and exchanges drop sessions without warning. This section adds the missing dimension: reliability.

We will start by turning the vague goal of "high availability" into concrete reliability objectives for both trading and market data paths. We then design redundancy and failover topologies that can meet those objectives without quietly destroying the latency characteristics we worked so hard to achieve. Along the way we will be explicit about where latency hides in failover logic itself, and how to keep recovery times in the sub-second range without destabilizing order routing or duplicating orders.

## From "Always Up" to Quantified Reliability

Most teams talk about availability in slogans: "four nines" or "no more than a few minutes a month of downtime." To design real architectures, we need more precise targets:

- **Target availability:** Often expressed as a percentage per year. For serious electronic trading, targets of 99.9%–99.99% for the core trading path are common. That translates to at most tens of minutes of unplanned outage per year.
- **Recovery Time Objective (RTO):** How quickly a specific failure mode must be mitigated. For example, "If a single gateway host fails, we must restore order entry capability within 500 ms."
- **Recovery Point Objective (RPO):** How much state you are allowed to lose across a failure. For a trading gateway, the RPO for order state is effectively zero: you cannot "forget" about outstanding orders.

For low-latency trading, these objectives must be stated separately for two main flows:

- **Market data path:** From the exchange price feed to the strategy's local view of the order book. Here, a brief disruption of a few hundred milliseconds may be tolerable if it happens rarely and is clearly visible in monitoring, but longer gaps or frequent flaps can lead to stale decisions or missing opportunities.
- **Order and risk path:** From the strategy's decision to the exchange acknowledgment. Here, even seconds of outage during a critical market move can cause severe losses, but an equal or

greater danger is inconsistent state: believing an order is dead when it is actually live at the exchange, or sending duplicate orders.

Before choosing technologies, you should list the critical flows and assign targets. A typical example for a single venue might look like:

- Order entry availability: 99.99% during trading hours.
- RTO for a single gateway process crash: 200 ms.
- RTO for a single server failure (host down): 1 s.
- RPO for in-flight order state: zero loss; any ambiguity must be resolved via exchange queries before resuming normal trading.

These numbers will drive how much redundancy you build, how complex your failover logic must be, and how much background state replication you need.

## Common Failure Modes Along the Trading Path

Once objectives are clear, the next step is to enumerate where things can break. For a simplified trading stack, typical failure modes include:

- **Process-level failures:** A gateway, strategy, or risk engine crashes or deadlocks.
- **Host failures:** The machine running one or more critical processes reboots, loses power, or experiences hardware errors.
- **Network failures:** A top-of-rack switch reloads, a link to the exchange drops, or a misconfiguration causes packet loss or routing black holes.
- **Storage and configuration issues:** A corrupted configuration file or failed log volume causes processes to exit or behave unpredictably.
- **External venue problems:** The exchange drops the session, replays market data with gaps, or goes into a degraded mode.

Each failure has a characteristic scope (single process, single host, entire rack, entire datacenter, or external) and a characteristic timescale of detection and recovery. Good redundancy architecture matches mechanisms to these scales. For instance, you do not need cross-datacenter failover to handle an individual process crash, but you cannot rely on restarting a single process to cover a full data center outage.

## Redundancy Patterns: Active–Active vs Active–Standby

Redundancy means having more than one instance of a component so that if one fails, another can take over. The two most important patterns for trading gateways and market data handlers are *active–active* and *active–standby*.

- **Active–active:** Two or more instances are simultaneously in service. They may share the load (e.g., half of client sessions on each gateway) or all handle the same data (e.g., two independent market data receivers). If one instance fails, the others are already hot and usually need no special activation.

- **Active–standby:** One instance is primary; one or more are backups. Only the active instance processes live traffic. Upon failure, a standby is promoted to active via a failover decision.

Intuitively, active–active architectures minimize failover time because the backup is already working. However, they are more complex to reason about when components hold state that must be globally consistent, such as session sequence numbers or per-order identifiers. Active–standby designs simplify state management but introduce an explicit failover step, which can add latency and risk if implemented poorly.

Immediately after this conceptual introduction, it is helpful to visualize how these patterns look for a trading gateway cluster.

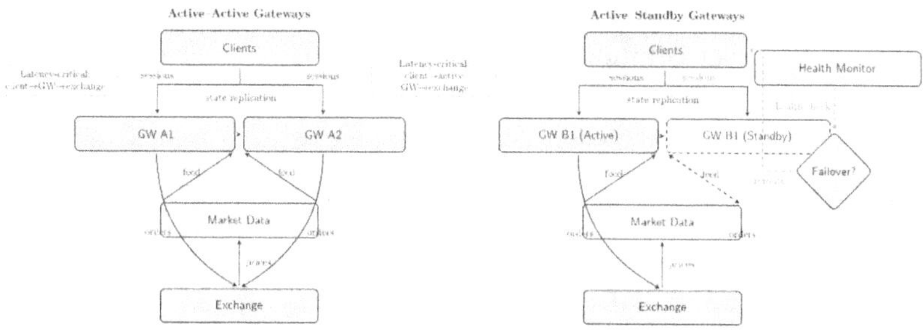


## State, Sessions, and Why Failover is Hard

Before we dive into topologies, it is worth emphasizing why trading gateways are not just stateless load balancers. They typically maintain:

- Session state with the exchange (sequence numbers, heartbeats, replay windows).
- Session state with upstream clients or strategies.
- Per-order state: mappings from internal identifiers to exchange order IDs and statuses.
- Risk-related counters and throttles (per symbol, per client, per venue).

If you lose this state, or if it diverges between two instances, failover can cause serious harm. Examples include:

- Sending a cancel for an order that your new primary does not know about.
- Re-sending a new order message the exchange interprets as a duplicate.
- Failing to enforce limits that were already hit on the old instance.

Designing redundant architectures is therefore a problem of state management as much as it is a problem of networking. The guiding principle is:

Do as much state replication and preparation as possible in the background, so that the moment of failover only switches traffic, not logic.

## Active–Active Designs for Latency-Critical Components

In an active–active design, both instances are live. There are two main patterns depending on where the state boundary lies.

### Stateless or Locally Stateful Components

For components that are naturally stateless or hold only local, easily reconstructible state—for example, market data normalization processes or purely stateless risk filters—active–active is straightforward. You can run two identical instances on separate hosts, feed each from independent network paths, and let upstream components either:

- Use both outputs and choose the "better" (e.g., lowest latency, or majority vote), or
- Shard the load so each instance handles different symbols or clients.

If one instance fails, the other continues without any special coordination. Your RTO becomes the time it takes routing or subscription logic to recognize that one path is down and stop expecting data from it, which can be well under 100 ms.

### Stateful Active–Active Gateways

The more challenging case is a trading gateway cluster where you want both nodes serving live clients concurrently. To make this safe:

- **Partition state carefully.** One clean pattern is to partition clients or strategies across gateways so that each client's orders are owned by one gateway at a time. This reduces the risk of cross-node conflicts.

- **Replicate state continuously.** Even if a gateway "owns" a client, the current order book and order states for that client should be replicated, in near real-time, to at least one other gateway. This lets a standby gateway quickly take over the ownership of that client if needed.

- **Decouple exchange sessions.** In some venues you can run multiple independent sessions to the exchange. Each gateway can maintain its own session, which confines sequence number state to that node. Clients can be re-bound across sessions on failover, at the cost of a small reconnection delay.

The key latency benefit of active–active is that there is no cold start. The alternate gateway has ongoing heartbeats with the exchange, hot caches, and warm CPU paths. Failover is fundamentally a routing problem: which clients and symbols send orders to which gateway.

However, active–active is not a free lunch. You must:

- Ensure that your client-side routing is deterministic and stable under partial failure. For example, if you hash client IDs to pick a gateway, that hash function must be consistent across code versions and deployments.

- Guard against split-brain scenarios where, due to a network partition, both gateways believe they own the same client or symbol. Mitigations include explicit leader election for each partition (client or symbol group) and conservative "fail closed" behavior when health information is ambiguous.

## Active–Standby Designs and Failover Control Planes

Active–standby designs place more logic into the failover decision itself. A typical layout for an order gateway is:

- One *active* gateway maintains the exchange session and handles all client traffic.

- One *warm standby* gateway keeps up-to-date replicas of critical state and, if the venue allows, may maintain a passive session to the exchange or a secondary session kept in sync.
- A separate health-monitoring component watches the active gateway's heartbeats and error rates and decides when to promote the standby.

The benefit is simpler state reasoning: there is a single writer of state at any time. However, the cost is the complexity of the control plane: losing the active gateway is now a two-step process.

- **Detection:** Recognize that the active gateway is down or unhealthy.
- **Promotion:** Promote the standby to active, including taking over the exchange session or opening a new one, and redirecting clients.

Each step can hide latency if done naively:

- Health checks that run every few seconds will delay detection. In low-latency trading, health checks for critical components should run at tens of milliseconds granularities, with multiple signals (heartbeats, queue depths, error logs) to avoid false positives.
- Promotion logic that requires manual confirmation, or a heavyweight leader election algorithm, will slow down RTO. For single-venue gateways, simpler deterministic schemes can suffice (for example, pre-designated priority ordering of nodes).

A common pattern is to treat the health monitor as almost part of the latency-critical path, even if it is logically separate:

- It must have redundant network paths to both gateways.
- It must itself be redundant, typically through a small, highly available cluster.
- Its decision logic must be well-tested and deterministic.

## Hot, Warm, and Cold Standbys

The terms *hot*, *warm*, and *cold* refer to how ready a standby is to take over.

- **Hot standby:** Fully initialized, processing the same inputs as the active instance, and maintaining matched state. Failover is essentially instantaneous; traffic is already flowing, and only routing or final role labels change.
- **Warm standby:** Initialized and patched up-to-date with state snapshots and log replay, but not in the direct traffic path. On failover, some last bits of state catch-up or session establishment are required.
- **Cold standby:** Not running until failure occurs. Failover involves provisioning, loading configurations, connecting to the exchange, and possibly replaying historical state from storage.

For ultra-low-latency trading:

- **Hot standbys** are appropriate for gateway processes and market data handlers where sub-second RTO is required.
- **Warm standbys** are reasonable for less critical, but still important, components such as batch risk reports or analytics-services where a few seconds of unavailability does not threaten client money.
- **Cold standbys** are rarely appropriate for anything in the live trading path, but may be adequate for disaster recovery environments that only need to come online if an entire site is lost.

The main challenge with hot standbys is state replication overhead: every piece of state written on the primary must be efficiently streamed to the standby. The trick is to separate what must be replicated synchronously from what can be replicated asynchronously:

- Synchronous replication for minimal, critical state needed to avoid inconsistent order behavior (for example, order ID mappings and outstanding order lists).

- Asynchronous replication for logs, detailed telemetry, and bulky caches.

By keeping the synchronous set small and optimized, you can stay within tight latency budgets while still being able to promote the standby in under a second.

## Fast Failover Paths in the Network Layer

Redundancy at the process level is only part of the story. The network itself must offer quick alternative routes:

- **Redundant links and switches:** Dual-homing gateways to two top-of-rack switches, with redundant connections towards the exchange. If one switch reloads, traffic quickly shifts to the other.
- **Fast convergence:** Use network designs that converge quickly when a link fails, such as equal-cost multipath (ECMP) routing or carefully tuned static routes, rather than complex dynamic routing protocols that take seconds to converge.
- **Separate paths for market data and orders:** This allows you to isolate failures and maintain at least partial functionality (for instance, still receiving prices while investigating order path issues, or vice versa).

From a latency perspective, each redundant link and switch adds the potential for extra hops and jitter. The rule is to keep the *active* path as short and deterministic as possible and treat the backup path as a slightly more expensive insurance policy that is used rarely. Avoid complex in-band signaling that attempts to discover and re-optimize routes during an incident; pre-configured, simple backup routes are generally more reliable and predictable.

## Market Data Redundancy and Gap Handling

Market data paths face a slightly different reliability problem: you care about both timeliness and continuity. Common strategies include:

- **Dual feed handlers:** Two independent processes, potentially on different hosts, subscribe to the same exchange feed. Downstream, a merger component takes the earliest valid tick and monitors for discrepancies.
- **Primary and secondary feeds:** Many venues offer multiple feeds (for example, multicast A and B groups). Systems can subscribe to both, using one as primary and the other as a backup, with logic to fill gaps if one stream experiences packet loss.
- **Sequence-aware gap filling:** Feed protocols typically include sequence numbers. On detecting a gap, your handler can request a replay from the exchange, reconstructing the missing portion of the book.

Latency hides in these gap-handling mechanisms. A system that immediately triggers a replay on any small gap might block the consumer of the feed, causing a stall longer than the original loss. A better pattern is:

- Detect the gap using sequence numbers.
- Immediately mark the affected symbols or book levels as "possibly stale," so upstream strategies know to degrade gracefully or pause.
- Request a replay in a separate path, while continuing to process subsequent ticks, if the protocol allows.
- Merge replayed data back into the live stream, clearing the stale flag when consistent.

Redundancy helps because a gap on one feed might be filled by clean data on the other. Your merger logic should prefer the fastest valid packet, not blindly trust a single source.

## Keeping Failover Out of the Hot Path

So far we have considered the structures of redundant systems. The final, subtle issue is how to keep failover machinery from hurting you when nothing is failing.

The temptations to avoid include:

- **Synchronous health checks in the trading loop:** For example, verifying the standby's state before sending each order. This adds needless latency and couples performance to the slowest component.
- **Leader election on every request:** Some coordination frameworks encourage frequent consensus operations. In a trading gateway, the leader should be stable over many requests, and leader changes should be rare events.
- **Overly aggressive automatic failover:** Failing over on every minor glitch can cause oscillation, where traffic flips between nodes, destroying cache locality, warming costs, and latency predictability.

Instead, design your failover components along these lines:

- **Background replication:** State changes are streamed to standbys asynchronously, with bounded delay and explicit metrics. The trading path simply writes to a well-optimized replication queue.
- **Simple health indicators:** Each gateway exports a small, clear set of metrics (e.g., heartbeat count, backlog depth, error rate) that a separate monitor interprets according to a known policy.
- **Hysteresis and cool-downs:** Once a failover occurs, do not fail back immediately when the old primary recovers. Require a stability period and explicit operator review to avoid thrashing.

In other words, aim for architectures where:

> In steady state, redundancy costs only a small, predictable overhead, and in failure state, switchover happens quickly and deterministically according to a plan you have already tested.

## Testing Switchover and Avoiding Split-Brain

Redundancy architectures look impressive on diagrams, but their value depends entirely on predictable behavior under stress. At a minimum, you should routinely test:

- **Process crash scenarios:** Kill the active gateway process and measure time until clients can successfully send new orders via the standby.
- **Host failures:** Power-cycle or otherwise disable an entire host and verify that both order and market data paths recover within RTO.
- **Network partitions:** Simulate loss of connectivity between health monitors and gateways to ensure you do not create split-brain conditions.

Split-brain refers to a situation where two instances believe they are active simultaneously, often due to inconsistent views of the network. This is particularly dangerous in trading because it can lead to duplicate orders or breach of predefined limits. To avoid it:

- Require that any node claiming to be active must see a quorum of health monitors or shared resources.
- In ambiguous conditions (e.g., a node can reach the exchange but not the monitor), err on the side of failing closed: stop sending new orders and raise an alarm, rather than assuming activity is safe.
- Keep a simple, auditable source of truth for which node is primary for each partition of state (e.g., per symbol group or per client).

These tests and safeguards turn redundancy from a comforting idea into an operational asset. Combined with the measurement and monitoring practices discussed in later sections, they allow you to maintain both reliability and the deterministic, low-latency behavior that defines serious electronic trading systems.

## 10.2 Monitoring and Alerting for Latency

Redundancy and failover give your trading system ways to survive failures without going dark. That only works, however, if you can see what the system is doing in real time. You must know not just whether it is "up," but whether it is still fast enough to be competitive.

This section focuses on building that visibility. We will construct a telemetry stack that measures latency where it actually matters: at successive hops along the trading path. Then we will turn those measurements into concrete service level objectives (SLOs), per-hop latency budgets, and alerts that distinguish real performance degradation from harmless noise.

The goal is simple to state: when latency moves, you should know *where*, *by how much*, and *whether it matters right now*. Achieving that in a complex trading platform requires some discipline and structure.

### What to Measure: End-to-End and Per-Hop

The most natural number to look at is end-to-end order round-trip time: how long it takes from the moment your strategy decides to send an order until it receives the exchange acknowledgment (or reject). This captures everything that can delay a trade:

- Network from your strategy host to the gateway.
- Processing in the gateway (including risk checks and protocol translation).
- Network from the gateway to the exchange.
- Processing at the exchange gateway and matching engine.
- Network and processing for the acknowledgment on the way back.

End-to-end latency is the right metric for traders and business stakeholders. From an engineering point of view, however, it is a *composite* metric. If it drifts from 400 microseconds to 800 microseconds, you cannot tell which part of the path is responsible. To fix problems quickly, you must break this number down into *per-hop* contributions.

A simple conceptual decomposition for an order path is:

- **Strategy decision latency:** Time from market data arrival on the strategy host to the strategy deciding to place an order.
- **Strategy-to-gateway network latency:** Time on the wire between the strategy process and the local gateway.
- **Gateway processing latency:** Time spent in the gateway, including risk checks, throttling, serialization, and any persistence on the hot path.
- **Gateway-to-exchange network latency:** Time on the wire between your infrastructure and the exchange entry point.
- **Exchange processing latency:** Time between the exchange receiving the order and sending an acknowledgment or execution report.

For each of these segments, the telemetry system should be able to produce latency distributions over time. The goal is not to isolate every microsecond, but to be able to answer questions of the form:

> "Our overall p99 latency is 200 microseconds worse than usual right now. Is that because of our own software, our network, or the exchange?"

To answer this reliably, your measurements must be:

- **Consistent:** Timestamps at different points must be comparable.
- **High resolution:** Microsecond or better where possible, not millisecond-only counters.
- **Statistical, not single-point:** You need distributions (for example, medians and tail percentiles), not just averages.

## Clock Synchronization and Timestamping

All latency measurement starts with timestamps. If two components' clocks disagree, per-hop measurements become meaningless. In low-latency trading, you typically rely on hardware-assisted time synchronization:

- Precision Time Protocol (PTP) with network cards and switches that support hardware timestamping.
- In some data centers, a local GPS-disciplined time source that keeps one or more grandmaster clocks aligned with UTC.

The exact technology is less important than the principle: every host in the trading path should know time to within a tight bound, often on the order of tens of nanoseconds to a few microseconds. More importantly, you must *record* the quality of time:

- What is the offset between this host and the grandmaster?
- When was the last time synchronization event?
- Has the time discipline process reported any large corrections?

These details should be part of your telemetry. When analyzing a latency anomaly, you want to be confident that you are not chasing artifacts from a drifting clock.

Once clocks are sound, instrument each component to add timestamps at key boundaries:

- When a market data packet is received from the network.
- When a market data update is delivered to the strategy.
- When the strategy makes a trading decision and enqueues an order.
- When the gateway receives that order.
- When the gateway emits the corresponding order message to the exchange.

- When the acknowledgment or execution returns from the exchange.

Prefer timestamps as early and as late in each step as you can reasonably get them, to avoid hiding internal queueing delays.

## Latency Distributions: Medians and Tails

Averages are poor summaries for latency. They hide the rare slow events that matter most in trading. Instead, think in terms of a distribution: for a given time period, what fraction of events completed within a given time?

Common percentiles include:

- **p50 (median):** Half of all events are faster than this. Good for baseline behavior.
- **p95:** 95% of events are faster than this. Shows the edge of the "typical" range.
- **p99 and p99.9:** The slowest 1% or 0.1% of events. These tails often reveal problems such as queue contention, garbage collection, or occasional retries.

In trading, it is common to see systems whose p50 latency is excellent but whose p99 is erratic. That can translate directly into missed opportunities or inconsistent execution quality. Your telemetry infrastructure should therefore track at least p50, p95, and p99 over rolling windows, at both end-to-end and per-hop levels.

Variance over time also matters. A system that occasionally exhibits slow outliers is one thing; a system whose tail latency gradually worsens over hours under heavy load is another. Both patterns should be visible on your dashboards.

## From Latency Measurements to SLOs

Armed with per-hop latency distributions, you can now define service level objectives. An SLO is a precise statement of intended performance, typically over a given time window. For example:

- "During continuous trading hours, 99% of orders should receive an acknowledgment from the exchange within 800 microseconds, measured end-to-end from the strategy host."
- "For this venue, our gateway processing p99 latency should remain below 150 microseconds in any 5-minute window."

These SLOs should build logically on the reliability objectives from the previous section. There, you asked: "How often can we be down?" Here, you ask: "How slow can we be before we consider ourselves out of spec, even if we are technically up?"

To be actionable, SLOs must be tied to:

- **Specific paths:** Per-venue and sometimes per-strategy. Different venues have different network distances and exchange behaviors.
- **Time windows:** Short enough to catch real-time degradation, long enough to smooth out noise. Common windows are 1, 5, or 15 minutes.
- **Business impact:** A mild SLO breach in the middle of a quiet trading day may matter less than the same breach during a volatile opening auction. Some firms weight breaches by market regime.

Once you have end-to-end SLOs, you can start allocating *budgets* to each hop.

## Per-Hop Latency Budgets

A latency budget is a target slice of the overall SLO assigned to a component or step. Suppose your end-to-end p99 SLO for a particular venue is 800 microseconds. A plausible budget decomposition might be:

- Strategy decision: 200 microseconds.

- Strategy-to-gateway network: 50 microseconds.
- Gateway processing (including risk): 150 microseconds.
- Gateway-to-exchange network: 300 microseconds.
- Exchange processing: 100 microseconds (not under your control, but part of the observed total).

These numbers are illustrative; the important aspect is the structure. Each component team now has a concrete target, and telemetry can show:

- Whether the component is meeting its own budget.
- Whether global SLO breaches are due to local budget overruns or external factors.

Budgets also guide optimization work. If your gateway consistently runs at 50 microseconds p99 against a 150 microsecond budget, while your strategy host occasionally exceeds its 200 microsecond budget during bursts, you know where to focus.

Per-hop budgets are not rigid constraints but design tools. It is acceptable for one component to exceed its budget if others are comfortably under, so long as the end-to-end SLO holds. That said, persistent budget overruns should trigger analysis before they turn into SLO regressions.

After introducing SLOs and budgets, it is helpful to see how they appear visually on an operations dashboard.

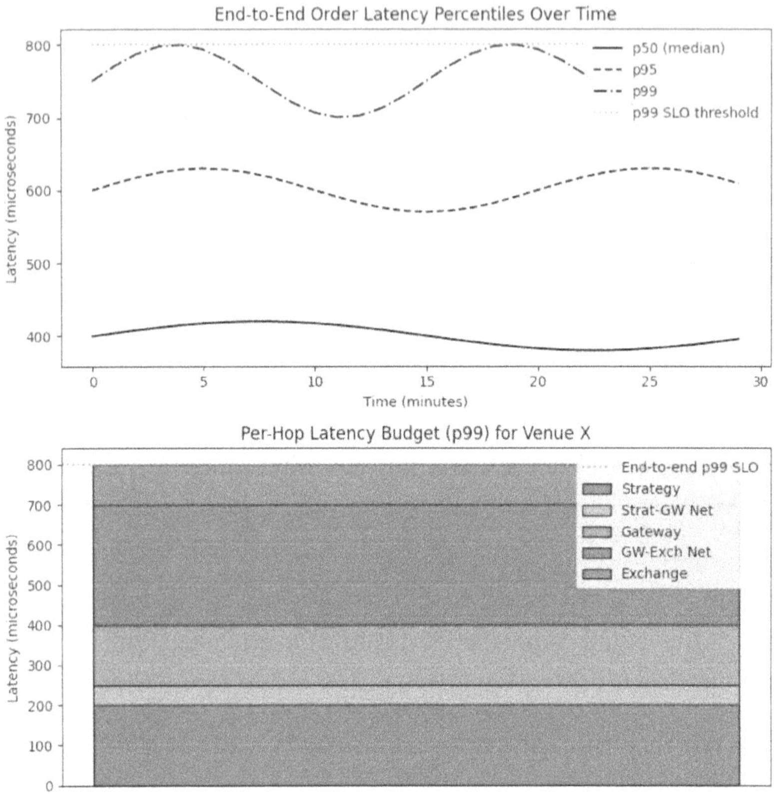


## Designing Dashboards that Separate Signal from Noise

With SLOs and budgets defined, the next step is to present them in a way that operators and developers can use during live trading. A well-designed latency dashboard should:

- **Start at end-to-end:** The first view should show p50, p95, and p99 over time for each key venue, with clear SLO lines visible.
- **Offer quick drill-downs:** From a venue-level chart, a single click or selection should reveal the per-hop contributions for the

same time window.

- **Separate internal and external sources:** By plotting exchange processing and external network separately from internal components, you can avoid chasing problems that lie outside your control.
- **Highlight changes rather than raw values:** Operators learn what "normal" looks like; dashboards should emphasize deviations from that baseline.

Avoid clutter. It is tempting to show every percentile, for every strategy, on one screen. In practice, that becomes unreadable. A practical pattern is:

- A high-level "trading health" dashboard showing a handful of key venues and summary metrics.
- Per-venue drill-down dashboards with detailed per-hop breakdowns and strategy-specific overlays.
- Specialized diagnostics dashboards used for deeper investigations, not for day-to-day monitoring.

The visual style matters. Distinct line styles (solid, dashed, dotted) are easier to distinguish when printed or viewed on low-quality displays than subtle colors. Clear labels and legends reduce the risk of misinterpretation during an incident.

## Alerting: When Should the System Shout?

Monitoring without alerting is passive: you only notice problems when someone actively looks at a dashboard. Alerting turns telemetry into a safety net by notifying you when metrics cross predefined thresholds.

However, naïve alerting can be worse than none. If the system pages people for every brief p99 spike, they will learn to ignore alerts. Your design must balance sensitivity with stability.

Key design choices include:

### Which Metrics to Alert On

Not every metric deserves an alert. Good candidates are:

- End-to-end p99 latency for high-priority venues.
- Component-level p99s for gateways, risk engines, and market data ingestion.
- Derived metrics such as queue depth or the gap between p99 and p50 (an indicator of growing jitter).

Avoid alerting on medians; p50 typically moves gently and mainly reflects normal load variation.

### Thresholds and Windows

Instead of alerting the moment a metric exceeds its threshold, require sustained breaches over a window:

- For transient network jitter, a 30-second spike may not justify intervention.
- For genuine regressions (for example, a misconfigured gateway), the metric will remain elevated over multiple minutes.

A common pattern is to define SLOs over longer windows (for example, a week) and then derive *alerting* thresholds using shorter windows. In practice:

- Use short windows (1–5 minutes) for "page" alerts that wake humans only when there is a strong, ongoing breach.
- Use longer windows (15–60 minutes) for "ticket" alerts that require investigation but are not urgent.

### Severity Levels

Not all alerts are equal. Establish clear severity levels, for example:

- **Critical:** SLO breach on end-to-end p99 for a major venue, sustained over several minutes, or loss of critical data paths.

- **High:** Component-level regressions that may soon impact end-to-end performance, such as gateway processing p99 doubling relative to baseline.
- **Medium/Low:** Slow drifts or anomalies worth investigating but not emergencies.

Each level should have predefined response expectations: who is notified, expected reaction time, and whether trading should be throttled or paused.

## Automated Responses and Safe Rollbacks

Alerts do not always need to result in human action. Some classes of latency regression are best handled automatically. Examples include:

- **Rolling back a deployment:** If latency metrics for a gateway or strategy degrade sharply immediately after a code release, an automated system can roll back to the previous version while raising an alert for deeper investigation.
- **Draining a node:** If one gateway instance shows abnormal processing latency or error rates, traffic can be gradually drained away to other instances while the suspect node is quarantined.
- **Adjusting throttles:** If market data ingestion starts falling behind, non-critical downstream consumers (for example, some analytics) can be temporarily slowed or paused to preserve the primary trading path.

These actions should be designed with the same care as failover logic in the previous section. They must be:

- **Deterministic:** The same conditions lead to the same action, and operators understand why.
- **Reversible:** There is a clear path back to normal operation once the underlying issue is resolved.
- **Auditable:** Decisions and their triggers are logged for post-incident review.

## Integrating Latency Telemetry into Post-Trade Analysis

Telemetry is not only for real-time operations. Historical latency data is a valuable input to both performance engineering and trading analysis.

From an engineering perspective, you can:

- Identify time-of-day patterns where latency tends to worsen, pointing to capacity issues or background tasks.
- Correlate latency changes with code deployments, configuration changes, or infrastructure upgrades.
- Quantify the impact of optimizations by comparing distributions before and after changes.

From a trading perspective, you can:

- Evaluate how execution quality varies with your own latency, especially during volatile periods.
- Study whether certain strategies are more sensitive to tail latency than others.
- Support conversations with venues by providing evidence of changing exchange-side processing times.

To make this feasible, you must retain summarized latency metrics over meaningful horizons (weeks or months), even if you discard fine-grained raw data sooner. Aggregated percentiles, counts, and derived statistics are usually sufficient.

## Telemetry as a Design Constraint

Finally, effective latency monitoring should influence how you design and evolve the trading system itself. Some examples:

- **Instrumentation as a first-class requirement:** Whenever a new component is introduced into the hot path, part of its design should include how it will be timed and reported in the end-to-end trace.
- **SLO-aware development:** Feature work should respect existing latency budgets, and any anticipated changes should be visible as shifts in those budgets, not as silent degradations.
- **Performance gates in CI/CD:** Before deploying new code, automated tests can run representative workloads and measure whether latency distributions remain within expected bounds. If not, the deployment is blocked.

The overarching philosophy is that latency is not an after-the-fact measurement; it is a design target that you enforce continuously. Monitoring and alerting provide the feedback loop that keeps low-latency architectures honest long after the first deployment.

Together with the redundancy and failover mechanisms from the previous section, a robust latency telemetry stack turns your trading platform from a black box into a well-instrumented machine. You gain the ability not only to survive failures, but to maintain a quantifiable, reliable edge in how quickly you see and act on market information.

## 10.3 Chaos Testing in Trading Systems

Redundancy and monitoring tell you how the system behaves when components fail or slow down *in theory*. Chaos testing asks a harder question: *what actually happens when we break things on purpose?*

In a live trading environment, this is not a rhetorical question. A kill switch that fires too late, a circuit breaker that never triggers, or a gateway that hangs silently instead of failing fast can all lead to real losses. Traditional testing—unit tests, functional tests, user acceptance tests—helps, but it largely assumes a cooperative world: networks are stable, dependencies respond, and clocks are well behaved. Production is not like that.

Chaos testing is the deliberate, controlled injection of failures into a *realistic* environment so you can observe how your system detects, contains, and recovers from them. In this section we will tailor chaos engineering ideas to trading systems, with particular attention to validating:

- Kill switches that halt trading when risk limits are threatened or system behavior is abnormal.
- Circuit breakers that isolate failing components, venues, or strategies.
- Recovery behavior of gateways, risk engines, and market data pipelines under stress.

The central idea is to let you discover weaknesses on your own terms, at your own pace, instead of allowing the market to find them for you on a busy day.

## Why Traditional Testing is Not Enough

Previous sections gave you architectures and telemetry. You can stand up redundant gateways, monitor end-to-end latency, and page people when SLOs are breached. Why is that not sufficient?

There are three main reasons.

**1. Complex, Emergent Failures**

Trading systems are made of interacting parts: networks, hardware, operating systems, runtimes, custom code, exchange links, and external data sources. Each component may behave correctly in isolation, yet the *combination* can fail in surprising ways. For example:

- A minor increase in packet loss causes the market data handler to fall behind, which in turn causes strategies to see stale prices and overreact.
- A risk engine slows down under burst load, which pushes orders into larger queues on the gateway, which then hit operating system limits and start dropping connections.

These behaviors are hard to anticipate with unit tests aimed at individual modules.

**2. Time and Load Sensitivity**

Many bugs only appear under specific timing conditions or loads:

- A kill switch that checks certain thresholds once per second may work fine in a test environment but be too slow during a genuine runaway strategy event.
- A circuit breaker that trips after five consecutive errors might work under steady failure, but not when failures are mixed with partial successes.

Reproducing these timing patterns requires more than a simple test plan; it requires actively shaping the environment, which is what chaos testing does.

**3. Overconfidence in Rare Paths**

The logic paths that matter most in safety—"panic modes," emergency shutdown, and failover—are precisely those that are executed least often. If you never exercise them under realistic conditions, you cannot trust them. A shutdown button that has never been pressed in anger may or may not work when you need it.

Chaos experiments address this by making rare paths *less rare*: you deliberately trigger them, observe them, and refine them.

# Principles of Safe Chaos in Trading

Chaos engineering originated in web and cloud services, where the worst outcome of a bad experiment might be degraded performance or temporary outages for users. In trading, stakes are different: there is client money at risk, regulatory scrutiny, and the possibility of creating erroneous trades.

Therefore, trading-specific chaos testing must follow stricter principles.

**Start in Non-Production Environments**

Your first experiments belong in realistic but isolated environments:

- Simulated market data feeds or historical replays.
- Exchange-provided test or certification environments.
- Sandboxes where orders are never sent to live markets.

The goal is to push your architecture and kill switches to their limits *without* endangering real capital. Only once you understand behavior there should you consider tightly constrained production experiments.

### Use Representative Workloads

Chaos without realistic activity is misleading. A gateway that recovers gracefully when idle may behave quite differently under sustained quote bursts. For meaningful results, your experiments should run against:

- Recorded periods of high volatility and market stress.
- Strategy traffic patterns that resemble real trading days: bursts, pauses, cross-venue activity.
- Risk limit configurations that match production, so kill switches and limits fire in realistic ways.

### Define Clear Safety Guardrails

Before injecting any failure, you must articulate what *must not* happen. Examples:

- No experiment may cause a real order to be sent with size or price outside predefined simulation bounds.
- No experiment may weaken or disable external risk controls (for example, broker-level pre-trade checks).
- In production, no experiment may run without real-time human oversight and an immediate abort mechanism.

Guardrails should be part of the experiment definition, not an afterthought.

## Designing a Chaos Experiment

Think of each experiment as a scientific test: you have a hypothesis, an intervention, measurements, and criteria for success.

**Step 1: Formulate a Hypothesis**

A good hypothesis ties a specific failure scenario to an expected system response, with clear timing. For example:

- "If a primary order gateway process crashes, all new orders from affected strategies are blocked or rerouted within 100 milliseconds, and no duplicate orders are sent."
- "If market data for a symbol becomes corrupted, the strategy will stop trading that symbol within 50 milliseconds and raise a high-severity alert."
- "If the exchange starts delaying acknowledgments beyond 1 millisecond, our circuit breaker will reduce order rates within 200 milliseconds to avoid oversizing queues."

Each hypothesis points to a kill switch, circuit breaker, or recovery mechanism you want to validate.

**Step 2: Choose Failure Injection Mechanisms**

You then choose how to create the adverse condition. In trading systems, common failure injections include:

- **Process kills:** Abruptly terminating a gateway, strategy, or risk engine process. This simulates crashes and unhandled exceptions.
- **CPU and resource stress:** Consuming CPU or memory on a host to simulate noisy neighbors or runaway processes.
- **Network partitions and degradation:** Blocking traffic between specific components, introducing packet loss, or adding artificial latency.
- **Message corruption or drops:** Altering or discarding a fraction of market data messages or order acknowledgments.

- **External dependency failures:** Simulating slow or failing calls to reference data services, pricing libraries, or internal APIs.

Each mechanism must be precise and reversible. For instance, instead of randomly dropping packets across the entire network, you might drop every tenth message on a single market data multicast group for a 30-second window.

**Step 3: Instrument and Observe**

You cannot run meaningful chaos experiments without visibility. The monitoring and alerting stack from the previous section is your primary tool:

- Measure end-to-end and per-hop latencies during the experiment.
- Track order rates, rejection rates, error logs, and queue depths.
- Record when each kill switch or circuit breaker triggered and with what parameters.

It is also useful to tag your telemetry with experiment identifiers and start/end times, so you can easily separate experiment-induced behaviors from background noise.

**Step 4: Define Success and Abort Criteria**

Before starting, decide:

- What counts as a successful outcome? For example: kill switch triggered within 100 milliseconds, no orders leaked after threshold breach, circuit breaker opened as expected.
- What conditions require you to abort the experiment? For example: unexpected surge in rejected orders beyond test scope, unexpected high latency on unrelated venues, or internal alarms indicating risk exposure.

These criteria protect you from drifting into unsafe territory and keep experiments focused.

## Validating Kill Switches

Kill switches are mechanisms that halt trading quickly when certain conditions are met. In many firms, they are implemented at several layers:

- **Strategy-level switches:** Stop a single strategy or symbol when it behaves abnormally.
- **Gateway-level switches:** Block outbound orders from a group of strategies or clients.
- **Firm-level switches:** Halt all trading activity, often by instructing upstream brokers or clearing members.

Chaos tests for kill switches focus on both correctness and timing.

**Scenario: Runaway Strategy**

Hypothesis: "If a strategy starts sending orders at ten times its normal rate, the gateway-level kill switch will block new orders from that strategy within 200 milliseconds and log the event."

Experiment design:

- In a replay environment, configure a strategy instance to ignore its usual rate limits and fire orders as fast as possible for selected symbols.
- Monitor gateway-side rate counters and the kill switch threshold.
- Observe when the switch trips, how quickly order rates drop, and how the strategy is notified.

Questions to answer:

- Did any orders slip through after the kill switch should have triggered?
- Did the switch affect unrelated strategies or clients?

- Was the event clearly surfaced to operators and logged for future analysis?

**Scenario: Loss Limit Breach**

Hypothesis: "If intraday realized loss for a desk exceeds a predefined threshold, new orders from that desk will be blocked within one second, while existing working orders are canceled promptly."

Experiment design:

- Use a simulated P&L feed to the risk system, artificially accelerating losses for a given desk.
- Confirm that, once the threshold is crossed, the risk system signals the gateway to block new orders and send cancels for active ones.
- Check that the trading UI and alerts reflect the situation clearly.

This type of test validates the entire chain from P&L calculation through risk logic to gateway enforcement and operator awareness.

## Exercising Circuit Breakers and Throttles

Circuit breakers are mechanisms that sense failing or overloaded components and isolate them. Throttles adjust the rate of activity to keep the system within safe operating bounds. In trading architectures, you may have:

- Per-venue or per-gateway circuit breakers that stop sending orders when error rates or latencies spike.
- Per-client or per-strategy throttles that limit orders per second.
- Market data circuit breakers that stop consuming corrupted feeds.

Chaos testing can validate these in several ways.

### Scenario: Exchange Latency Spike

Hypothesis: "If exchange-side processing latency for orders exceeds 2 milliseconds for more than 30 seconds, our venue circuit breaker will reduce order rates by 50% and, if conditions persist, fully halt new orders while allowing cancels."

Experiment design:

- In a test environment, introduce artificial delays into acknowledgments and execution reports from the simulated exchange.
- Monitor end-to-end latency and the derived metric for exchange processing time.
- Observe when the circuit breaker logic engages partial throttling and when it escalates to a full stop.

Key checks:

- Are thresholds and time windows calibrated realistically, or are they too sensitive/too lax?
- Do throttles ramp down smoothly, or is the behavior erratic?
- Are cancel messages still being processed quickly even when new orders are blocked?

### Scenario: Market Data Corruption

Hypothesis: "If we detect malformed or inconsistent market data messages for a symbol, the market data circuit breaker will mark that symbol as "trading disabled" and prevent strategies from acting on it until the feed is healthy again."

Experiment design:

- Inject occasional malformed messages into the market data stream for specific symbols in a replay environment.
- Validate that parsing errors or book consistency checks raise a flag.

- Confirm that, while flagged, strategies cannot place orders for those symbols and that alerts are raised.

This kind of experiment protects against silent, bad data—a common root cause of trading incidents.

# Testing Recovery Behavior

Failover architectures are built with assumptions about how components will restart and recover state. Chaos testing challenges those assumptions.

**Gateway Crash and Restart**

Hypothesis: "When a primary gateway crashes during active trading, the standby gateway takes over within 300 milliseconds, and all order state is consistent."

Experiment design in a non-production environment:

- Run active trading traffic through a primary gateway while a standby gateway maintains replicated state, as designed.
- Abruptly kill the primary gateway process.
- Observe:
  - Time until the standby is declared active and starts accepting new orders.
  - Whether pending orders are still correctly tracked and whether cancels work.
  - Whether duplicate orders are sent due to replay or re-submission.

Compare the observed recovery time and behavior to the expectations set in your reliability objectives. If reality is worse, you now have concrete data to improve state replication and failover logic.

**Network Partition Between Strategy and Gateway**

Hypothesis: "If the network link between a strategy and its gateway is interrupted, the strategy will stop placing new orders immediately, cancel any in-flight ones when possible, and either reconnect cleanly or fail over to another gateway according to policy."

Experiment design:

- In a controlled setup, begin normal trading activity.
- Introduce a network rule that drops packets between the strategy host and its gateway.
- Watch how quickly:
  - Heartbeats fail and the disconnection is detected.
  - The strategy stops sending new orders or attempts to reconnect.
  - Any configured failover to alternative gateways or venues occurs.

This tests not only technical behavior but also the strategy's logic for handling partial connectivity loss.

## What Not to Test in Production

Some organizations are tempted to run aggressive chaos experiments directly against production to "really know" how systems behave. In trading, this is often too risky. A prudent division is:

**Safe for Carefully-Controlled Production Experiments**

With strict guardrails, you might consider:

- Restarting a redundant, non-primary gateway during off-peak hours to confirm that failover is seamless.
- Introducing a tiny amount of additional latency or rate limiting on *non-critical* internal services to verify that latency alerts fire and automated rollbacks work.

- Temporarily draining a single node from a gateway cluster to exercise load redistribution, under watchful human supervision.

These experiments should always be reversible, with a clear rollback path, and announced to relevant teams.

**Never Chaos-Test Live**

Certain actions should remain firmly in the realm of non-production:

- Corrupting live market data streams or altering price information.
- Intentionally dropping live orders or exchange acknowledgments.
- Disabling or bypassing external risk controls or regulatory reporting paths.

The potential damage to clients, counterparties, and your firm's reputation far outweighs the benefits.

## Operationalizing Chaos: From One-Off Tests to Discipline

To be effective, chaos testing must evolve from occasional ad hoc exercises into a regular practice.

**Scheduling and Runbooks**

Define a cadence, such as:

- Monthly themed chaos weeks in non-production environments, focusing on one class of failures (for example, gateway crashes this month, market data next).
- Quarterly major incident simulations that involve both technical and operational teams.

For each experiment type, maintain a runbook:

- Steps to prepare the environment and verify that guardrails are in place.
- Exact commands or configurations used to inject failures.
- Metrics and dashboards to watch before, during, and after.
- Checklist of success and abort criteria.

This documentation turns chaos testing into a repeatable process rather than an art.

**Integrating with Release Pipelines**

Some chaos experiments can become part of your regular release process:

- Before promoting a new gateway version, run a standard suite of crash-and-restart experiments in the staging environment.
- Before enabling a new kill switch or circuit breaker in production, validate it through targeted chaos tests in replay environments.

Automating these steps where appropriate ensures that new code does not silently weaken your safety posture.

**Feeding Back into Architecture and Monitoring**

Every experiment, successful or not, should result in concrete learning:

- Did some alert trigger too late or not at all? Update monitoring thresholds or instrumentation.
- Did a component recover functionally but with degraded latency? Adjust redundancy design or capacity plans.
- Did operators find dashboards confusing during the experiment? Improve visualizations and training.

Over time, this feedback loop tightens the connection between architecture, observability, and operations. Your system does not just become more resilient; your *confidence* in its resilience becomes grounded in repeated, observed behavior.

### From Fear of Failure to Informed Confidence

Chaos testing in trading systems is not about recklessness. It is about replacing vague fear—"What if the gateway fails during a fast market?"—with informed confidence: "We have repeatedly crashed the gateway under realistic load; failover happens in 250 milliseconds, kill switches trip as designed, and operators know what to look for."

Combined with redundancy, failover architectures, and robust latency monitoring, chaos testing completes the reliability picture. You not only design for safety and speed; you continually verify that those designs survive contact with the messy reality of live markets.

## 10.4 Compliance, Audit Trails, and Data Retention

So far in this chapter we have focused on keeping the trading system fast and resilient: redundant architectures, latency monitoring, and chaos tests. In production, however, you are never only optimizing for speed. You also operate under regulatory and contractual obligations: you must be able to prove what happened, when it happened, and that records have not been tampered with.

This section explains how to satisfy those obligations—timestamping, signing, and retaining trading records—while keeping compliance input/output and storage work off the latency-critical path. The challenge is to design auditability as a parallel system: always present, always accurate, but never blocking the flow from market data to trading decision to order.

### What Regulators and Stakeholders Need

Different jurisdictions and asset classes impose different rules, but the core themes are remarkably consistent. Regulators, clients, and internal control functions all need you to provide at least the following:

- **Precise timestamps:** Events must be time-stamped according to a documented time source (for example, synchronized to UTC) with known accuracy and drift bounds.
- **Reconstructible order lifecycles:** For each order, you must be able to reconstruct the full chain of events: who initiated it, which systems touched it, what messages went to and from the exchange, and how it was modified or canceled.
- **Immutability and integrity:** Once records are written, they must not be silently altered. If corrections are needed, they must be additive (for example, new records that supersede old ones) with clear audit trails.
- **Retention:** Records must be stored for years, sometimes a decade or more, in a way that allows retrieval for regulatory inquiries and internal investigations.
- **Support for surveillance and best execution:** Data must be rich enough for surveillance teams to detect suspicious activity and for best-execution analysis to verify that client orders received appropriate handling.

All of this must be provided even when the trading system is under stress or experiencing partial failures. From an architectural perspective, that means:

> You must separate the *latency-critical trading path* from the *compliance and audit path*, while ensuring the latter still reliably receives all the necessary information.

## Separating Hot Path from Compliance Path

Recall the core latency-critical chain:

Market Data → Strategy → Risk → Gateway → Exchange

Every additional operation you insert into this chain—disk writes, compression, encryption, remote calls—adds variability. Compliance requirements, on the other hand, often encourage heavy-weight operations: durable storage, cryptographic signatures, multiple copies of data.

The key design principle is therefore:

> The trading path should emit a minimal, structured stream of events to an *asynchronous* audit pipeline, which handles the heavy work outside the hot loop.

Concretely, this leads to a two-lane view of the system:

- A **hot lane** where decisions are made and orders are transmitted with minimal and deterministic overhead.
- A **compliance lane** that processes a copy of those events, enriches them, signs them, and writes them to durable storage.

The engineering challenge is to define the interface between these lanes so that:

- The hot lane only pays a small, bounded cost for emitting events.
- The compliance lane can lag slightly behind in time but must *never* lose events.

## Designing the Audit Event Stream

The first step is to define what, exactly, you emit from the trading path. Think of this as an internal "audit protocol" that describes all the important events and their fields. Typical event types include:

- **Order events:** New order, modify, cancel, partial fill, full fill, reject.
- **Session events:** Logon, logout, connection drop, reconnection, sequence resets.
- **Risk and limit events:** Limit checks, breaches, kill switch activations, throttling actions.

- **Market data reference events:** Key price updates used in decision making, especially around important orders or risk decisions.

For each event, you typically capture:

- A high-precision timestamp (with time source and accuracy documented elsewhere).
- Unique identifiers: internal order ID, client ID, strategy ID, venue, and any external exchange order IDs.
- The event type and relevant parameters (for example, price, size, side, symbol).
- The identity of the component that produced the event (strategy name, gateway instance, risk engine).

Well-designed identifiers are crucial. A single immutable internal order ID that follows the order across all systems, plus explicit mapping to exchange-assigned IDs, makes later reconstruction vastly easier. Similarly, stable identifiers for strategies, desks, and clients help both surveillance and performance analysis.

## Low-Overhead Emission from the Hot Path

Once you know what to emit, the next question is how to do it without harming latency. A few patterns are particularly effective:

### In-Memory Write-Ahead Buffers

Instead of writing events directly to disk or over the network from the trading loop, each process appends them to an in-memory buffer or queue. Characteristics of a good buffer:

- **Lock-free or low-lock:** Writing to the buffer should be almost as cheap as writing to a thread-local structure.
- **Bounded and monitored:** The buffer has high but finite capacity, and metrics track how full it becomes.

- **Single-responsibility consumer:** One or a small number of dedicated threads or processes read from this buffer and handle onward transmission to the compliance lane.

From the trading code's point of view, emitting an event is a local memory operation and a pointer update, which can be made very cheap and predictable.

### Batching and Append-Only Queues

The consumer reading from the write-ahead buffer can batch events into larger units before writing them to disk or sending them over the network. Batching amortizes the cost of system calls and network headers:

- Instead of flushing every event, flush at regular intervals (for example, every few milliseconds) or when a batch reaches a certain size.
- Use append-only log structures, where writes are sequential and do not require expensive seeks or updates.

Append-only designs are naturally aligned with audit needs: they produce a chronological sequence of events that is easy to hash, compress, and replicate.

### Asynchronous Flow Control

What if the compliance lane is slow or temporarily unavailable? You must not let backpressure from audit storage propagate into the hot path.

Mechanisms to achieve this include:

- **Generous buffering:** Sizing in-memory queues and local disk logs to handle plausible bursts and temporary downstream outages.
- **Graceful degradation policies:** If buffers begin to fill, it is better to fail over to local disk logging (with later upload) than to block trading threads. In extreme conditions, firm-level risk controls may require you to slow or halt trading rather than trade without audit trails; that policy decision must be explicit.

- **Clear metrics and alerts:** Rising buffer occupancy should trigger operator awareness well before it threatens the trading path.

The architectural rule is that the hot path never waits for a remote compliance component in the normal case. Only explicit, high-level control decisions (for example, "we do not trade if we cannot create audit records for $N_{minutes}$") should connect compliance health to trading availability.

## Signing and Integrity Without Hot-Path Penalties

Regulators and auditors care not only that records exist, but that they have not been silently altered. Cryptographic signing and hashing are common tools for this. The challenge is to apply them without putting heavy cryptographic work into the trading thread.

An effective pattern is to sign or hash *batches* of events rather than each event individually:

- The compliance lane aggregates events into blocks (for example, thousands of events or a few megabytes of data).
- For each block, it computes a hash (such as a cryptographic digest) and stores that hash in a separate, possibly more secure store.
- Optionally, blocks can be chained: the hash of each block includes the hash of the previous block, forming a tamper-evident chain.

This design has several advantages:

- Cryptographic computations occur off the hot path, executed by dedicated processes or hardware.
- The cost per event is tiny, as one hash covers many events.
- Any later modification of the stored data breaks the chain, making tampering detectable.

Depending on legal and internal requirements, you may use:

- Digital signatures with private keys held in hardware security modules for the highest assurance.
- Simpler keyed hashes stored in restricted, replicated databases where only a small, well-audited service can write.

The crucial point is that signing is applied to already-collected audit blocks, not enforced synchronously on every order decision.

## Timekeeping and Timestamp Documentation

Earlier we emphasized synchronized clocks for latency measurement. The same time discipline underpins legal audit trails. For each deployment, you should be able to document:

- The primary time sources (for example, PTP grandmasters, GPS receivers).
- The accuracy and maximum drift between host clocks and those sources.
- Procedures for handling leap seconds, time source failures, and clock adjustments.

In many regimes, the requirement is not perfection but traceability. If, years later, a regulator asks, "How do you know these timestamps were accurate to within $X$ microseconds?", you should be able to provide:

- Configuration records and change logs for your time synchronization systems.
- Periodic measurements of clock offsets stored alongside operational metrics.
- Any incident reports related to timekeeping problems and their remediation.

Crucially, some of this meta-information should be linked to the audit trail itself. For example, you might include in daily audit summaries:

- The identity and status of time sources used that day.
- The maximum observed offset for trading hosts.
- Any failover events between time sources.

This way, questions about timestamp reliability get concrete, data-backed answers instead of vague assurances.

## Reconstructing Order Lifecycles

One of the most demanding uses of audit data is reconstructing an order's full history in response to an inquiry. This is where earlier design choices about identifiers and event structure pay off.

To make reconstruction straightforward:

- Use a single immutable *internal order ID* from the moment a strategy decides to place an order. This ID should appear in:
  - Strategy logs and audit events.
  - Gateway logs and in-flight state.
  - Mapping tables to exchange order IDs.
- Record every state transition as a separate event: created, routed, acknowledged, partially filled, modified, canceled, rejected.
- Avoid overwriting or in-place updates in audit stores. Instead, append new events that refer to the internal order ID and describe state changes.

When a regulator asks, “Why was this client order filled at that price?”, an investigator should be able to:

1. Search the audit store by client ID and external reference to find your internal order ID.

2. Retrieve all events with that internal order ID, sorted by timestamp.
3. Inspect related events: risk checks, kill switch activities, strategy signals, and any manual interventions.

To support this, audit storage systems typically provide:

- Indexes on key fields (internal order ID, client ID, symbol, venue).
- Efficient retrieval by time range (for example, "all events on this date for this desk").
- Access controls so only authorized teams can perform sensitive searches.

Again, these features belong to the compliance lane. The trading hot path only needs to ensure that each emitted event contains the fields required for later indexing and analysis.

## Retention and Tiered Storage

Regulatory retention periods often span years. Storing all raw data at the same performance and cost level as recent data is usually wasteful. A tiered storage strategy balances cost and access patterns:

- **Hot storage:** Recent weeks or months of data stored on relatively fast, query-friendly systems. Used for day-to-day surveillance, incident triage, and performance analysis.
- **Warm storage:** Older data compressed and stored on cheaper media but still reasonably accessible (for example, slower disks, object stores). Used for less frequent queries and regulatory audits.
- **Cold storage / archives:** Very old data placed in long-term archival systems, often with higher retrieval latency but lower cost, sometimes with write-once-read-many properties.

The compliance lane is responsible for aging data between tiers. This process should be:

- **Automatic and logged:** Data movement should follow defined policies and generate its own audit events.
- **Integrity-preserving:** Hashes or signatures must remain valid across moves, or new integrity markers must be generated and linked.
- **Non-disruptive:** Archival jobs should not contend with active trading workloads; schedule them when markets are closed or system load is low.

Retention policies must also cover derived data sets: surveillance summaries, best execution reports, and operational incident timelines. These may have different retention horizons than raw event logs, but they should reference original records via stable identifiers.

## Cost Controls Without Cutting Corners

Compliance infrastructure can become expensive: storage, compute for processing and signing, and staff to maintain it. The temptation is to economize in ways that quietly reduce coverage or fidelity. Better approaches manage cost without compromising obligations:

- **Summarization with raw backups:** Keep detailed, query-optimized summaries for recent data while archiving raw logs in cheaper formats. This allows common analyses to be fast while preserving the ability to perform rare, detailed reconstructions.
- **Compression tuned to access patterns:** Compress older data more aggressively, accepting higher CPU overhead on rare reads, while keeping recent data lightly compressed for frequent access.
- **Scope-aware storage:** Separate highly sensitive, tightly regulated records from more routine operational logs so that the most stringent (and costly) controls only apply where necessary.

Cost discussions should be explicit about risk trade-offs. For example, if you propose to reduce the resolution of certain telemetry logs after three months to save space, you should state how that might affect future forensic capabilities or best-execution analyses.

## Operational Considerations and Failure Modes

Even well-designed compliance pipelines can fail. Disks fill, processes crash, and network segments become unavailable. You must treat the compliance lane as a first-class system with its own reliability objectives:

- **Redundancy:** Just as you replicate trading gateways, replicate key compliance components: log collectors, signing services, and storage endpoints.
- **Monitoring and alerts:** Track ingestion lag, buffer occupancy, error rates, and signing service health. Alerts should fire long before you risk data loss.
- **Disaster recovery:** Ensure that audit stores are replicated offsite according to policy and that recovery procedures are tested.

A particularly important failure mode is silent data loss: events that never reach the audit store. To minimize this risk:

- Use at-least-once delivery semantics when moving events from hot-path buffers to compliance storage. This may result in duplicates, but duplicates are easier to handle than missing records.
- Include sequence numbers or unique event IDs in audit messages, allowing downstream systems to detect and de-duplicate events.
- Periodically reconcile counts: compare the number of events emitted by trading components with the number ingested by audit stores, per time window and event type.

If reconciliation reveals discrepancies, investigate immediately and treat unexplained gaps as serious incidents. Regulatory regimes often assume that incomplete records are worse than explicit negative records.

### Bringing It All Together

Compliance, audit trails, and data retention can feel like a burden added on top of trading. Architecturally, however, they are a natural extension of the themes already developed in this chapter:

- From *redundancy and failover*, you borrow the idea of parallel paths and resilient infrastructures for critical functions.
- From *monitoring and alerting*, you inherit techniques for timestamping, latency measurement, and health reporting—applied here to audit pipelines.
- From *chaos testing*, you can devise experiments that simulate compliance component failures and verify that trading either continues safely or halts according to policy.

By treating compliance as a carefully designed, asynchronous companion to the hot trading path, you can satisfy strict regulatory obligations without sacrificing latency. Orders continue to flow at microsecond speeds, while in the background a robust pipeline captures, signs, and preserves the evidence that proves you did the right thing.

## 10.5 Incident Response Playbooks

The previous sections of this chapter focused on building systems that are robust by design and constantly monitored: redundant architectures, latency telemetry, chaos testing, and compliant audit trails. Even with all of that, incidents will still happen. Markets change, exchanges misbehave, software has bugs, and humans make mistakes.

This section is about what happens *next*: how your team responds in the first seconds, minutes, and hours after something goes wrong. The quality of that response often matters more to clients and regulators than whether the system was perfect to begin with. A disciplined response can contain losses, preserve evidence, and build trust. A chaotic response can turn a recoverable glitch into a lasting reputational problem.

An *incident response playbook* is a set of agreed procedures that tells everyone what to do under stress. It defines roles, communication patterns, decision trees, and forensic steps. The aim is not to script every detail, but to remove ambiguity when time is short.

## What Counts as an Incident?

The first step is deciding which situations trigger the playbook. Not every small glitch justifies an incident declaration; otherwise the process becomes noise. At the same time, you must not ignore early signs of serious issues.

Typical trading incidents include:

- **Latency blowups:** End-to-end or component p99 latency suddenly doubles or worse, especially during active market periods.
- **Misrouted or erroneous orders:** Orders going to the wrong venue, wrong symbol, or wrong account; orders with unintended size or price.
- **Stale or incorrect prices:** Strategies acting on outdated market data, or internal prices diverging from venue prices.
- **Partial outages:** Some venues, strategies, or client flows are unavailable or degraded while others are fine.
- **External venue issues:** Exchange session drops, halts, asymmetric behavior (for example, one side of the book not updating).

A practical approach is to define *severity levels* based on impact:

- **SEV 1 (Critical):** Potential or actual financial loss above a threshold, regulatory breach, widespread client impact, or loss of control over trading behavior.

- **SEV 2 (High):** Significant degradation (for example, inability to trade a major venue) but with risk still under control.
- **SEV 3 (Medium):** Limited impact to a particular strategy or client, or degraded performance with safe fallbacks in place.
- **SEV 4 (Low):** Minor anomalies worth tracking but not requiring immediate coordinated action.

The playbook should state who can declare each severity and how. A useful guideline is: *when in doubt, temporarily declare a higher severity*. It is easier to downgrade an incident after gaining clarity than to explain why you waited too long to escalate.

## Roles in a Trading Incident

Incidents are stressful. Without clear roles, everyone talks and no one decides. A good playbook assigns responsibilities explicitly. In a trading context, common roles include:

- **Incident Commander (IC):** Owns the overall response. Decides priorities, assigns tasks, and has the final say on actions such as invoking kill switches or halting trading. There is exactly one IC at any time.
- **Trading Liaison:** Represents the trading desk(s). Communicates trading priorities, risk tolerance, and client impact. Provides context (for example, "this symbol is core to a major client").
- **SRE/Engineering Lead:** Coordinates technical diagnosis and remediation. Delegates to specialists for networking, gateways, databases, and so on.
- **Communications Lead:** Manages information flow to internal and external stakeholders: senior management, client coverage, potentially regulators. Ensures messages are consistent and clear.

- **Compliance and Risk Observer:** Ensures that regulatory obligations and internal risk limits are respected during the response. Advises on when to escalate to formal reporting.

In smaller organizations, one person may wear multiple hats, but the *roles* must still be conceptually distinct. For example, if the same individual acts as both IC and Communications Lead, they must be aware when they are making technical decisions versus drafting client messages.

The playbook should specify:

- How these roles are assigned (for example, rotation schedules, on-call rosters).
- How handovers occur if an incident runs long.
- Who acts as backup if a primary role holder is unavailable.

Clarity here prevents confusion during the first few minutes of an incident, when fast decisions matter most.

## Communication Channels Under Stress

In a trading outage, you may not be able to rely on normal channels. For example, your internal messaging platform could be affected by the same network issues that hit trading. Playbooks should therefore define:

- **Primary incident channel:** A dedicated chat room or bridge for the incident team. This is where real-time decisions and updates happen.
- **Secondary channel:** A fallback (for example, phone bridge, alternative messaging system) to use if the primary is degraded.
- **Out-of-band contact list:** Phone numbers or other contact methods for key roles, stored somewhere accessible even if internal systems are down.

Simple rules keep communication effective:

- The IC controls the main incident channel, keeps discussion focused, and periodically summarizes the situation.
- All key decisions and their timestamps are written into the channel, not only spoken, so they become part of the incident record.
- Side issues go to secondary or one-to-one discussions to avoid cluttering the main channel.

From the perspective of later analysis and compliance, the incident channel's transcript is part of the forensic trail. It complements the system logs and audit events already discussed in earlier sections.

## Immediate Actions: Stabilize First, Then Optimize

When an incident is detected, the first instinct of many engineers is to "debug" by changing things: restarting processes, tweaking configurations, or deploying fixes. The playbook should enforce a more controlled approach:

1. **Detect and declare:** As soon as someone observes a serious issue (for example, SLO alerts fire, traders report unexpected behavior), they raise a potential incident. The appropriate severity is declared, and the IC is assigned.
2. **Stabilize the system:** The immediate goal is to reduce risk exposure, not to fully diagnose root cause. Examples:
   - Invoke kill switches or throttles to halt or slow new trading on affected venues or strategies.
   - Switch order flow to backup gateways, venues, or less aggressive strategies if safe to do so.
   - If in doubt about data quality, stop trading on symbols with questionable prices.
3. **Preserve evidence:** Ensure that logs, packet captures, configuration snapshots, and telemetry from the period of interest are preserved and not overwritten.

4. **Only then, investigate and remediate:** Once the system is in a safer state (risk contained, trading paused or limited), focus shifts toward diagnosis and repair.

The ordering matters. Many of the worst trading incidents in history were made worse because teams prioritized keeping trading going over ensuring that it was still *safe* to trade.

## Decision Trees for Common Incident Types

To reduce decision time under pressure, playbooks often include simple decision trees for recurring scenarios. These are not rigid scripts, but starting points.

**Example: Latency Blowup on a Single Venue**

1. **Confirm the signal:** Do monitoring dashboards and on-desk observations agree that end-to-end p99 latency has degraded materially on venue X?
2. **Check scope:** Is the problem:
   - Only on this venue?
   - Only for certain strategies or client flows?
   - Coincident with known exchange events (for example, auction, halt)?
3. **Assess risk:** Is the increased latency causing:
   - Execution quality issues (for example, frequent price slippage)?
   - Risk limit breaches or near misses due to delayed risk checks?
4. **Decide on action:** Depending on answers:
   - *Mild impact:* Continue trading with heightened monitoring; consider temporarily reducing aggressiveness or order size.

- *Moderate impact:* Route flow away from affected gateway instance or network path; activate alternate routes if available.
- *Severe impact:* Halt new orders on the venue while allowing cancels; escalate to SEV 1 if risk is high.

5. **Communicate:** Trading liaison informs desks about the change; Communications Lead prepares internal update and, if needed, client messaging.

### Example: Suspected Mispricing or Bad Market Data

1. **Validate data:** Compare internal prices for the symbol against:
   - Alternative feeds (for example, backup multicast group, consolidated feed).
   - Exchange reference data (for example, last trade, indicative auction price).
2. **If discrepancy confirmed:**
   - Immediately disable trading in the affected symbol(s) or venue(s) for all strategies that depend on that feed.
   - Mark feeds as "suspect" in monitoring systems.
3. **Investigate cause:** Is the issue:
   - External (exchange sending bad data)?
   - Internal (bug in parser, dropped sequence, incorrect replay)?
   - **Decide on reopening:** Only after clear evidence that prices are correct and feeds stable should trading be re-enabled, possibly with initial limits.

### Example: Runaway Strategy or Kill Switch Trigger

1. **Confirm the trigger:** Did the kill switch fire due to:
   - Volume/rate limits?

  - P&L losses?
  - Error rates or anomalous behavior?

2. **Freeze and contain:**
   - Ensure that no new orders are emitted from the affected strategy.
   - Cancel outstanding orders if not already done.
   - Verify that related risk limits are enforced across all venues.

3. **Assess market impact:** Were clients or counterparties affected? Is there residual exposure?

4. **Communicate and investigate:** Inform trading and risk; begin root cause analysis with logs and telemetry.

5. **Re-enable only with care:** Strategy restarts should require explicit approval from risk and trading, not just a technical "fix and go".

Embedding such decision structures in the playbook shortens response time and reduces the chance of inconsistent behavior between different incidents or shifts.

## Forensic Data: Capturing the Right Evidence

When something goes wrong, one of the most common regrets is: "We wish we had more data from the critical window." The monitoring and compliance sections of this chapter already described how to collect and retain rich telemetry and audit trails. During an incident, the playbook should specify additional steps to preserve evidence:

- **Snapshot key logs:** Copy relevant logs (gateway, strategy, risk engine, network devices) from impacted hosts for the incident timeframe. Mark them as "do not rotate" until the investigation is complete.

- **Capture network traces:** If feasible and legal, start or preserve packet captures on critical links (for example, exchange connections, market data feeds) to analyze protocol-level behavior.

- **Record configuration state:** Save current versions of important configuration files, risk limit settings, and routing tables. Many incidents are driven by unintended config changes.
- **Tag telemetry:** Mark in monitoring systems when the incident began and when major actions occurred. This annotation simplifies later correlation.

It is important that these steps do not themselves destabilize the system. Large-scale packet captures or log-level increases can hurt performance if done indiscriminately. The playbook should therefore:

- Define lightweight default capture actions that are safe to apply immediately.
- Provide guidance on heavier capture actions that require IC and engineering lead approval.

From a compliance standpoint, preserving these artifacts is essential. They form the factual basis for explaining the incident to regulators and clients, and for demonstrating that you responded appropriately.

## Coordinating with Compliance, Legal, and Clients

Trading incidents are rarely purely technical. They have legal, regulatory, and client-relations dimensions. The playbook should outline:

- **When to notify compliance and legal:** For example, any SEV 1 incident, any event with potential client detriment, or any situation that might trigger mandatory regulatory reporting.
- **Who can speak externally:** Typically, only designated individuals (for example, Communications Lead, senior management, or legal) communicate with clients, regulators, or the media. Others should route inquiries through them.
- **What to avoid saying:** Do not speculate, assign blame, or promise timelines prematurely. Focus on known facts and immediate steps being taken.

A simple and honest message such as "We are experiencing a technical issue affecting trading on venue X; we have halted new orders while we investigate and will update you again in N minutes" is often better than silence or overly detailed guesses.

Clear communication reduces the secondary damage from an incident: loss of trust. It also helps align expectations internally so that technical teams are not pressured into unsafe quick fixes.

## Ending the Incident and Returning to Normal

At some point, the system is stable again: risk is under control, trading has been safely resumed or adjusted, and no further immediate action is needed. The playbook should describe how to formally *close* the incident:

- The IC announces closure in the incident channel, with a brief summary of what happened, what was done, and what remains to be followed up.
- Monitoring is set to heightened watch for a defined period (for example, the rest of the session), in case the issue recurs.
- Any temporary measures (for example, disabled strategies, reduced limits) are documented along with their planned rollback conditions.

Closure does not mean forgetting. It means that the response shifts from real-time operations to retrospective analysis.

## Post-Incident Reviews: Learning Without Blame

A post-incident review (often called a post-mortem) is where you turn an unpleasant experience into lasting improvement. The playbook should mandate such reviews for significant incidents, with the following characteristics:

### Timely and Structured

Hold the review soon after the incident (for example, within a week), while memories are fresh. Use a structured format:

- Timeline of events: detection, declaration, key actions, and closure.
- Impact: financial, client-facing, operational.
- Technical cause(s): proximate triggers and deeper contributing factors.
- Response evaluation: what worked well, what slowed you down.
- Action items: concrete steps with owners and target dates.

### Blameless but Honest

People are more likely to reveal useful information if they are not afraid of punishment. The goal is to improve the system, not to shame individuals. At the same time, the review must be honest about:

- Design flaws or missing safeguards.
- Inadequate or misleading monitoring.
- Playbook gaps (for example, undefined decision paths).
- Human errors, viewed as symptoms of deeper systemic issues (for example, overly complex procedures, insufficient training).

### Connecting Back to Architecture and Operations

Finally, the review should explicitly feed its conclusions back into:

- **Architecture changes:** Adjusting redundancy, failover, or compliance pipelines to prevent recurrence or limit impact.
- **Monitoring and alerting:** Adding or refining metrics and alerts that would have detected the problem earlier or more clearly.
- **Chaos testing plans:** Designing new experiments that simulate the incident conditions to verify improved resilience.
- **Playbook updates and training:** Updating decision trees and running drills so future teams are better prepared.

Action items should be tracked like any other work: in backlogs, with prioritization based on risk and impact. Otherwise, lessons fade, and the same patterns recur.

### From Ad Hoc Reactions to Operational Discipline

A mature trading organization treats incidents as inevitable but manageable. The difference between a fragile and resilient firm is less about the absence of bugs and more about the presence of disciplined, well-practiced responses.

Incident response playbooks are the bridge between the technical mechanisms described earlier in this chapter and the human processes that activate them under pressure. They ensure that:

- Kill switches, circuit breakers, and failover paths are used correctly and promptly, not improvised.
- Monitoring data is interpreted consistently, with clear triggers for action.
- Evidence is preserved in a way that supports both technical debugging and regulatory obligations.
- Clients and regulators see a coherent, responsible response rather than confusion.

Ultimately, the goal is a culture where every incident, large or small, leaves the system and the organization stronger: architectures are refined, monitoring gets sharper, playbooks get clearer, and teams gain confidence in handling the next challenge without sacrificing the latency edge that makes electronic trading worthwhile.

## 10.6 Capacity Planning and Continuous Improvement

By this point in the chapter, we have built a trading platform that is structurally robust, carefully monitored, tested under deliberate failure, and compliant with audit obligations. The remaining question is: *will it stay that way as markets and business grow?*

Markets do not stand still. Message rates on major venues have trended upward for years, with sharp spikes during macro events. Your own strategy mix evolves, often becoming more data-hungry and latency-sensitive over time. Hardware ages; software accumulates features. A system that is comfortably fast and stable today can drift toward saturation and fragility if you do not plan and adjust.

This section focuses on capacity planning and continuous improvement: using historical load and latency data to forecast capacity needs, guide hardware and network upgrades, and prioritize optimization work. The aim is to keep your system reliably fast not only under average conditions, but also during the most stressful days you are likely to encounter.

## Inputs to Capacity Planning

Effective capacity planning begins with data, not guesses. Fortunately, previous sections already equipped you with much of what you need: detailed latency telemetry, audit trails, and incident records. For capacity, we focus on the following inputs.

### Historical Message Rates

For each venue and feed, gather:

- **Order flow:** Number of new orders, modifications, cancels, and acknowledgments per unit time (for example, per second or per millisecond window).
- **Market data:** Tick rates, book update rates, and snapshot frequencies.
- **By symbol or product group:** Concentration can matter more than totals; a handful of symbols may generate most of the load.

These should be collected over months and, ideally, across different market regimes: quiet days, typical days, and high-volatility days.

### Intraday Seasonality

Load is not uniform over the trading day. Typical patterns include:

- Spikes at market open and close.
- Surges around macroeconomic announcements or scheduled events.
- Lunch-time lulls in some regions.

Plotting message rates and latencies over the course of a day helps identify recurring peaks and the times when you are closest to saturation.

### Utilization of Key Resources

For each major component—strategy hosts, gateways, market data handlers, risk engines, databases, and network links—track:

- CPU utilization and core-level saturation (not just averages across the host).
- Memory usage and garbage collection or paging behavior.
- Network throughput and packet rates, including NIC-level statistics such as drops or errors.
- Storage I/O: read/write throughput, queue depths, and latency for any disks involved in the trading path or critical logging.

These metrics tie observed performance to underlying physical constraints.

### Latency Distributions Under Stress

Not all load is equally dangerous. You should pay particular attention to:

- Latency distributions (p50, p95, p99) during the busiest periods of observed traffic.
- How these distributions change as load increases—for example, whether p99 grows much faster than p50 as message rates climb.

- Latency behavior during past incidents, even if they were handled successfully.

This data reveals the system's "knee points"—where a small increase in load starts causing a large increase in latency.

## Simple Capacity Models

Capacity planning does not require a complex mathematical model. Often, a few simple relationships are enough to guide decisions.

At a high level, think of each component as having a *throughput limit* and a *latency curve*:

- Up to some load, latency remains flat and low; the system has headroom.
- Beyond a certain point, queues build up and latency rises sharply; you are near or above capacity.

In practice, you can estimate these characteristics by:

- **Analyzing historical data:** Plot observed latency against load for each component. Look for regions where latency begins to curve upward.
- **Synthetic load tests:** In controlled environments, drive components with increasing artificial load (for example, replaying market data at 1.5x, 2x, 3x normal rates) and measure how latency responds.

From this, you can derive approximate capacity metrics such as:

- "Gateway cluster A handles up to 100,000 messages per second while keeping p99 processing latency below 150 microseconds."
- "Market data handler B starts to show p99 increases above 2x its baseline when tick rates exceed 1.8x the average of the past year."

These simple models are more useful than they may appear. They let you translate business questions—"What if we double our trading volume on this venue?" or "What if message rates spike to 2x last year's high?"—into engineering answers about whether the current platform can cope.

## Defining Capacity Headroom Targets

Capacity headroom is the safety margin between normal load and the maximum load you are willing to handle while still meeting performance objectives. In trading, you generally want enough headroom to absorb:

- Organic growth in message rates over the next planning horizon (for example, one year).
- Short-lived spikes during volatile events, sometimes several times higher than typical daily peaks.
- Degraded conditions such as partial hardware failures, where some fraction of your capacity is temporarily offline.

A practical way to define headroom targets is:

- Identify the maximum load observed in the last $N$ months, by venue and component.
- Multiply that by a factor capturing growth and stress tolerance (for example, 2x or 3x).
- Require that your capacity models show that the system can sustain that load while keeping key SLOs (for example, p99 latency) within acceptable bounds.

For example:

> "For venue X, we observed a peak of 50,000 messages per second over the last year. Our planning target is to handle 150,000 messages per second (3x) with end-to-end p99 latency remaining under 800 microseconds."

Headroom targets give you a clear test: run synthetic load or replay experiments at the target load and see whether SLOs hold. If they do not, you know you must either optimize or scale.

## Identifying Early Warning Signs of Saturation

Systems rarely jump from "comfortably fast" to "catastrophically overloaded" in one step. There are usually early warning signs:

- **Growing queue depths:** Internal queues in gateways, risk engines, or message buses take longer to drain as load increases.
- **Rising jitter:** The spread between p99 and p50 latencies widens, even if medians look stable.
- **Resource utilization plateaus:** CPU or network utilization seems "stuck" near a high percentage during peaks, leaving little room for variability.
- **Increased error rates:** Timeouts, retransmissions, or dropped messages become more frequent under load.

Your monitoring stack should track these as first-class signals, not just side metrics. For example:

- Set non-paging alerts when p99–p50 gaps exceed a certain threshold for sustained periods.
- Trend queue depths and utilization over weeks and months to see whether peaks are creeping upward.
- Use dashboards that correlate latency with load, so you can visually identify when capacity boundaries are being approached more often.

These early warnings are the raw material for capacity planning discussions: they tell you when the system is drifting toward the edges of its comfort zone.

## Deciding Between Optimization and Hardware Upgrades

Once you know that capacity will become a problem, you have two main levers:

- **Optimize the software:** Make the system do less work per message, or do it more efficiently.
- **Upgrade hardware or add more of it:** Faster CPUs, more cores, better NICs, more bandwidth, or additional instances.

Choosing between them is both a technical and an economic decision.

### When Optimization Makes Sense

Optimization is attractive when:

- Profiling shows clear hotspots: specific components or code paths where a significant portion of time is spent.
- The same software inefficiency would limit you even on better hardware.
- Changes are low risk and well understood (for example, removing redundant serialization, tightening data structures, tuning threading).

Optimization often yields "double benefits": it increases capacity and improves latency at current loads, making the system more competitive.

### When Hardware is the Right Answer

Hardware or topology upgrades are preferable when:

- You are fundamentally bound by physical constraints (for example, CPU cycles to handle cryptography, line-rate NIC limits).
- The software is already well optimized, and further changes would be complex, risky, or offer diminishing returns.

- You need a quick, low-intrusion capacity boost to bridge a near-term gap while planning deeper changes.

Examples include:

- Upgrading to NICs with larger receive queues or better offload capabilities.
- Moving latency-critical components to hosts with higher single-thread performance.
- Adding more gateway instances and load-balancing order flow across them, provided your redundancy and state-management design supports it.

### Back-of-the-Envelope Comparisons

You do not need perfect precision to compare options. Rough estimates are often enough. For instance:

- If you expect message rates to double and your current gateway cluster runs at 60% of comfortable capacity, you might see that a small optimization (say 30% faster processing) plus a 50% hardware increase will comfortably cover the expected load.
- Conversely, if profiling suggests that a particular component could be made twice as fast with a modest effort, it might be more sensible to optimize first and revisit hardware later.

These decisions should be documented, including the assumptions about growth and performance. When reality deviates from those assumptions, you have a clear record to revisit.

## Using Historical Incidents as Capacity Signals

Not all capacity problems show up as slow, smooth trends. Some appear as sharp incidents: bursts of latency, partial outages, or degraded performance under unusual conditions. Incident post-mortems, discussed earlier, are valuable inputs to capacity planning.

For each relevant incident, ask:

- **Was capacity a contributing factor?** For example, did a gateway become overloaded after a failover concentrated more flow on fewer instances?
- **Did redundancy assumptions hold?** Perhaps a "backup" path worked functionally but had significantly lower capacity, leading to latency blowups.
- **Did monitoring provide early warnings?** If not, what additional metrics could have spotted the approach to saturation?

Lessons from incidents often lead to:

- Adjusted headroom targets (for example, accounting for the possibility that a whole rack might be lost).
- Changes in traffic distribution (for example, more even sharding of load across gateways).
- Concrete capacity projects (for example, adding instances, splitting feeds, or separating workloads).

In this way, "failure stories" become quantitative drivers for future capacity decisions rather than isolated anecdotes.

## Continuous Improvement as a Feedback Loop

Capacity planning is not a one-time exercise aligned with annual budgets. In a live trading platform, it should be a continuous loop that connects operations, engineering, and business.

A useful mental model has four stages:

1. **Observe:** Collect ongoing metrics on load, latency, utilization, and incident frequency.
2. **Analyze:** Periodically review these data with both engineering and trading stakeholders. Identify trends, outliers, and gaps between headroom targets and reality.

3. **Decide and Prioritize:** Convert findings into a prioritized backlog of improvements: optimizations, hardware changes, architectural refinements, and monitoring enhancements.

4. **Act and Validate:** Implement changes, then validate their impact using the same metrics and, where appropriate, chaos tests or synthetic load.

This loop mirrors the scientific method: you form hypotheses about where performance will break, design interventions, and test whether they work.

## Embedding Capacity Awareness in Daily Operations

To make continuous improvement sustainable, capacity awareness must be embedded into everyday processes:

**Change Management**

Every significant change—new strategies, additional venues, configuration changes, or software releases—should include a brief capacity impact assessment:

- How will this change affect message rates or computational load?
- Does it concentrate risk or traffic on specific components?
- Are existing headroom targets still satisfied after the change?

Even if the answer is "impact is negligible," writing it down forces conscious consideration and makes assumptions explicit.

**Performance Gates in CI/CD**

As part of your release pipeline, include automated performance tests that:

- Run representative workloads against the new code.
- Measure latency distributions and resource usage.

- Compare them to baselines, failing the build or requiring sign-off if regressions exceed agreed thresholds.

This helps prevent gradual erosion of performance as features accumulate.

**Operational Reviews**

Schedule regular operational reviews that include:

- Capacity dashboards for each major venue and component.
- Summaries of recent high-load days and how the system performed.
- Follow-ups on previous capacity-related action items.

Involving trading and risk teams ensures that technical findings are interpreted in business context: some venues or products may warrant larger safety margins than others.

## Avoiding Overreaction and Waste

While under-provisioning is dangerous, over-provisioning can be costly. The goal is not to build an infinitely overpowered system, but a *well-targeted* one. A few guidelines help avoid unnecessary waste:

- **Distinguish critical and non-critical paths:** Latency-critical, high-volume paths (for example, primary order and market data flows) deserve generous headroom and top-tier hardware. Supporting paths (for example, some analytics, reporting, backtesting) can accept more variability and run on less expensive infrastructure.
- **Use real peaks, not imagined worst cases:** Basing capacity solely on theoretical worst-case scenarios can lead to extreme overbuild. Instead, use historical peaks plus sensible stress multipliers, and revisit them as more data accumulate.

- **Scale incrementally:** When in doubt, favor changes that can be scaled up or down in discrete steps (for example, adding gateway instances) rather than massive, irreversible investments.

This discipline ensures that capacity planning remains anchored in observed reality and well-motivated risk tolerance rather than in fear.

## The Long View: Evolving with Markets and Strategies

Finally, capacity planning and continuous improvement are not only about "keeping up" with markets; they also enable strategic choices:

- **Adopting more demanding strategies:** If you know that your platform has significant headroom, you may be willing to deploy more aggressive or complex strategies that push higher message rates or rely on more real-time calculations.
- **Entering new venues or products:** Capacity analysis can tell you whether you can onboard a new venue in a region with very different load patterns without endangering existing flows.
- **Technical innovation:** Data from capacity and performance efforts often reveal architectural bottlenecks that, once addressed, unlock new design possibilities (for example, refactoring a monolithic gateway into a set of specialized microservices with clearer scaling properties).

In other words, a strong capacity discipline is not just defensive; it makes your trading platform a more flexible and powerful tool for the business.

Capacity planning and continuous improvement tie together many threads from this chapter:

- Redundancy and failover architectures define how the system can redistribute load under failure; capacity planning ensures that those failover paths themselves have enough headroom.

- Monitoring and alerting provide the detailed metrics and SLOs that make capacity analysis quantitative rather than anecdotal.
- Chaos testing reveals how the system behaves at and beyond its limits, informing realistic headroom targets.
- Compliance and incident response ensure that, when capacity is exceeded despite your efforts, the consequences are documented, controlled, and learned from.

Together, these practices move you away from a brittle "build once and hope" mindset and toward an evolving, measured approach: the trading system is treated as a living organism that must adapt as markets, strategies, and technologies change, while continuing to deliver the low-latency performance that underpins your edge.

www.ingramcontent.com/pod-product-compliance
Lightning Source LLC
LaVergne TN
LVHW052013200926
848481LV00005B/1476